Authors
Damian Strojek, Jerzy Kluczewski, Robert Wszelaki, Marek Smyczek
English translation
Joanna Margowniczy

COMPUTER NETWORKS IN PACKET TRACER

FOR BEGINNERS

The book: "**COMPUTER NETWORKS IN PACKET TRACER FOR BEGINNERS**" contains advices for people who want to learn how networks work and the hardware that makes up the modern network architecture. Beginners will learn how to download the simulator software and how to start working with it.

The reader will find here the basics of configuring network devices. You will learn about network services such as **TELNET, SSH, FTP, EMAIL, DHCP, DNS** and routing protocols RIP, EIGRP, OSPF. Learn how to design and deploy VLANs. The authors, when describing the issues of administering computer networks, use many examples and exercises.
Proprietary names of companies, organizations, and products are used in the book solely to identify them.

Cover design: **Marcin Król**
Edited and composed of: **Marek Smyczek** and **Marcin Kaim**
English translation: Joanna Margowniczy

IT Publishing House
http://www.itstart.pl
email: itstart@itstart.pl

This publication has been developed in order to facilitate the assimilation of practical content related to computer networks and as a textbook supporting teaching in the professions: IT Technician and ICT.

ISBN 978-83-65645-84-5

First Edition – Piekary Śląskie 2023

TABLE OF CONTENTS

CHAPTER 1

INTRODUCTION

COMPUTER NETWORKS
IN PACKET TRACER

FOR BEGINNERS

1 INTRODUCTION

The book **PACKET TRACER FOR YOUNG BEGINNERS ADMINS** contains advice for people who want to learn how networks work and the hardware that makes up the modern network architecture. Beginners will learn how to download the simulator software and how to start working with it.

The reader will find here the basics of configuring network devices. You will learn about network services such as TELNET, SSH, FTP, EMAIL, DHCP, DNS and routing protocols RIP, EIGRP, OSPF. Learn how to design and deploy VLANs.

The authors, when describing the issues of administering computer networks, use many examples and exercises.

The book is an updated compilation of the publications of our Publishing House from the Packet Tracer series for CISCO courses, has a described changed interface of the currently latest Packet Tracer software and contains a set of new examples and exercises.

In order to facilitate learning, the authors have prepared numerous examples and exercises supporting the teaching process, which have been placed on a special website of our publishing house, at the following address: **http://cninptbeg.itstart.pl**. To get full access to the files, you must log in with the login: **cninpt1** and password: **cninpt!BEG**.

The files have been divided into two categories: examples and exercises, and are located in subdirectories, with the names: (**examples** and **exercises**)

Note: To open and use them, you must have Packet Tracer at least version 8.2.0 installed. The publisher and authors are not responsible for the malfunction of files in other versions of Packet Tracer.

In this book there are definitely some small bugs, according to Murphy's Law, if something goes wrong, it will happen.

1.1 Main Changes in the Packet Tracer 8.2

On July 28th, 2022 the version 8.2 of the program Packet Tracer was released. The main changes compared to the previous version are:

- simplified way of logging in (**the option of logging in the visitor is not available any more**),
- the mistakes have been improved (e.g. in VTP the Transparent mode works correctly),
- the visualization of transferring devices and wiring in the patch cabinet.

1.2 Detailed Comments Applying to the Program Version.

- The files made in Cisco Packet Tracer in 7.2.2 version or older might work differently in Cisco Packet Tracer 8.2 version.
- Depending on the efficiency of your computer, running Packet Tracer Activity (**PKA**) files or Packet Tracer (**PKT**) might take a **few minutes!**
- Not all offered functionalities work correctly!

1.3 Keep me logged in Option

„Keep me logged in" option was designed to ensure the access (for 3 months) to Cisco Packet Tracer without the necessity of logging in again each time .

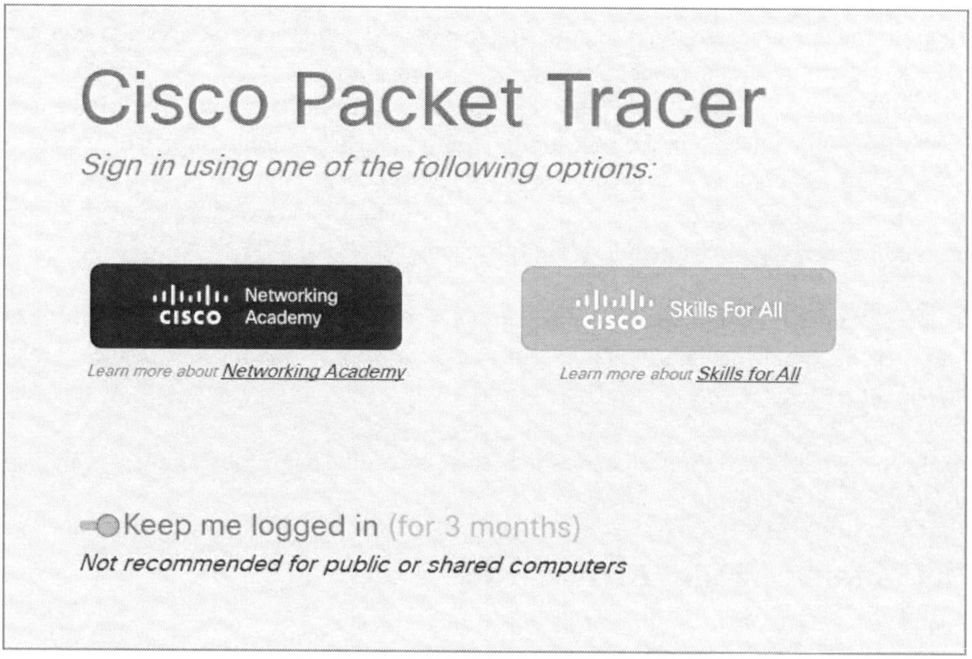

Figure 1.1 Keep me logged in option

Using „**Keep me logged in**" option is recommended for private computers.

If you use public or any shared computer, DO NOT use "Keep me logged in" option or log out before closing Cisco Packet Tracer to unable the other users of the computer the access to PT using Your credentials.

1.4 The minimum System Requirements.

Part 1. System requirements for Cisco Packet Tracer 8.2 (64 bit).

- operating systems: Microsoft Windows 8.1, 10, 11 (64bit), Ubuntu 20.04 LTS (64bit), macOS 10.14 or newer versions
- amd64(x86-64) CPU
- 4GB of free RAM
- 1.4 GB of free disk space

Part 2. System requirements for Cisco Packet Tracer 8.2 (32 bit).

- operating systems: Microsoft Windows 8.1, 10 (32bit)
- x86 compatible CPU
- 2GB of free RAM
- 1.4 GB of free disk space

CHAPTER 2

DOWNLOADING AND INSTALLING CISCO PACKET TRACER

2 Downloading and Installing Cisco Packet Tracer

This chapter describes how to register with **Netacad.com** and how to download and install Packet Tracer.

2.1 Downloading from NETACAD

How to obtain Cisco Packet Tracer?

Cisco Packet Tracer is available free of charge to all Cisco Networking Academy instructors, students, and alumni.

Please follow these instructions to download the software from the NetAcad.com learning environment:

1. **Log in to Cisco NetAcad.com;**

2. **Select Resources → Download Packet Tracer**;

You can also sign up for the free "**Getting Started with Cisco Packet Tracer**" on SkillsForAll.com to learn how to download, install, and get started.

What if I do not have NetAcad.com account?

The latest version of Cisco Packet Tracer requires user authentication. A NetAcad.com or a SkillsForAll.com account is required to sign in when you launch Cisco Packet Tracer.

Remark. Due to the possibility of infecting the program, it is not recommended to download the program from other unknown Internet resources than **Cisco Networking Academy**. You can use the latest versions of **Cisco Packet Tracer (8.2.0)** in two ways: as **a Guest** or when you log in to the Cisco Networking Academy:

- way one: as a **guest;**
- the second way: as a **student** of the Academy;

The **first method** is characterized by the fact that the number of records of practice **PKT** and **PKA** files is limited. The Packet Tracer program is free of charge and can be used without restrictions (after obtaining an account in the Academy).

To use **the second way**, i.e. to use the program without restrictions, you should:

- Register for the course "Getting Started with Cisco Packet Tracer"
- Create your own Cisco Networking Academy account
- Log in to your Academy account

Alternatively, download the correct version of the installation file and install the program if Cisco Packet Tracer is not installed in the lab.

Start the program for the first time (any questions in the dialog boxes should be answered positively).

Step 1. In your browser, go to the **https://www.netacad.com/** website

Figure 2.1 Cisco Networking Academy Website Window

Step 2. On the official website of the Academy, at the bottom of the Academy, find an item called [**Packet Tracer**] and then click on it

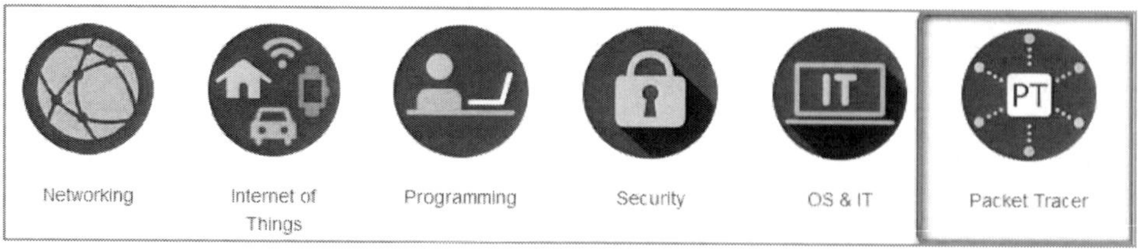

Figure 2.2 Packet Tracer on the Cisco Networking Academy website

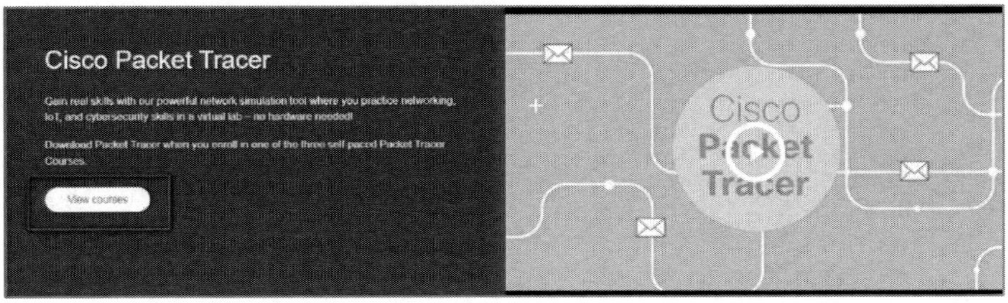

Figure 2.3 Cisco Packet Tracer – View courses Button

Step 3. A page will appear informing you about the enrolling the Getting Started with Cisco Packet Tracer

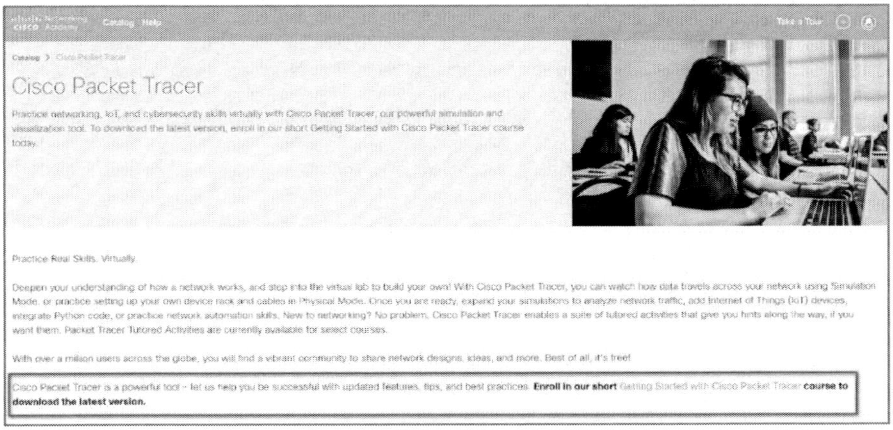

Figure 2.4 Cisco Packet Tracer website

Step 4. A page will appear informing you about the procedure for Getting Started with Cisco Packet Tracer

Figure 2.5 Button [Get Started] in Getting Started with Cisco Packet Tracer

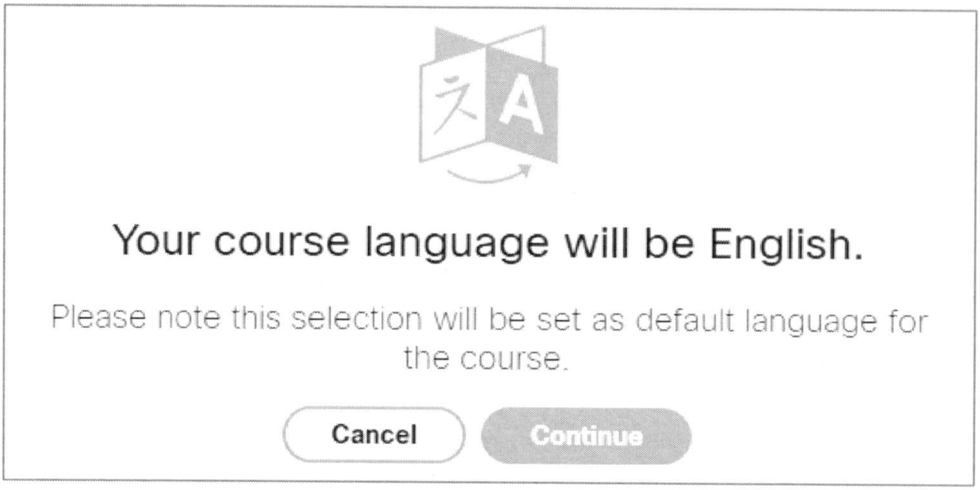

Figure 2.6 Button [Continue] in Getting Started with Cisco Packet Tracer

The course Getting Started with Cisco Packet Tracer is free - No purchase required, anytime. Estimated time to complete, but finish it in your time - 2 Hours. Level of the course: beginner.

Step 5. Log in with your existing account or sing up, if don't have an account.

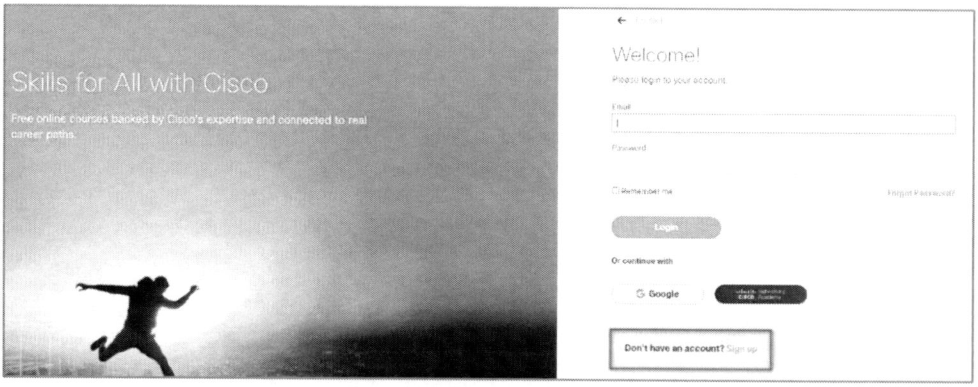

Figure 2.7 Log in or Sign up screen

Step 6. Sing up, if don't have an account.

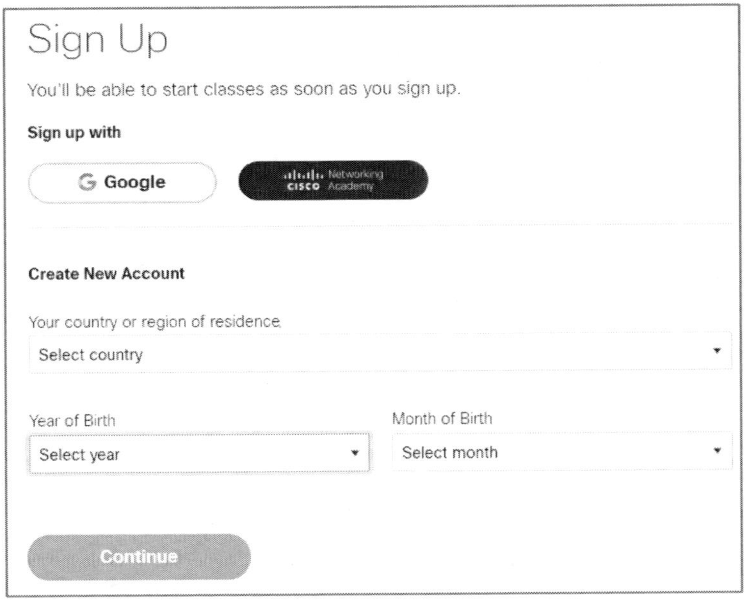

Figure 2.8 Sign Up screen

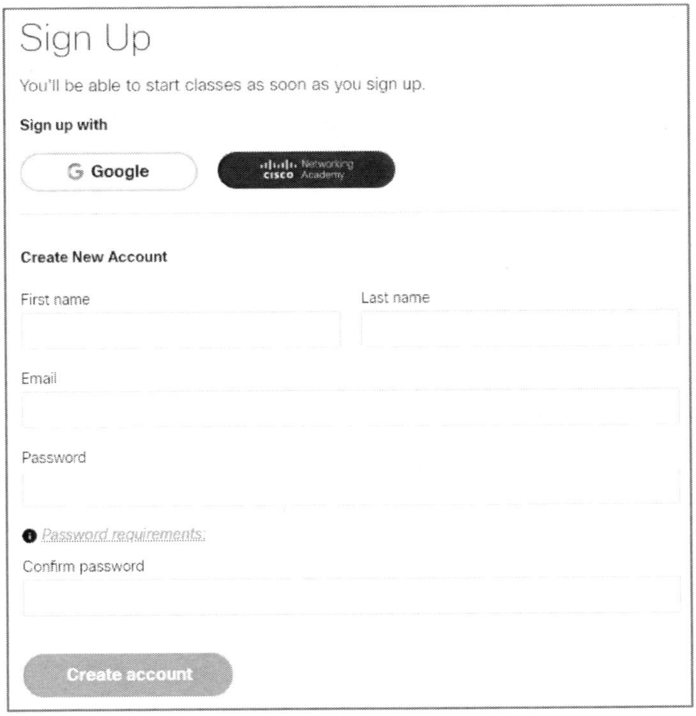

Figure 2.9 Sign Up screen

Step 6. After registering, you can login to your account

Figure 2.10 Log in screen

Step 7. Select Resources → Download Packet Tracer

To do this, find the top menu and **[Resources]** and then select **[Download Packet Tracer].**

Figure 2.11 Menu [Resources] in Networking Academy

Step 8. Select the appropriate operating system type and platform (32-bit or 64-bit) and download the appropriate file.

Figure 2.12 Saving install file on your local disk

2.2 Installing the Packet Tracer (Version 8.2.0)

Step 1. Run the installer **CiscoPacketTracer_820_Windows_64bit.exe**

or any other suitable version of your choice.

Step 2. Accept the License Agreement

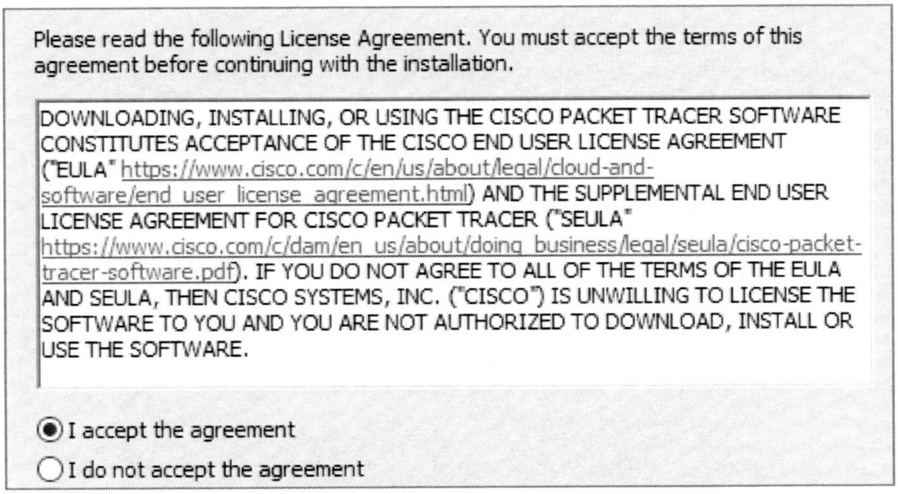

Figure 2.13 Accepting the License Agreement

Step 3. Select Destination Location (the best practice principle – leave the default setting)

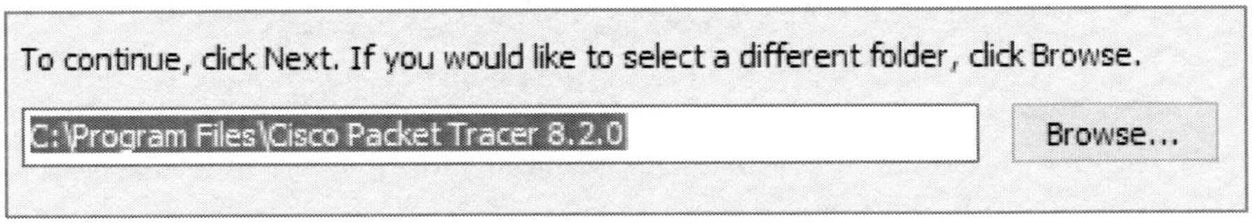

Figure 2.14 Selecting the Destination Location

Step 4. Select Start Menu Folder (the best practice principle – leave the default setting)

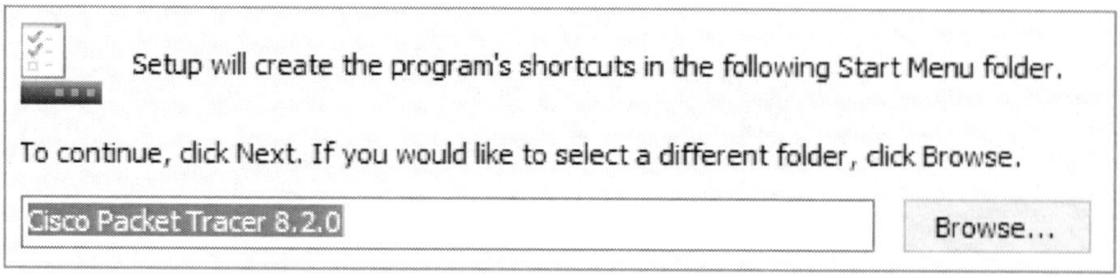

Figure 2.15 Selecting the Start Menu Folder

Step 5. Select Additional Tasks (the best practice principle – leave the default settings)

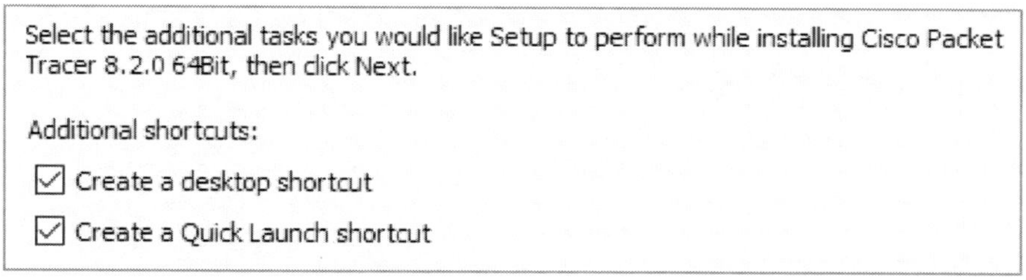

Figure 2.16 Selecting the Additional shortcuts: Desktop and Quick Launch

Step 6. Continue the installing process

2.3 The First Run of the Packet Tracer Program

Step 1. The first run of the program – boot logo.

Figure 2.17 The first run of the program – boot logo.

Step 2. The first run of the program – should the Multi-user mode be activated during application start? (it doesn't matter what is chosen).

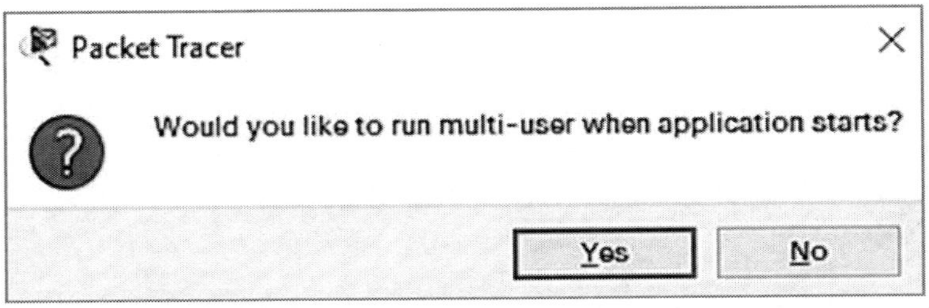

Figure 2.18 The first run of the program – activating a multi-user mode

Step 3. The first run of the program – it is necessary to enable the „**Keep me logged in**" option.

Step 4. The first run of the program - choose „**Networking Academy**".

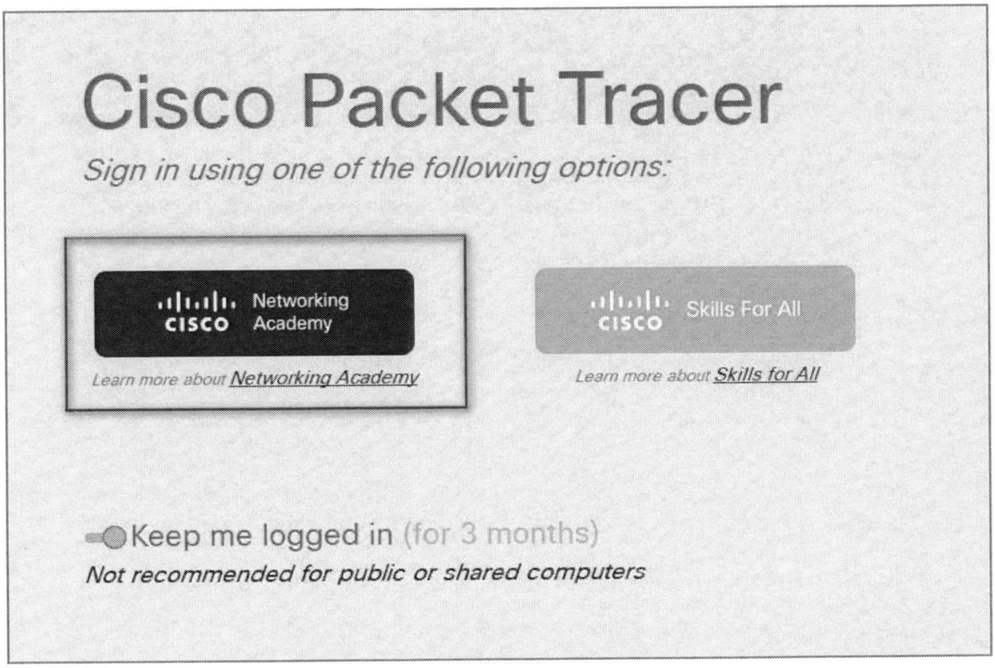

Figure 2.19 The first run of the program - choosing Networking Academy

Step 5. The first run of the program - you should check if the newest version of the Packet Tracer has been run. From the main menu choose **Help → About** and check the version.

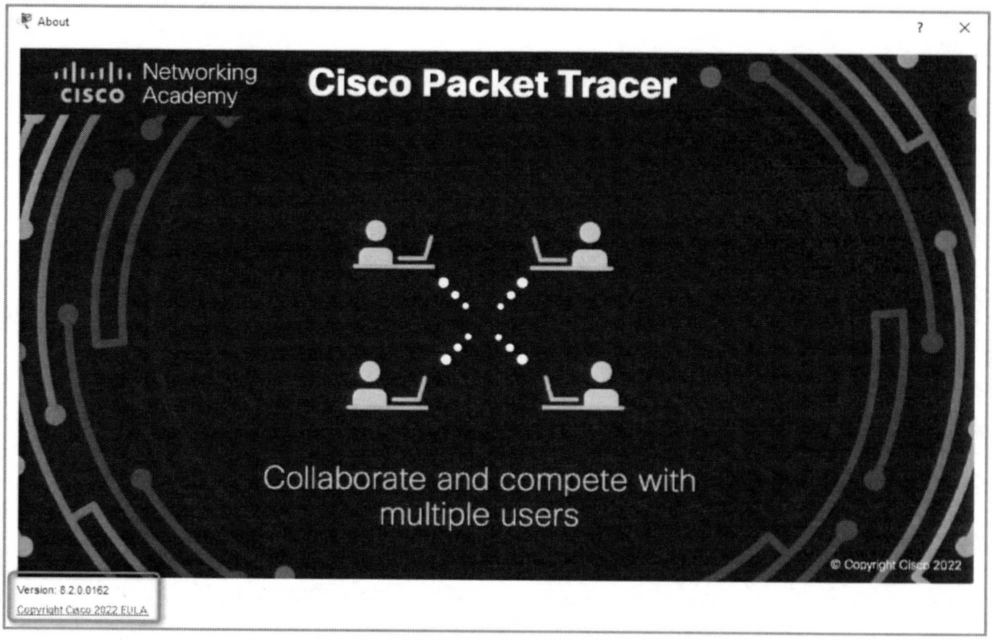

Figure 2.20 The first run of the program – check the version.

CHAPTER 3

GETTING STARTED WITH THE CISCO PACKET TRACER

3 Getting Started with the Cisco Packet Tracer

This chapter is intended for beginners and describes the main elements of Cisco Packet Tracer.

3.1 The Main Program Window

When you start **Cisco Packet Tracer**, the default view of the main program window will appear, shown in the figure, where the most important areas of the packet tracer are described and shown below.

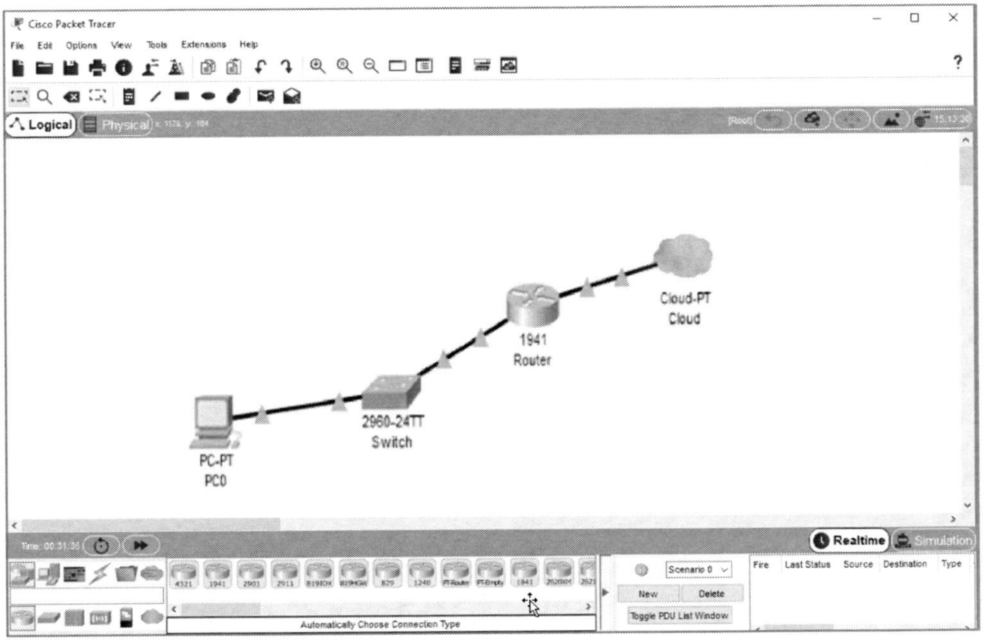

Figure 3.1 The main Packet Tracer window

3.2 The Main Areas of the Program Window

Below there are brief descriptions of the areas of the Main window.

Description of the Area
The menu bar contains commands: **File, Edit, Options, Extensions, Help**. Here you can perform, among others, operations: **Open, Save, Save as, Print**. 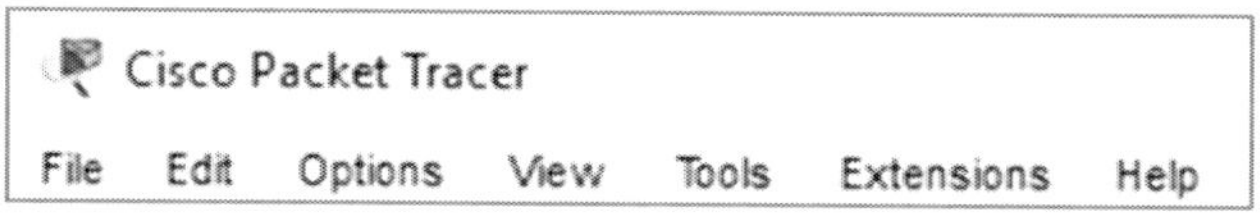
The toolbar contains icons for performing the following operations, among other things: **New, Open, Save, Print, Copy, Paste, Undo, Redo, Zoom In, Zoom Reset, Zoom Out, Drawing.** 
General purpose toolbar: **Select**, **Move Layout**, **Place Note, Delete**, **Inspect Resize Shape**, **Add Simple PDU**, and **Add Complex PDU.** 
Logical/Physical - a tool that allows you to switch between the view of the **logical** and **physical** topology of the network. 
A switch that allows the program to work **in real-time mode** and network **simulation mode**. The simulation mode is used to observe the transmission of frames and packets.

Area containing buttons for working in clouds and for the IoT simulation window

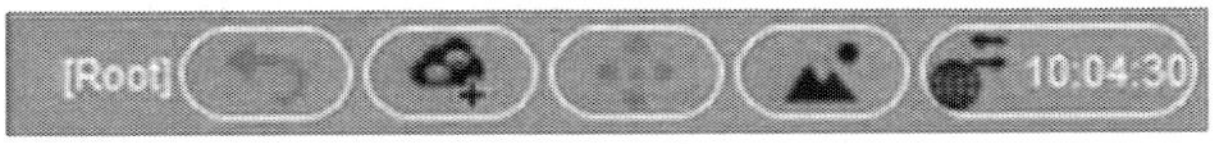

The workspace where you create your network, configure devices, and simulate network operation.

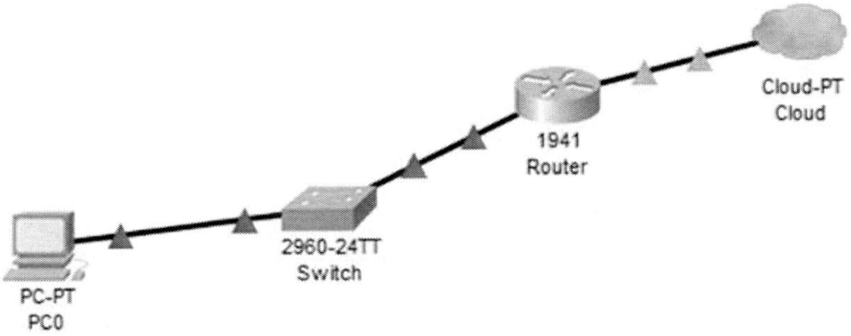

The area containing the current working time and buttons: **[Power Cycle Devices]**, **[Fast Forward Time]**

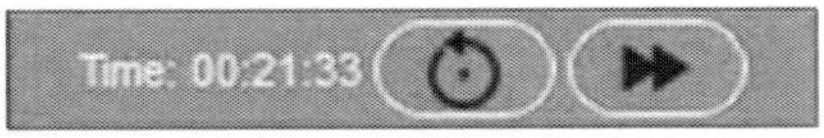

The **[Power Cycle Devices]** button is used to delete the configuration of all devices without any means, and after this operation, all routers and switches will have the default configuration (unless you first execute the copy running-config startup-config command). Therefore, it should be used with caution.

The **[Fast Forward Time]** button is used to speed up network convergence, which is very useful for large networks (convergence time can be reduced from many minutes to seconds).

An area that allows you to choose network components: network devices and cables.

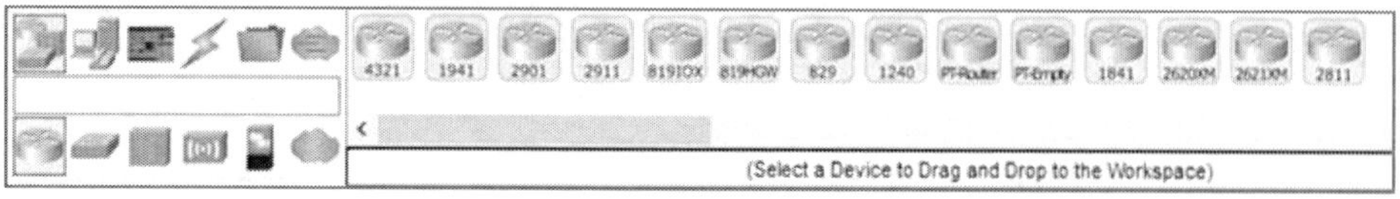

An area that allows you to select the type of network device or cable.

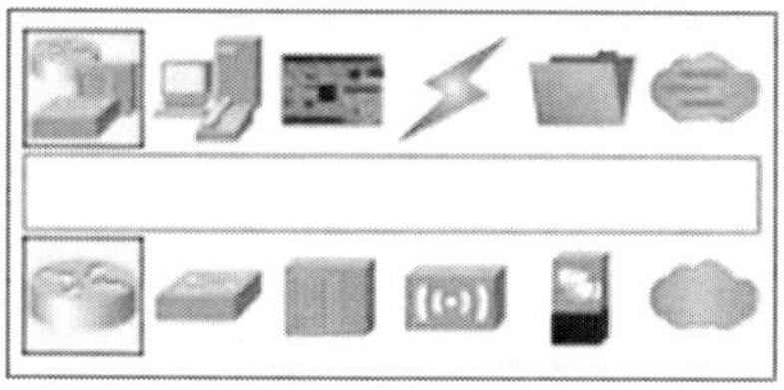

An area that allows you to select a specific network device or a specific cable.

An area used to observe packets during simulation.

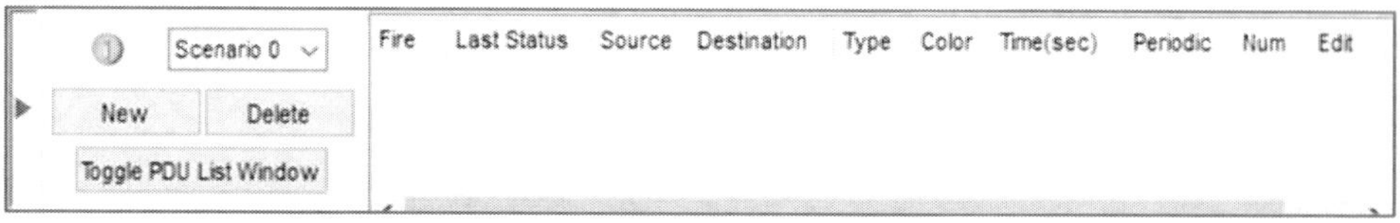

Table 3.1 Descriptions of areas of the main Packet Tracer window

3.3 Toolbar Icons

Below, there are brief descriptions of the icons in the toolbar.

Icon appearance	**Icon description (operation)**

	New – Create a new file
	Open – Open a file
	Save – save a file
	Print – Print a file
	Network Information – Displaying the window 'Network Description'
	User Profile – Displaying the "User Profile" window (containing the fields: Name, E-Mail, Additional Info)
	User Profile – Displaying the "User Profile" window (containing the fields: Name, E-Mail, Additional Info)
	Copy
	Paste
	Undo

	Redo
	Zoom In
	Zoom Reset
	Zoom Out
	Show Workspace List (Show window containing a list of devices) The window contains data: name, device model, location coordinates, connection status
	View Command Log
	Custom Devices Dialog (Dialog box for creating new devices) – based on existing devices (Dialog box for creating new devices) – based on existing devices
	Cluster Associations Dialog (logical topology structure mapping dialog box to physical topology structure)

Table 3.2 Icon descriptions in the Packet Tracer toolbar

3.4 General Purpose Toolbar Icons

Below, there are brief descriptions of the icons in the general use toolbar.

Icon appearance	**Icon description (operation)**	**Key**
	Select	Esc
	Inspect	I
	Delete	Del
	Resize: Draw Line, Draw Rectangle, Draw Ellipse	Alt+R
	Place Note	N
	Draw Line	L
	Draw Rectangle	R
	Draw Ellipse	E

	Draw Freeform	F
	Add Simple PDU	P
	Add Complex PDU	C

Table 3.3 Icon descriptions in the Packet Tracer General Utility Toolbar

CHAPTER 4

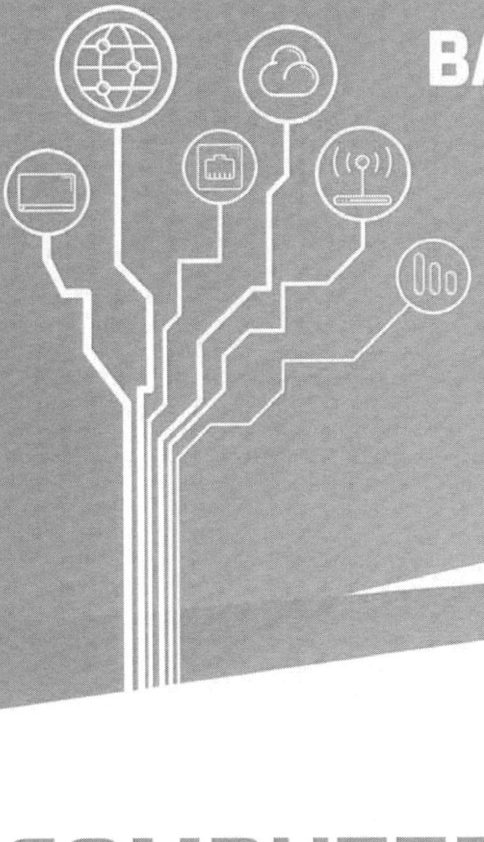

BASICS OF WORKING WITH THE CISCO PACKET TRACER

COMPUTER NETWORKS IN PACKET TRACER

FOR BEGINNERS

4 Basics of Working with the Cisco Packet Tracer

4.1 First Steps

This chapter shows you how to create your first network connections, basic devices, necessary wiring, and appropriate device configurations.

Note – Warning: Remember to periodically save the file state during exercises (keyboard shortcut CTRL+S)

4.1.1 Working with Devices

Suppose the first task will be to directly connect two computers with a network cable without additional devices. What will you need? Of course, two computers that you should look for in the device block in the End Devices section. If you want to diversify the task a little, you can combine a desktop computer with a laptop.

If you want to add a device, grab it with the left mouse button and drag it into an empty workspace of the program. The end result should look like the following figure.

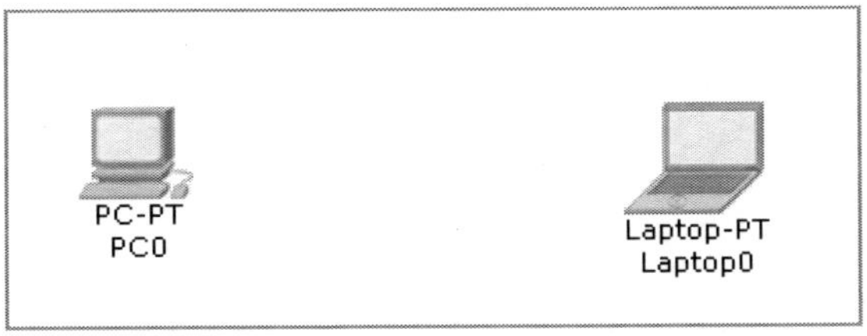

Figure 4.1 Devices placed in the workspace

Of course, at any time you can move any object or selected group of objects to another place in the workspace. To do this, hold the element and drag it to another place.

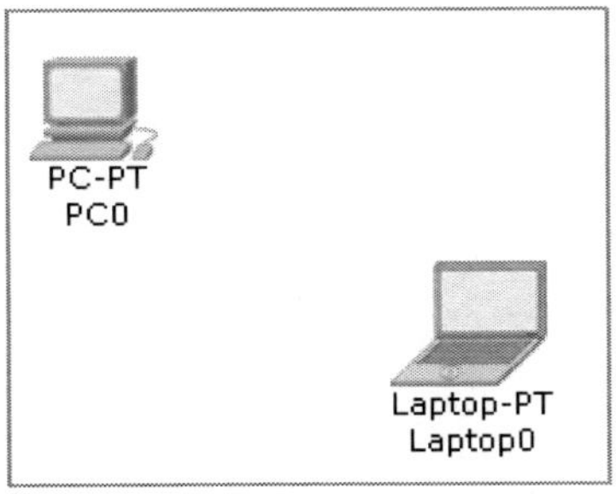

Figure 4.2 Moved devices to other locations in the workspace

It may also happen that when working with placing elements on the matrix, some device turns out to be superfluous or redundant and there will be a need to remove it. Then, on the top toolbar, click the Delete button  then the cursor turns into a cross and you can indicate the device to be removed, as shown in the figure below. After doing this, the delete mode is still open, so to return to normal operation, press the Esc button on the keyboard.

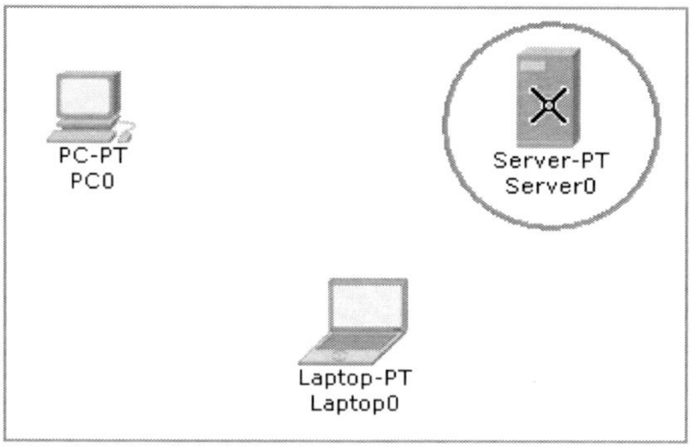

Figure 4.3 Remove an unnecessary device

4.1.2 Replacing and Adding Modules

Theoretically, devices are prepared for connection, however, sometimes there is a need to install a different network adapter in the device than the one that is in its equipment by default, which must be done before making the wiring. These steps are described in this section of the book.

By default, computers have Fast Ethernet network adapters with a bandwidth of 100Mbps installed. Assuming that you are connecting computers in the same technology, but with a higher bandwidth, i.e. 1Gbps. To do this, both devices need to replace the current network adapters with new ones. To do this, it is required to click on the icon of the computer located in the workspace, which will result in the window shown in the following figure.

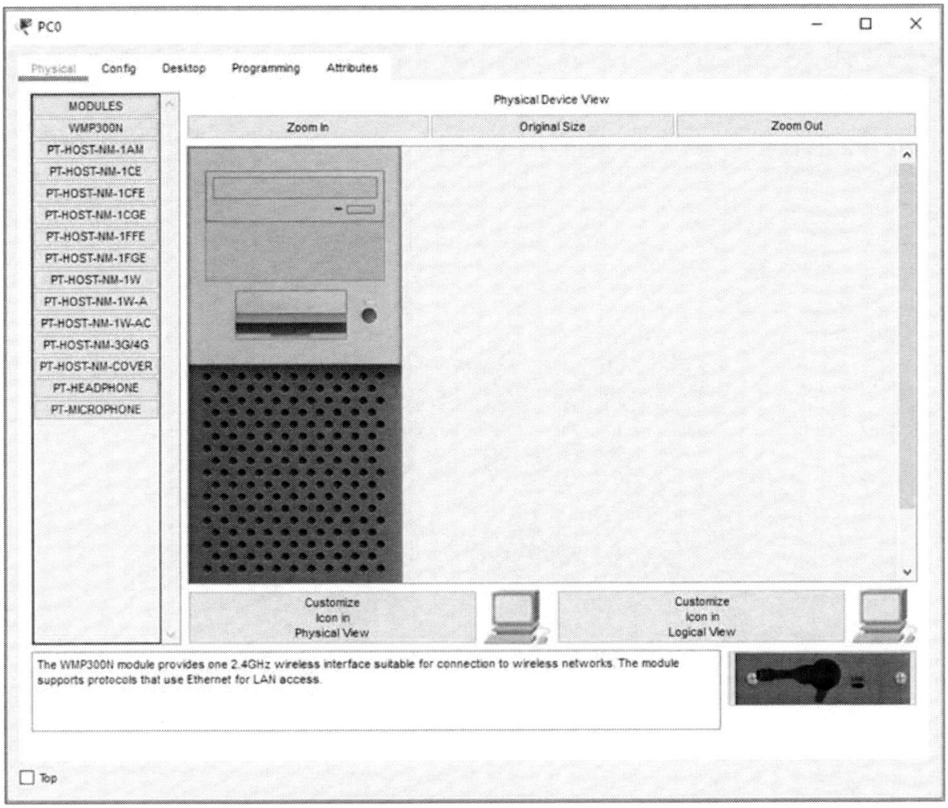

Figure 4.4 Desktop configuration window

The window consists of four tabs, of which you will need the first of them, i.e. Physical, to replace the network card. It consists of two parts: on the left side there are components that can be installed, and on the right there is a view of the central unit of the computer.

The Packet Tracer is a tool that almost realistically reflects the real-world environment, so to remove the current network adapter, you must first shut down the computer. To do this, place the mouse cursor near the power button and click on it, after which the LED light will turn off, which means that the central unit is turned off.

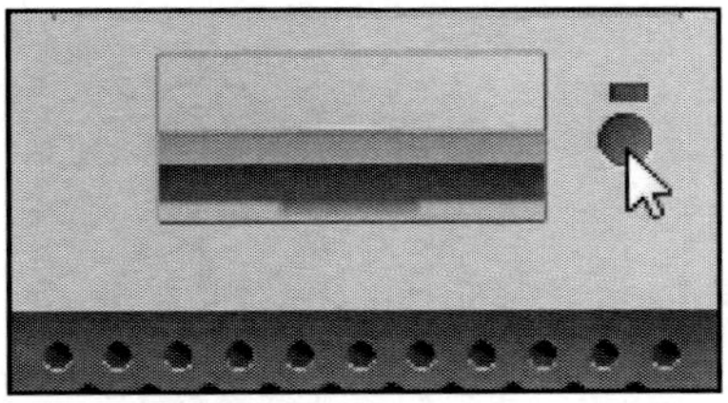

Figure 4.5 Disabling the central unit of the PC.

After the computer is turned off correctly, you can proceed to remove the unnecessary network adapter located in the central processing unit. To do this, move the computer view slightly down so that you can see the network adapter, then grab it with the left mouse button and move it to the left, above the list of devices to install, and then release the mouse button.

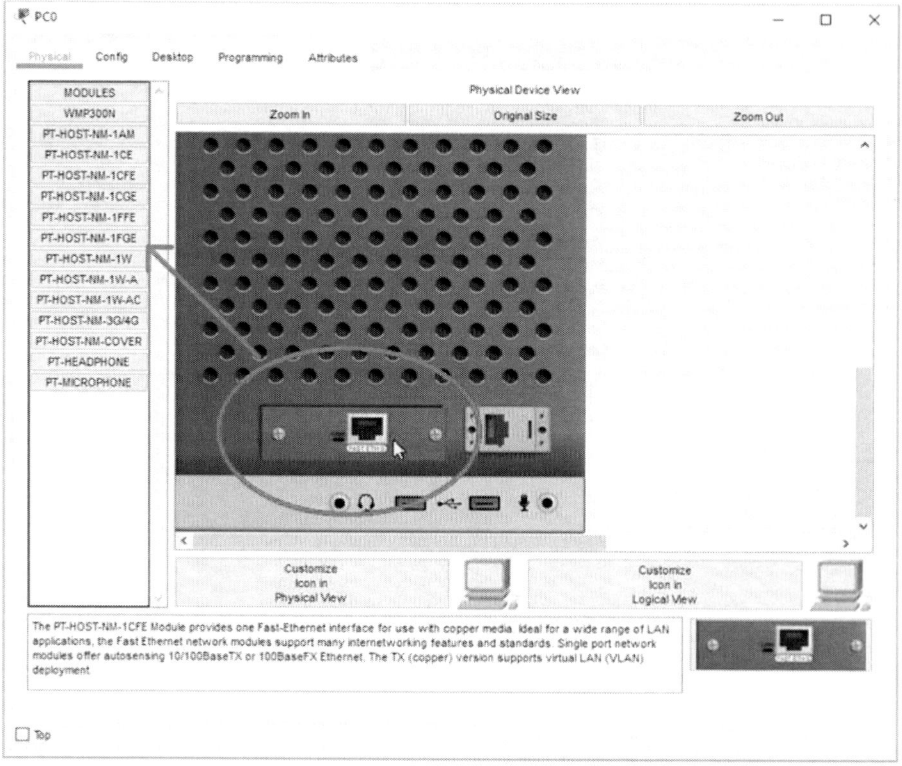

Figure 4.6 Remove a network adapter from the computer's central processing unit

After a while, the slot in the central unit should be empty, which means that the network adapter has been removed, as shown in the figure below.

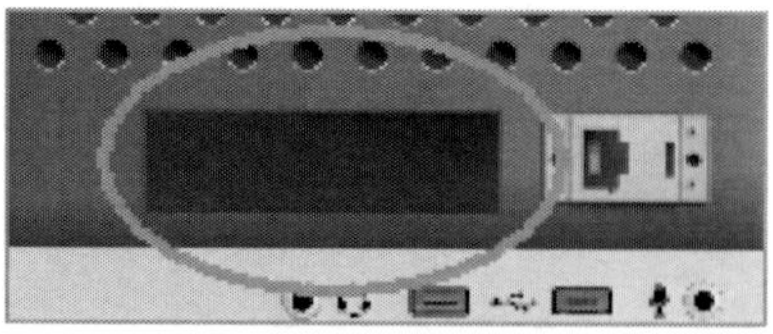

Figure 4.7 An empty slot on a desktop computer when you remove a network adapter

At this point, you can proceed to the installation of the correct card, but before that you need to make an overview of all devices that can be installed and connected to the central unit. The type of device can be recognized by the photo, and its full specification by its description. The devices have been divided into the following groups:

1.  Ethernet UTP network adapters:
    - **PT-HOST-NM-1CE** – Ethernet port, designed for working with copper media, which can be used for LAN connections with a bandwidth not exceeding 10 Mbps, able to support up to six PRI connections of ISDN lines - 24 synchronous / asynchronous ports.
    - **PT-HOST-NM-1CFE** – Fast-Ethernet port, designed to work with copper media. Ideal for a wide range of LAN applications. Single network modules with automatic detection of 100BaseFX(copper) Ethernet ports. The version supports virtual LANs (VLANs).
    - **PT-HOST-NM-1CGE** – Gigabit Ethernet port, providing copper connectivity in LAN networks as well as for access routers with 1Gbps speed. The module is supported by Cisco 2691, Cisco 3660, Cisco 3725 and Cisco3745 series routers. This module has one Gigabit network interface (GBIC).
2.  Ethernet Fiber Optic Network Adapters:
    - **PT-HOST-NM-1FFE** – Fast-Ethernet port using fiber optic media. Ideal for a wide range of LAN applications, high-speed Ethernet modules supporting multiple functions in a 10/100Mbps Internet environment with automatic port detection.
    - **PT-HOST-NM-1FGE** – Gigabit Ethernet port, providing optical connectivity with 1Gbps bandwidth for access routers. The module is supported by Cisco2691, Cisco 3660, Cisco 3725 and Cisco3745 series routers.
3.  Wireless network adapters:
    - **Linksys-WMP300N** – Linksys 2.4 GHz wireless interface, suitable for connecting wireless networks. The module supports Ethernet protocols for connection to LAN-WIFI.
    - **PT-HOST-NM-1W** – 2.4 GHz wireless interface, suitable for connection to wireless networks. The module supports Ethernet protocols for connection to the LAN.

- **PT-HOST-NM-1W-A** – 5GHz wireless interface, suitable for connection to 802.11a wireless networks. The module supports protocols that use Ethernet to connect to the LAN.

4. Calling cards:

- **PT-HOST-NM-1AM** – A calling card equipped with two RJ-11 connectors that are used for basic dial-up service connections. It uses one port to connect to a standard phone line, and the other port can be connected to the base analogue line for use when the modem is at rest.
- **PT-HOST-NM-3G/4G** – GSM telephony card providing access to the 3G/4G generation wireless network.

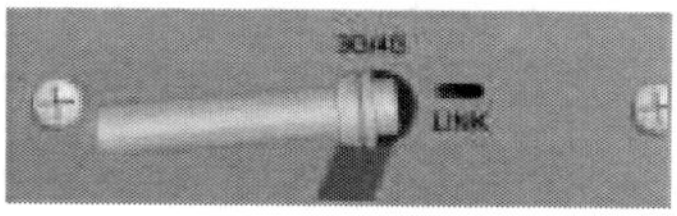

5. Other external devices:

- **PT-HEADPHONE** – Headphone output allows you to listen to music and sounds from your computer.
- **PT-MICROPHONE** – Microphone input that allows you to record audio.
- **PT-CAMERA** – A device that allows you to capture images and videos.
- **PT-USB-HARD-DRIVE** – USB hard drive, external storage space.

Please note that the peripherals listed in position 5 are not connected to the expansion socket, but to the USB or MINI-JACK port in the computer case, as shown in the figure below.

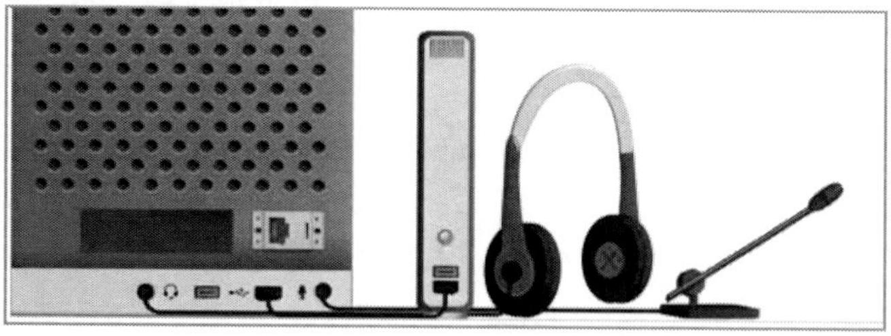

Figure 4.8 Additional peripherals connected to the computer

Returning to the main content of the task (i.e. installing a network card based on copper media with a bandwidth of 1 Gbps in the computer), in this case you should mount network cards in both computers: PT-HOST-NM-1CGE.

4.1.3 Network Cabling

Once your computers have expansion cards of the appropriate standard that provide bandwidth at a certain speed, you can turn on the central processing units and proceed to connect the hardware.

Before connecting the equipment, the basic types of wires that will be used for this purpose will be discussed. In order to display all types of wires, click the lightning-like icon (Connections) in the hardware block and the wiring department.

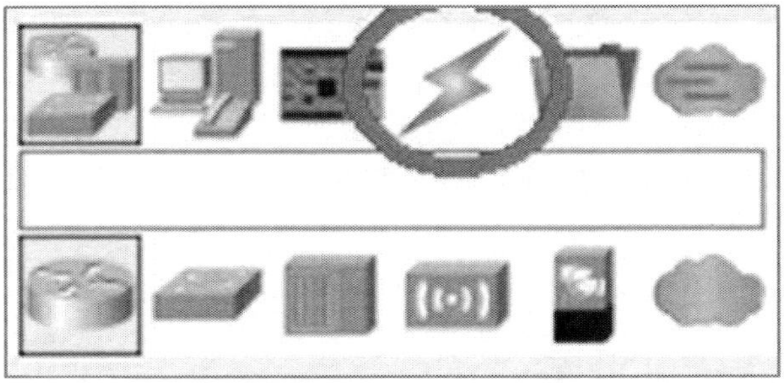

Figure 4.9 Entrance to the network cabling department

After clicking on the icon, on the right side all available types of wires that you can use as they are displayed. Due to the fact that the program can run on computers with different resolutions and can be opened in a smaller window, not all wires will be immediately visible. To do this, either use the horizontal slider to move the current view or stretch the window size so that you can see all the devices at once. Ways to work with this block are shown in the figure below.

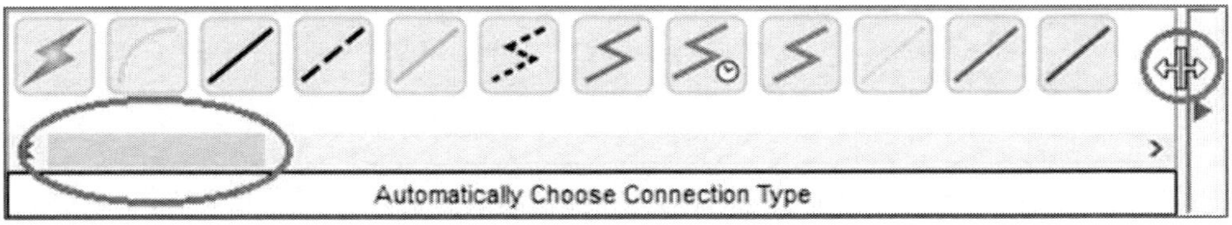

Figure 4.10 Move the current view and stretch block size: wiring

When the wiring block takes a sufficient size, all the wires that we will use in a moment will appear in it, as shown in the figure below.

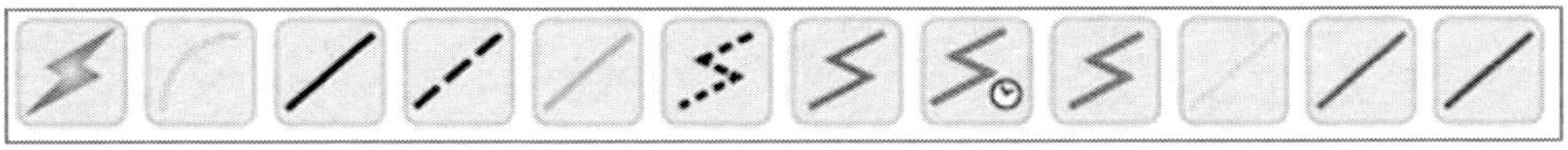

Figure 4.11 All cable icons, usable in the program

We will now discuss the meaning of the icons that symbolize the type and standard of a given cable:

- **Automatic cable**  - using this cable, it will automatically adapt to the network card installed in the device, does not require the user to have basic knowledge of cabling.
- **Console cable**  - used to connect computers to network devices such as routers, switches to configure them through Terminal Services.
- **UTP cable (straight twisted pair cable)**  - one of the most commonly used cables of general application for connecting devices such as: computer-switch, switch-router, etc.
- **UTP cable (cross-over twisted pair cable)**  - as in the above case, but to connect two identical groups of devices as: computer-computer, switch-switch, router-router.
- **Fiber optic cable**  - for general applications where the use of optical media is required.
- **Telephone cable**  - for use in telephone calls (e.g. for connecting an analogue phone to a VoIP gateway).
- **Coaxial cable**  - used in cable networks and as a signal cable in terrestrial and satellite television.
- **Serial cable (clock speed)**  - for serial connections in WAN networks.
- **Serial cable** (without clock speed)  - for serial connections in WAN networks.
- **USB cable**  – to connect to devices via USB.

- **Octal cord**  – connects the access server or terminal server to routers and switches console cables in your lab.
- **IoT Custom Cable**  – it is a cable that allows you to create computer networks that will contain uniquely identifiable IoT (Internet of Things) devices that can directly or indirectly collect, process and send data.

4.1.4 Connecting Devices

The previous section describes typical devices and network cabling, and this subsection will describe how to connect network devices.

The first way is to use an automatic cable. From the cable group, select  and click one of the computers. In the figure you can see that the wire has been connected to it and now you need to point the cursor towards the second of them, after which you can click the left mouse button again.

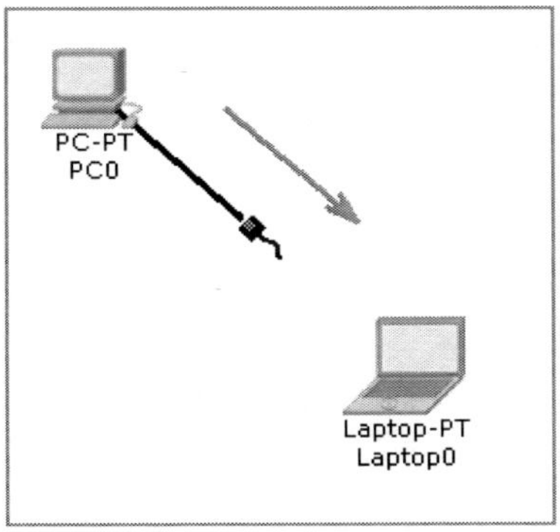

Figure 4.12 Connecting two devices via an automatic cable

After a while, a wire will be connected between the computers, in the form of a dotted line, which is characteristic of a UTP patch cable in the Cisco Packet Tracer.

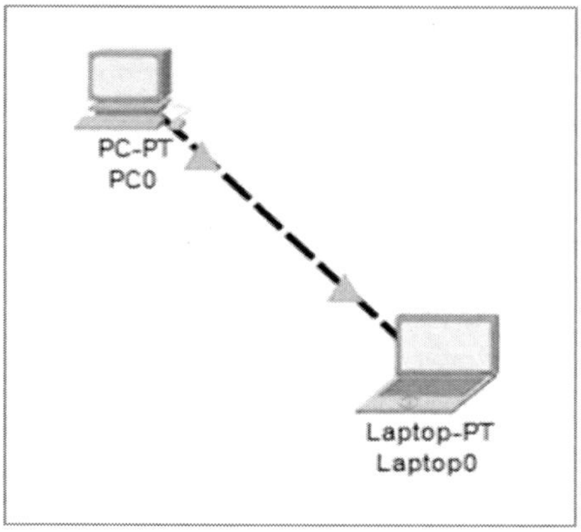

Figure 4.13 Connected computers via UTP patch cable

However, it will not always be possible to use an automatic connection, because, for example, if there is a need to insert it into the appropriate port, and not into the first free one, this way will be unreliable. Therefore, another way is presented, explaining how to directly use a cable of a given type, without using an automatic connection.

First of all, you should choose the UTP patch cable , point the cursor over the first computer and left-click, and a pop-up menu appears from which to select the appropriate port for your connection type, in which case it will be Fast Ethernet. Then drag the cable to the other device and select the appropriate port.

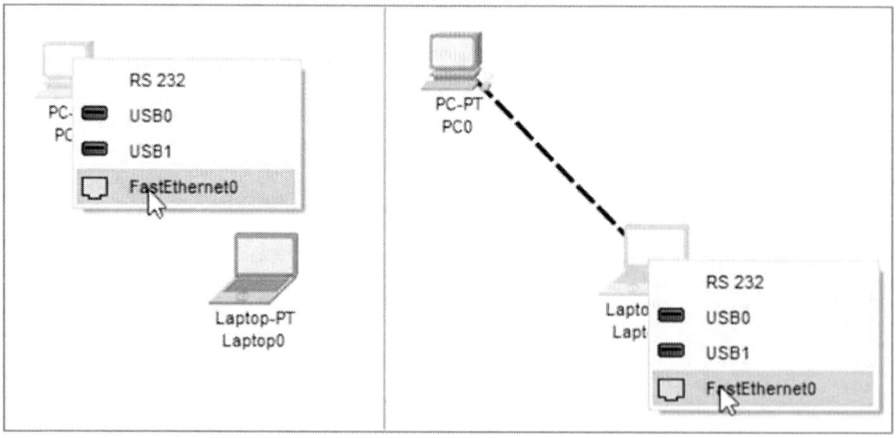

Figure 4.14 Connecting devices via manual mode

4.1.5 Basic Device Configuration

After making the appropriate connections between the devices, for the proper operation of the network, its configuration is required. For proper operation of the LAN (local area network), it is enough that each device has a unique IP address and subnet mask.

This section does not describe the principles of building IP addresses, address classes and dividing addresses into private or public. The subsection describes the necessary conditions to be met when addressing IP addresses. In this case, all devices must have the same class address and the same network mask but with a different host ID. This example uses a network with the address **200.200.200.0** and a network mask of **255.255.255.0** (another notation is: **200.200.200.0/24**, which means that the mask consists of 24 ones (24 bits)).

4.1.5.1 Global Configuration Mode

Depends on clicking the icon of the computer to be configured, and then the following window opens with the **Config** tab active.

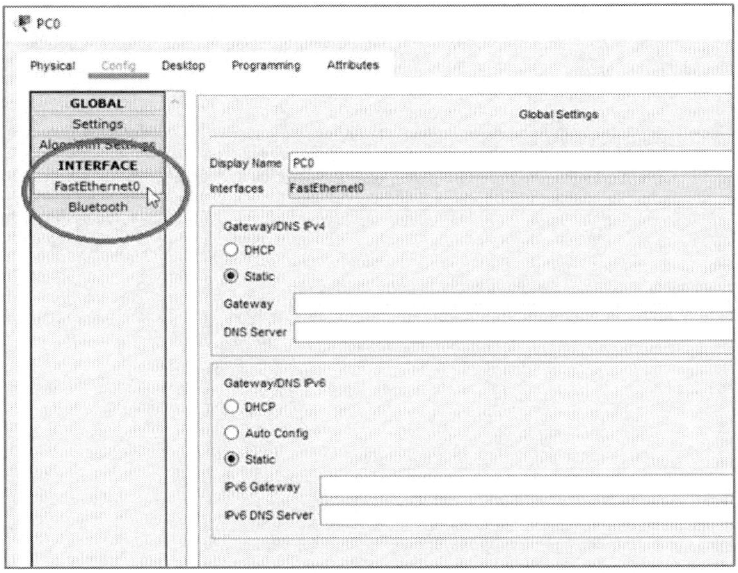

Figure 4.15 Config tab of the PC configuration window

On the default tab in the left window, click on the interface to which the IP address will be assigned, in this case it will be **FastEthernet0.**

Note: To switch to static addressing, type the network address in the IP Address field, type **200.200.200.1** and Subnet Mask the default network mask for this network class, which is **255.255.255.0**. After doing this, basically, the computer was prepared to work on the network.

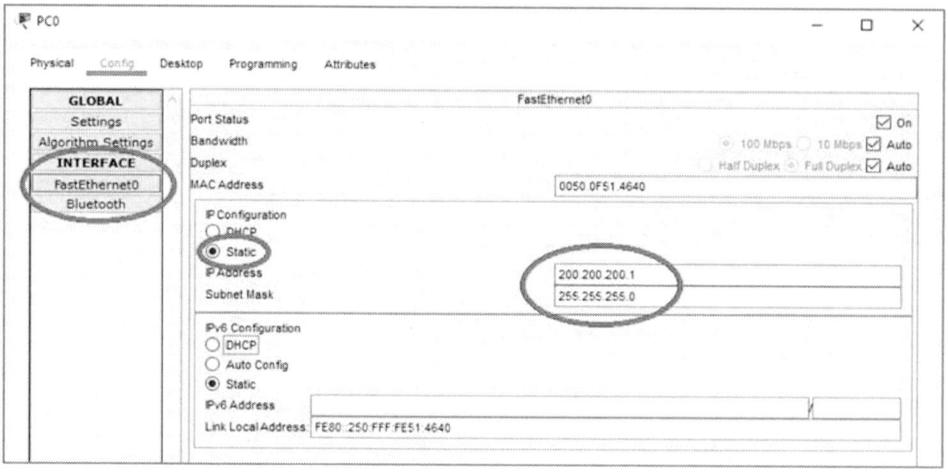

Figure 4.16 Assigned IP address and network mask to the computer

4.1.5.2 Desktop Tools

The second method of configuring the device is to go to the virtual desktop of the computer where it can be configured. After clicking the computer icon, with the left mouse button, go to the Desktop tab and click on the first of the available icons – **IP Configuration.**

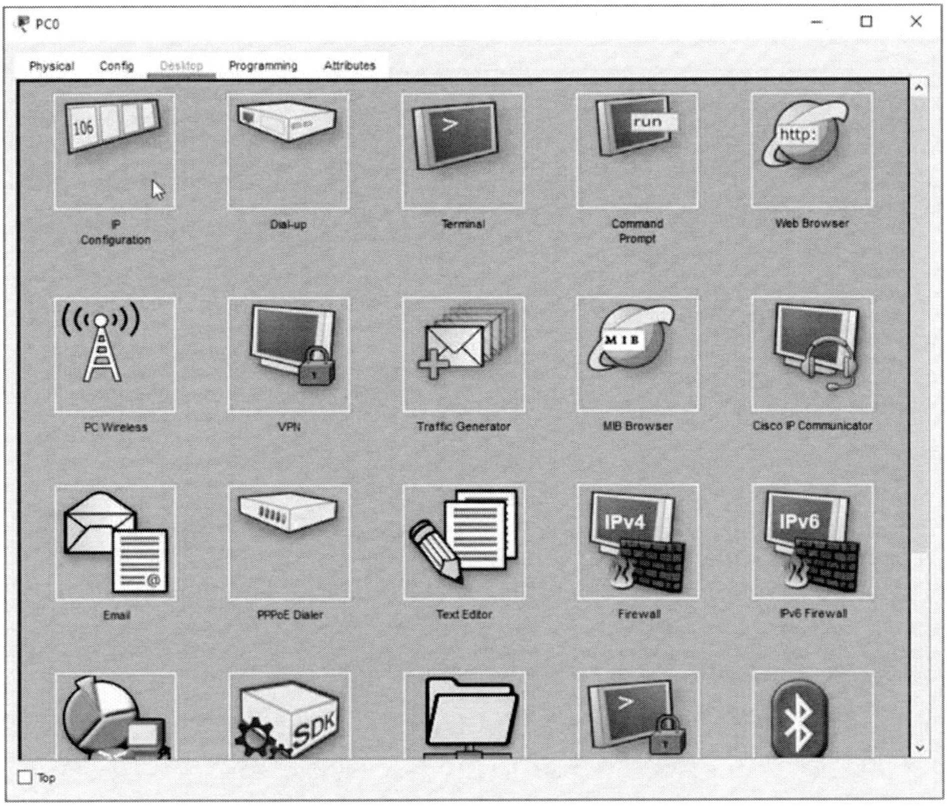

Figure 4.17 Computer desktop contents

After a while, a window with the same name as the selected icon on the computer's desktop appears. Select **Static** and type the IP address and network mask.

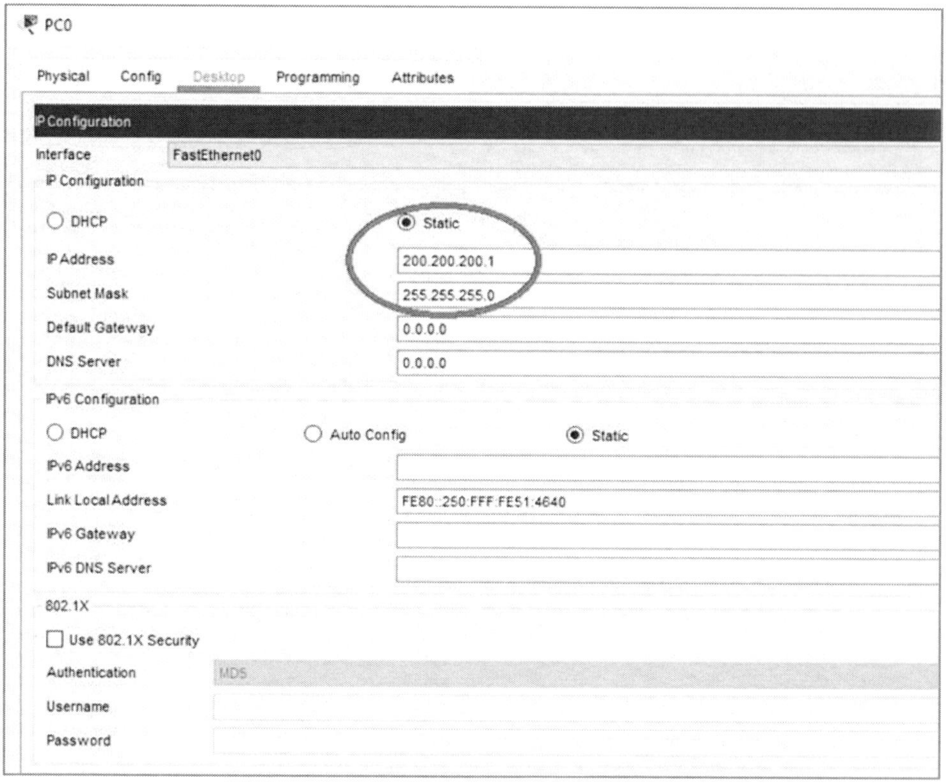

Figure 4.18 Computer Configuration Through IP Configuration

It should be remembered that no matter which method the configuration of computers was performed, it is important that everyone who will have to work on the network has an IP address and a mask configured.

4.1.6 Check the Status of Your Configuration

When working with the program, at various stages of working with the network, you should check the configuration status of the devices that make up it.

4.1.6.1 Status of Network Adapter LEDs

The basic element used for verification is to check the status of the network adapters of the devices visible at the ends of the cables connecting them.

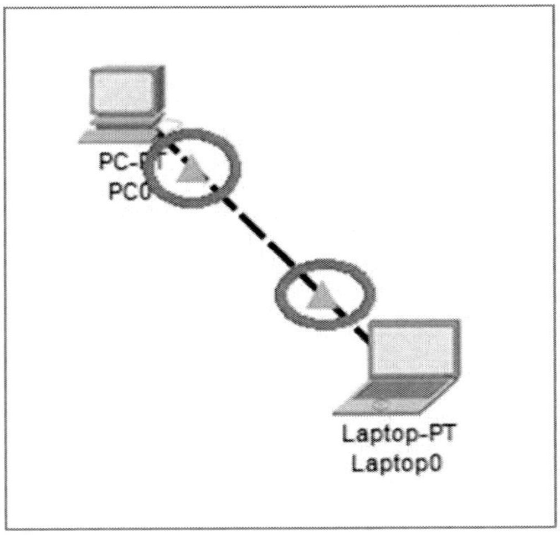

Figure 4.19 Port status of connected network devices

The LEDs at both ends should be **green**. What if this is not the case? There may be several reasons for this... Here are the most likely causes:

- Incorrect wire (e.g. in this case, if a straight wire was used).
- Network device disabled (via power button).
- Disabled device port (**On** must be selected, which is described as **Port Status** for the network adapter or interface of the selected device).
- Different speed of network adapters of connected **Bandwidth** devices (the best choice is to select **Auto**).
- Different types of **Duplex** transmission (the best choice is to select **Auto**.

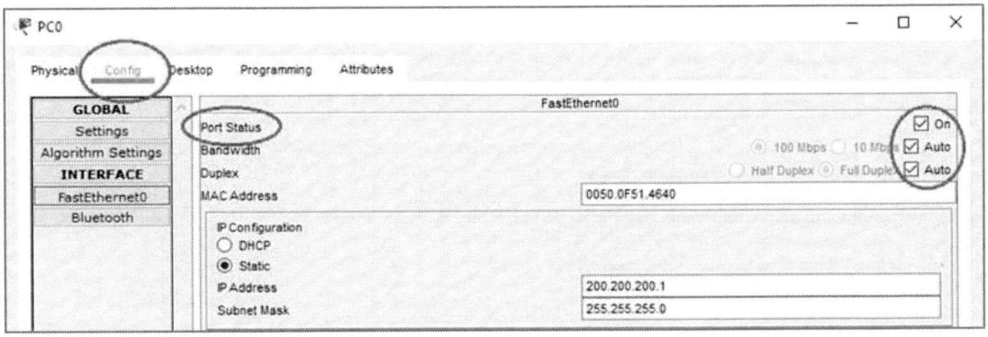

Figure 4.20 Conditions for correct configuration of computer ports

4.1.6.2 IP Address Display

When the port LEDs are green and the physical devices are running, you can check the IP address of the computer that is visible on the logical topology. The first and fastest way is to set the mouse cursor over the icon of the computer whose IP, you want to display for a while and after a while a dialog box is displayed in which you can see the basic parameters (the subnet mask, MAC address, default gateway address, DNS server address, as well as physical location will also be displayed), as shown in the figure below.

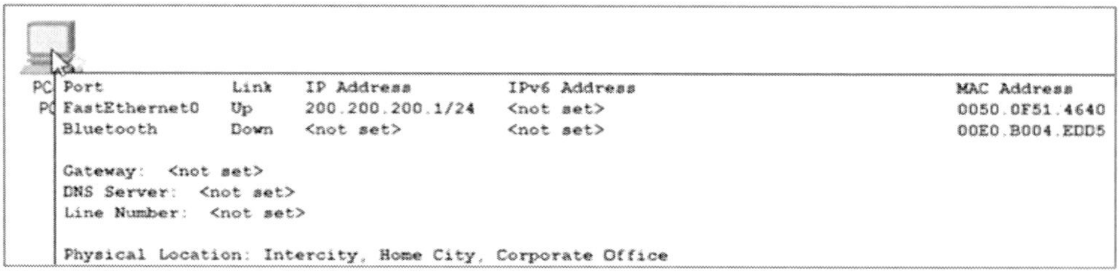

Figure 4.21 IP address and network mask of the computer displayed

4.1.6.3 Inspect Tool

Another way is to use the Inspect tool  from the top tool tray and left-click on the computer. From the context menu, select **Port Status Summary Table**, as shown in the figure below.

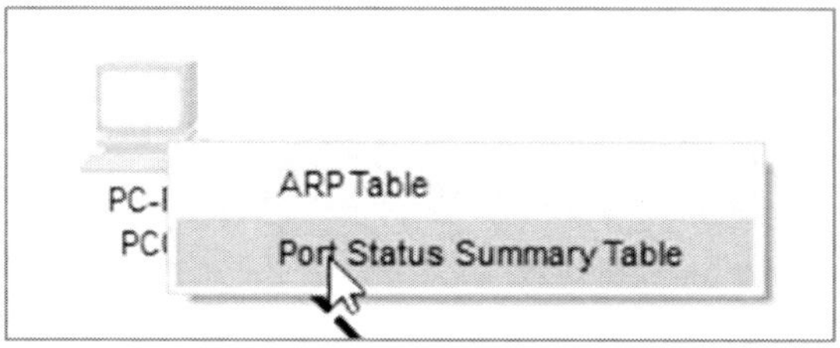

Figure 4.22 Use inspect to display your computer's IP address

After a while, a window will appear in which all the necessary configuration data will be presented.

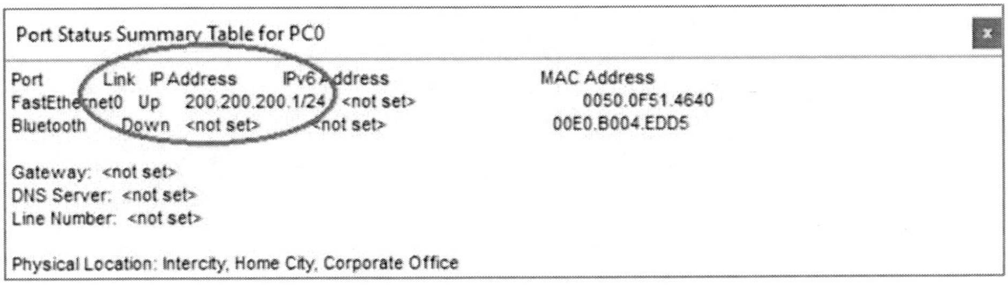

Figure 4.23 Computer Port Array

4.1.6.4 Command Line for PC

The command line is designed for advanced people who have more experience working with a real computer environment. These people often use the **command line** to display the IP address of the computer or to configure the PC or SERVER device.

The Cisco Packet Tracer implements a console that offers a poorer list of commands compared to the Console of the Microsoft Windows family, but a list of these commands for basic tasks is quite enough. To start the console for a computer, you must left-click on the computer, then go to its desktop and select a tool called **Command Prompt.**

Figure 3.4.24 Command line icon available on the desktop of your PC

After opening the command line, you can first check the commands available in the console by typing **help** or ?, after which you should press **Enter**. All available commands that can be used will be displayed.

```
Packet Tracer PC Command Line 1.0
C:\>help
Available Commands:
  ?            Display the list of available commands
  arp          Display the arp table
  cd           Displays the name of or changes the current directory.
  delete       Deletes the specified file from C: directory.
  dir          Displays the list of files  in C: directory.
  exit         Quits the CMD.EXE program (command interpreter)
  ftp          Transfers files to and from a computer running an FTP server.
  help         Display the list of available commands
  ide          Starts IoX development environment
  ioxclient    Command line tool to assist in app development for Cisco IOx
               platforms
  ipconfig     Display network configuration for each network adapter
  ipv6config   Display network configuration for each network adapter
  js           JavaScript Interactive Interpreter
  mkdir        Creates a directory.
  netsh
  netstat      Displays protocol statistics and current TCP/IP network
               connections
  nslookup     DNS Lookup
  ping         Send echo messages
  python       Python Interactive Interpreter
  quit         Exit Telnet/SSH
  rmdir        Removes a directory.
  snmpget      SNMP GET
  snmpgetbulk  SNMP GET BULK
  snmpset      SNMP SET
  ssh          ssh client
  telnet       Telnet client
  tracert      Trace route to destination
C:\>
```

Figure 4.25 Displaying a list of available commands at the command line

To view the IP address configuration of the computer, use the **ipconfig** command, or (more specifically) **ipconfig /all**.

```
C:\>ipconfig /all

Bluetooth Connection:(default port)

   Connection-specific DNS Suffix..:
   Physical Address................: 00E0.B004.EDD5
   Link-local IPv6 Address.........: ::
   IP Address......................: 0.0.0.0
   Subnet Mask.....................: 0.0.0.0
   Default Gateway.................: 0.0.0.0
   DNS Servers.....................: 0.0.0.0
   DHCP Servers....................: 0.0.0.0
   DHCPv6 Client DUID..............: 00-01-00-01-D2-6A-15-B1-00-50-0F-51-46-40

FastEthernet0 Connection:

   Connection-specific DNS Suffix..:
   Physical Address................: 0050.0F51.4640
   Link-local IPv6 Address.........: FE80::250:FFF:FE51:4640
   IP Address......................: 200.200.200.1
   Subnet Mask.....................: 255.255.255.0
   Default Gateway.................: 0.0.0.0
   DNS Servers.....................: 0.0.0.0
   DHCP Servers....................: 0.0.0.0
   DHCPv6 Client DUID..............: 00-01-00-01-D2-6A-15-B1-00-50-0F-51-46-40
```

Figure 4.26 Displaying the IP address of the computer via the command line

4.1.7 Testing Connection (Real Mode)

If you want to test the correctness of the connection along with the configuration, you can use various tools.

4.1.7.1 Simple Way - Graphic PING

The first way is to use a special tool available from the **Add Simple PDU icon** . When you select the **Add Simple PDU icon** an envelope will be "glued" to the cursor, which must be "added" to the computer that is to send the test signal (selection of the so-called source host).

Then click "add" the envelope to the target computer (selecting the so-called destination host), as shown in the figure below.

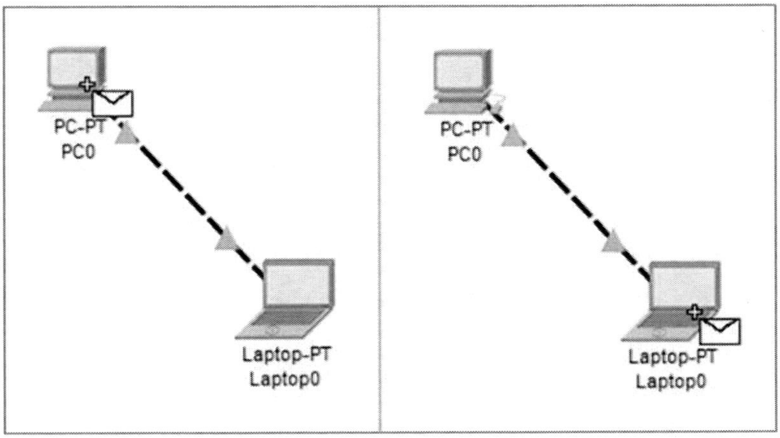

Figure 4.27 Sending simple test information

When everything is connected and configured correctly, a red icon should appear in the field located in the lower right corner of the program window, symbolizing the sending of the package, and next to it the **Successful** status.

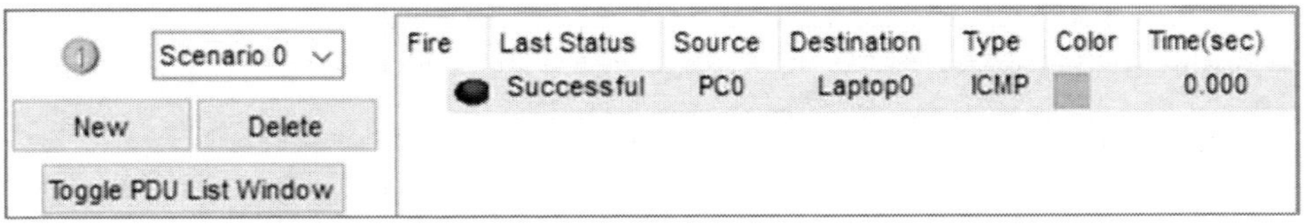

Figure 4.28 Successful delivery of the test package

Sometimes, however, especially when working with larger networks, it may turn out that the network configuration is correct, but the status takes the form of **Failed.** This is because only one test packet is sent during this type of activity, which for various reasons may not be delivered correctly (e.g. the ARP or routing protocol process has not yet been completed).

Then you do not need to send a new test package, but to refresh it correctly. To do this, point the mouse over the icon of the sent packet and double-click it with the left mouse button. After a while, the **In Progress** status will be displayed, and if everything is correct, it should change to **Successful**. This is illustrated in the figure below, if after several sent attempts the status still assumes the **Failed status**, it means that you need to check the correctness of the wiring or configuration of the devices.

Fire	Last Status	Source	Destination	Type	Color	Time(sec)
	Failed	PC0	Laptop0	ICMP		0.000

Fire	Last Status	Source	Destnation	Type	Color	Time(sec)
	In Progress	PC0	Laptop0	ICMP		0.000

Fire	Last Status	Source	Destination	Type	Color	Time(sec)
	Successful	PC0	Laptop0	ICMP		0.000

Figure 4.29 Refreshing a test package

If you want to be 100% sure that the transmission works correctly in both directions, you can perform the same test, only the other way around. To do this, proceed in the same way as above, but change the order of the indicated computers. After a while, the status in the second case should also get the **Successful state**, as the figure below illustrates.

Fire	Last Status	Source	Destination	Type	Color	Time(sec)
	Successful	PC0	Laptop0	ICMP		0.000
	Successful	Laptop0	PC0	ICMP		0.000

Figure 4.30 Checking the connectivity test in both directions

4.1.7.2 Standard Method - PING via Command Line

A more professional way to perform a connectivity test between devices is to use the command line, as if you were to display your computer's IP address. When you open the command line, type **ping** in the console, and after the space bar, the **IP address** of the computer to which you want to send the test information. In this case, it will be **ping 200.200.200.2**. After a while, four test packets will be sent automatically, and if the connection is correct, then four responses. Lack of response, indicates incorrect connection

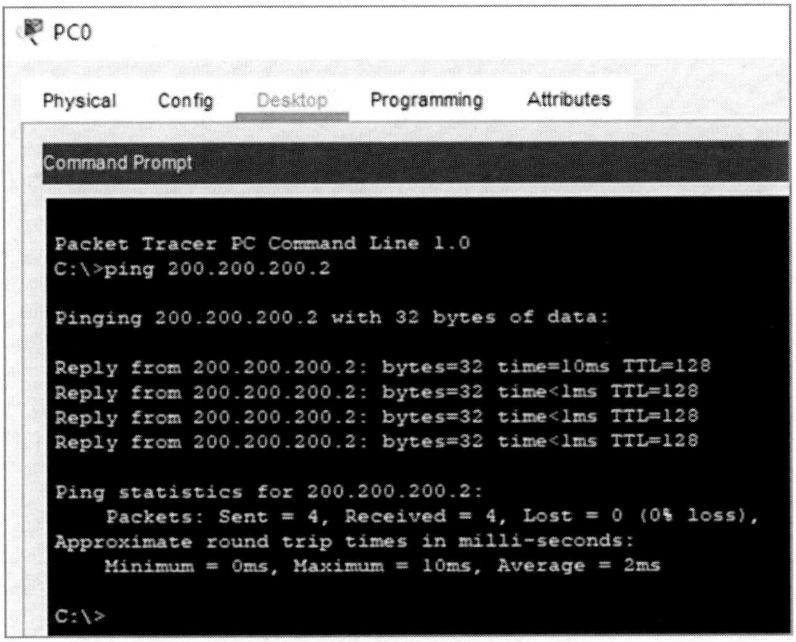

Figure 4.31 PING connection test

4.1.7.3 Advanced Graphic PING

When testing a connection, the Cisco Packet Tracer has a number of tools designed to do so. Another of them is advanced graphic Ping, if you want to use it, select **Add Complex PDU**  from the toolbar.

Then, as in the standard graphics ping, click the source computer, and then the **Create Complex PDU** dialog box opens, as shown in the figure below.

An important element to check is the **Outgoing Port** field, which should contain the interface from which the PING is to be sent, in this case it will be **FastEthernet0** (you can also select **Autoselect Port**).

Next, you can select the service that needs to be checked, in this case it will be PING and fill in the **Destination IP Address**: field (or click with the left mouse button on the target computer and the field will be filled in automatically).

An important element is to fill in the **Sequence Number** field (equivalent to the amount of sending test information), **Size** (the size of test information, expressed in bytes), as well as in the **Simulation Settings** section, select options (enter parameters appropriate for a single or multiple test): (**One Shot**) or if ping is to be sent cyclically, select the option (**Periodic**) and specify what, how many seconds – option (**Interval**).

Figure 4.32 Defining complex ping parameters

As in the previously described tests, in the lower right corner of the program window, you should see the **Successful** information, which is appropriate for the correct delivery of test information.

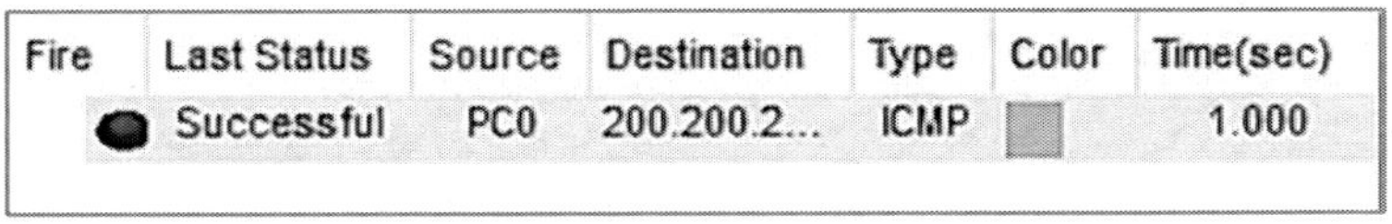

Figure 4.33 Correct provision of test information

4.1.8 Testing Connection (Simulation Mode)

The Cisco Packet Tracer also allows you to test in simulation mode, i.e. with visualization of network operation. To switch to simulation mode, use the button in the lower-right corner of the screen (Realtime or Simulation mode), as shown in the figure below.

Figure 4.34 Switch From Realtime to Simulation

After doing this, the **Simulation Panel** appears on the right side of the program window, in which all services and protocols to be tested are visible at the bottom of the window. However, if a simulation were made with these settings, too many test packets would be transmitted at once, and as a result, the simulation itself would be illegible.

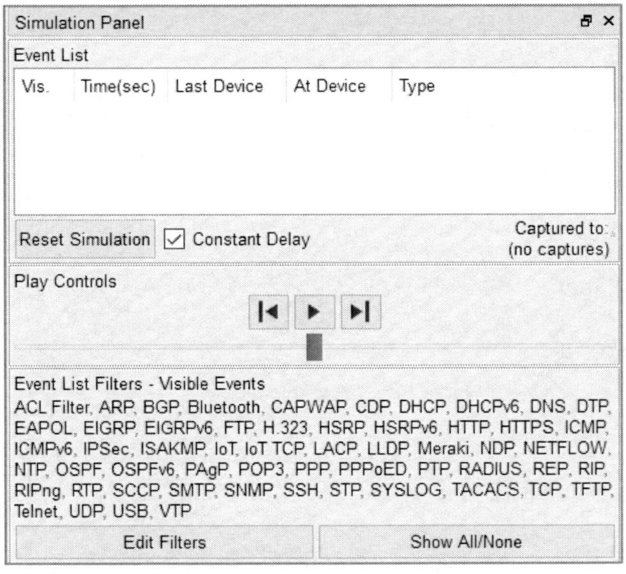

Figure 4.35 Simulation Panel window

If you want to test only the correctness of the connection, it is enough to simulate the ICMP protocol itself. To do this, click on the **Edit Filters** button, then to deselect all selected protocols, left-click **Show All/None**, and then ICMP.

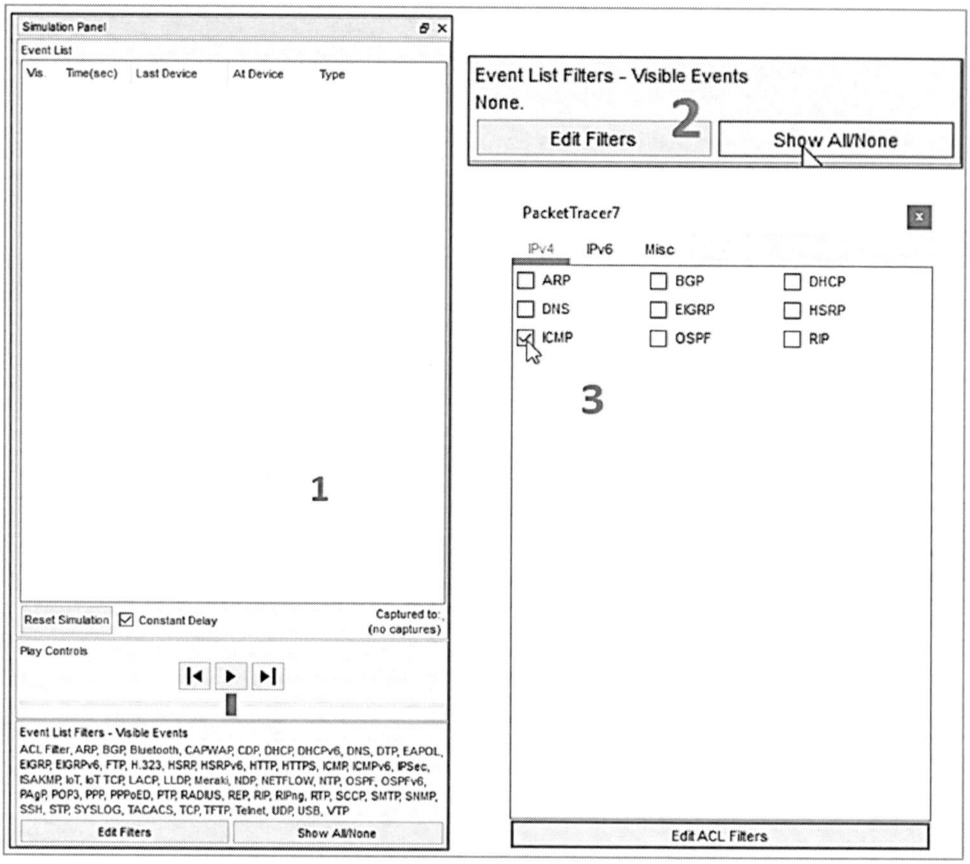

Figure 4.36 Selecting protocols for simulation

Legend:

1 – Simulation Panel

2 – Event List Filters

3 – Edit Filters

After that, you should proceed as it was in the mode of sending a simple graphic PING, i.e. click on **Add Simple PDU**  and proceed in the same way as in Realtime mode (click on the source computer, then the destination computer). After a while, an envelope will appear in the workspace above the source computer, in the waiting state – the prepared package for shipment.

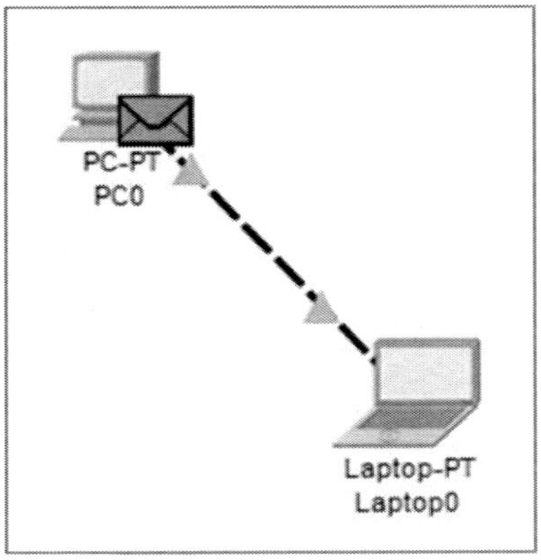

Figure 4.37 Ready-to-ship test package in Simulation mode

After completing the described actions, the ICMP package that has been prepared for shipment appears in the **Simulation Panel** window. At its bottom there is a slider through which you can set the speed of the simulation by moving it to the right or left. To begin with, it is recommended to leave the default position of the slider, after which you can press the **Play** button to start the simulation.

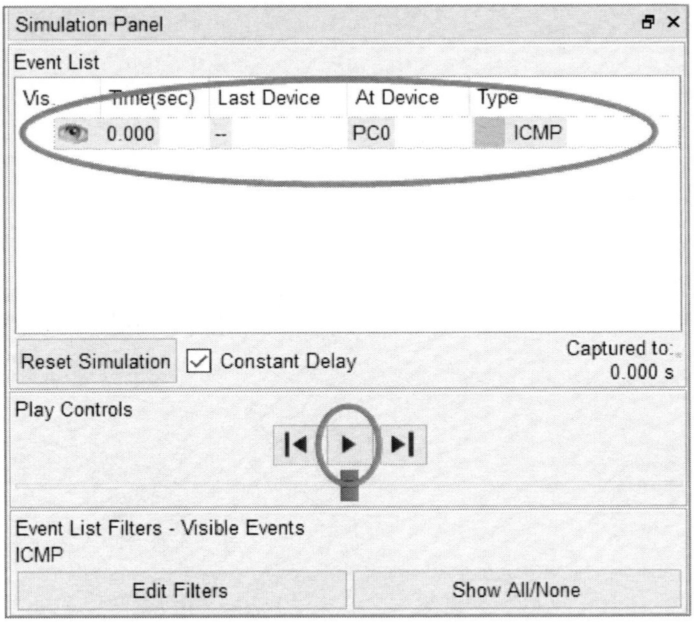

Figure 4.38 Simulation Panel view

After the simulation starts, the envelope moves from the source computer towards the target computer, and after reaching the goal (which is tantamount to sending a Ping query), the packet should be reversed towards the source computer (which is equivalent to sending a response to the Ping query).

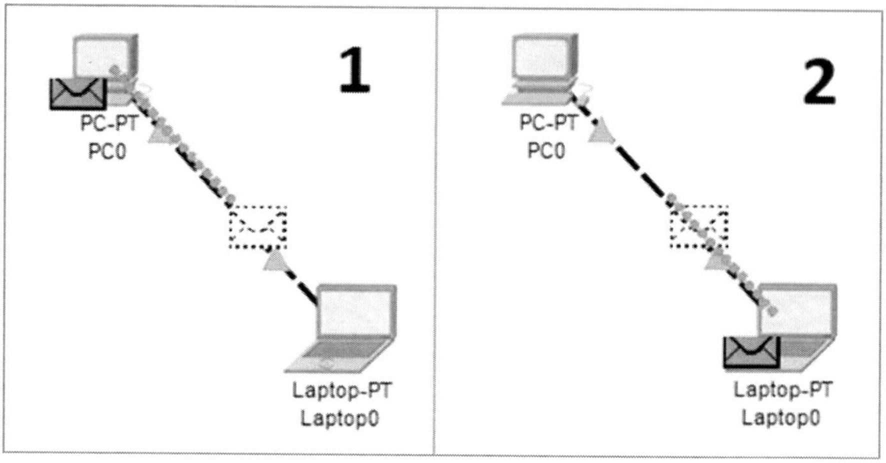

Figure 4.39 Graphical transmission of the PING package

Eventually, when the response is delivered to the sender, the icon at PC0 should appear, as in the figure below.

Figure 4.40 Graphical designation of the received PING packet

This means that the response is delivered correctly, while if a different icon is displayed, it means that the return packet has not been received. In the upper part of the simulation panel, you can also observe its individual stages, as shown in the figure below.

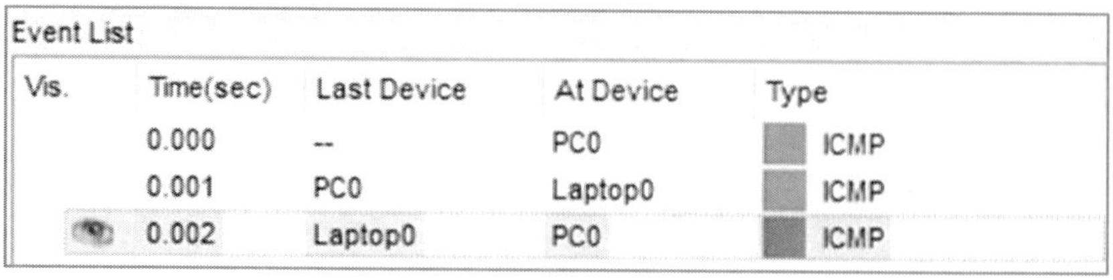

Event List

Vis.	Time(sec)	Last Device	At Device	Type
	0.000	--	PC0	ICMP
	0.001	PC0	Laptop0	ICMP
	0.002	Laptop0	PC0	ICMP

Figure 4.41 Individual simulation steps in the Simulation Panel window

CHAPTER 5

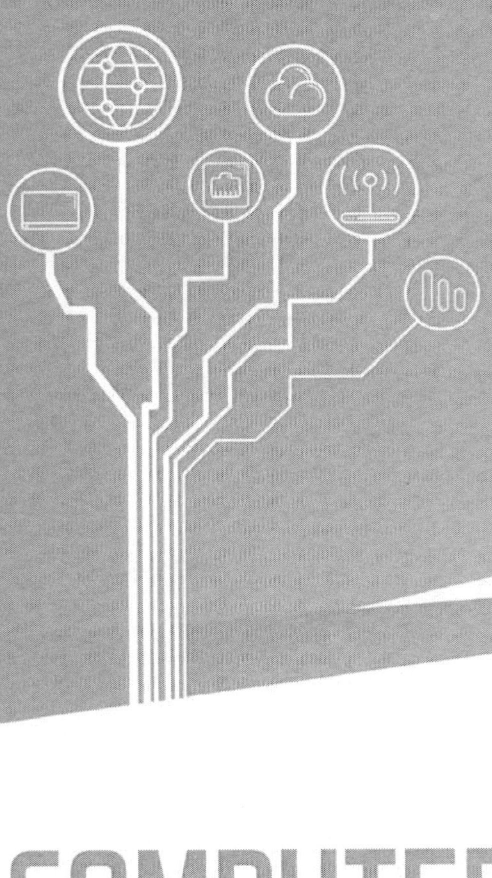

DEVICES USED TO CREATE NETWORK

COMPUTER NETWORKS IN PACKET TRACER

FOR BEGINNERS

5 Devices Used to Create Network

We have already discussed the configuration of PCs and tested the first connections. Now we will deal with slightly extensive networks, consisting of several end devices, exchanging information with each other.

5.1 Hubs

A **network hub** (commonly called a **hub**) is a device (also called a repeater) that allows you to connect many network devices to a computer network with a star topology. The hub is dedicated solely to transmitting and amplifying electrical signals from one port to all other network ports. The hub creates conflicting domains. A **collision domain** is a part of the network in which the transmission must be carried out by the device in a way that excludes transmission by other devices at the same time.

Types of network hubs can be found in the Hubs section, after selecting the Hubs section, 3 devices are available: **Hub**, **Repeater** and **Coaxial Spliter**. In our case, you will need the first device that can be placed in the working area.

Figure 5.1 Network devices available in the Hubs section

After clicking on the hub with the left mouse button, you should enter its settings, but it is an unmanaged device and cannot be configured (hence the **Config** tab is empty), but on the **Physical** tab, you can exchange network modules in it, exactly the same as it was in a desktop computer.

Figure 5.2 Physical view of the hub available in the program

By default, the hub is equipped with the six Fast Ethernet network interfaces and has an additional four empty ports, which allows for a maximum of ten end devices. In this subsection there is no description of the replacement of components, but only the construction and operation of the network based on this type of device will be presented.

To begin with it, 100% of its already installed interfaces will be used to create a LAN consisting of five PCs and one network printer. The arrangement of devices in the workspace is arbitrary, and the following figure illustrates an example of their arrangement.

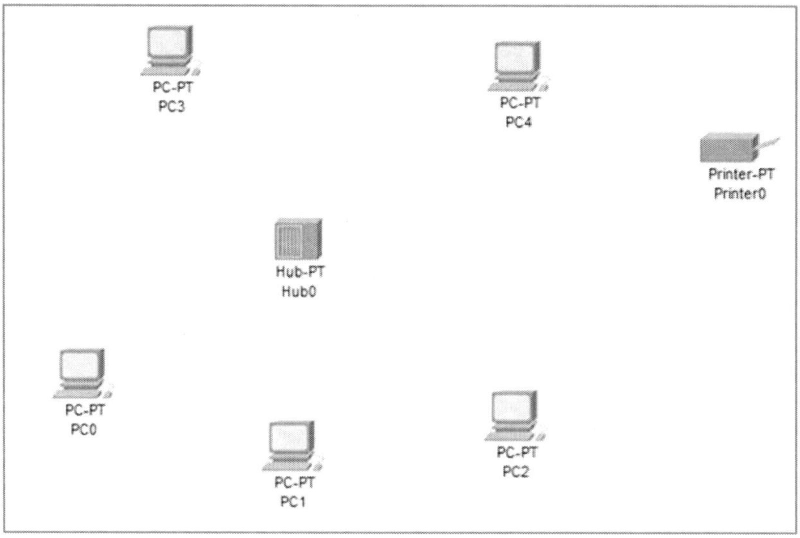

Figure 5.3 Arrangement of network devices in the program workspace

After you have placed all the devices in the workspace, you can proceed to connect them. Of course, you can use the tool for automatic cable selection for this purpose  or do it manually. When using the second method, keep in mind that you should use a Copper Straight-Through .

When computers are connecting to the hub manually, remember to select additional ports for given devices.

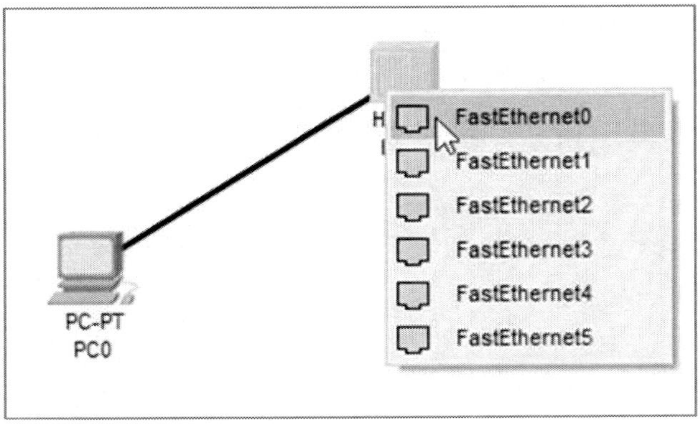

Figure 5.4 Manually connect your computer to the hub

When all devices have been connected, all LED should turn green, and the topology should look as shown in the figure below.

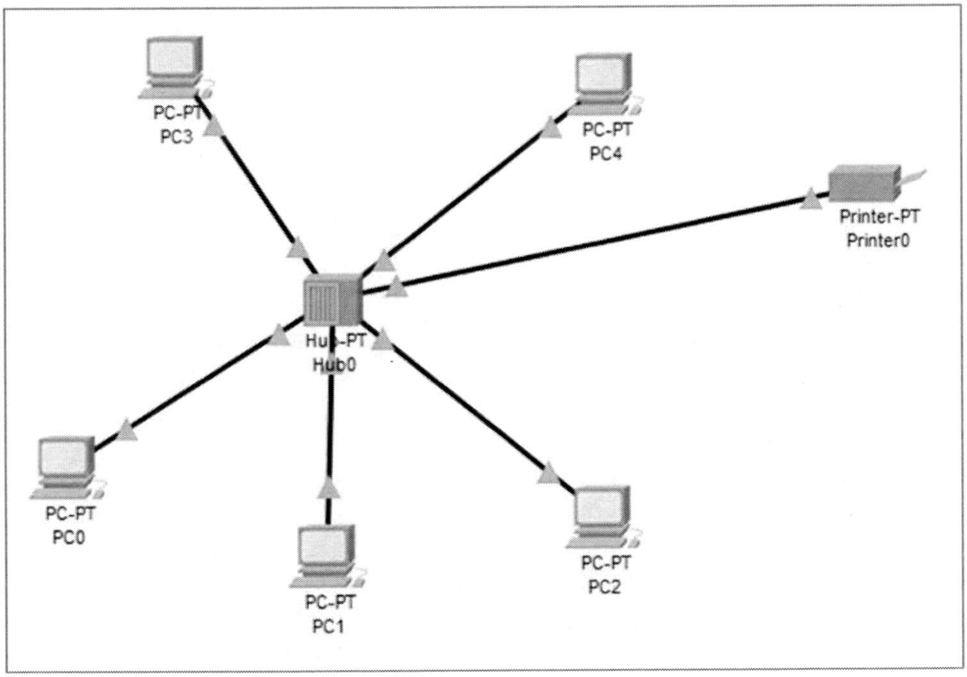

Figure 5.5 Correct connection of devices with the hub

Assumption: address class A 10.0.0.0/8 used, i.e. with network address 10.0.0.0 and mask 255.0.0.0. A device that we have not yet encountered in our book is a network printer, its physical appearance is shown in the figure below. Of course, the network card can be replaced with another type.

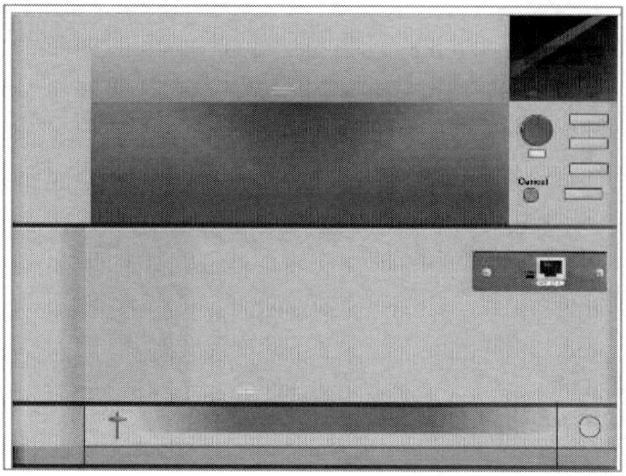

Figure 5.6 Physical appearance of a network printer

The IP configuration window of the network printer is illustrated in the figure below. On the **Config** tab, left-click on the printer port (in this case it will be **Fast Ethernet**) and configure the network address of the printer.

Figure 5.7 Network Printer IP Setup

When the network begins to take on slightly larger sizes, it is worth controlling it, and thus it is worth using comments in the form of notes that we can place in the work area of the program. For this purpose, we use the icon tool located on the toolbar – it is **Place Note**

.

You can use notes to identify computers faster. The created notes, containing the IP addresses of network devices, on the program board are illustrated in the following figure.

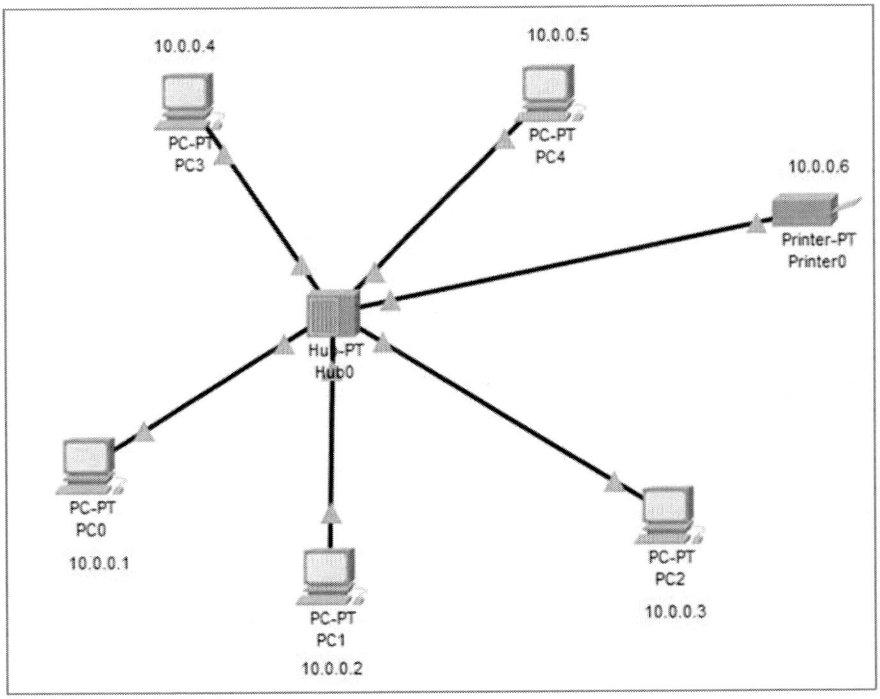

Figure 5.8 Notes placed on the program board

In the example presented above, all devices have been given IP addresses and network masks, network tests should be carried out. The network has been configured correctly, but to be sure you need tools that will be used to check the status of the hub, which is **Inspect** . After selecting this tool and clicking the hub with the left mouse button, the following window is displayed, where you can observe the status of all ports of the network device.

Port Status Summary Table for Hub0

Port	Link
FastEthernet0	Up
FastEthernet1	Up
FastEthernet2	Up
FastEthernet3	Up
FastEthernet4	Up
FastEthernet5	Up

Physical Location: Intercity, Home City, Corporate Office, Main Wiring Closet

Figure 5.9 Hub port status displayed

After confirming the status of the hub, you can enter the simulation mode.

In simulation mode, you can use ICMP to check the route of packets. For example, you need to send a test package from **PC0** to a **Printer0** network printer. During the simulation, when the test package passes through the hub, it separates into as many parts as there are devices connected to the hub and each of them goes to the device connected to a given port. This situation is not a mistake, but actually reflects the operation of the hub, which distributes input information to all active ports, without analyzing to which host they were addressed.

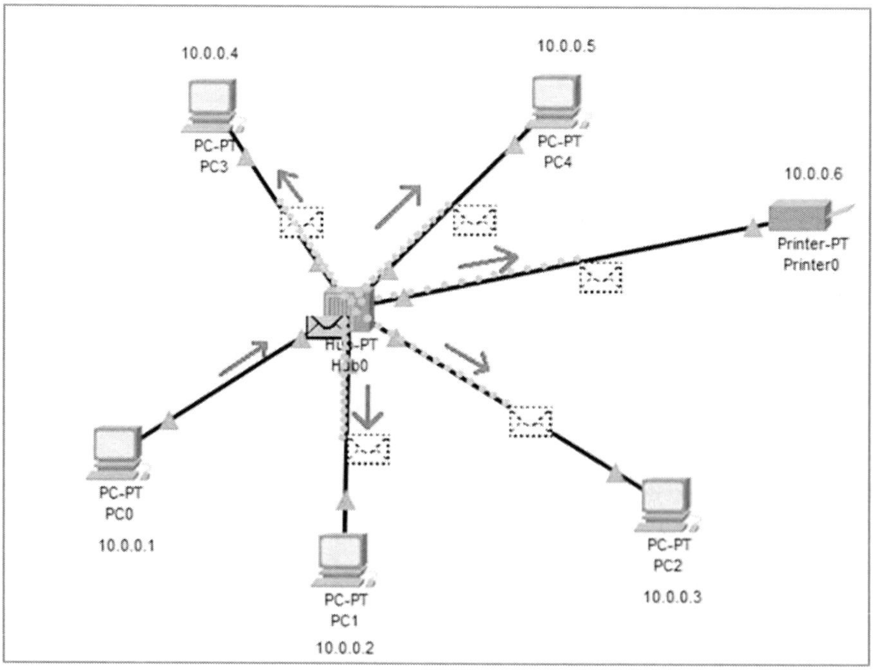

Figure 5.10 Cloning process of an ICMP packet passing through a hub

When the separated packets reach their goal, they are rejected by devices to which the test information was not addressed, as shown by the red "**X**" crosses displayed on the supplied envelopes. In this case, the packets are received only the "recipient" is a network printer, above which a green "**V**" or no "**X**" is displayed.

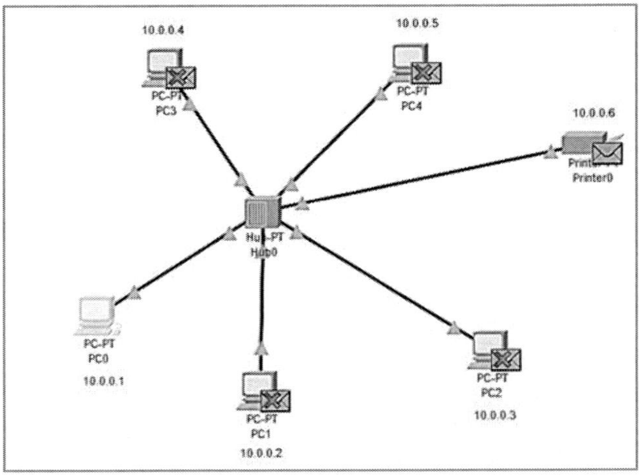

Figure 5.11 Test information provided for the network printer

After the package is delivered to the printer, the response to the query sent from PC0 will be transmitted. Due to the fact that the response will also pass through the hub, it will also be sent to all other computers, but it will only be accepted by the sender of the query, which will be marked with a "V" on pc0.

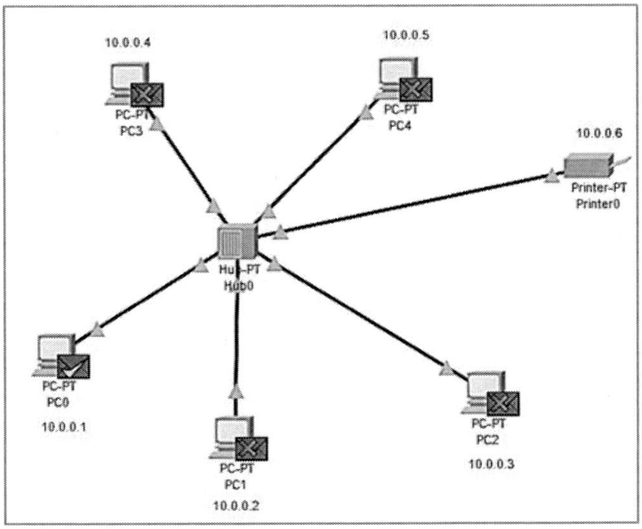

Figure 5.12 Delivering a response from a network printer to a PC0

After the simulation is complete, you can check the **Simulation Panel** window, specifically the **Event List**. Compared to the simulation carried out on only two connected computers, you can see that there are many more events, and they correspond to all stages of the simulation.

Event List

Vis.	Time(sec)	Last Device	At Device	Type
	0.000	–	PC0	ICMP
	0.001	PC0	Hub0	ICMP
	0.002	Hub0	PC1	ICMP
	0.002	Hub0	PC3	ICMP
	0.002	Hub0	Printer0	ICMP
	0.002	Hub0	PC4	ICMP
	0.002	Hub0	PC2	ICMP
	0.003	Printer0	Hub0	ICMP
	0.004	Hub0	PC0	ICMP
	0.004	Hub0	PC1	ICMP
	0.004	Hub0	PC3	ICMP
	0.004	Hub0	PC4	ICMP
	0.004	Hub0	PC2	ICMP

Figure 5.13 A list of the events of the simulation

In addition to the advantage that the hub has, which is the speed of operation and the ease of adding more hosts to the network, it is characterized by a huge disadvantage, which is the inability to transmit two packets at the same time.

This phenomenon is called a collision.

Below is a simulated collision. To perform the simulation, it is best to remove the previous package and add two packages from scratch. Assume that PC0 and PC2 will want to communicate with the printer at the same time.

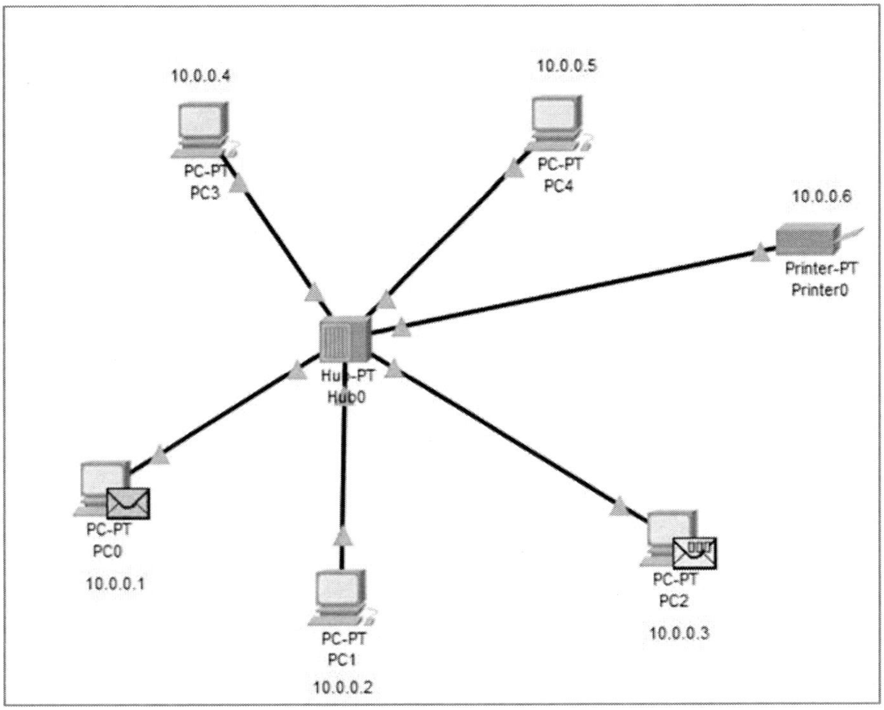

Figure 5.14 Waiting packages to start the simulation

To validate the addition of packages, do so in the Event List event window, as shown in the figure below.

Fire	Last Status	Source	Destination	Type	Color	Time(sec)
	In Progress	PC0	Printer0	ICMP		0.000
	In Progress	PC2	Printer0	ICMP		0.000

Figure 5.15 Visible packages in the Event List window

After checking all the guidelines described above, you can run the simulation. Packages begin to move towards the hub at the same time. When they reach the central point of the network, a collision occurs between them, which in the program is symbolized by red flare, as illustrated in the figure below.

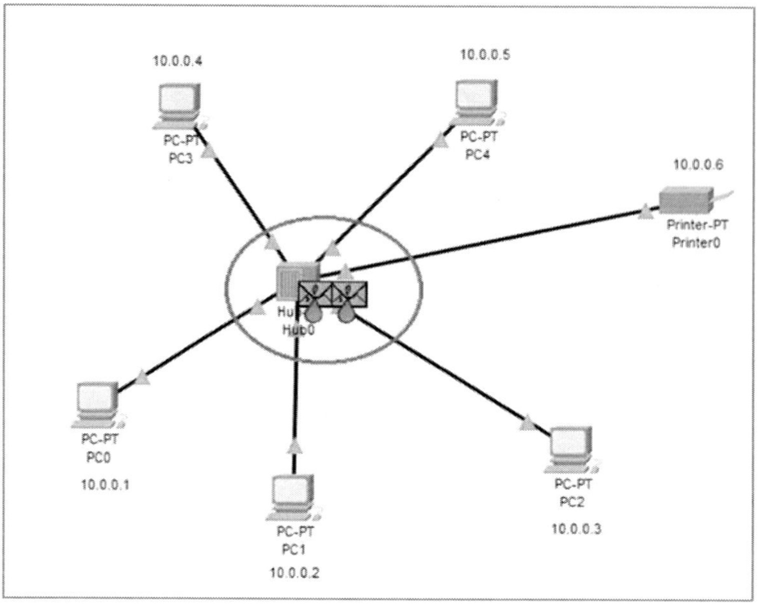

Figure 5.16 Collision inside the HUB

Due to the hub feature, the packets will be duplicated according to the number of ports used and in an unreadable form for terminal devices will be delivered to computers and the printer, as shown in the figure below.

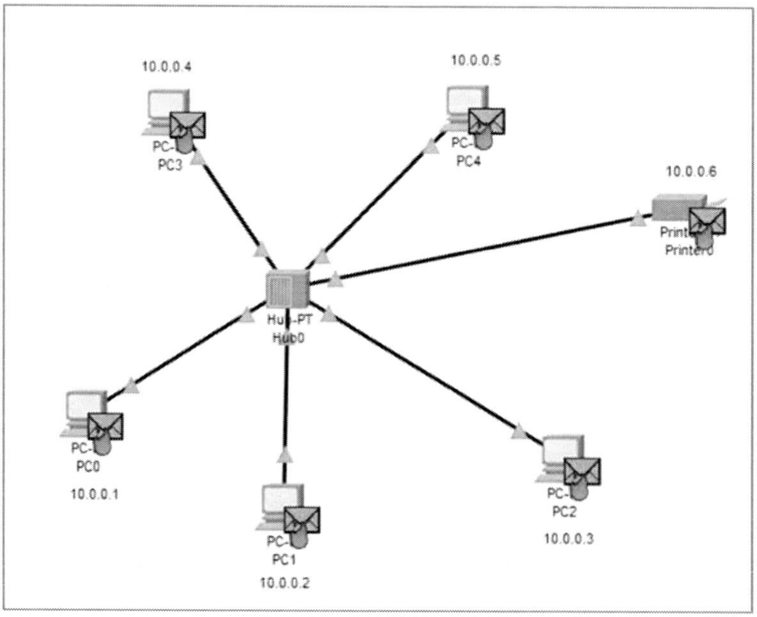

Figure 5.17 Duplicate collision packages delivered to terminal equipment

5.2 Repeaters

A device with the same properties as a hub is a signal amplifier (repeater). By default, it has two ports of the same type.

With the help of a repeater, it is certainly impossible to create a network with a star topology, because you can connect only two devices to it. However, it can be used to amplify the signal and increase the distance between computers.

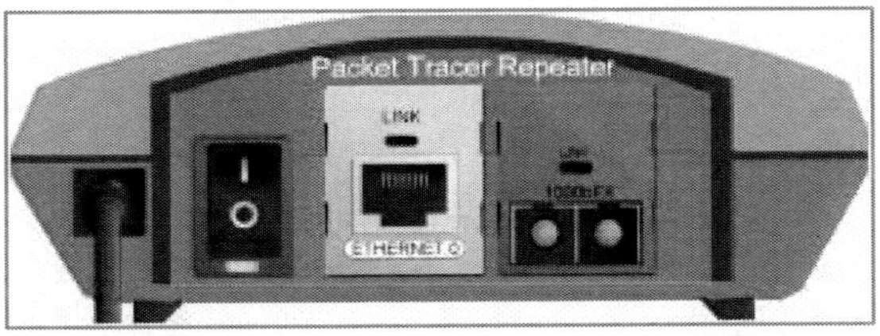

Figure 5.18 Repeater with Fast Ethernet and Fiber Optic port

This example assumes that two computers need to be connected to each other, but the distance between them is about 500 m, which is more than 100 m.

According to standards and norms, the length of the cable (Ethernet segment) should not be longer than 100 m, so use devices that amplify the signal between network segments, e.g. two repeaters. All devices are placed in the work area of the program, as shown in the figure below.

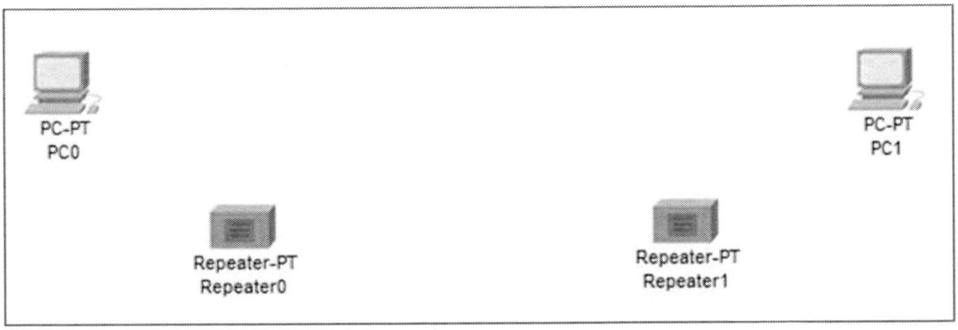

Figure 5.19 Deployed network devices

In order to configure networks containing repeaters, add them to the network, left-click on the icon of the first repeater, then replace one of the ports from Ethernet to optical and do the same with the second repeater.

Then you need to connect the computers to the devices using a **Copper Straight Through** Ethernet cable and connect the repeaters using an optical cable (**Fiber**) .

The connection should be as shown below. The optical wires in the area of the main board of the program take the colour **red**.

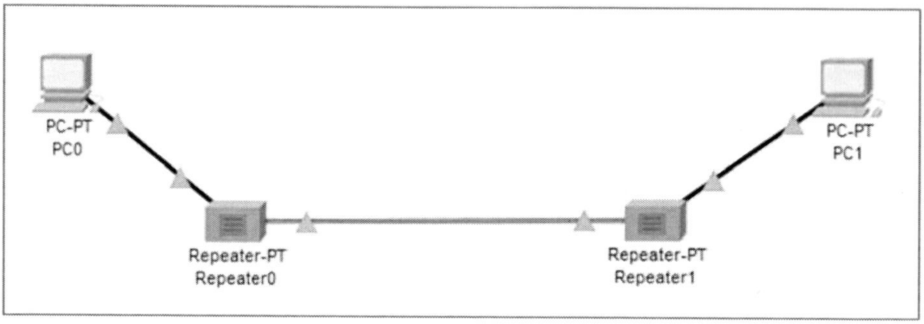

Figure 5.20 Correct connection of network devices

You can then proceed to perform device addressing to finally perform link tests in both **Realtime** and **Simulation** mode.

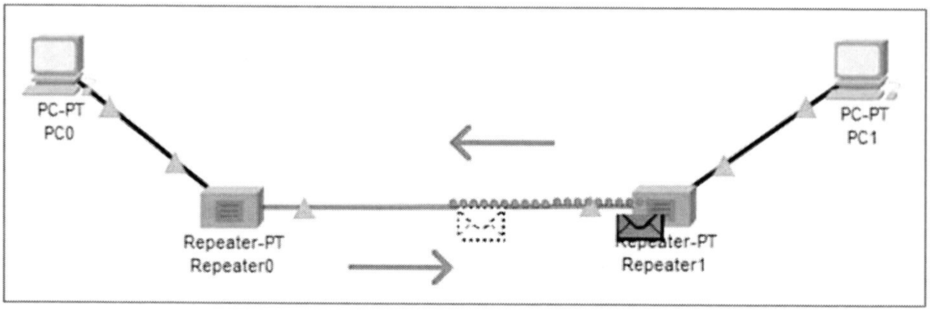

Figure 5.21 Link test in Simulation mode

5.3 Bridges

Bridges are used to limit the collision domain, e.g. to divide one LAN segment into two collision segments (domains) or to separate physical networks, e.g. copper cable network from fiber optic cable network.

5.3.1 Two-segment Network Built with Two Hubs

Before it is presented what is the point of using bridges, this subsection will describe how a two-segment network made of two hubs behaves. Hubs with Ethernet ports are connected to each other by a patch cable.

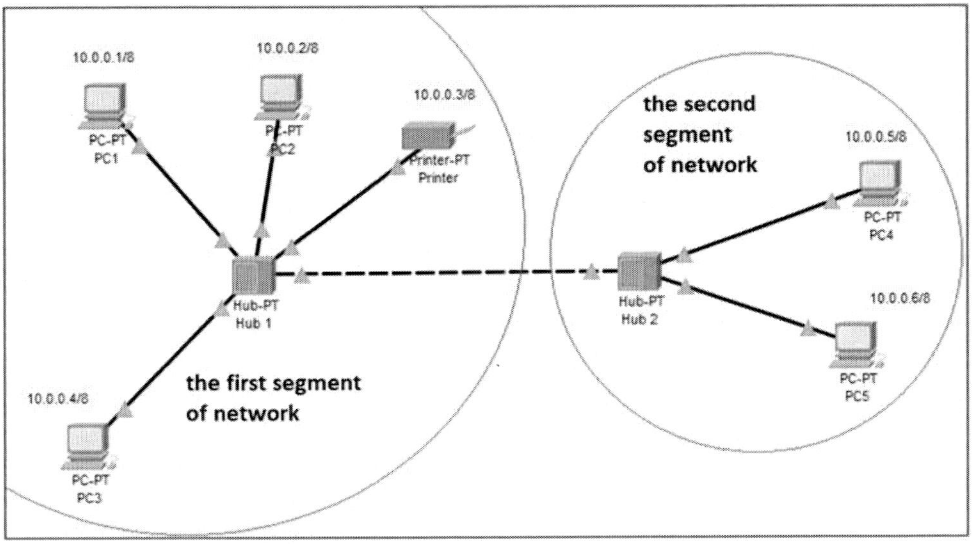

Figure 5.22 Two connected LAN segments

After going to the simulation and sending the test packet from the PC3 to the printer, which is in the same segment, then due to the feature of the hub, it will also be delivered to the second segment, it will also be duplicated to all connected ports. So you can see that the collision domain (the area where packet collisions can occur) has expanded to include a second LAN segment.

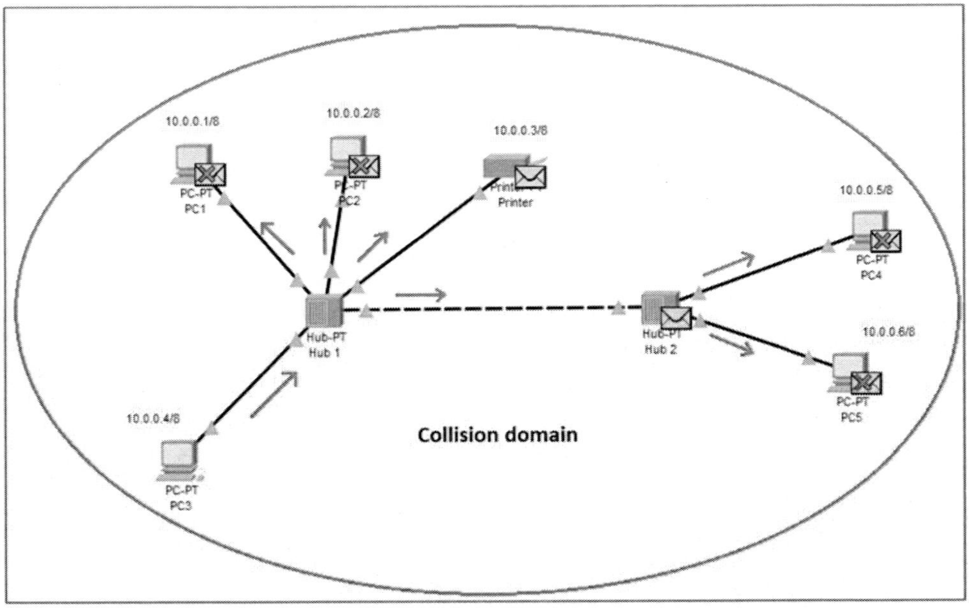

Figure 5.23 Collision domain covering two LAN segments

If the simulation comes to successful, you will notice that the printer correctly accepted the sent packet, after which it will send a response to PC0, the response, like the query, will also be redundantly distributed to the second LAN segment.

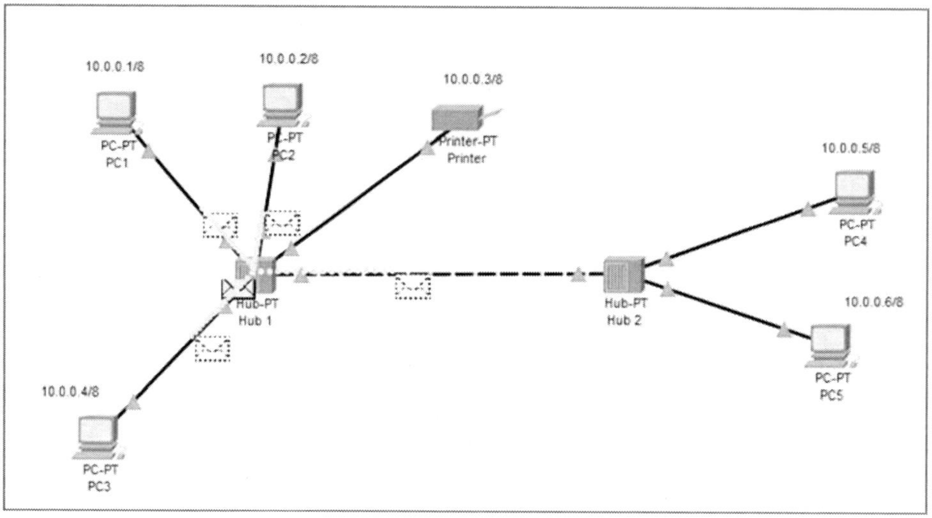

Figure 5.24 Distribute packets to two network segments

5.3.2 Sample Network with a Bridge

To limit a collision domain to a single LAN segment, you can use a **bridge**. Bridge devices are located in the **Switches section**, which is a device in the list of available devices called **PT-Bridge**.

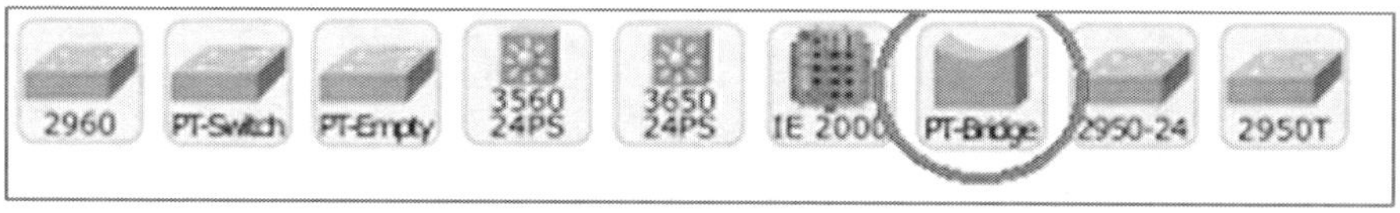

Figure 5.25 Select a bridge from the list of switches

The physical view of the bridge in the Cisco Packet Tracer looks like the following figure. The device is not configurable, it has two Ethernet ports, which of course can be exchanged for others according to the previously learned methods.

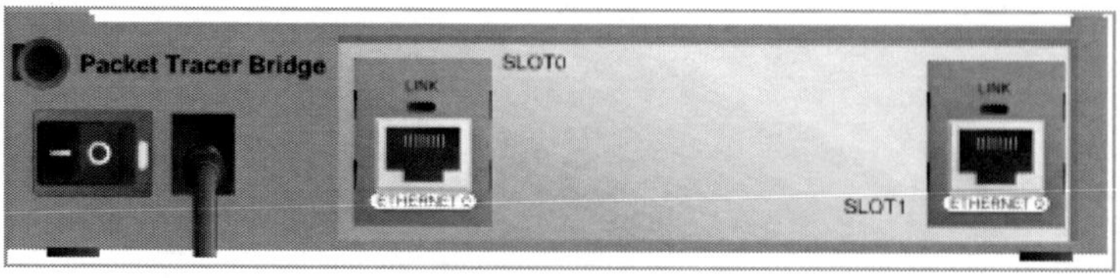

Figure 5.26 Physical view of the network bridge

If you want to separate two LAN segments with a bridge, disconnect the connection between the two hubs using the **Delete tool** , available has a toolbar.

After that, in the working area you need to put a bridge and connect the hubs with the bridge, the patch wire. LED sirens next to the bridge first light up in orange, only after a while they take on the green status. This is a normal symptom that consists in first of all in reading the MAC addresses of connected computers in a given segment.

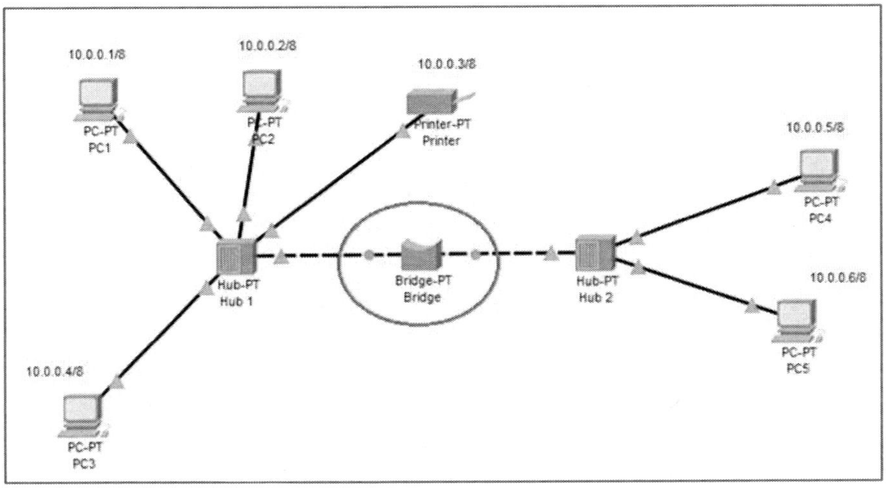

Figure 5.27 Network bridge connecting two LAN segments

To check the bridge configuration, you must generate some traffic from one network segment to another. Then you can use the **Inspect tool** , applied to the bridge, which you can click with the left mouse button, and then select **MAC Table** from the context menu, as shown in the figure below.

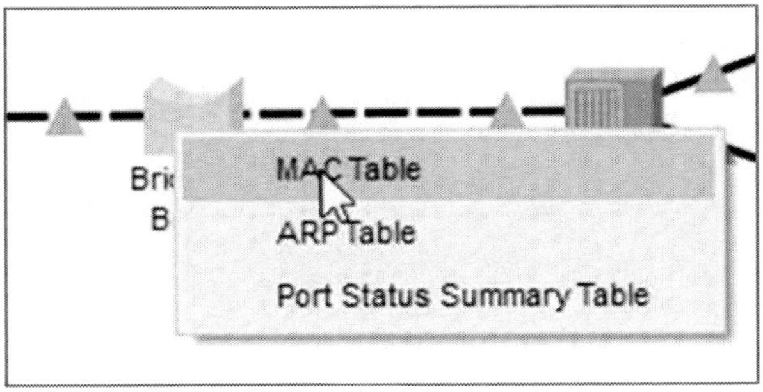

Figure 5.28 Selecting MAC Table

After that, a window will be displayed on the screen with an array of MAC addresses in the devices and the port number of the bridge to which they are attached.

MAC Table for Bridge

VLAN	Mac Address	Port
1	0006.2A1B.B3A8	Ethernet1/1
1	000C.CF37.3675	Ethernet0/1
1	000C.CFE9.4562	Ethernet0/1
1	0030.F2D7.7D5E	Ethernet0/1
1	0060.2F05.2D23	Ethernet1/1

Figure 5.29 Example array of MAC addresses in the bridge

What happens when a test packet is sent from PC0 to the printer in simulation mode? The bridge will distribute packets to all devices, but when the bridge receives the MAC address of the recipient of the packet (that is, the printer) and checks that it is on the same (left) segment of the network, it passes the packet further (to the same collision domain), as shown in the figure below.

If the MAC address of the packet recipient is on a different (right) network segment, the bridge will pass the packet further (to another collision domain).

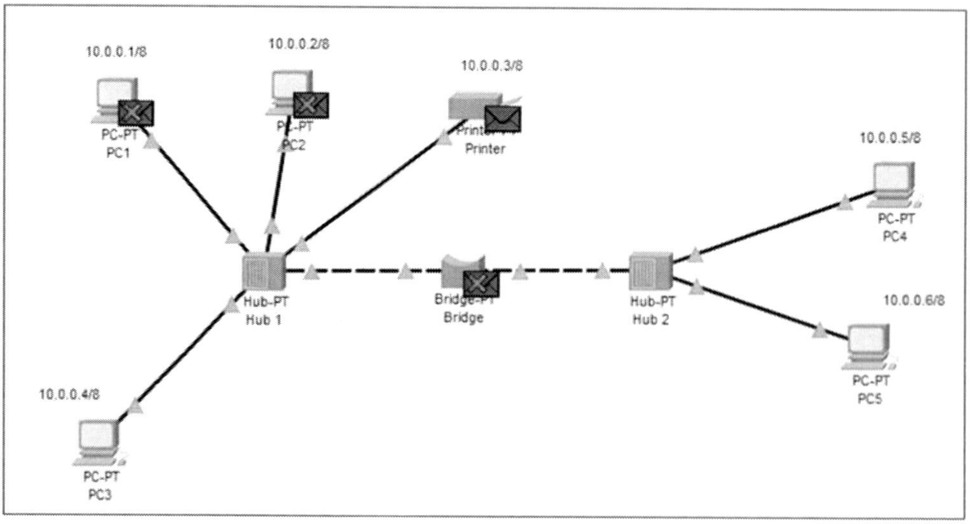

Figure 5.30 Limit the collision domain over the bridge

If the packet were addressed to any computer located in the right segment of the network, e.g. PC5, the bridge would simply pass the packet.

5.4 Switches

This section shows the basic network switches, also called switches, which can be used in the Cisco Packet Tracer. In the Cisco Packet Tracer we have a full range of them at our disposal. If you want to see the entire library of devices, select the **Switches section** from the bottom tray, and then all available switches appear on the right side, as shown in the figure below.

Figure 5.31 Network switch models available in the Cisco Packet Tracer

In the program, the available devices can be divided into two categories: real devices used on a daily basis and virtual devices, which the user can freely modify. In real devices, components cannot be removed, added, or replaced. An example of this type of device is the basic Catalyst 2950 series 24-port switch, which is shown in the figure below.

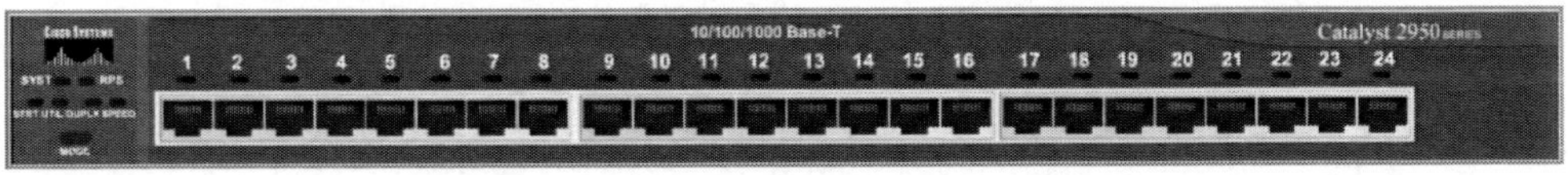

Figure 5.32 Switch Catalyst 2950

The another next real device is also the basic 24-port Catalyst 2960 series switch.

Figure 5.33 Switch Catalyst 2960

Both of the above series of switches belong to the group of fully configurable devices with a built-in IOS system, but for a user who will not apply changes in the so-called "zero configuration" there will be no differences between this type of devices.

The another next device in this group is the basic **Catalyst 3560 series multilayer** switch, which can work in two layers of the OSI model. Knowledge of the operation of this type of device will not be necessary in this part of the book. Detailed configuration of this type of switch requires advanced knowledge of computer networks.

Figure 5.34 Catalyst 3560 Series Multilayer Switch

In the Cisco Packet Tracer, there are two types of virtual devices (switches) that can be freely modified for the needs of the network. These are switches marked in the program as **PT**.

The one of them is the **Switch-PT** switch, which by default has 4 Fast Ethernet and 2 Fiber optic ports and 4 empty ports, which gives a total of 10 ports at the disposal of the PT user.

Figure 5.35 Switch-PT

The another one is the **Switch-PT-Empty** switch, which has 10 empty ports. It gives you the opportunity to equip with appropriate interfaces, in accordance with the previously learned rules.

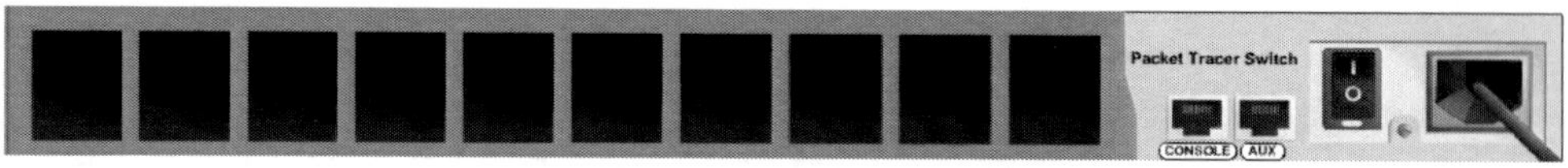

Figure 5.36 Switch-PT-Empty

The example topology contains 6 network devices and two segments.

Two **Switch-PT-Empty** switches were used. The topology should look like the following figure.

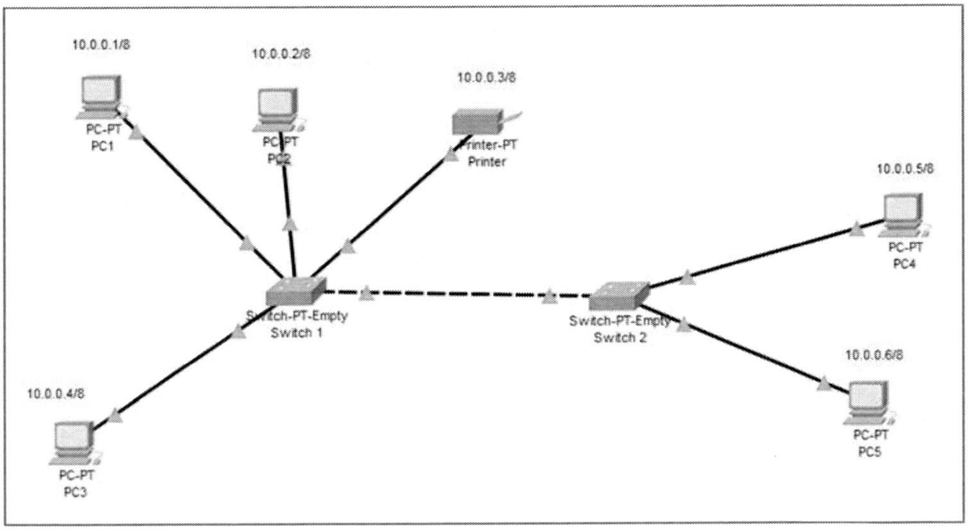

Figure 5.37 Example topology based on two network switches

After going to the simulation and performing a connection test between the PC3 and the printer, the packet passing through **Switch 1**, based on the physical MAC addresses of the end devices, will recognize the recipient and forward the packet only to the appropriate port, thus limiting excessive traffic.

In this situation, there are two independent network segments, during which each device together with a single switch port forms a single, small micro-segmentation of the LAN (micro-segmentation) called a **collision domain**.

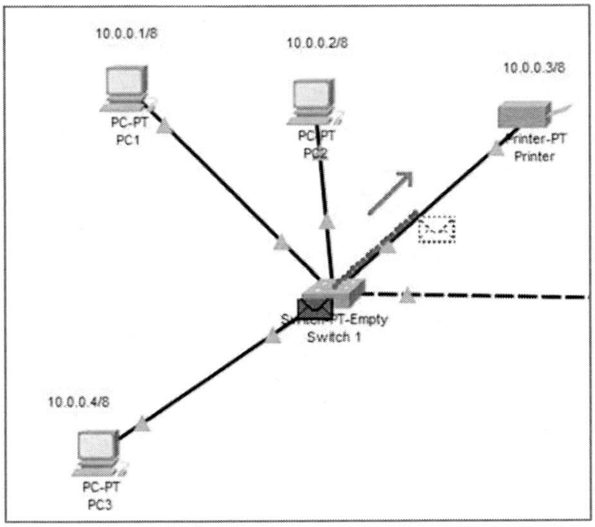

Figure 5.38 Packet route using switch

Sometimes, when simulating in slightly more complex networks, a message may appear at the very end of the network informing about a buffer overflow, as shown in the figure below.

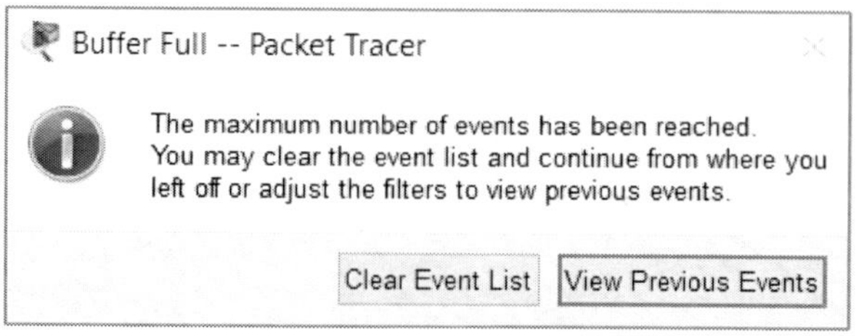

Figure 5.39 Overflowing list of events during simulation

Then press the **Clear Event List** button to clear the list of events and return to the simulation.

5.5 Access Points

If you want to make a network based on access points, i.e. wireless, you must use the appropriate devices, which are available in the **Wireless Devices** section. In this section there are 3 very similar devices that differ from each other in the frequency of work, and thus classes, e.g. A or N. If you want to make a network based on access points, i.e. wireless, you must use the appropriate devices, which are available in the Wireless Devices section. In this section there are 3 very similar devices that differ from each other in the frequency of work, and thus classes, e.g. A or N.

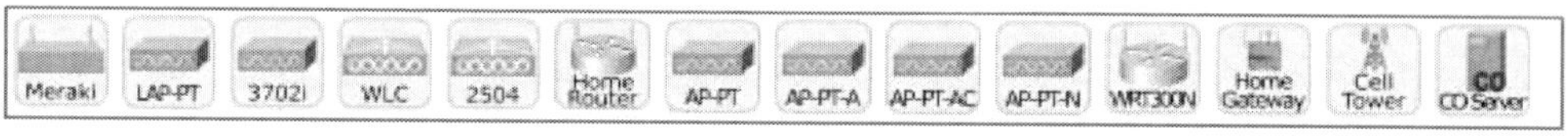

Figure 5.40 Types of wireless devices

The View of the Access-Point in the Cisco Packet Tracer is shown in the following figure. This is a typical device with one FastEthernet port, which of course can be exchanged for another network interface.

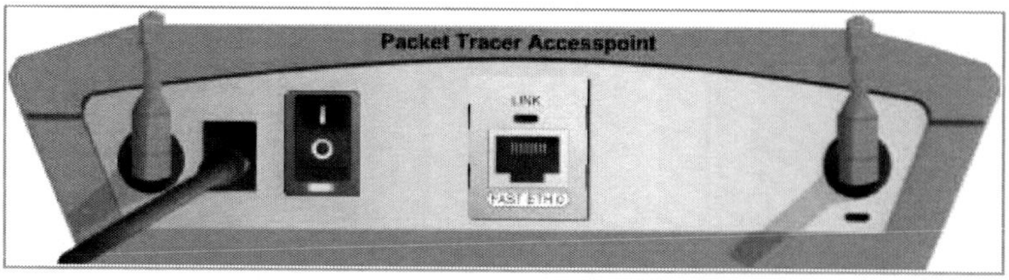

Figure 5.41 Physical view of the Access Point

You can build a network based on the same end devices as in the previous chapter, but often the role of switches and routers is taken over by access-points. However, creating such a topology will not be as easy as before. The first thing to do is to equip each computer with a wireless card. This action should not cause much difficulty, but when we put one Access Point in the workspace, the connections to it will be made automatically and when we put a second Access Point, there will probably be a problem that no end device wants to connect to the other access device. As is the case in the figure below.

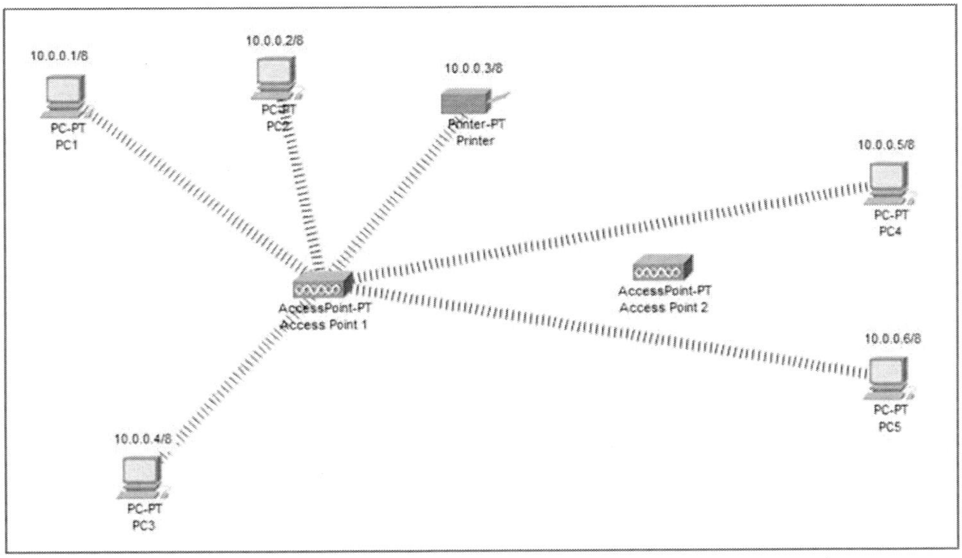

Figure 5.42 Connected end devices with one Access-Point

There are two ways to resolve this issue, which you should look for in the configuration of access devices. After clicking on the right Access Point 2 device with the left mouse button (to which no computer has connected), you need to go to the Config tab. Two ports are configured:

- Port 0 – responsible for the wired link of the device,
- Port 1 – responsible for the wireless link.

In our case, you go to Port 1 where the WIFI network was encrypted, for example, we will use the WPA2 key, entering the password: **cisco321**. After applying the changes, it will not change much in our topology, because you still have to manually connect computers to the encrypted WIFI network.

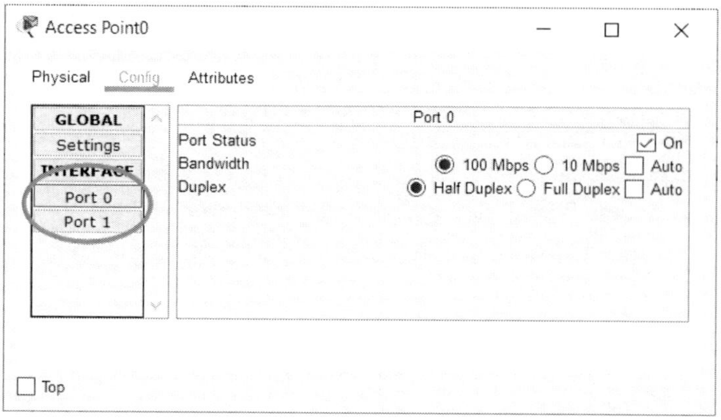

Figure 5.43 Fast Ethernet port configuration window in Access-Point

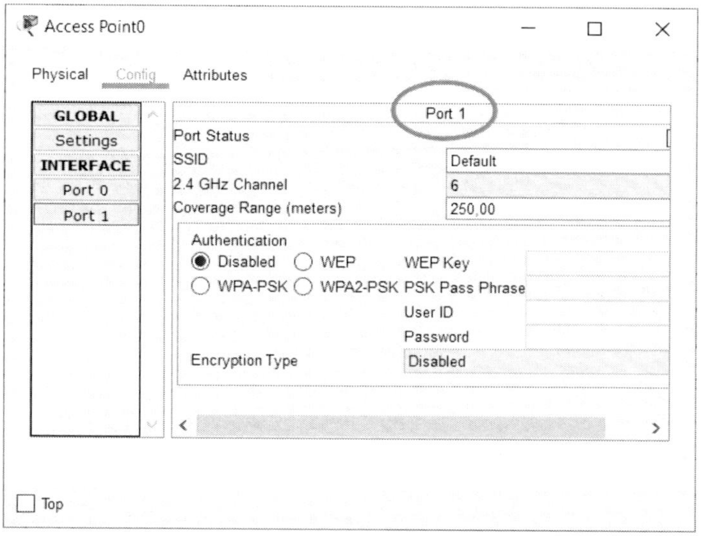

Figure 5.44 Wireless port configuration window in Access-Point

Now you need to encrypt access to the second access point using **WPA2-PSK** encryption and the password "**cisco321**". You can connect selected computers to it by setting the same type of encryption on them and providing a password. To do this, click on PC5 with the left mouse button and go to the **Config** tab. Then, in the list of interfaces, search for the Wireless port in which in the **Authentication** section select **WPA2-PSK** encryption and enter the password: **cisco321** in the Pass Phrase field.

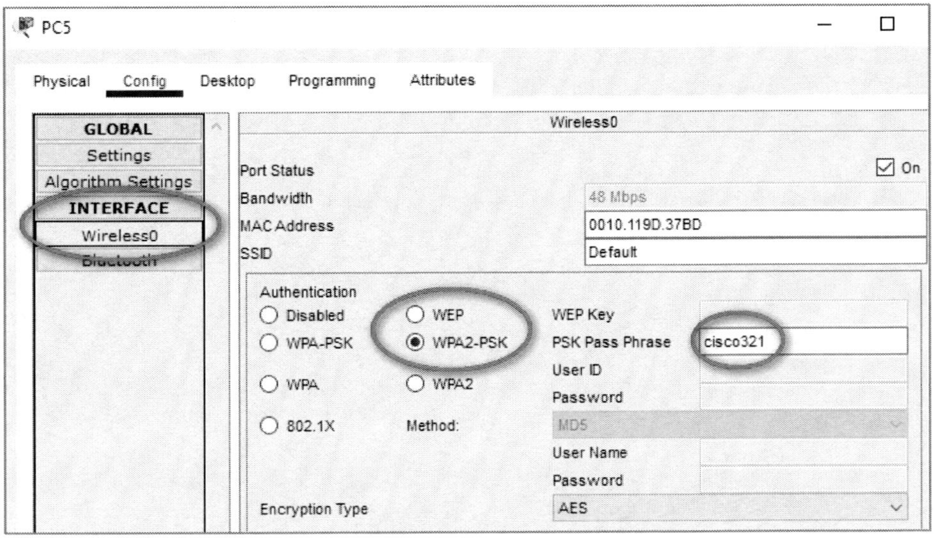

Figure 5.45 Selecting encryption on your computer's wireless card

After leaving the configuration window, after a while the connection will be made automatically. When all the computers in a given segment are connected, the topology should look as shown in the figure below.

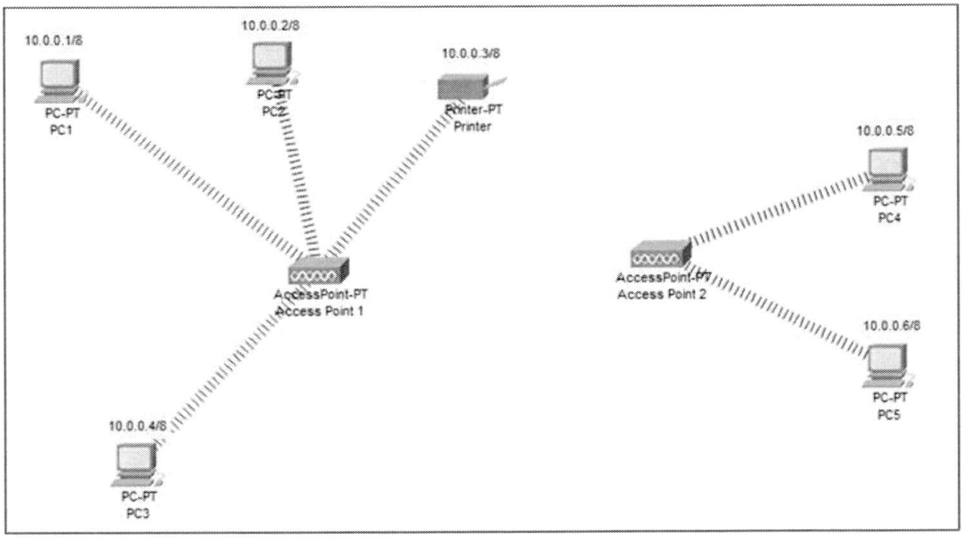

Figure 5.46 Connected terminal equipment to the appropriate access points

In order to connect access-points with each other, a patch cable in the **FastEthernet** standard should be used. Ultimately, the topology should take the following form.

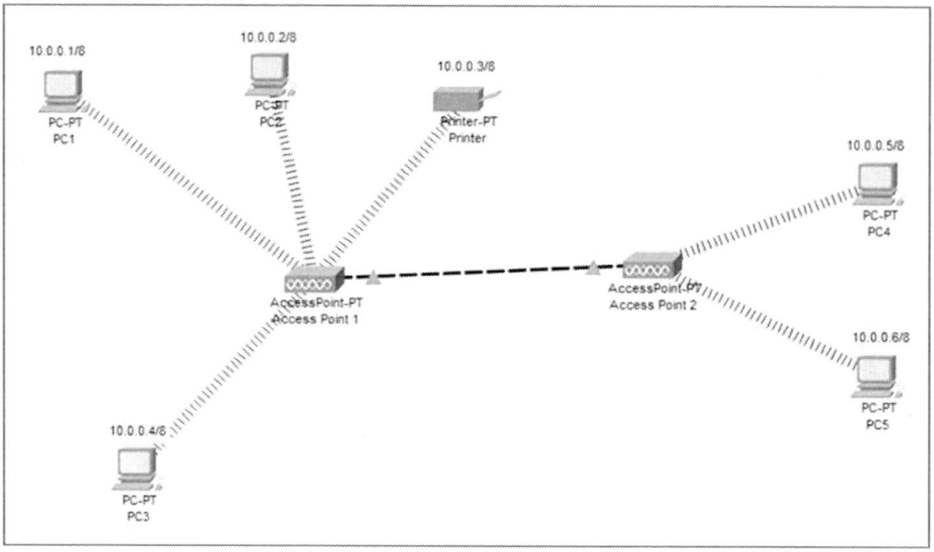

Figure 5.47 Connection of two wireless LAN segments

The prepared network is already ready for simulation, assuming that **Access Point 1** does not encrypt the signal, and **Access Point 2** connects computers using **WPA2** encryption. Due to the fact that you should not leave the Wi-Fi network open, but you should encrypt the signal, you could be tempted to set **Access Point 1** to encrypt with a different key or type of encryption.

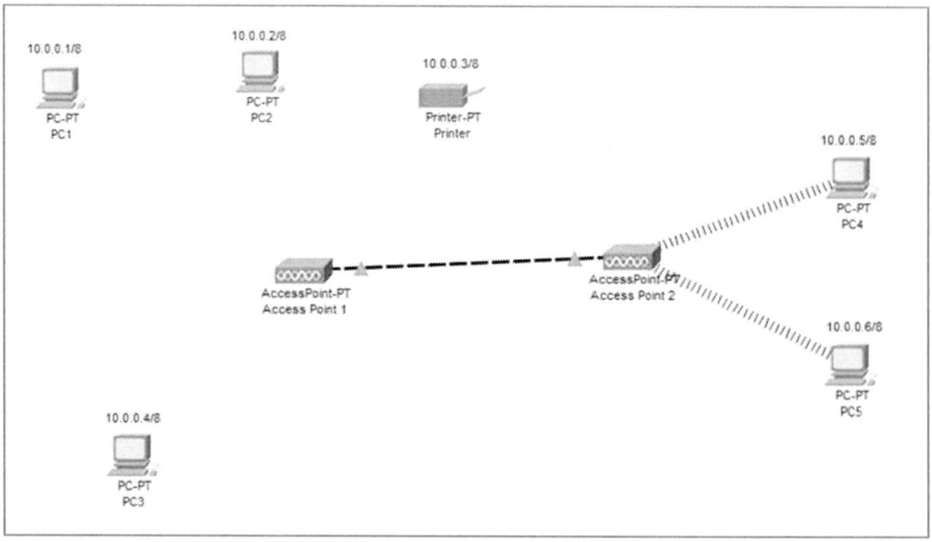

Figure 5.48 Disconnected network devices after changing wireless network settings in Access Point 1

In this case, there will be no signal encryption for simulation purposes, but you must intentionally rename the **SSID** so that the computers disconnect the automatic wireless connection, achieving the situation shown in the following figure. For the purposes of the exercise, the new SSID name is **AP1**.

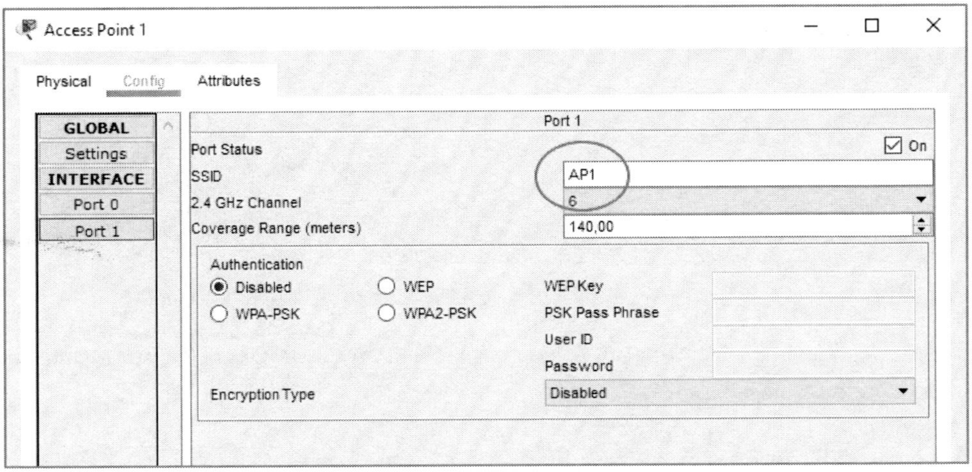

Figure 5.49 Setting the SSID on the Access Point

You need to manually connect each computer by clicking on it with the left mouse button and going to the **Config** tab to finally enter **AP1** in the **SSID** field. When you close the window, the connection will be made automatically.

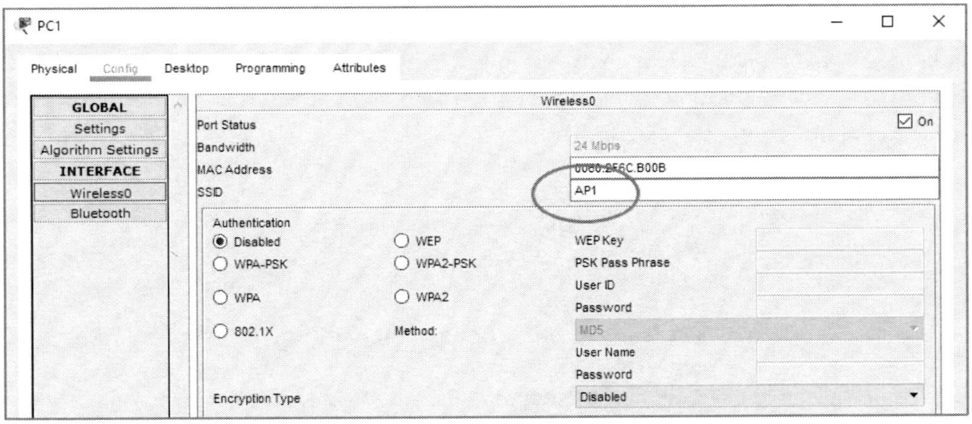

Figure 5.50 Setting the SSID on the computer's wireless card

5.6 Other Access Point Wireless Devices

5.6.1 LAP-PT Devices

The **LAP-PT** is part of the wireless access point group and is used only for Wi-Fi operations. You can configure static addresses, possibly dynamic via DHCP: gateway address, DNS address and radio signal access range in meters (**maximum 1000 m**).

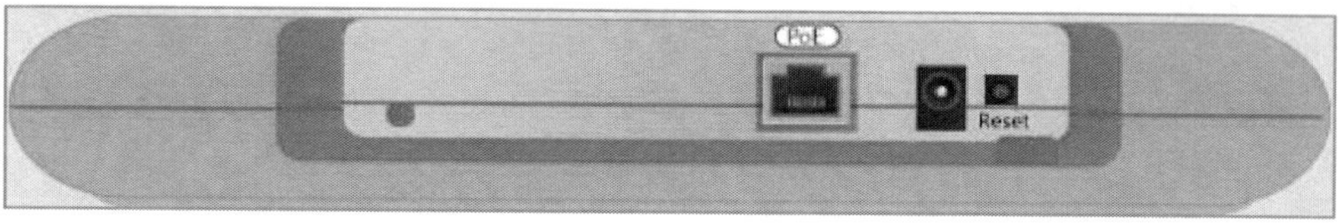

Figure 5.51 View of the LAP-PT device available in the program

The device has only one **Gigabit Ethernet** port and a built-in **Dot11Radio** module for radio communication.

5.6.2 3702i Device

The **3702i** belongs to the group of wireless devices such as the **Cisco Aironet** access point controller.

It is used to operate the Wi-Fi network in which WLC controllers are located. You can configure the static address of the Wireless Controller (WLC). The following static or dynamic addresses can be configured for the internal network: gateway address, DNS address and radio signal access range in meters (maximum 1000 m). The more accurate operation and configuration of this device is beyond the scope of this book, and therefore these capabilities will not be described.

Figure 5.52 View of the 3702i available in the program

The device has only one Gigabit Ethernet port and a built-in Dot11Radio module for radio communication.

5.6.3 WLC-PT Device

The **WLC-PT** device belongs to the group of wireless devices such as the **Wireless LAN Controller**. It is used to operate the Wi-Fi network in which **WLC** controllers are located. You can configure a static address for the management interface called **Management**.

Figure 5.53 View of the WLC-PT available in the program

The device has only one Gigabit Ethernet port (without the possibility of its configuration) and a built-in Dot11Radio module for radio communication. It is equipped with two ports:

- GigabitEthernet0
- Management
- Wireless LAN, AP Groups

The following static addresses can be configured for the internal network in the **Management** interface: IP address, subnet mask, default gateway address, DNS address. The **Wireless LAN** module allows you to configure, among others: type of authorization, RADIUS server configuration, encryption type. The **AP Groups** module allows you to configure, among others: LAN groups, SSID names belonging to groups. You can also freely configure the DHCP addressing pool on the device.

The more accurate operation and configuration of this device is beyond the scope of this book, and therefore these capabilities will not be described.

5.6.4 WLC-2504 Device

The **WLC-2504** belongs to the group of wireless devices of the Access Point Controller type (the so-called **Wireless LAN Controller**), in which only the **Management** interface can be configured.

Figure 5.54 View of the WLC-2504 available in the program

The device is equipped with:

- 1000 Mbps Gigabit Ethernet interfaces (**GigabitEthernet0-GigabitEthernet3**)
- one **Management** interface where you can configure the following static addresses: IP address, subnet mask, default gateway address, DNS address.

More accurate operation and configuration of this device is beyond the scope of this book and therefore these capabilities will not be described.

5.7 Wi-Fi Access Routers

The next device that we will present will be an access router, that is, a device containing 3 different functions:

- Switch
- access-point
- router

The Integrated Services Router in the Cisco Packet Tracer looks like the following figure.

Figure 5.55 Physical appearance of the access router in the Cisco Packet Tracer

5.7.1 Standard Configuration of the Wi-Fi Router

An example network is a LAN consisting of 3 computers, two of which are connected directly to the Wi-Fi router using a simple cable in Fast Ethernet technology, while the third computer is equipped with a Linksys WMP300N wireless network card (the use of this card will allow you to configure the router via the WWW later in this chapter).

From the WAN side, a server or cloud emulating Internet behaviour is connected to the Wi-Fi router – connected to the WAN port. On the WAN side there is a Laptop, which is connected by a patch cable to the router. The described situation is illustrated in the figure below.

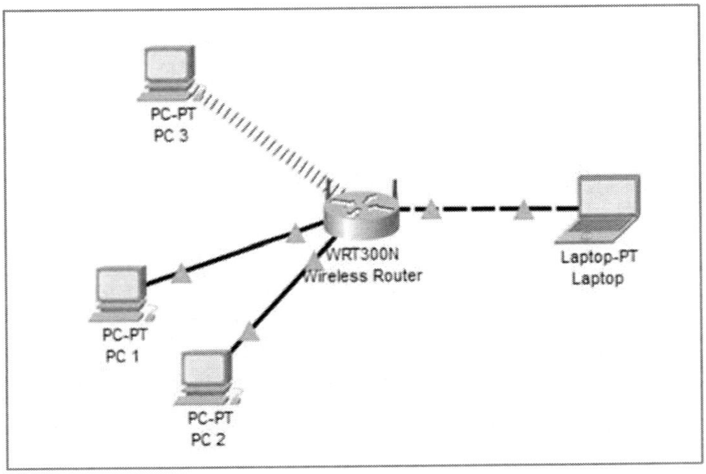

Figure 5.56 Connected devices to the access router

After making the necessary connections, you may notice that the computer connected wirelessly received an IP address automatically, while the computers connected by wire did not. Automatic wireless addressing is accomplished through the router's built-in **DHCP** service, which is responsible for assigning IP addresses to computers.

In order for computers connected by wires to also receive IP addresses, it is necessary to change the **STATIC** option to **DHCP** in the **IP Configuration** section, on the **Config** tab and the **Fast Ethernet** port, for each computer.

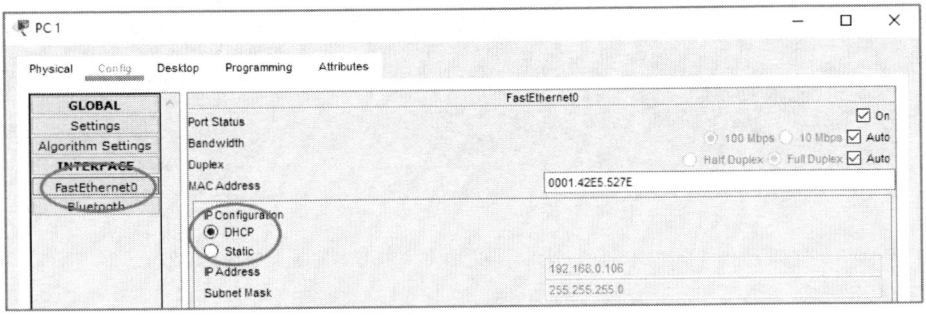

Figure 5.57 Automatic setting

After some time, you will be able to see that in the IP Address and Subnet Mask fields for PC 1 and PC 2, the network parameters obtained from the router will appear.

It should also be remembered that the second option to switch a computer to automatic acquisition of IP addresses is to use the tool available on the desktop of each computer, and this is the IP **Configuration** tab.

The result of the automatic operation (DHCP) of address assignment is described in the following figure.

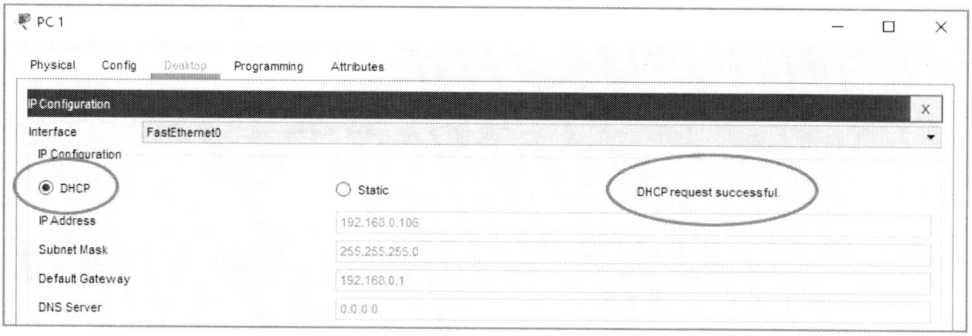

Figure 5.58 Setting automatic IP address assignment

Another network parameter has been assigned by the router, not yet described, which is Default Gateway. **Default Gateway**, which is the IP address of the router as seen from the LAN side. It is not needed for communication between computers located on the same LAN subnet, but it will be required to communicate with a Laptop connected to the WAN port of the router. Checking whether all the necessary parameters have been obtained is also possible through the command line, using the **ipconfig** command.

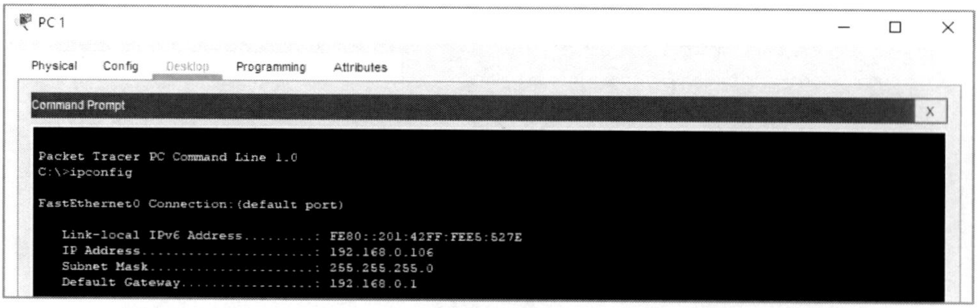

Figure 5.59 Checking the received IP address by the computer

In order to check the configuration of the WIFI router, click on it with the left mouse button and go to the **Config** tab, and then to the LAN section. In the **LAN** section, you can see the IP address of the router, which is also the IP address of the **Default Gateway**.

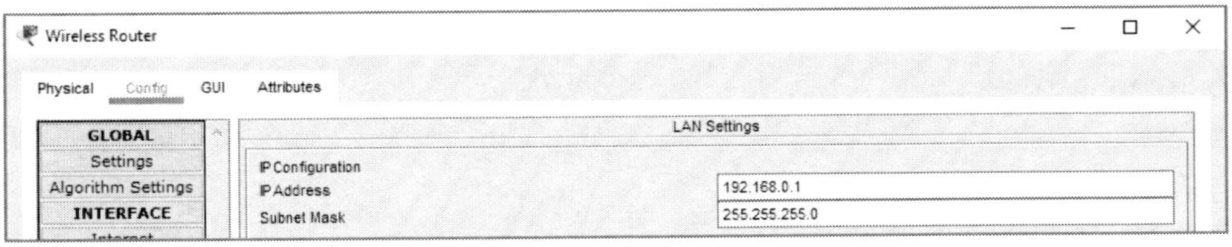

Figure 5.60 Router LAN Configuration

On the **Config** tab, in the **Wireless** section, you can configure the settings of wireless (internal) network parameters.

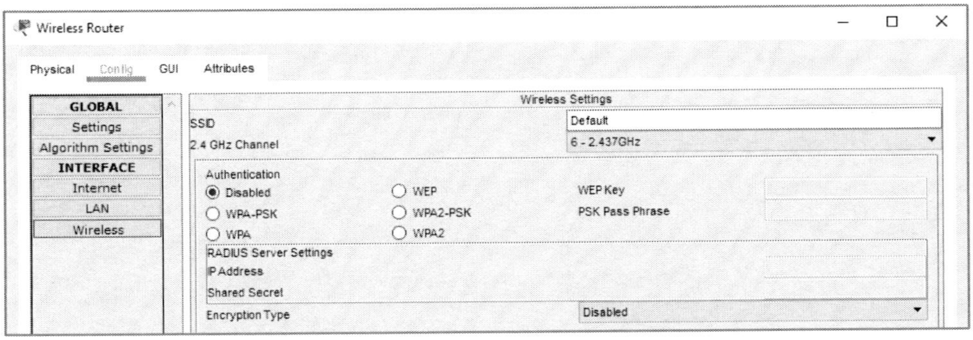

Figure 5.61 Router wireless network settings

On the Config tab, in the Internet section, you can configure the settings of WAN (external) network parameters.

A cloud that emulates Internet behavior has an IP address of 10.0.0.1 and a mask of 255.0.0.0. The laptop should be assigned the address 10.0.0.2 with the same network mask, since it is located on the external network Internet.

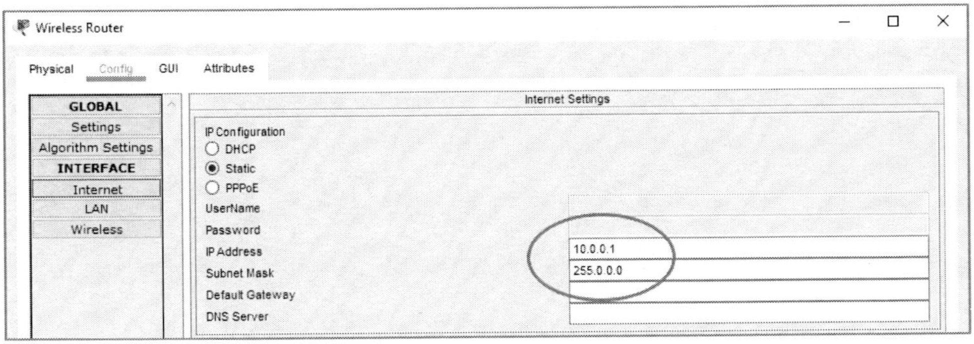

Figure 5.62 Router WAN Port Configuration

Execution of several simulations for transmission between LAN and WAN networks.

The first simulation is an ICMP packet sent from a computer from the LAN and we send the ICMP packet from PC 3 to a laptop connected to the WAN port. The packet passes through the router, reaches the recipient, after which the response is transmitted. The answer comes to PC 3.

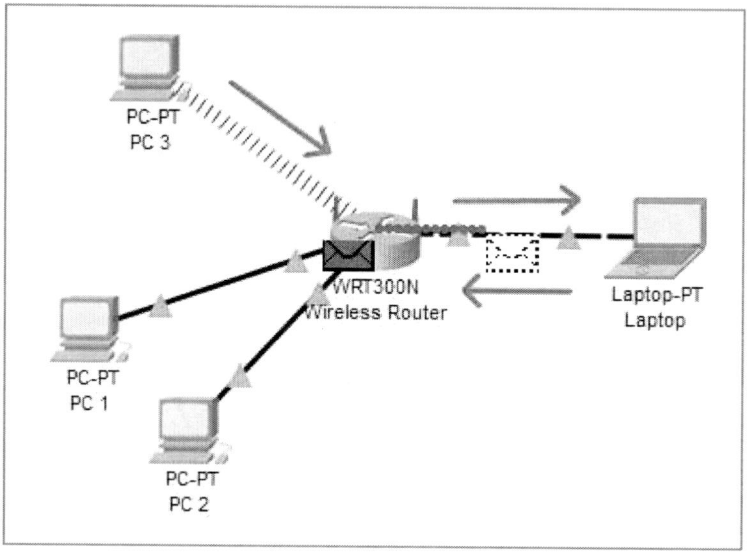

Figure 5.63 Transmission of ICMP packet from LAN to computer in WAN

The situation is different if you reverse the direction of transmission and send a packet from a computer connected to the WAN interface to any computer in the LAN.

The second simulation is an ICMP packet sent from a laptop from a WAN from Laptop to PC 3 or PC 2, or PC 1, connected to LAN ports.

In each access router, the default firewall of the local network works, thanks to which it will not pass such a packet further, and thus there will be no response to the ICMP (ping) packet formulated in this way. This situation is shown in the figure below.

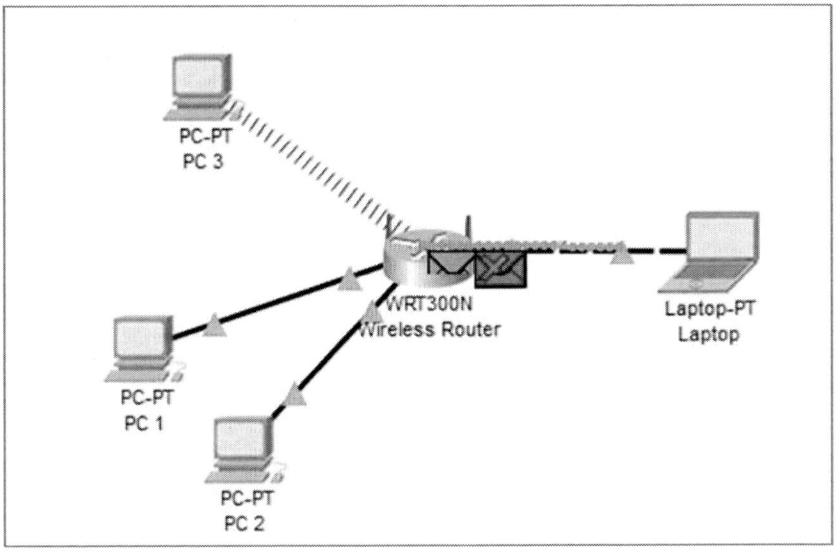

Figure 5.64 Block a packet from WAN

5.7.2 Configuration of Wi-Fi Router via HTTP

The second way to configure a Wi-Fi access router is to configure using a website using a browser. By default, the router has an IP address from the LAN side: **192.168.0.1**. Simply connect to any port on your device and enter the router's IP address and start setting up.

You must configure any address in the 192.168.0.0/24 pool on the computer, but different from the **192.168.0.1** address, for example, **192.168.0.2** and the subnet mask for this network class/24, which is 255.255.255.0. and the gateway **192.168.0.1**.

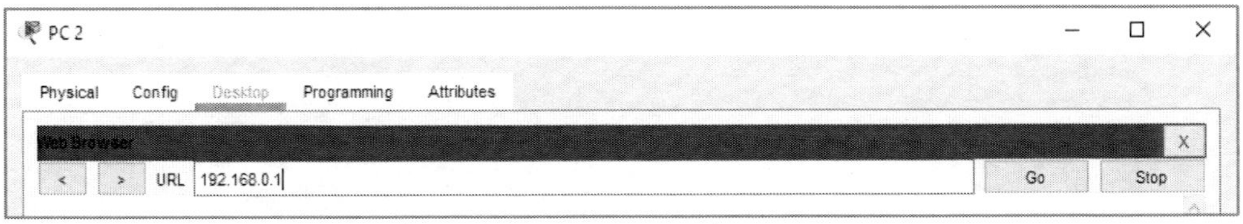

Figure 5.65 Enter the IP address of the router in the web browser window

If your computer is not responding to an IP address, your computer's address is misconfigured, or the mask or gateway or network cable is incorrectly connected.

Correctly entering the router's IP address in the browser window should result in the router login window appearing. With the default settings, the login and password are the same, i.e. you log in by providing the following parameters: **admin**, **admin**.

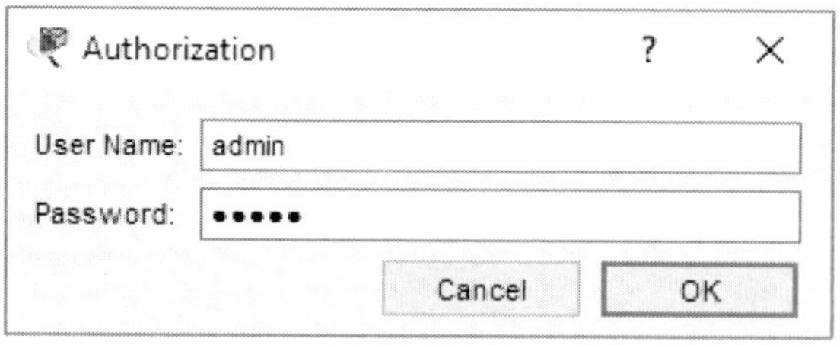

Figure 5.66 Logging in to your router

After logging in to the router, a window will appear, configuring the router, which is shown in the figure below. It should be remembered that in many network devices, configuration via the http protocol gives more convenient options in operation and many greater possibilities than via the command line (e.g. ASA 5506 devices).

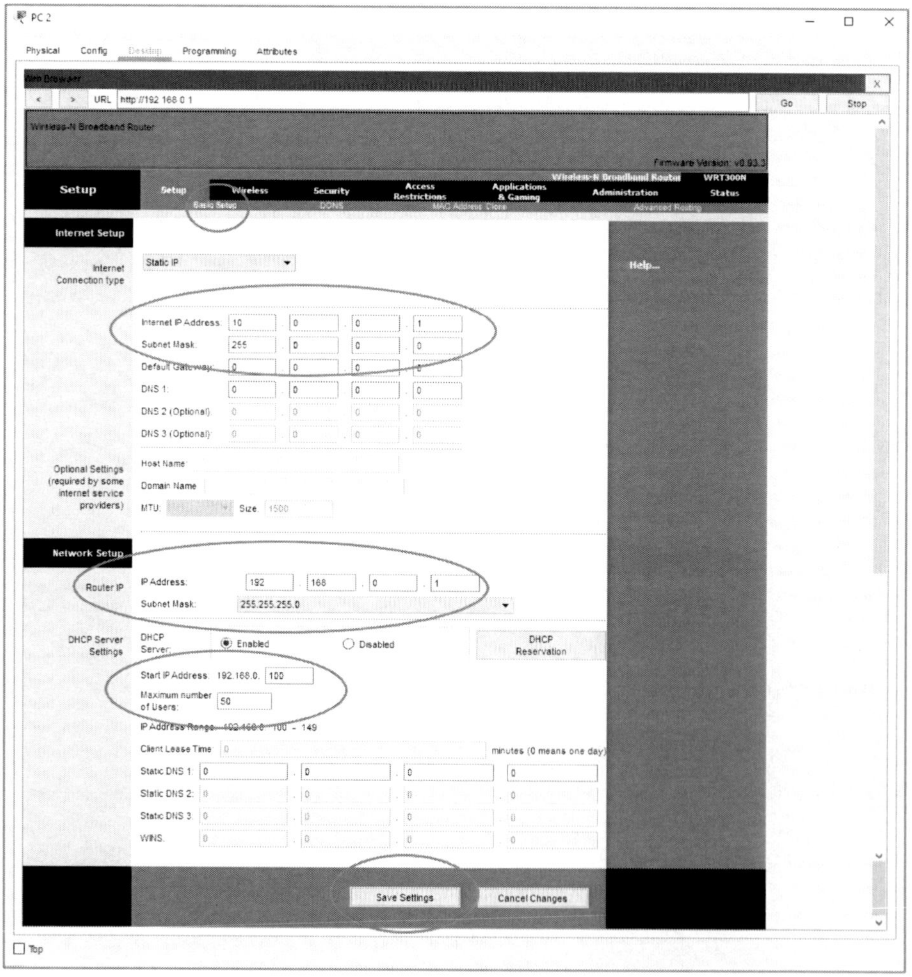

Figure 5.67 Basic Router configuration options

First of all, pay attention in our topology whether the Static IP option is selected on the **Setup-Basic Setup** tab in the **Internet Connection Type** section. The most important options (data) to configure are:

- Internet Address (Internet IP Address and Subnet Mask) WAN
- Internal address (**IP Address** and **Subnet Mask**) LAN
- DHCP Server Settings

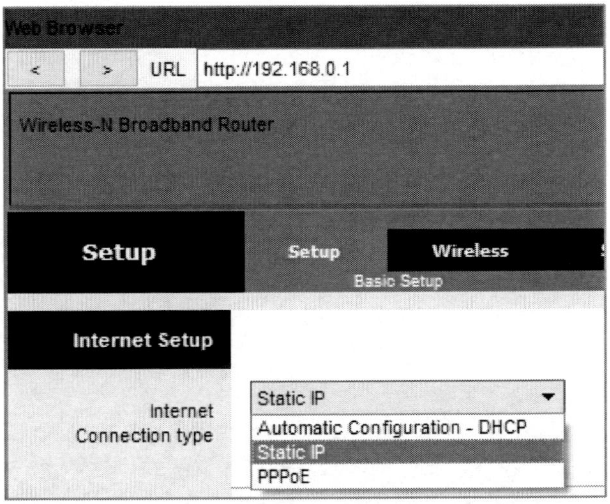

Figure 5.68 Selecting static WAN port addressing

In this example, you must manually set the IP address for the Internet (WAN) port to 10.0.0.1/8. Due to the fact that usually the access router from the WAN side connects to another router, you need to enter the IP address of the next device in the **Default Gateway** field, in this case it will be the IP address of the laptop connected to the Wi-Fi router (10.0.0.2). In the **IP Router** section, leave the default IP address of the router from the LAN side (i.e. for now we do not change the default parameters **192.168.0.1/24**).

Then, in the **DHCP Server** section, set the **Enabled** parameter to enable dynamic addressing of computers on the LAN side. An important element is to set the DHCP pool, i.e. from which number IP addresses will be assigned and how many computers will obtain network parameters. To do this, configure in the **Start IP Address** field (default 192.168.0.100), and in the **Maximum number of Users** section (50 by default). The final step to save your changes is to click the **Save Settings** button at the bottom of the window. After performing the above actions, the following window will appear, in which information about the correctness of saving changes is given.

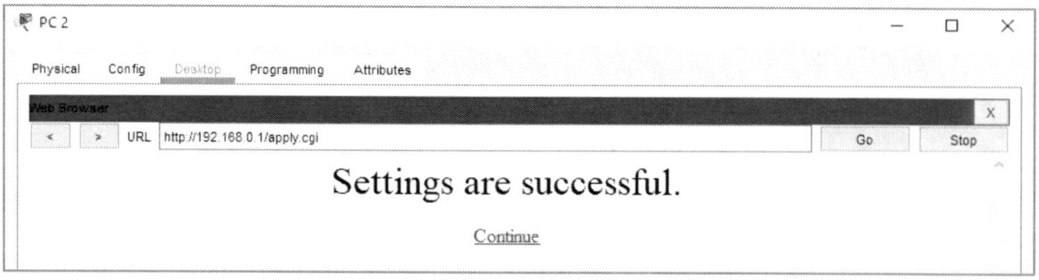

Figure 5.69 Saved changes on the router

After making changes to the router settings, close the window. Computers should receive IP addresses. Also, it should be remembered that if any computer has not received network parameters, it is advisable to check whether it is enabled in DHCP mode or refresh the network parameters of computers when changing DHCP parameters. This can be done, for example, through the command line. Just type **ipconfig /release** (to release the IP address) and then **ipconfig /renew** (to renew), as shown in the figure below.

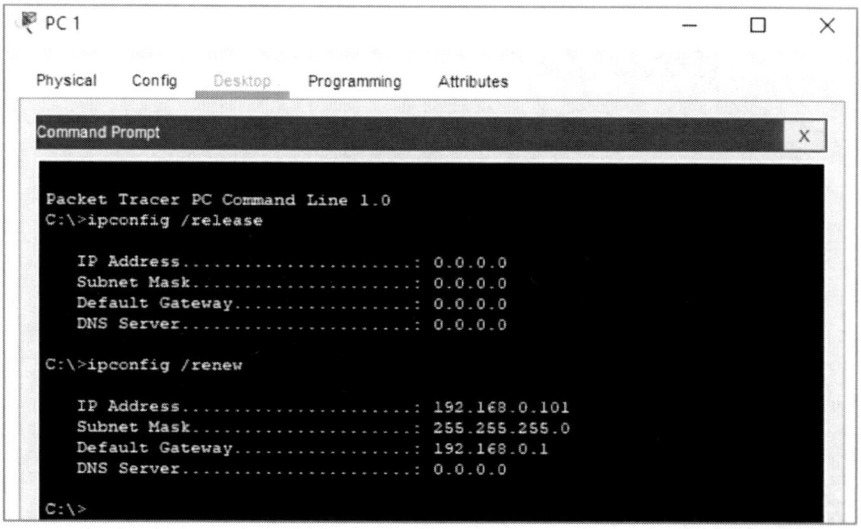

Figure 5.70 Release and renewal of the IP address via the command line

A common problem when configuring a router from the LAN side is changing the default address pool. This is the case when, for example, we want our router to allocate addresses from the network (for example, **200.0.0.0**). Then, we start by assigning an IP address to the router (**200.0.0.1**), as shown in the figure below, and the DHCP pool has remained unchanged and cannot be reconfigured in this step. In this case, first press the **Save Settings** button to save the changes on the router.

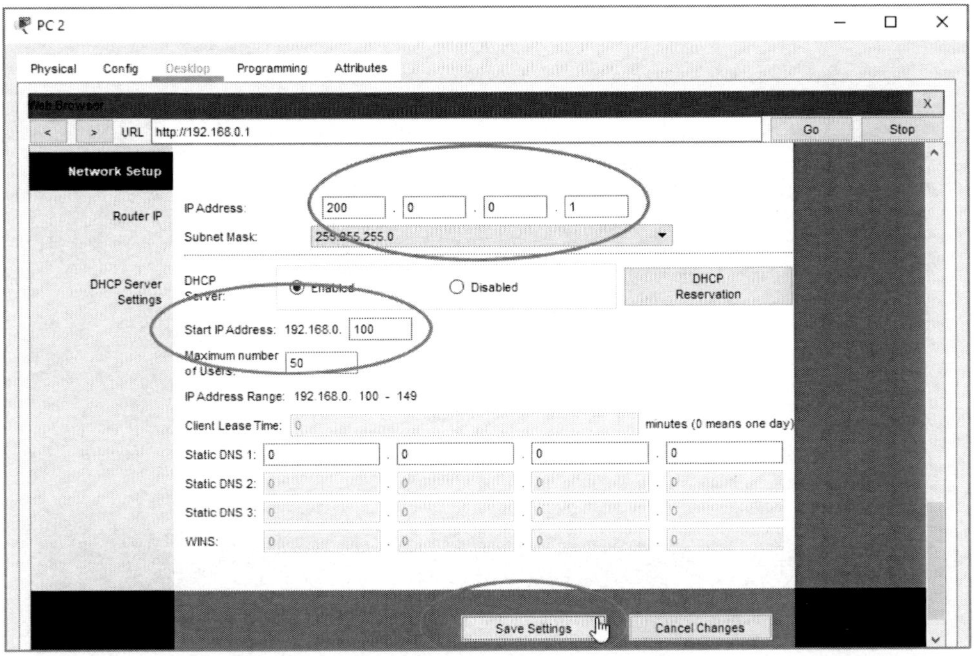

Figure 5.71 Saving router configuration changes

After saving the changes, you can observe that the browser window displays a message about the exceeded waiting time and the connection to the router has been interrupted, as the figure below illustrates. This is because the router already has a different IP address, so all computers connected to the LAN should refresh the IP address (if they receive it from DHCP) or enter manually from the new pool, for example **200.0.0.2/255.255.255.0**.

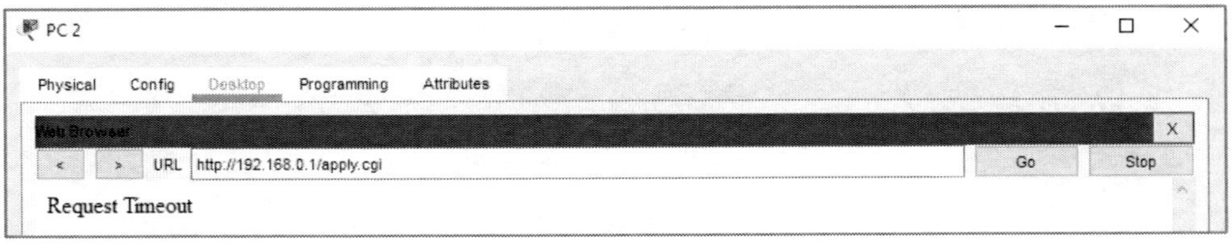

Figure 5.72 Interrupted connection to the router after changing the IP address

After successfully reconnecting with the router, you should go to the second **Wireless** tab, where you can configure the Wi-Fi settings. The first section is **Basic Wireless Settings** in which you can change the network mode (**B, G, N**), the **SSID** name with which computers connect to the network or set the parameters whether the **SSID** is to be broadcast on the Wi-Fi network or not.

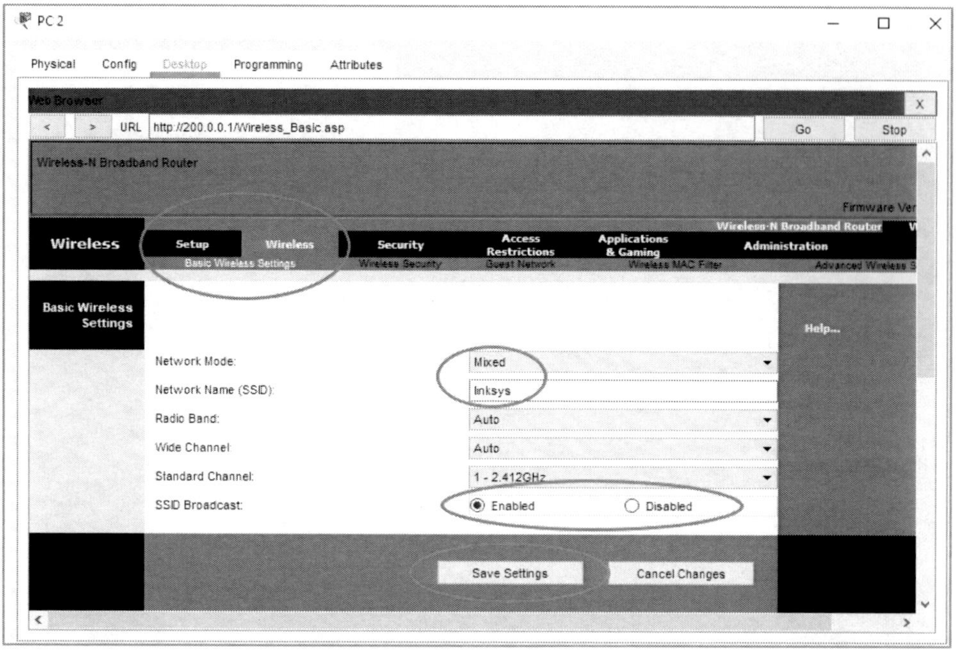

Figure 5.73 Basic Wi-Fi settings

The next section is **Wireless Security**, where you can set the network encryption type and password, for example, **WPA2 Personal** and sample password: **cisco321**.

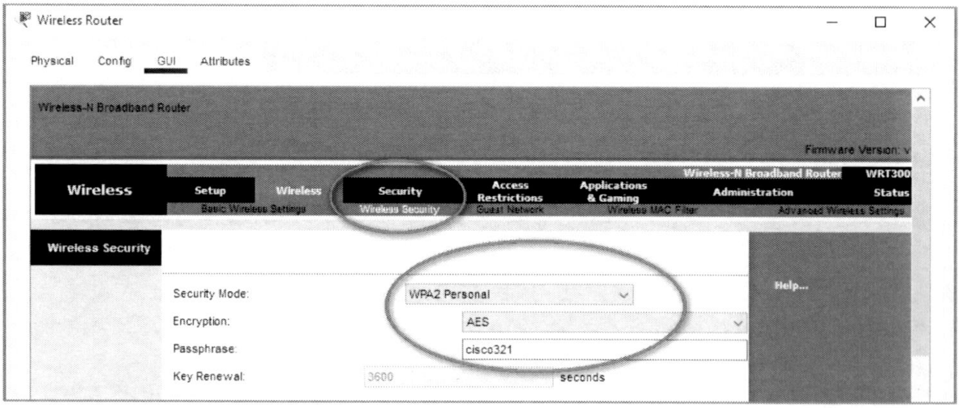

Figure 5.74 Wi-Fi security setting

After saving the changes to the Wi-Fi router, you need to configure the computer(s) to connect it to the new network parameters. We can do this through the standard configuration of the computer, but in this example we will do it through the tool available on the computer's desktop.

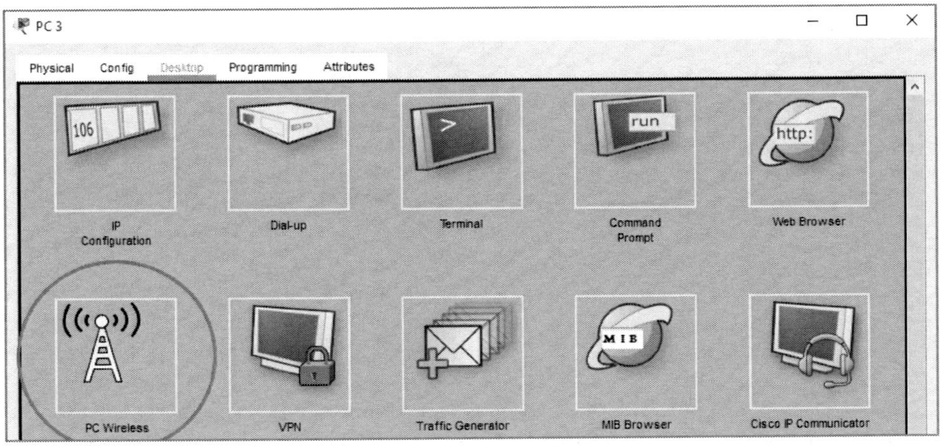

Figure 5.75 Wi-Fi configuration tool via the desktop utility of the computer

A prerequisite for connecting the computer to the Wi-Fi network through this tool is to install a LINKSYS wireless card in the computer. To start the configuration, run the **IP Wireless** utility shown in the figure above from the computer's desktop, and then the following window should open.

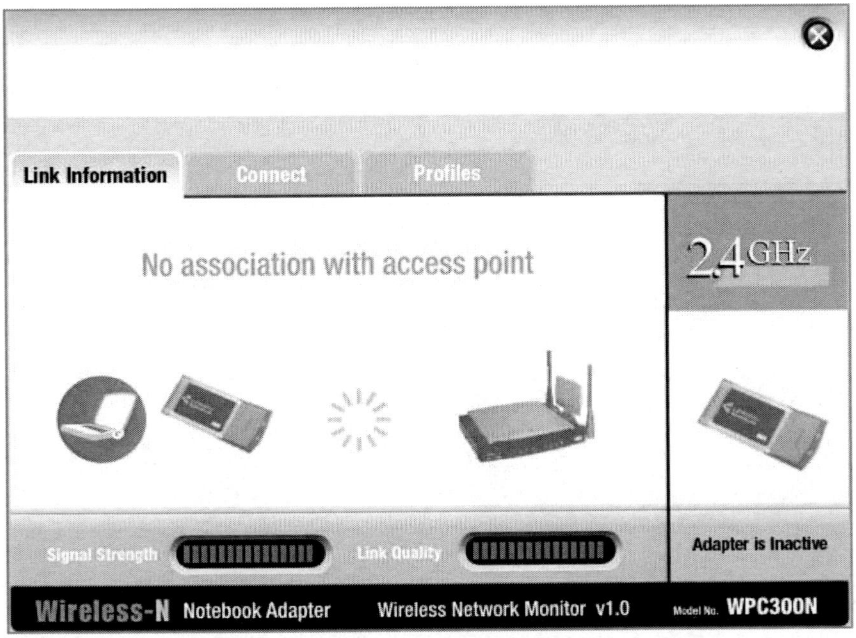

Figure 5.76 Tool for Wi-Fi configuration of computers equipped with the LINKSYS wireless card

Go to the second **Connect** tab, then press the **Refresh** button to display the available Wi-Fi networks, and then the **Connect** button to connect to it.

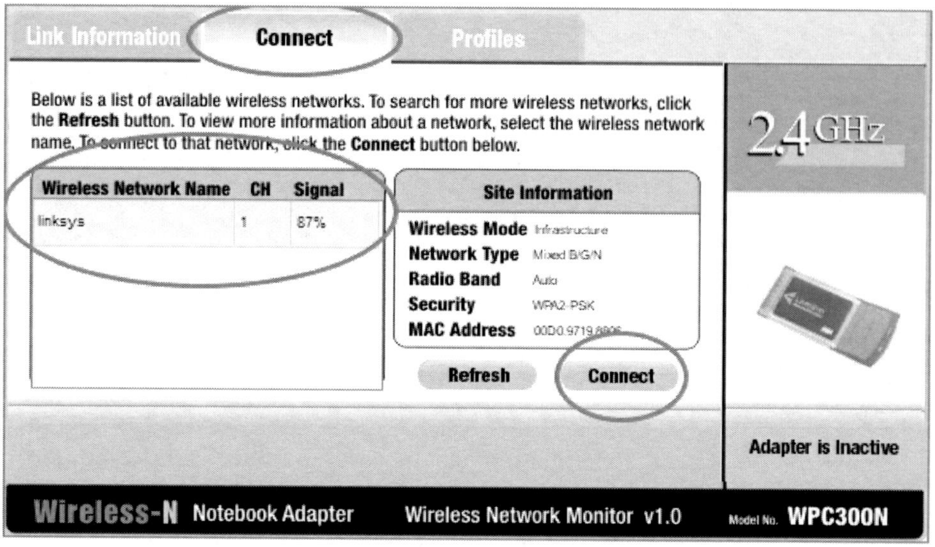

Figure 5.77 Connecting to the selected Wi-Fi network

After a while, another window will appear in which you need to select the encryption type and enter the appropriate password and press the **Connect** button again. When all the specified parameters meet the specified rules, a wireless connection will occur.

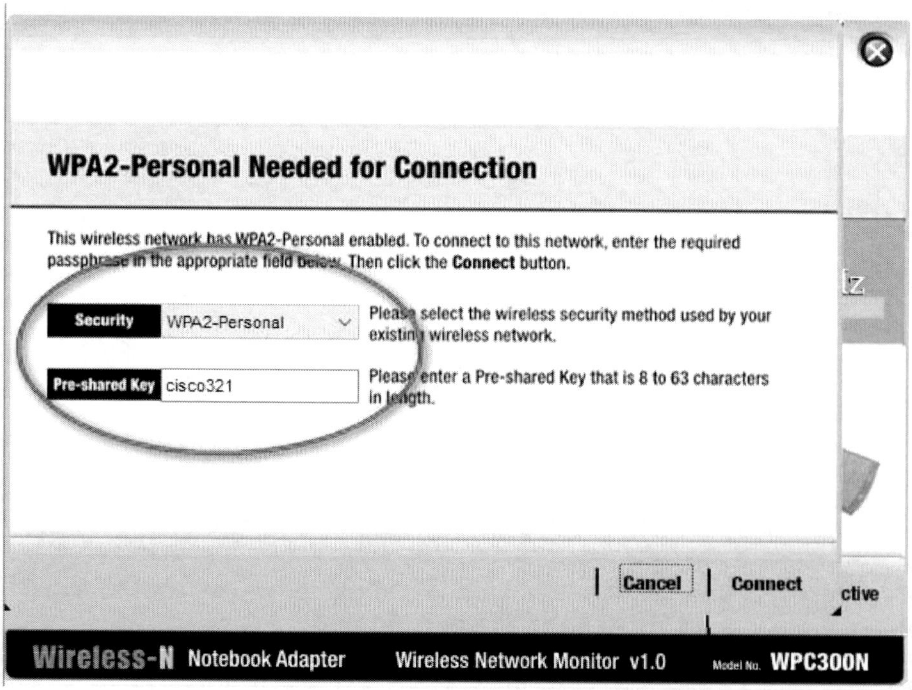

Figure 5.78 Choose encryption and enter your password (Pre-shared Key)

Another tab of the **Wireless** section is the **Wireless MAC Filter**, where you can configure which computers connected via Wi-Fi will have access to the network and which will not. In order to better illustrate the issue, you should connect 3 additional computers to our local network, which are equipped with LINKSYS wireless cards. Computers should be properly configured to connect, as shown in the figure below.

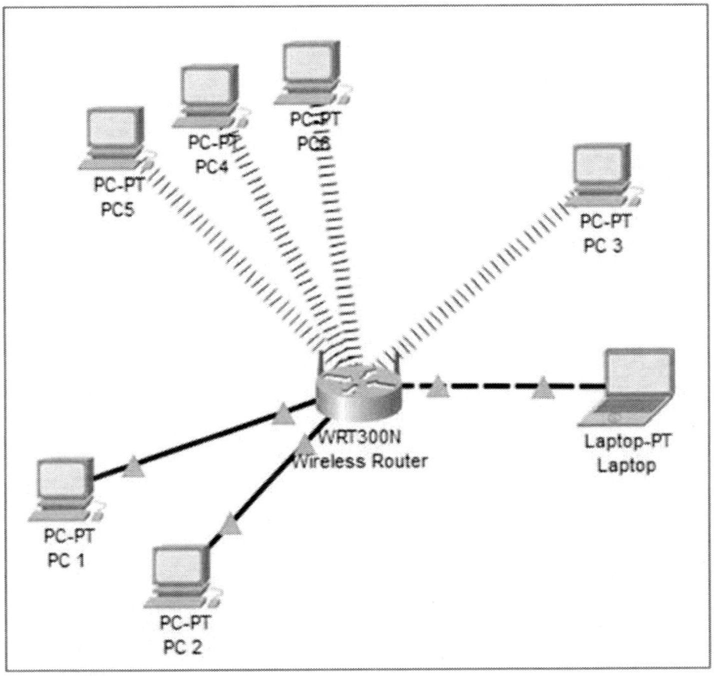

Figure 5.79 Connected additional computers to Wi-Fi

Assume that you filter the list of computers that you want to have access to the network and that you do not. In this case, PC3 and PC4 will be connected, and PC5 and PC6 will not be connected. First, read the physical (MAC) addresses of the computers you want to access (PC3 and PC4). Here are three ways to obtain MAC addresses. The first way is to point the mouse cursor over the icon of a given computer and after a while a window will appear in which the physical address appears.

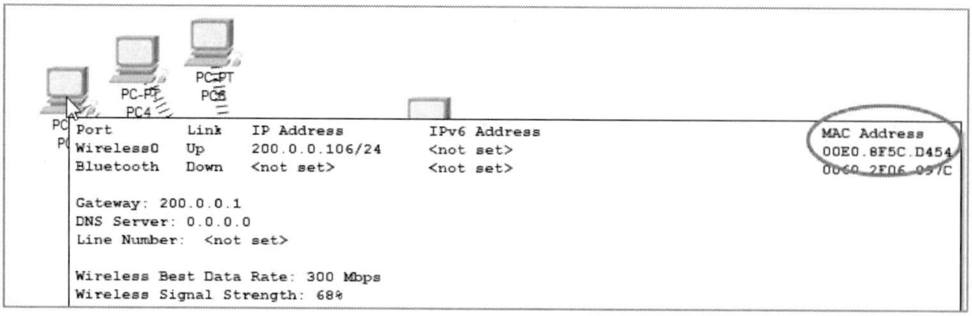

Figure 5.80 The first way to get your computer's MAC address

The second way is to enter the configuration window of a given computer interface and in the **MAC Address** field, you can read the physical address.

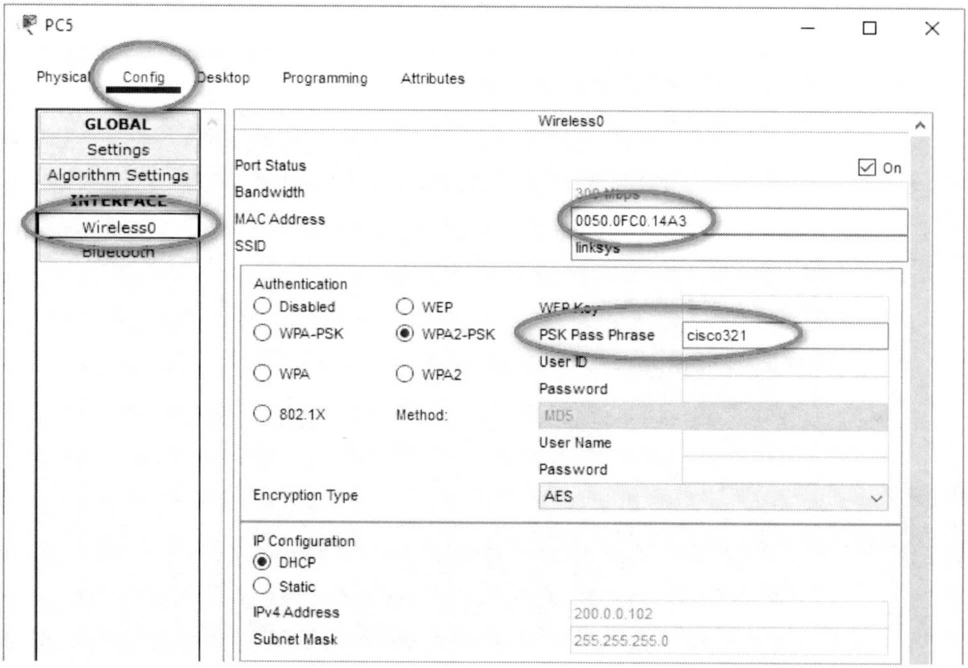

Figure 5.81 The second way to get a physical address

The third way is to enter the previously known **ipconfig /all** command in the console window:

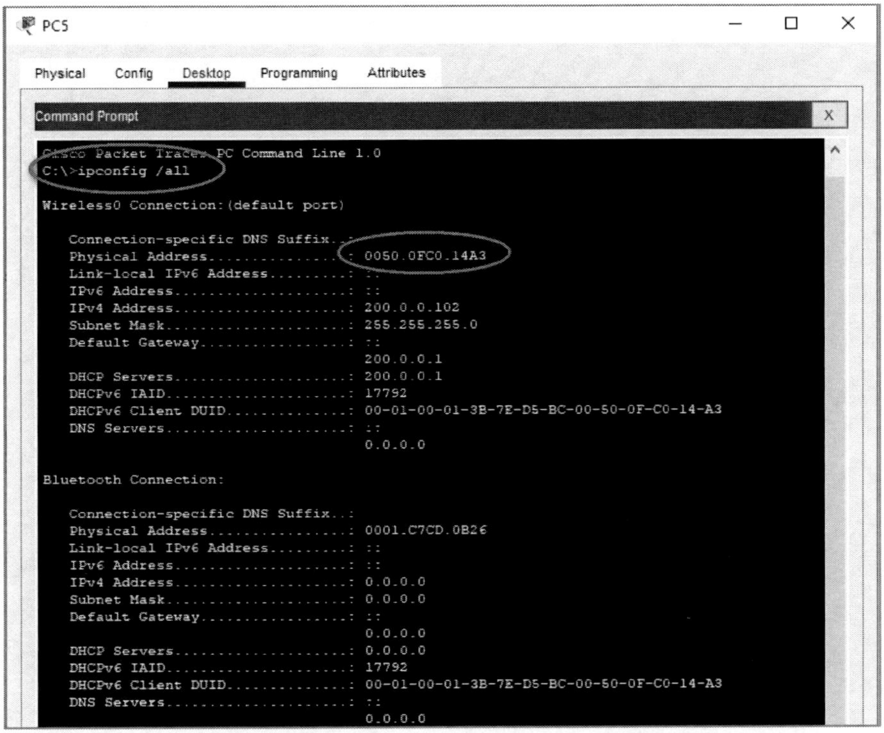

Figure 5.82 The third way to get a MAC address

Knowing the different ways to obtain MAC addresses, choose one of the ways and copy the MAC addresses of PC3 and PC4, then in the **wireless MAC Filter** router window, select **Enabled**.

Note: MAC addresses in presenting examples, which you see may be variable, **because the Cisco Packet Tracer randomizes addresses. We use addresses as examples in this book only**.

To allow the following computers: PC3 and PC4 to connect to the network, select the section: **Permit PCs listed below to access wireless network** and finally enter the physical addresses of the computers in the **MAC 01** and **MAC 02** fields.

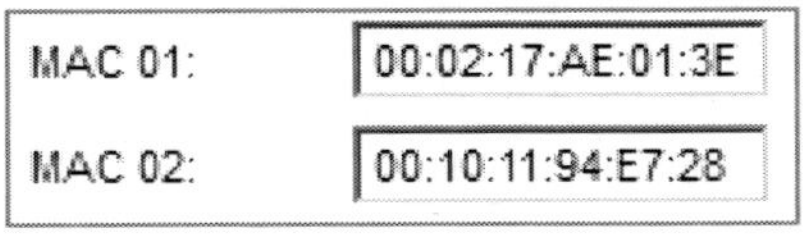

Figure 5.83 MAC Address List

Then save the settings. To save your changes, click the **Save Settings** button at the bottom of the window.

Figure 5.84 Saving the Wi-Fi Router Configuration

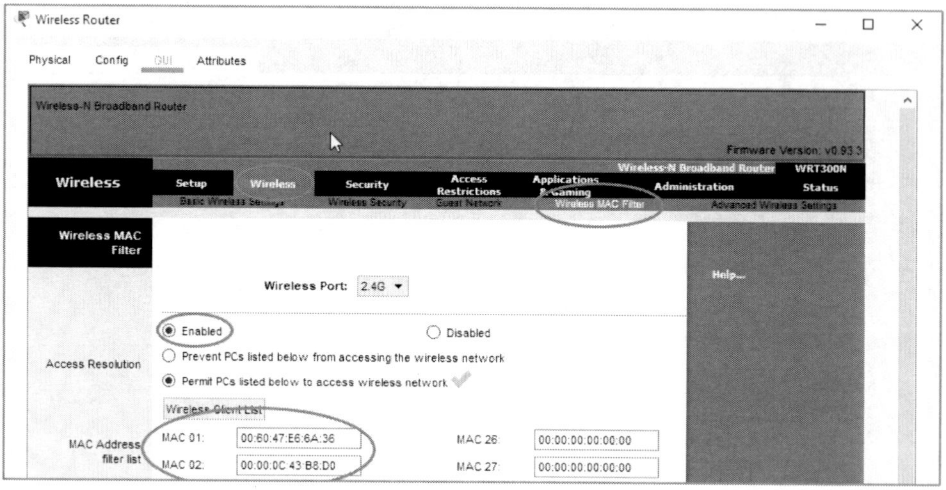

Figure 5.85 MAC address filtering

As a result of the saved changes, the situation shown in the figure below was obtained, noting that pcs PC5 and PC6 lost connection to the WiFi network.

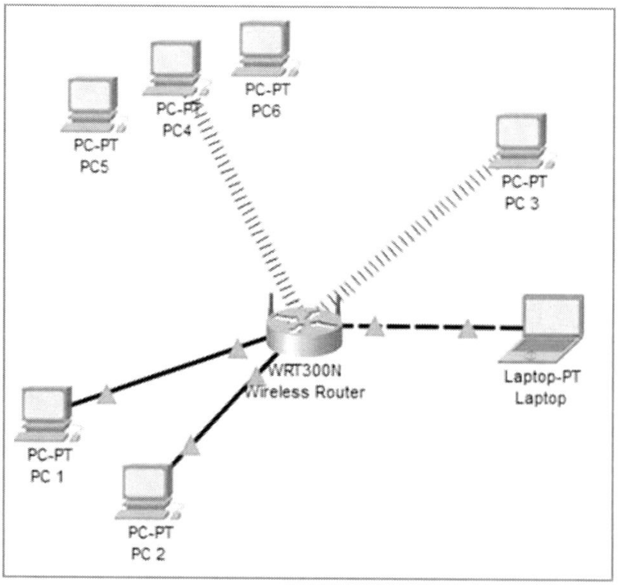

Figure 5.86 LAN after MAC address filtering

Note: After starting the Cisco Packet Tracer, MAC addresses may be different, so please update them on your router.

In addition, in the **Security** router tab, you can set parameters related to the Firewall and the ability to block or accept web scripts.

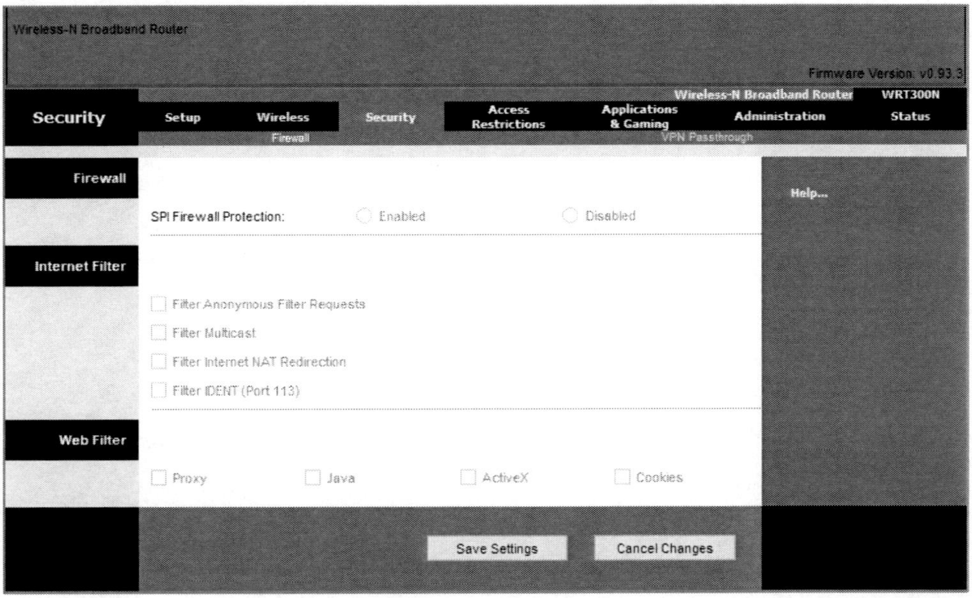

Figure 5.87 Firewall configuration on the router

By going to the **Access Restrictions** tab, you can configure a list (lists) according to which you can specify which computers can have access to specific applications, at what times, what websites and at what keywords will be blocked, as well as which port ranges will be allowed and which will not.

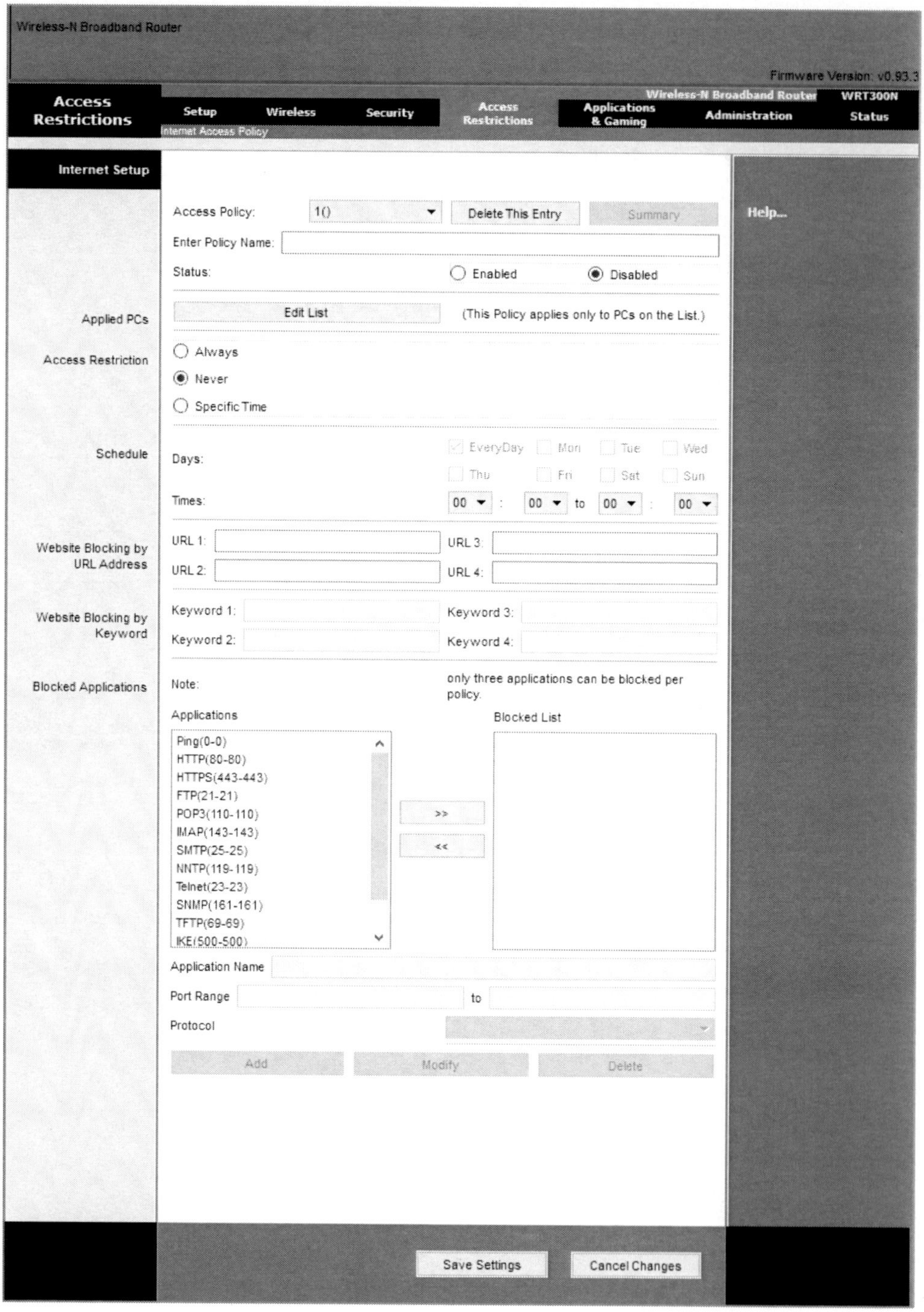

Figure 5.88 Configuring router access restrictions

In the **Applications & Gaming** tab in the **Single Port Forwarding** section, you can set options based on which the router will pass or block packets from specific network applications, directed to specific computers.

Figure 5.89 Packet filtering based on protocols and ports

On the same tab there is another section called **DMZ**, that is, the so-called Demilitarized Zone, in which most often there is a server or a group of servers that can be accessed from the WAN. In this section, you can specify the source address, the so-called trusted, and the destination address that you want to access from the WAN.

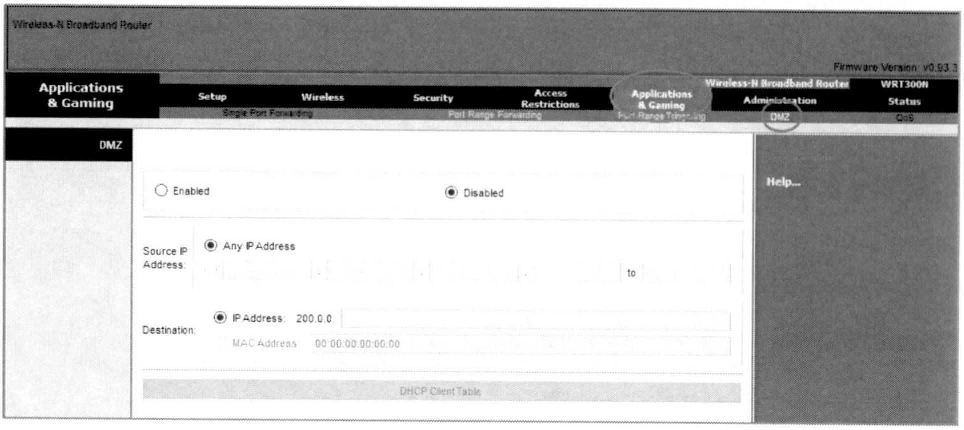

Figure 5.90 Configuring DMZ on the router

The next tab of the router is **Administration**, in which there is a **Management** section: it is recommended to change the default password: **admin**, to a new one, e.g. **packettracer**, after saving the changes you will be able to log in to the router with the following parameters: login: **admin**, password: **packettracer**. In addition to changing the password, you can also specify in this section what protocol will be used to be able to connect to the WIFI server (**HTTP** or **HTTPS**) and whether it will be possible to connect to the router remotely from the WAN.

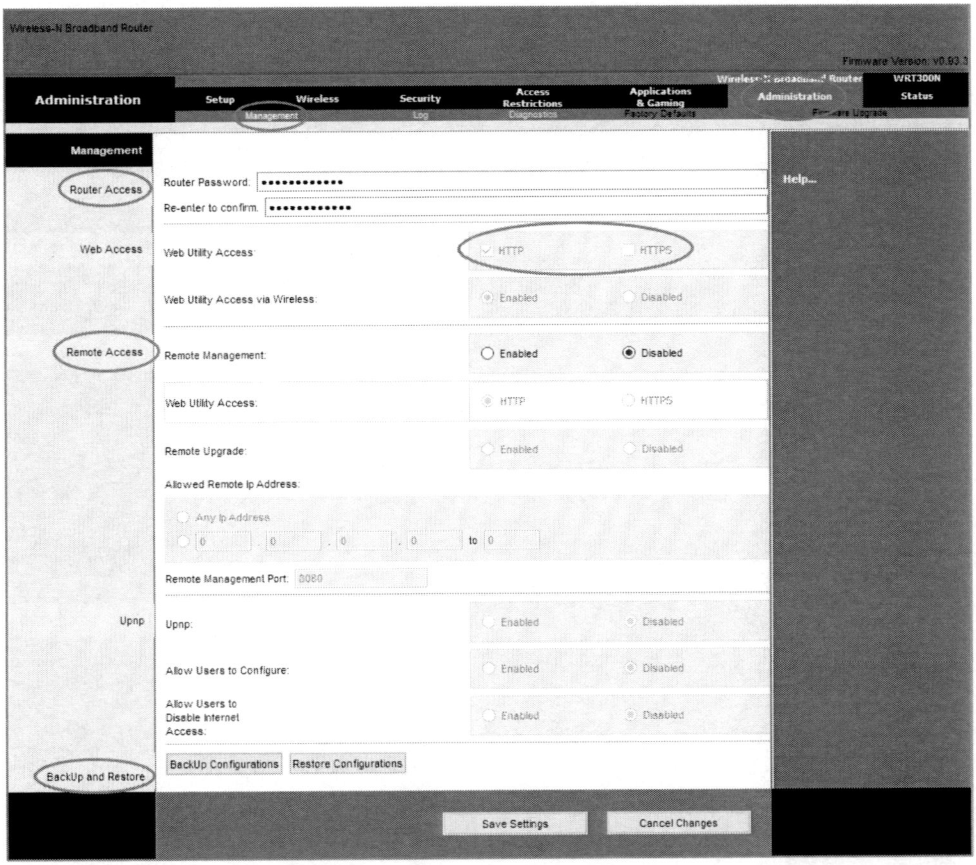

Figure 5.91 Options of the Management tab in the router

On the same tab there is also a **Factory Defaults** section, where using the **Restore Factory Defaults** button, you can restore the router to factory settings.

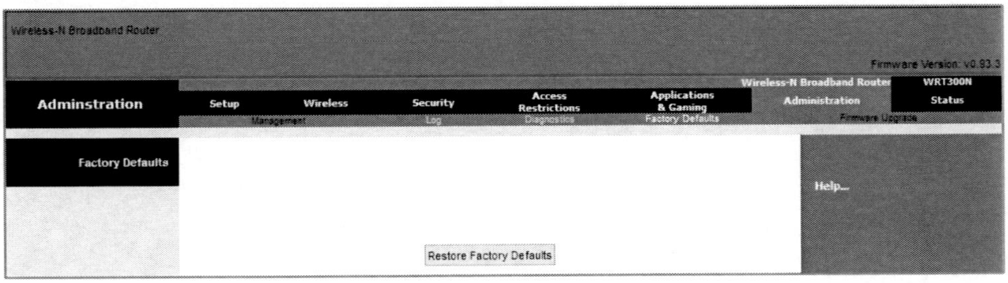

Figure 5.92 Restore default settings

The third section in the **Administration** tab is **Firmware Upgrade**, where you can update the router's service software from a file saved on our computer. This option should be handled very carefully – if the device works properly, it is not recommended to update firmware.

To upgrade a firmware, press the **Browse** button to point to the firmware update file, then click **Start to Upgrade** and watch the update installation progress.

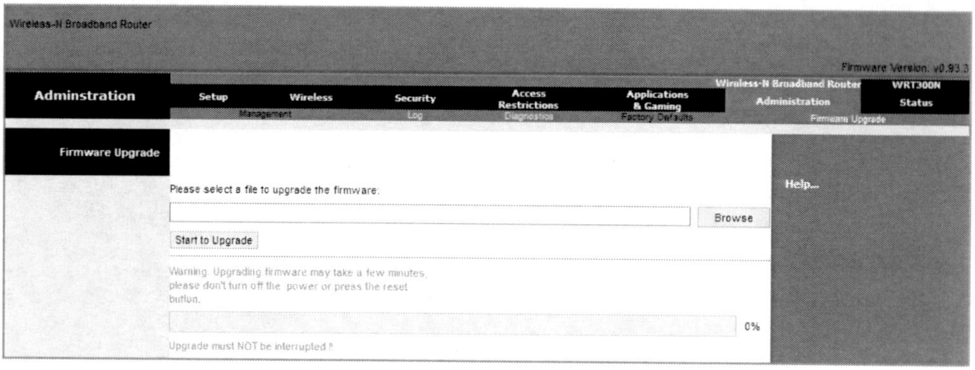

Figure 5.93 Router software update window

The last **Status** tab consists of three sections.

- Router Information
- Local Network
- Wireless Network

The first is **Router Information**, where you can see the basic data of the router and its LAN interface configuration.

Figure 5.94 Status tab and Router section

The next section is **Local Network**, where you can read data about the configuration of the router on the LAN side as well as information about the DHCP configuration.

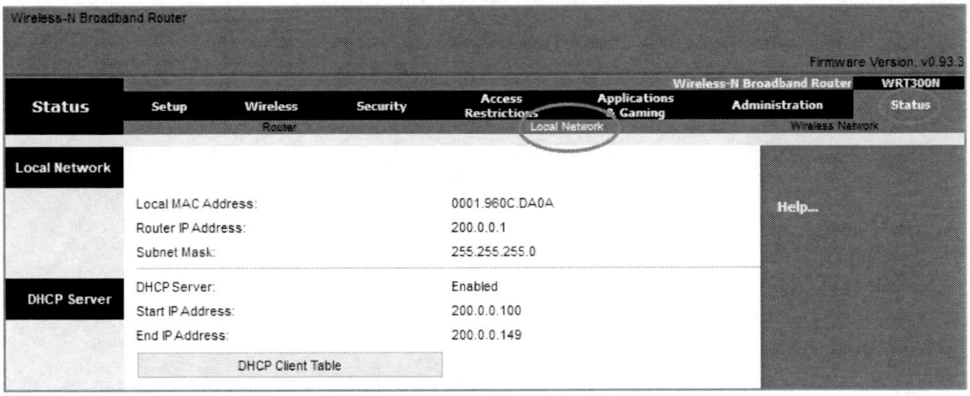

Figure 5.95 Status tab and Local Network section

The last section is the **Wireless Network**, where you can check the configuration of the wireless network, encryption and the name of the broadcast SSID.

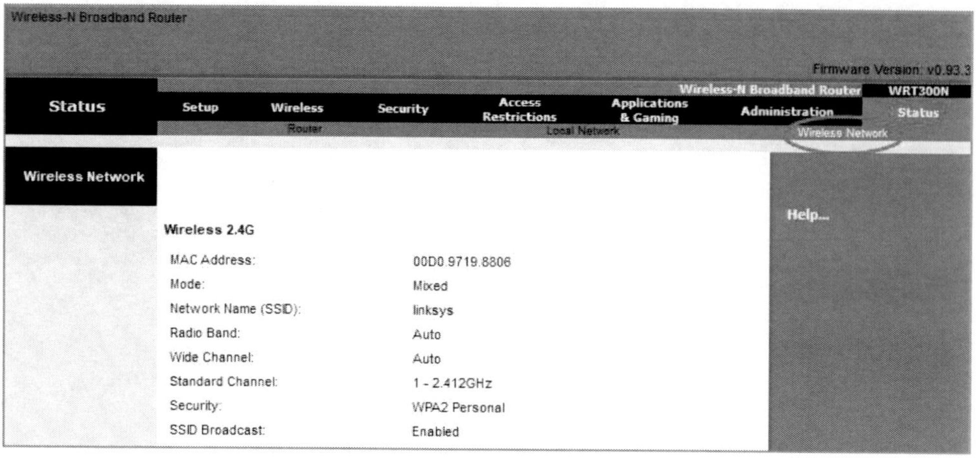

Figure 5.96 About Wi-Fi in the Wireless Network tab

5.8 Devices for Creating GSM Networks

In the Cisco Packet Tracer, the **BTS** base access station in a 3G/4G cellular network is simulated as a pair of two devices (**Cell-Tower** and **Central-Office-Server**) that must be connected to each other using a coaxial cable (the type of cable is **Coaxial**).

Figure 5.97 Appearance of the real BTS (Base Transceiver Station)

In the Cisco Packet Tracer, the BTS consists of an antenna (called as **Cell-Tower**) and a dedicated server (called as **Central-Office-Server**).

Cell-Tower acts as a sector antenna in the 3G/4G network for wireless connections. **Central-Office-Server** sets the default IP address for the cellular network and is responsible for communication with the WAN backbone.

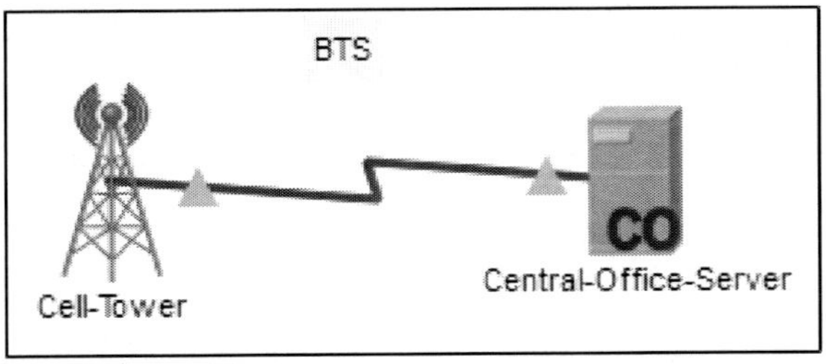

Figure 5.98 BTS simulation in the program

An example of a simple **3G/4G** network using **Cell-Tower** and **Central-Office-Server** is shown in the figure below.

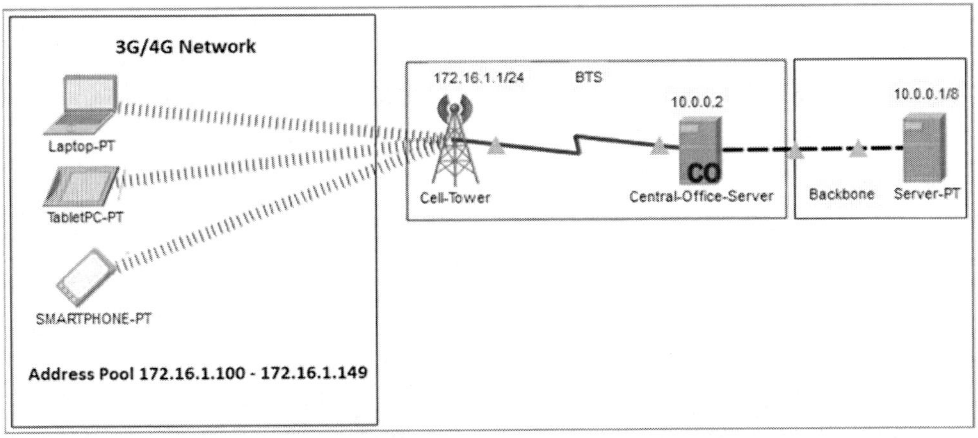

Figure 5.99 Simulation of a simple 3G/4G network

5.9 Hardware Firewalls

5.9.1 Meraki-MX65W Device

The **Meraki-MX65** is primarily designed to filter network traffic and isolate internal networks (LANs) from external networks (WANs).

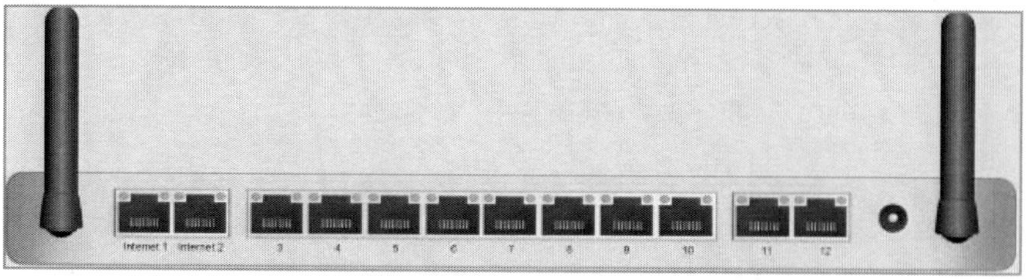

Figure 5.100 View of meraki-MX65 available in the program

The Meraki-MX65 comes standard with:

- 2 x 1000 Mbps interfaces (**Internet1**, **Internet2**) for WAN connection
- 8 x 1000 Mbps interfaces (**GigabitEthernet3** – **GigabitEthernet10**) for LAN connection
- 2 x 10 Mbps or 100 Mbps interfaces (**Ethernet11** – **Ethernet12**) for LAN connection

5.9.2 Meraki-Server Device

The **Meraki-Server** is used to support **Meraki-MX65** authentication using advanced procedures, accounts, passwords, and advanced network security techniques, as well as the **Meraki-MX65** serial number.

The **Meraki-Server** comes standard with one 1000 Mbps interface (**FastEthernet0**). The description of the interaction of these devices is very complicated and therefore will not be described in this book.

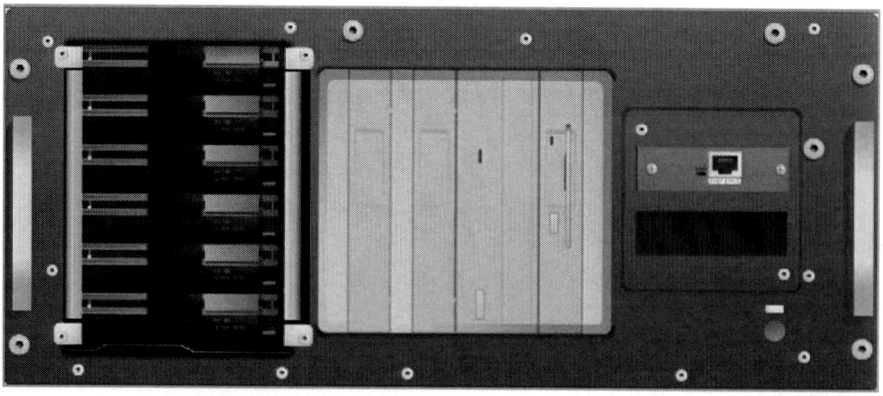

Figure 5.101 View of the Meraki-Server device available in the program

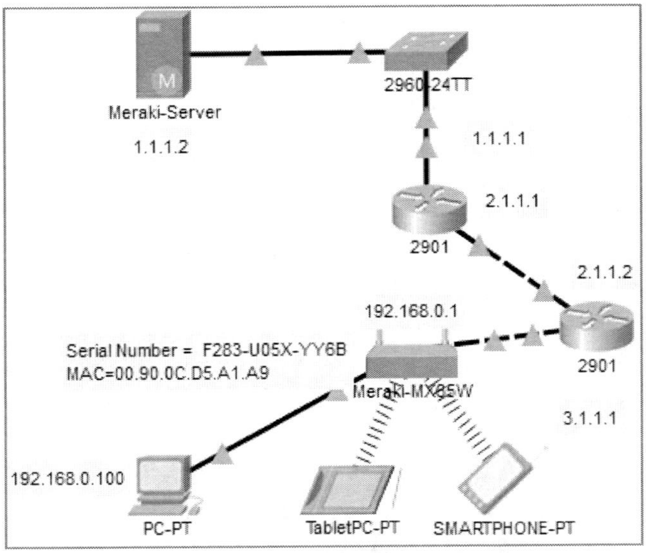

Figure 5.102 Example of topology for Meraki devices

5.9.3 ASA5505 and ASA5506 Devices

The Cisco Packet Tracer supports two so-called Adaptive Security Appliances (ASA): **ASA 5505** and **ASA 5506**, which act as advanced firewalls. In the Cisco Packet Tracer, in the **[Network Devices] [Security]** section, you can find Security Appliances (that is, advanced firewalls). Two devices are available: **ASA5505** and **ASA5506-X**.

Figure 5.103 Firewall devices available in the program

ASA devices are characterized by the following capabilities:

- IP packet filtering using ACL.
- Stateful filtering, i.e., the decision to pass or block a packet, is made based on port numbers and trust level.
- Act as a DHCP server or client.
- Support for static and dynamic address translation (static NAT, dynamic NAT, PAT).
- Support for dynamic routing protocols: RIP, EIGRP, OSPF and static routes.

- Define a group of objects that define a set of security (access) policies for greater configuration transparency.
- Support for Site-to-Site VPN tunnels.
- Supporting the AAA mechanism (authentication, authorization, settlement).

5.9.3.1 ASA 5505 Device

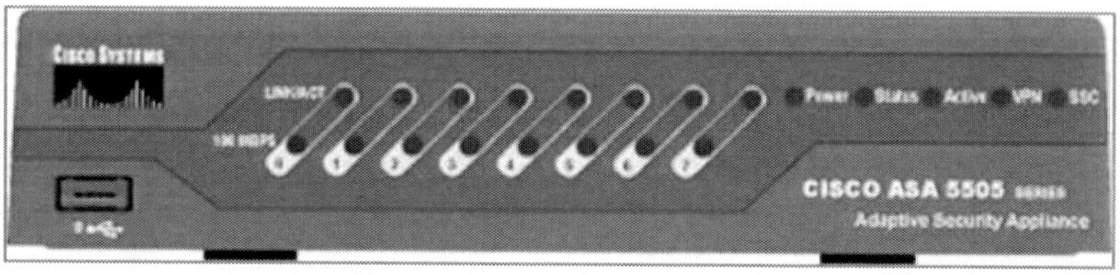

Figure 5.104 Appearance of the Cisco ASA 5505 front panel

Figure 5.105 Appearance of the Cisco ASA 5505 rear panel

5.9.3.2 ASA 5506 Device

Figure 5.106 Appearance of the Cisco ASA 5506 front panel

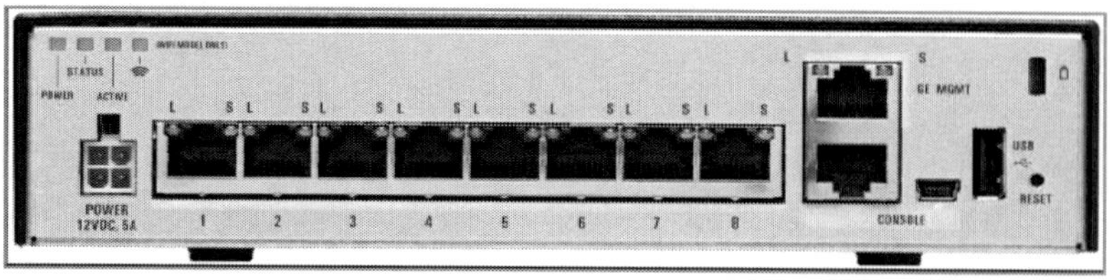

Figure 5.107 Appearance of the Cisco ASA 5506 rear panel

CHAPTER 6

BASICS OF DATA TRANSMISSION AND OVERVIEW OF NETWORK SERVICES

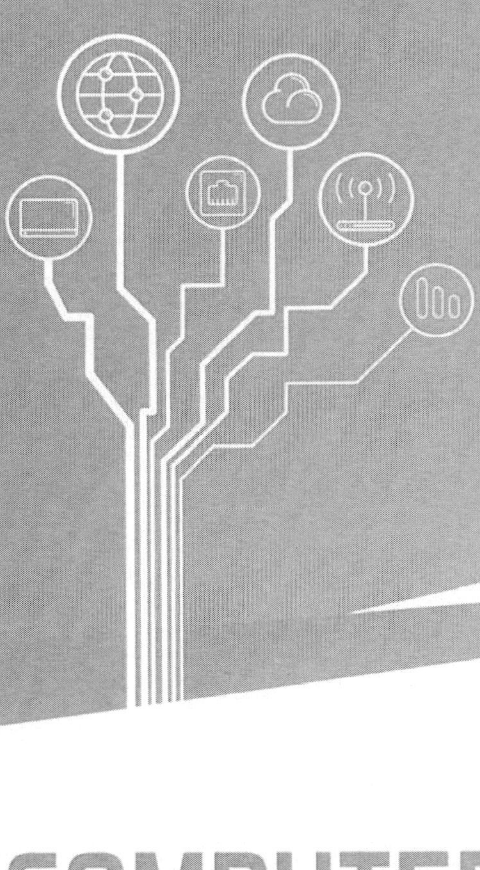

COMPUTER NETWORKS IN PACKET TRACER

FOR BEGINNERS

6 Basics of Data Transmission and Overview of Network Services

6.1 Transmission Types

This section discusses two types of transmission and how network devices behave when operating in a given mode.

6.1.1 Half Duplex

Half Duplex is a transmission during which data can run in both directions on one link, but not at the same time. The following network topology was used to analyse this issue, in which the connections between the two switches were configured in **Half Duplex** mode.

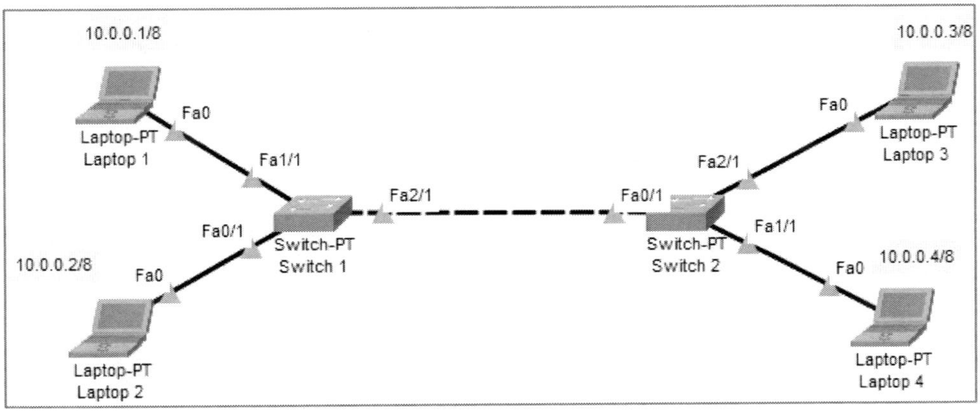

Figure 6.1 Half Duplex link between two switches

Until now, when creating a LAN, the automatic link speed and link type mode was used. If you want to change the default settings, you must first check which port number of the switch corresponds to the connection, and then make the appropriate settings. After reading the port number (in our case: Fa2/1 on the left switch and Fa0/1 on the right), click the left mouse button on the switch icon. Then go to the **Config** tab and select the port number.

Next, on the **Switch 1** switch, change the transmission type from **Auto** to **HALFDUPLEX**, as shown in the figure below. Similarly, perform the same action for the corresponding port on the right switch. On the **Switch 2** switch, change the transmission type from Auto to HALFDUPLEX.

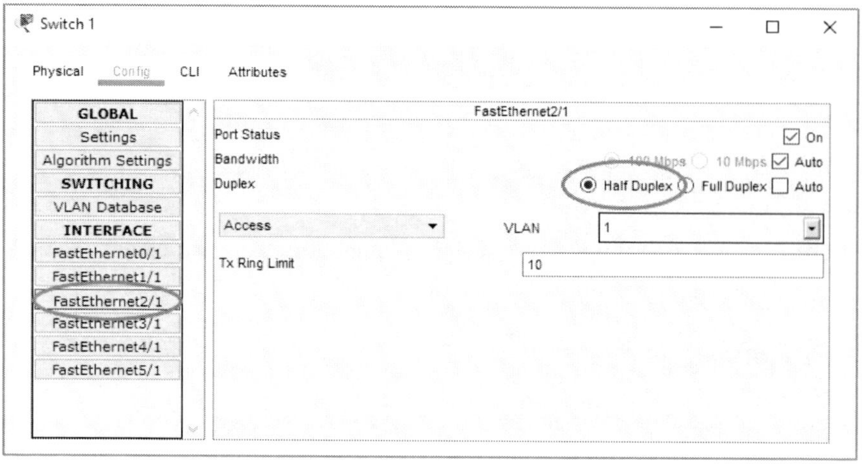

Figure 6.2 Setting the switch port to HALF DUPLEX mode

You can now observe the operation of the network in this mode, for this purpose you should switch to **Simulation** mode, and then send two test packets at the same time from the left segment of the network to the right and vice versa.

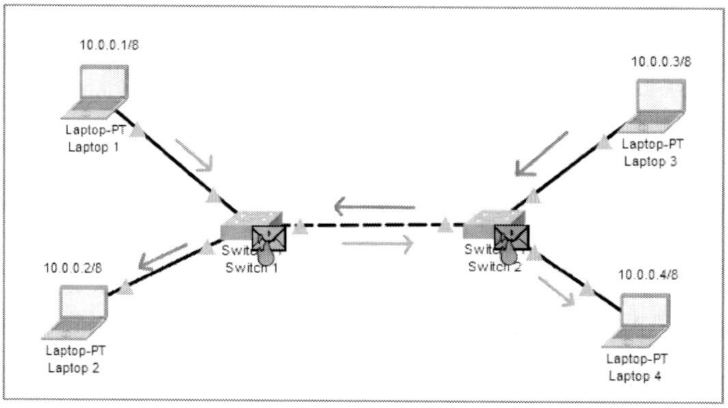

Figure 6.3 Collision on the HALF DUPLEX link

Both packets try to traverse the section of the link between the two switches, a collision occurs, as shown in the figure above. Then the transmission is resumed by the network devices, but in such a way that the right switch generates packets, and through the **HALF DUPLEX link** it will pass only one of them when the packet reaches the target.

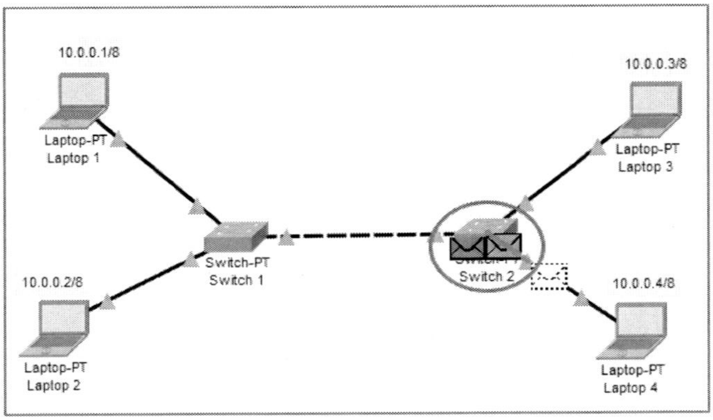

Figure 3.6.4 Packet caching by switch to avoid re-collision

6.1.2 Full Duplex

FULL DUPLEX transmission is definitely better (more modern), because it provides simultaneous movement through transmission media in both directions. If you want to test this transmission mode, you can use the same example as in the **HALF DUPLEX** transmission. Only in the configuration of the switch on the appropriate ports, set the **FULL DUPLEX** mode and proceed to the simulation. As you can see in the figure below, the simulation confirmed our theoretical expectations.

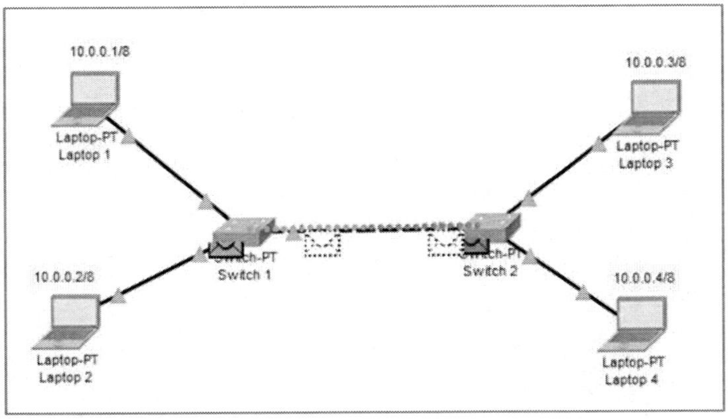

Figure 6.5 Full Duplex transmission on the link between switches

6.2 Configuring Network Services

This chapter describes the configurations of basic network services and protocols. **Note – Warning:** Remember to periodically save the file state (keyboard shortcut **CTRL+S)** during exercises.

6.2.1 DHCP

This section describes the DHCP service that is configured on the server. The following topology has been prepared for this purpose:

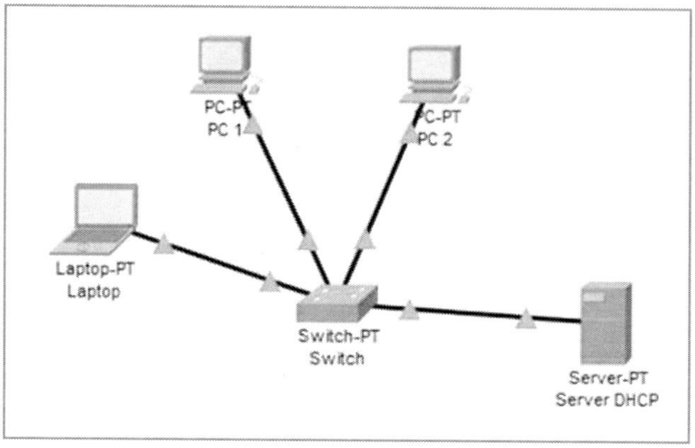

Figure 6.6 LAN with DHCP server

If you want to find a server among many devices, you should find it in the **End Devices** group, it is a device with the **Server-PT** name . The physical view of the device shows the following figure, which shows that by default one network adapter is installed on the server, with the possibility of attaching another.

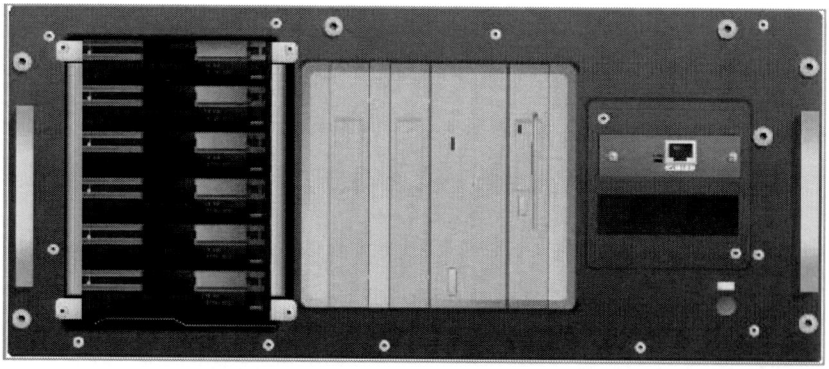

Figure 6.7 Physical view of the server

The topology is already prepared and includes a DHCP server. When you left-click on the server icon, you will see its physical appearance with the installed components. Now you will need the available services, so go to the **Services** tab.

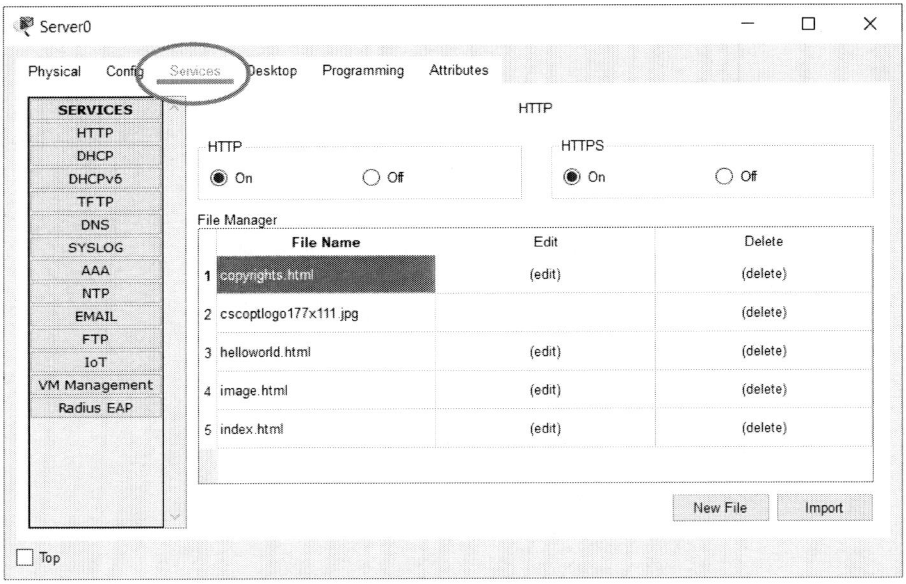

Figure 6.8 Window with configurable server services

Before you start configuring the DHCP service, it is necessary to give our server a static IP address so that it is located on the same LAN. Of course, as in the case of PCs, this is done in an almost identical way, using two methods:

- using the Config -> FastEthernet0 tab
- using the **IP Configuration** tool available on the server desktop,

We assume that each of us can do this action on our own, hence we will not describe it in detail, but enter the IP address for our server: **150.150.0.1/16**.

At this point, the server has been prepared to configure the DHCP service. The first step will be to enter the configuration and select the **DHCP** section, then the service will have to be enabled by selecting **On** in the **Service** section. Because different address pools can be stored on the server, you can assign different names to them. In this example, one is enough, so leave the **Pool Name** field unchanged. An important element is to set the parameter from which IP addresses are to be assigned, i.e. **Start IP Address**, in the described case it will be **150.150.0.10** with the same network mask as the server. It is still worth configuring the maximum number of computers, in this example it is enough to set it to **10**. The most important, and at the same time the last configuration step, is to save the settings, which should be done by pressing the **Save** button.

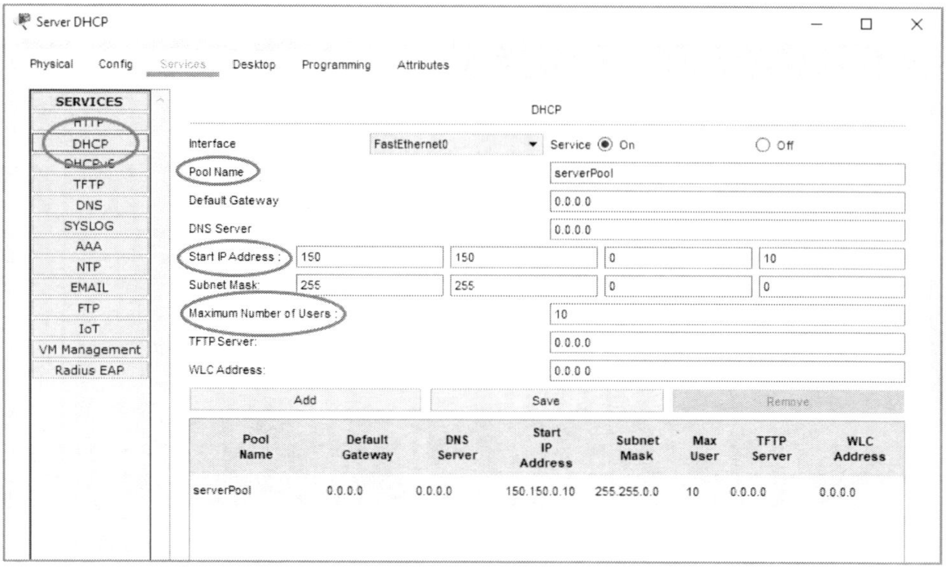

Figure 6.9 Configuring DHCP on the Server

All computers should be switched from static to dynamic addressing, after which they should receive an IP address, or you can refresh the IP address using one of the ways described in the previous chapters. After checking the addressing of the entire LAN, you can of course simulate the network to confirm the theoretical assumptions.

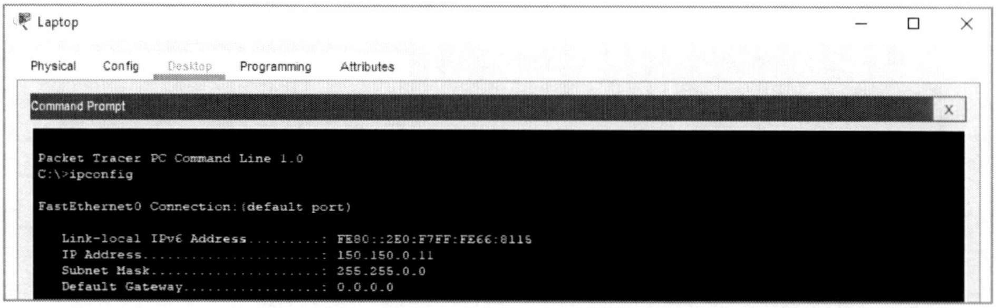

Figure 6.10 Obtained IP address from DHCP server via Laptop

The DHCP server does not necessarily need to be configured on the server, it is possible to configure it on the router, and this will be described later in the chapter on configuring routers using the console environment.

6.2.2 HTTP

Another service that will be described in this chapter is HTTP. Of course, you could place subsequent network services on one server, but we will allow ourselves to place each of them on a separate device. Therefore, you need to add another server to the topology that you will connect to the network and configure it according to the adopted address:**150.150.0.2/255.255.0.0**.

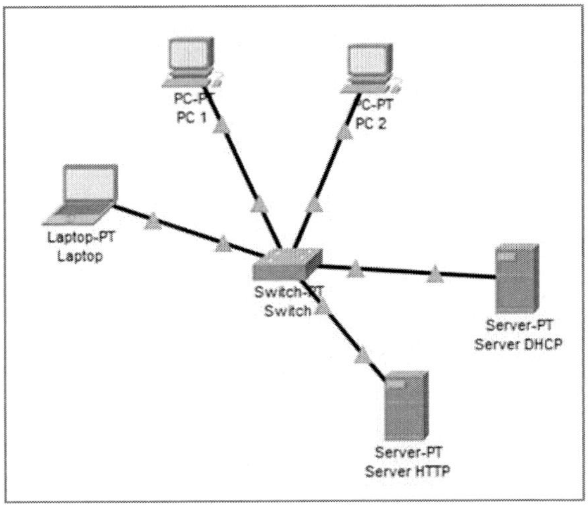

Figure 6.11 Attaching an HTTP server to the LAN

After completing the described steps, you can now take care of the HTTP configuration. To do this, left-click on the server icon and go to the **Services** tab, and then click on **HTTP**. The first thing to do is to make sure that the service is enabled, there are two options http and HTTPS. Note that the main file that will display the contents of the HTML code must be named **index.html**, otherwise you will not be able to view the web page. When you click on [edit] next to the **index.html** file name, a window opens in which the default code that contains the sample page is entered, along with two subpages with references. The rest of the files in this **[File Manager]** tab are files used by the HTML page.

By the way, it is also worth informing advanced readers that the HTTP server in the Cisco Packet Tracer also supports **CSS** files and **Java Scripts**.

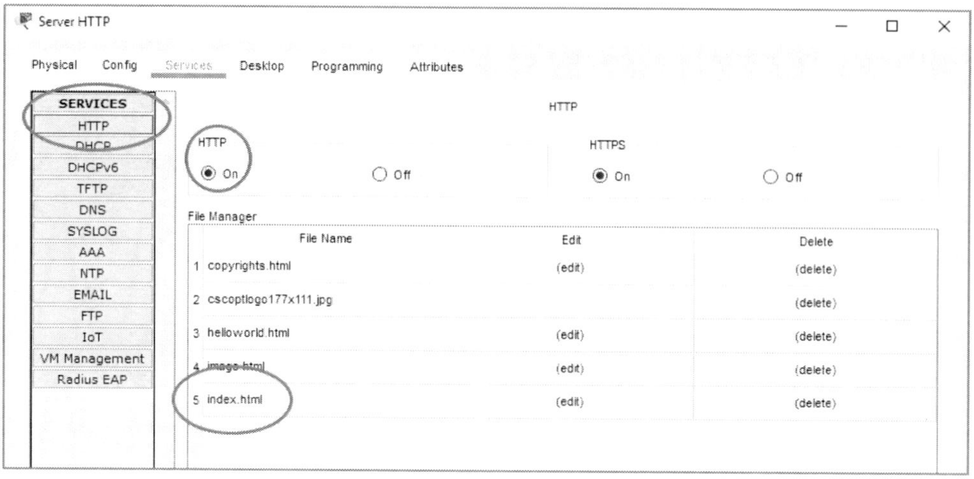

Figure 6.12 http Configuration

In fact, for starters, it's all to be able to display the content of a web page on any LAN computer. To do this, through any computer, go to its desktop, and then using a web browser enter the address of the web page, in this example it will be the IP address of the HTTP server (**150.150.0.2**).

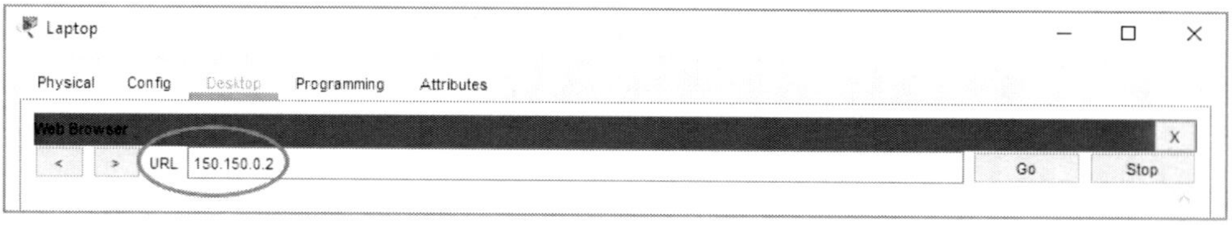

Figure 6.13 Type the HTTP server address

After pressing the **Go** button, the http page will be loaded.

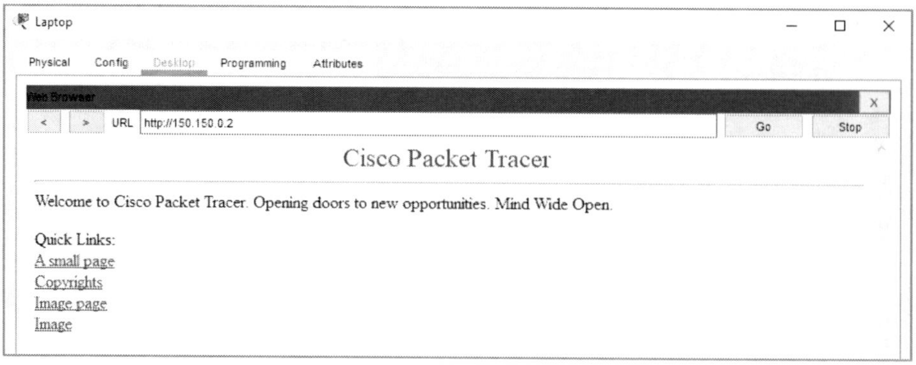

Figure 6.14 Contents of a sample web page displayed in your computer's browser

Of course, keep in mind that the default HTML code can be freely changed and modified. As a result of the changes, the sample page may look as shown in the figure below.

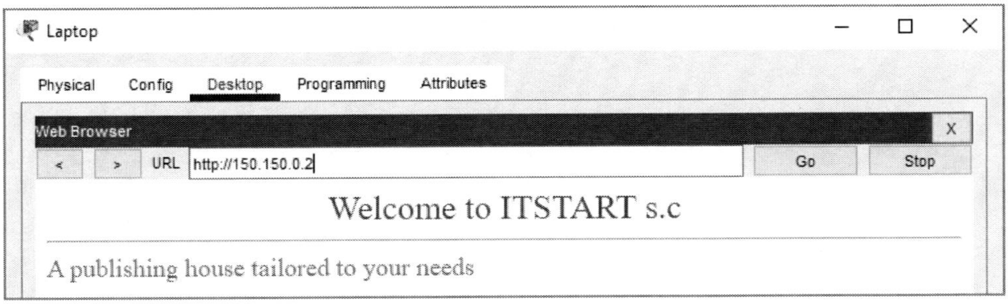

Figure 6.15 My Own website

6.2.3 FTP

Similarly to the previous cases, you can add an additional server on which to configure another FTP service. After adding another device, our LAN should already contain 3 servers. An FTP server is a file server. It allows us to download files from it and send files to it. We often deal with such servers on a daily basis – even by downloading a file from a platform.

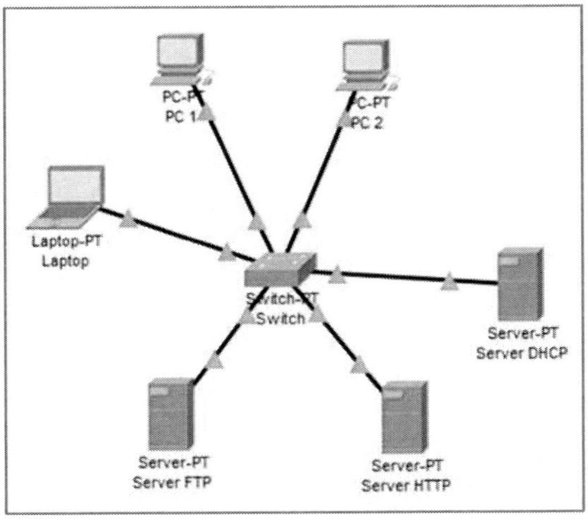

Figure 6.16 Adding an FTP server to the network

Then you need to go to the configuration of the service, which, of course, can be found in the **Services** section. At the very beginning, you should ensure that the service is enabled, then in the **User Setup** section, define access parameters (usernames and passwords). Below you can specify the access rights to files from the FTP level, while at the very bottom of the configuration window there are sample file names that can be downloaded from the server.

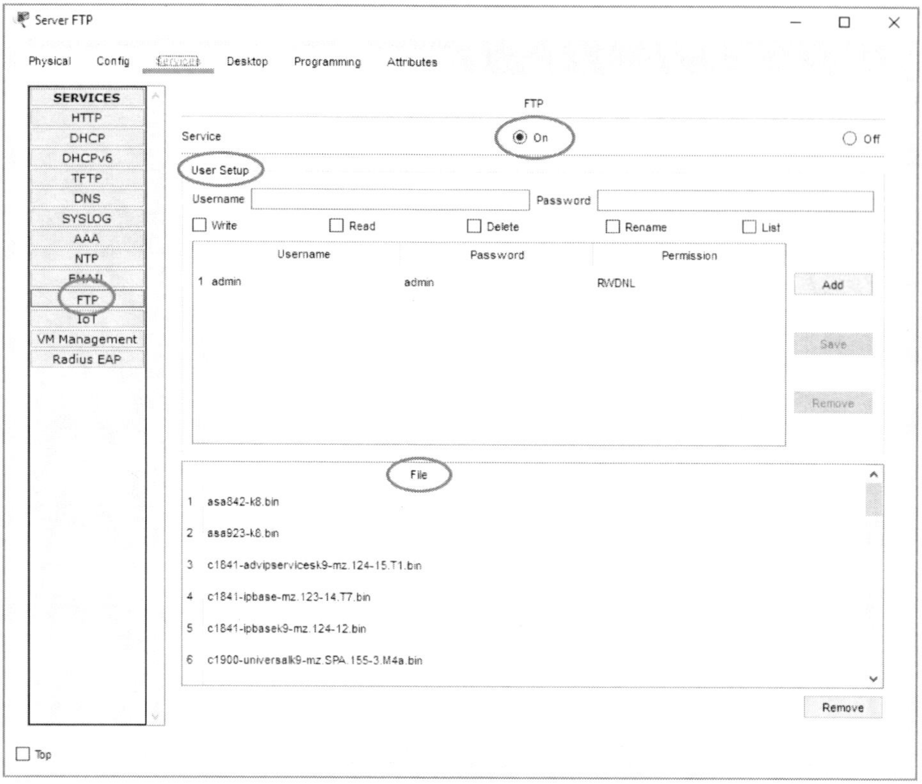

Figure 6.17 FTP configuration

Now you can add two new users, it will be **user1** with password **111** and **user2** with password **222**. Different access rights will be defined for each of them, for example, the first user will only be able to view the contents of the server and download files, while the second user will be able to additionally rename files and upload their files to the server.

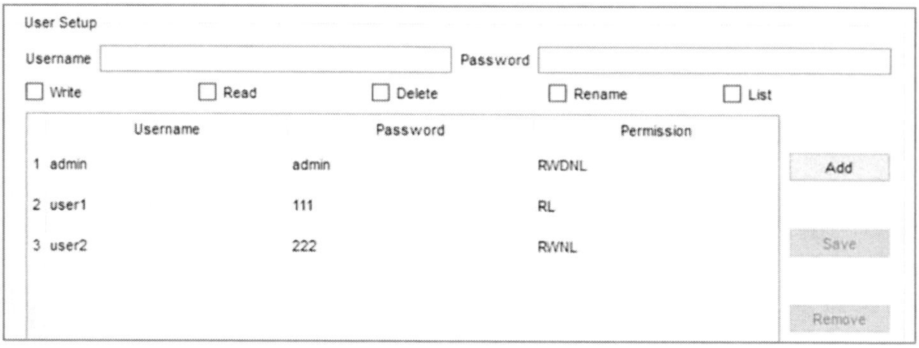

Figure 6.18 Defined FTP access rights for new users

File access rights on the FTP server:

- L – display of content (list of file names)
- R – reading files
- W – saving files
- D – deleting files
- R – renaming files

If you want to access the FTP server now, open a command line on any computer on the LAN and type **ftp 150.150.150.3** (the IP address matches the server address).

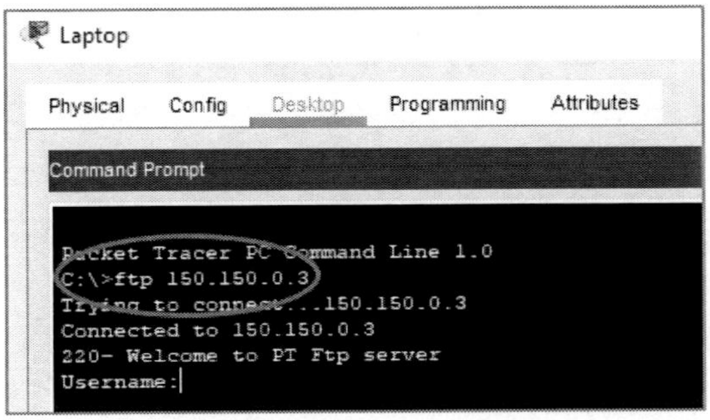

Figure 6.19 Connect to an FTP server using the command line

When you press Enter, you will be asked for your username and password. We must bear in mind that when entering a password, the characters that will be typed do not appear in the window, because for security purposes they are hidden, as shown in the figure below. When you connect to the server, you should see a message that you are connected to the service, and then the prompt from **PC>** to **FTP>** will be changed.

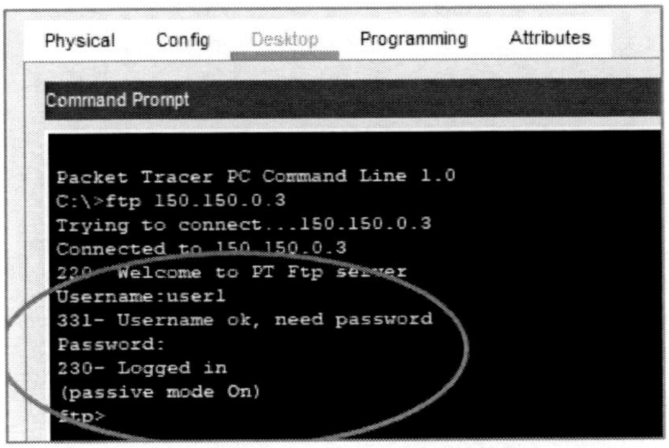

Figure 6.20 Log in to an FTP server

To find out what commands are available in this mode, you need to run a help command, or **help**.

```
ftp>help
              ?
              cd
              delete
              dir
              get
              help
              passive
              put
              pwd
              quit
              rename
ftp>
```

Figure 6.21 View help in FTP mode

Common commands on an FTP server are:

- **cd** (change directory) – change the current directory in the server
- **delete** – delete the file from the server
- **dir** (directory) – display the contents of the current directory on the server
- **get** – download the file from the server
- **put** – send the file to the server
- **pwd** (print working directory) – display the name of the current directory on the server
- **rename** – rename a file on the server
- **quit** – log out of the server

The next step will be to display the available files that are on the server, for this purpose the **dir** command will be used. There should be a fairly long list of files available for download. Why do they have such long and strange names? Well, these are images of the IOS system of routers that we will use when working with professional routers.

Therefore, at this stage of our adventure with the Cisco Packet Tracer program, we have to accept it and work on this type of files.

```
ftp>dir

Listing /ftp directory from 150.150.0.3:
0   : asa842-k8.bin                                   5571584
1   : asa923-k8.bin                                   30468096
2   : c1841-advipservicesk9-mz.124-15.T1.bin          33591768
3   : c1841-ipbase-mz.123-14.T7.bin                   13832032
4   : c1841-ipbasek9-mz.124-12.bin                    16599160
5   : c1900-universalk9-mz.SPA.155-3.M4a.bin          33591768
6   : c2600-advipservicesk9-mz.124-15.T1.bin          33591768
7   : c2600-i-mz.122-28.bin                           5571584
8   : c2600-ipbasek9-mz.124-8.bin                     13169700
9   : c2800nm-advipservicesk9-mz.124-15.T1.bin        50938004
10  : c2800nm-advipservicesk9-mz.151-4.M4.bin         33591768
11  : c2800nm-ipbase-mz.123-14.T7.bin                 5571584
12  : c2800nm-ipbasek9-mz.124-8.bin                   15522644
13  : c2900-universalk9-mz.SPA.155-3.M4a.bin          33591768
14  : c2950-i6q4l2-mz.121-22.EA4.bin                  3058048
15  : c2950-i6q4l2-mz.121-22.EA8.bin                  3117390
16  : c2960-lanbase-mz.122-25.FX.bin                  4414921
17  : c2960-lanbase-mz.122-25.SEE1.bin                4670455
18  : c2960-lanbasek9-mz.150-2.SE4.bin                4670455
19  : c3560-advipservicesk9-mz.122-37.SE1.bin         8662192
20  : c3560-advipservicesk9-mz.122-46.SE.bin          10713279
21  : c800-universalk9-mz.SPA.152-4.M4.bin            33591768
22  : c800-universalk9-mz.SPA.154-3.M6a.bin           83029236
23  : cat3k_caa-universalk9.16.03.02.SPA.bin          505532849
24  : cgr1000-universalk9-mz.SPA.154-2.CG             159487552
25  : cgr1000-universalk9-mz.SPA.156-3.CG             184530138
26  : ir800-universalk9-bundle.SPA.156-3.M.bin        160968869
27  : ir800-universalk9-mz.SPA.155-3.M                61750062
28  : ir800-universalk9-mz.SPA.156-3.M                63753767
29  : ir800_yocto-1.7.2.tar                           2877440
30  : ir800_yocto-1.7.2_python-2.7.3.tar              6912000
31  : pt1000-i-mz.122-28.bin                          5571584
32  : pt3000-i6q4l2-mz.121-22.EA4.bin                 3117390
ftp>
```

Figure 6.22 List of available files on the FTP server

If our permissions allow it, we can now download one of the files by typing the get command and after the space entering the full name of the file. In order not to be discouraged by typing long file names, we can select any of them with the mouse, copy and paste, but it should be remembered that the entire operation of copying the name should be done with the mouse, because keyboard shortcuts do not work.

```
ftp>get asa842-k8.bin

Reading file asa842-k8.bin from 150.150.0.3:
File transfer in progress...

[Transfer complete - 5571584 bytes]

5571584 bytes copied in 22.272 secs (57319 bytes/sec)
ftp>
```

Figure 3.6.23 Download a sample file from an FTP server

When the file is downloaded, the message **File transfer** in progress... is displayed, which means that this process is in progress. When the process is complete, another message will appear: **Transfer complete**, which informs you that the file has been downloaded correctly.

We will now try to present some other commands and permissions that we have assigned to the user on the server, which is why we will now try to delete the file using the delete command, as the figure below illustrates.

```
ftp>delete ir800_yocto-1.7.2.tar

Deleting file ir800_yocto-1.7.2.tar from 150.150.0.3: ftp>
%Error ftp://150.150.0.3/ir800_yocto-1.7.2.tar (No such file or directory Or Permission denied)
550-Requested action not taken. permission denied).

ftp>
```

Figure 6.24 Failed attempt to delete a file from an FTP server

The console window displays information that the requested file does not exist or we do not have sufficient permissions. Since we are sure that we have entered the file name correctly, we are 100% sure that we do not have permission to delete it. Our user **user1** can only view files on the server and download them, so now you need to log in to the second user **user2**, who admittedly can not delete files but can change names. To do this, type **quit** to disconnect from the server and **ftp 150.150.0.3** again and log in as **user2**.

```
C:\>ftp 150.150.0.3
Trying to connect...150.150.0.3
Connected to 150.150.0.3
220- Welcome to PT Ftp server
Username:user2
331- Username ok, need password
Password:
230- Logged in
(passive mode On)
ftp>rename asa842-k8.bin aaa.com

Renaming asa842-k8.bin
ftp>
[OK Renamed file successfully from asa842-k8.bin to aaa.com]
ftp>dir

Listing /ftp directory from 150.150.0.3:
0    : aaa.com                                              5571584
```

Figure 6.25 Rename a file on an ftp server

Then, after logging in correctly, type the command **rename asa842-k8.bin aaa.com** and after a while a message will be displayed informing about the correctly performed action. However, in order to see the effect of our actions, we list the files on the server using the dir command to finally check whether the file already has a new name, as shown in the previous figure.

We could now describe all the possibilities related to permissions, but we will leave it to the reader for his own exercises because it is done in the same way by using subsequent commands and defining the appropriate permissions.

6.2.4 SMTP/POP3

Once we have learned how to configure several well-known network services, the time has come for e-mail, so as in previous cases, we should add another server to our network, which will act as a server sending and receiving mail. The server address is: **150.150.0.4/255.255.0.0**. We will also choose two computers from the network that will send and receive (correspond) mail to each other. These will be PC1 and PC2.

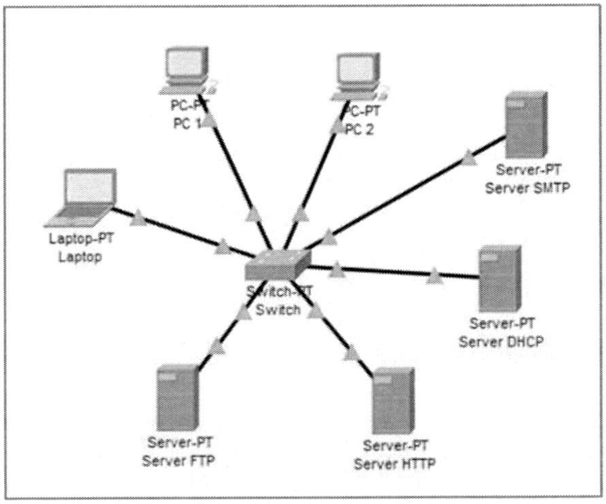

Figure 6.26 LAN with email server

After the correct IP configuration, you can go to the settings necessary for the proper operation of email. In the **Services** tab of the server settings, find the **Email** section where you need to enable both services: **SMTP** Service and **POP3** Service, responsible for sending and receiving mail.

We will set up two mail accounts:

Login	Password	Post Domain
George	George123	Itstart.pl
Marco	Marco456	Itstart.pl

Figure 6.27 Email configuration data

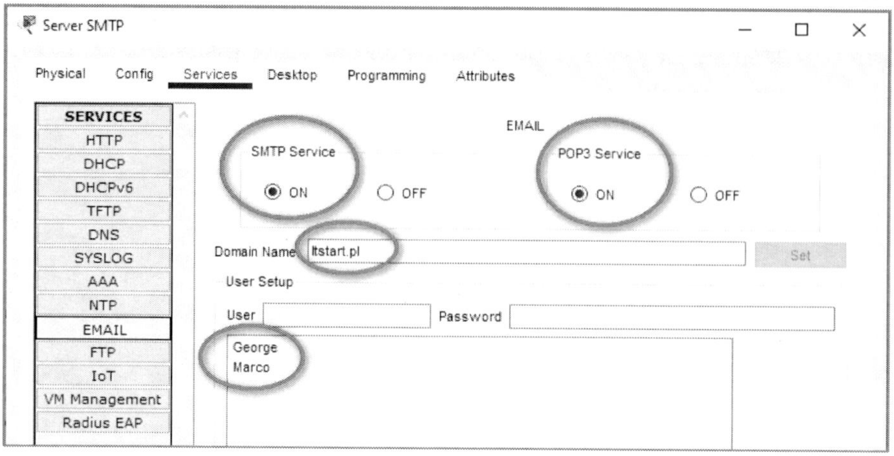

Figure 6.28 EMAIL Server Configuration

Next, we specify the domain name to type in the **Domain Name**: field, in this example we should type: **Itstart.pl**. Then we will create accounts of two users and assign them passwords. After the correct creation of user accounts, you can proceed to the configuration of mail clients, on those computers that will correspond with each other. To do this, on the selected computer, on the desktop, you need to left-click on the icon, which is shown in the figure below.

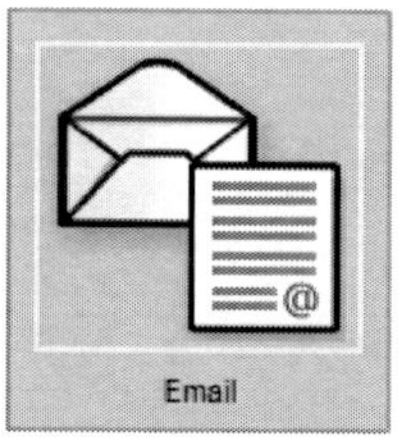

Figure 6.29 Email client icon, available on your computer's desktop

The first time you start the mail client, the mail configuration window opens automatically. In the **Your Name**: field, you can type any name that appears on the recipient's computer, in the **Email Address** field, type the email address, in this example it will be: **marco@itstart.pl**. In the **Incoming** and **Outgoing Mail Server** fields, and type the mail server address **150.150.0.4**. Finally, in the Fields **User Name**: and **Password**:, we enter the username and password that was assigned to the user directly on the server. After entering all the parameters, save the settings by pressing the **Save** button.

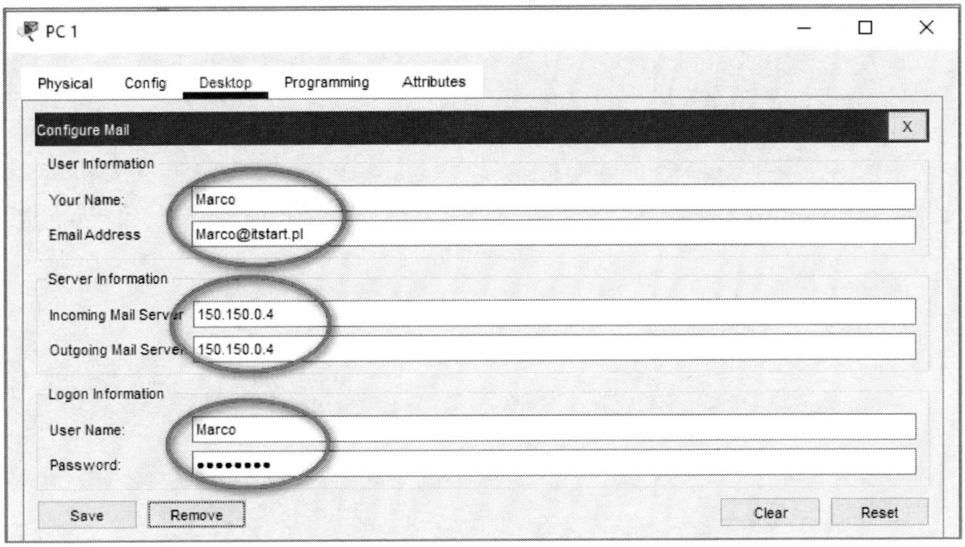

Figure 6.30 Mail client configuration on PC1

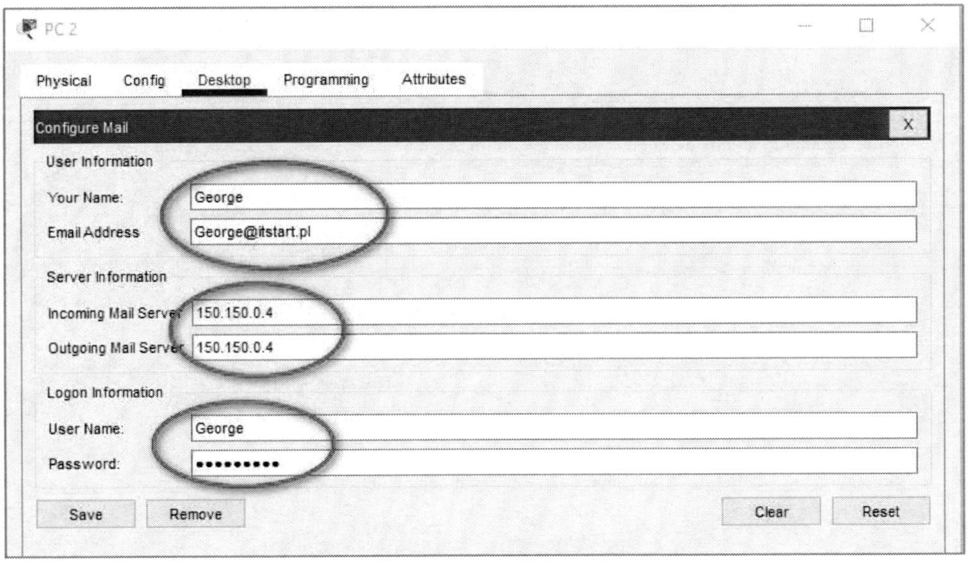

Figure 6.31 Mail client configuration on PC2

After saving the settings, the mail client window will automatically open in which you can compose, send and receive messages.

However, before we compose the first email, close this window and configure the e-mail program on the second computer so that you can carry out full correspondence between them.

So we will do one test to send sample message from Marco@Itstart.pl existing in PC1 to George@Itstart.pl existing in PC2.

The first message is edited by pressing the **Compose** button, after which the editor opens, in which we will be able to edit the first e-mail. Field **To**: is responsible for entering the recipient, **Subject**: entering the subject of the e-mail and at the bottom in the empty field enter the content.

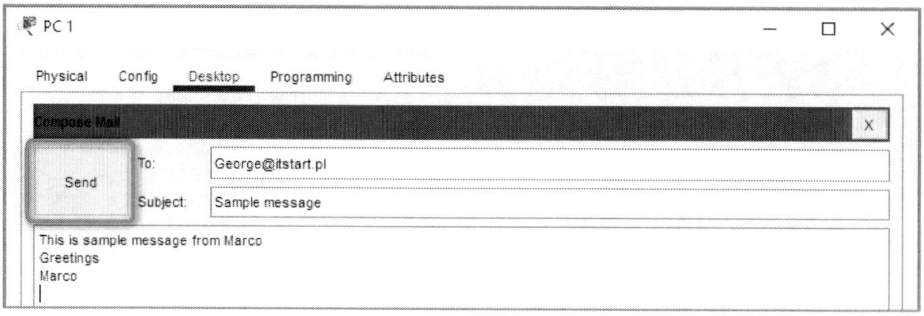

Figure 6.32 Compose and send a new message to George

The status of the sent message can be checked in the lower part of the window, where the following message should be displayed, informing about the correct sending of the e-mail.

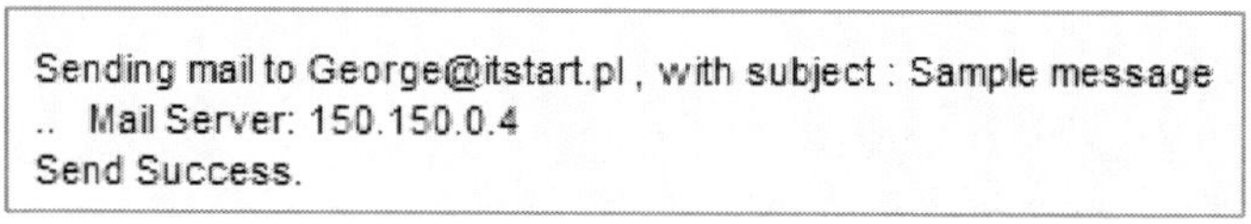

Figure 6.33 The status of the sent message displayed

Now, we can enable the e-mail program on the second, configured computer. Press the **Receive** button to check incoming messages. After a while, the header of the received email should appear in the window.

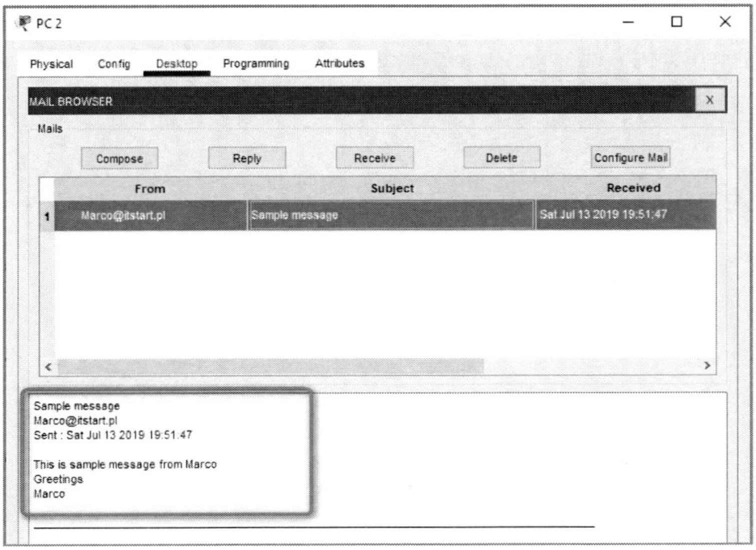

Figure 6.34 Received email

Now all that remains is to respond to the received e-mail, to do this we click on the **Reply** button. Then we respond to the received letter and press **Send** again. The message should be delivered to the sender's computer.

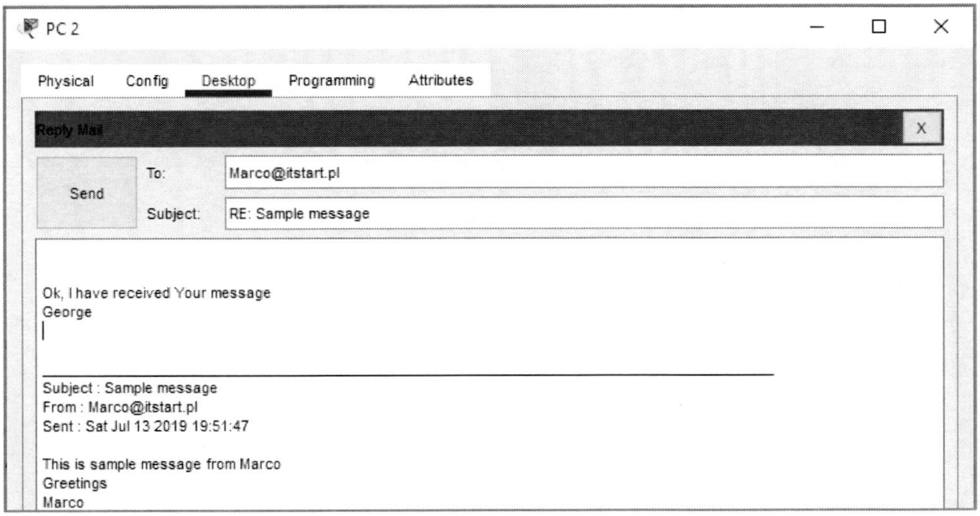

Figure 6.35 Reply to an email you receive

6.2.5 DNS

When most of the services have already been discussed, there is one more thing left - DNS. We deliberately left this service at the very end to be able to show its impact on the use of the network and other well-known services using the DNS (**Domain Name System**) protocol. According to the previously adopted principle, we add another server to our network, which we address: **150.150.0.5/255.255.0.0**.

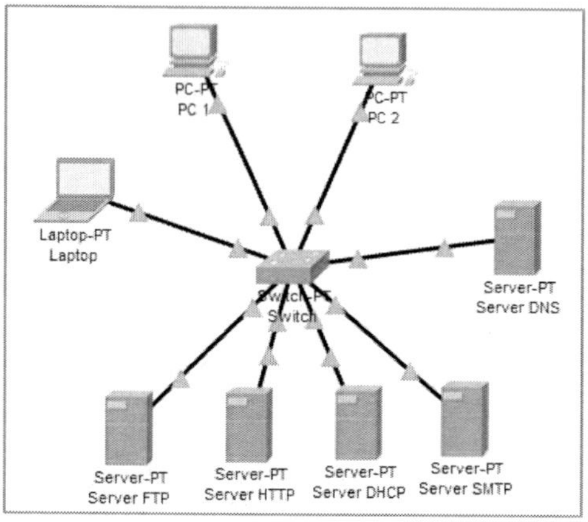

Figure 6.36 LAN after adding a DNS server

On the Server Services tab, select **DNS** and then configure it. First, the service must be enabled (**DNS Service On**). Then we add the names and addresses of the servers that we want to access through the names we provide, not by the IP address. Examples of addresses are shown in the figure.

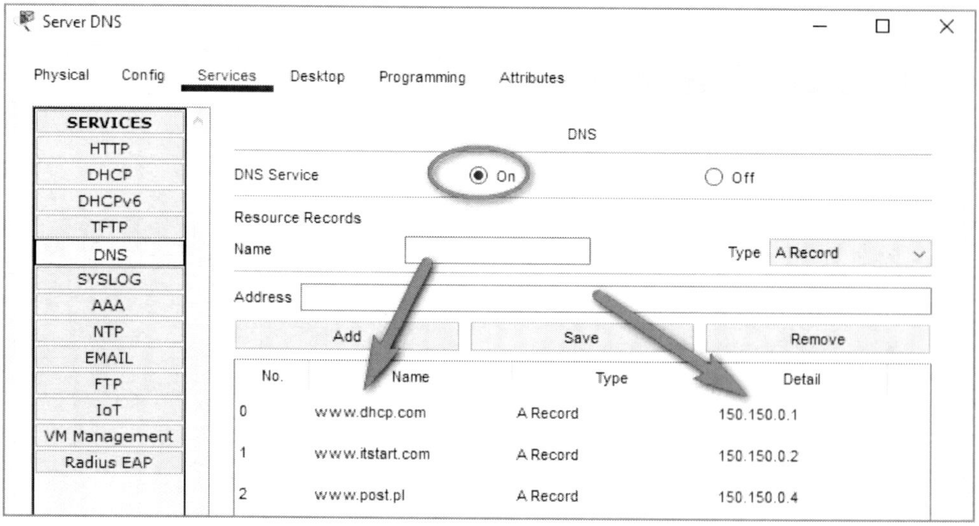

Figure 6.37 DNS Server Configuration

From the server's point of view, the configuration is complete, but the service will not work properly until each computer on the LAN is configured correctly. Because the DHCP server allocates addresses in our network, it does not yet pass the DNS server address to all computers, as shown in the figure below. Of course, you could enter the DNS address for each computer manually, but we will show you how this process can be automated.

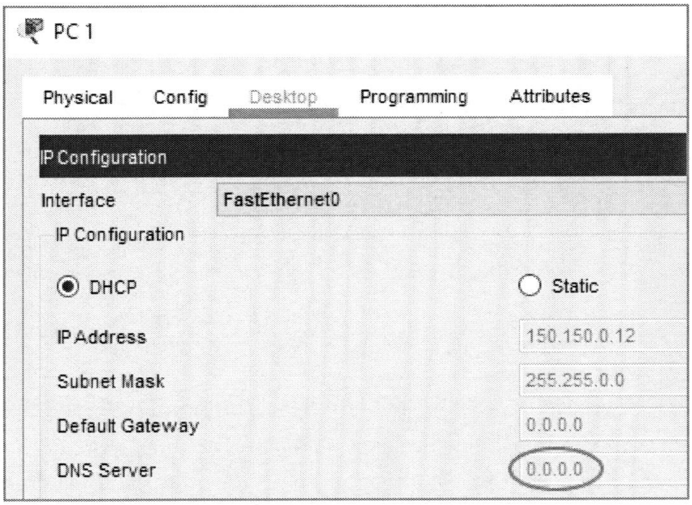

Figure 6.38 No DNS information on each LAN computer

So let's go to the DHCP server configuration, in which in the **DNS Server** field enter its IP address, and then in order to save the changes, click on **Save**.

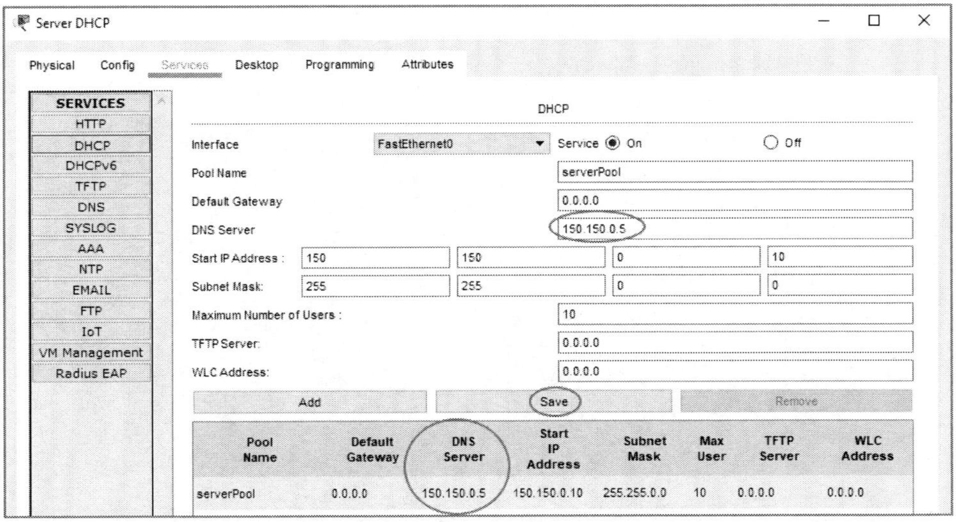

Figure 6.39 Append the DNS server address to the DHCP server settings

After performing the above steps, we refresh, by any means, the IP addresses of all computers and after a while they should receive information about the address of the DNS server, as shown in the figure below.

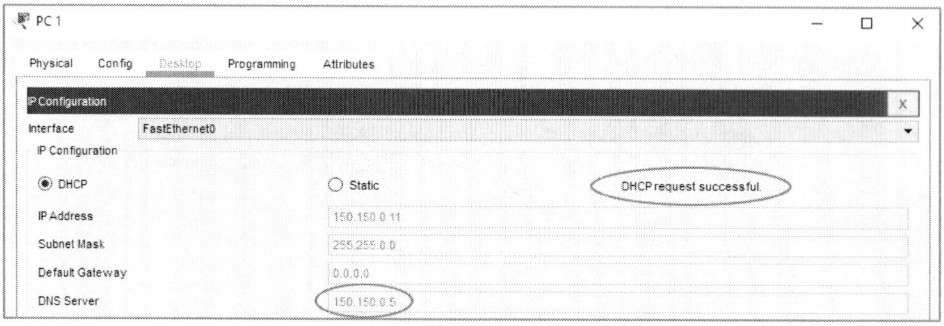

Figure 6.40 Received DNS server address

It would now be necessary to check whether DNS is working properly. First, test this by using the PING command on the command line of any computer. After you run Command Prompt, type ping **www.post.pl**. A positive response from the IP address 150.150.0.4 indicates that DNS is working correctly.

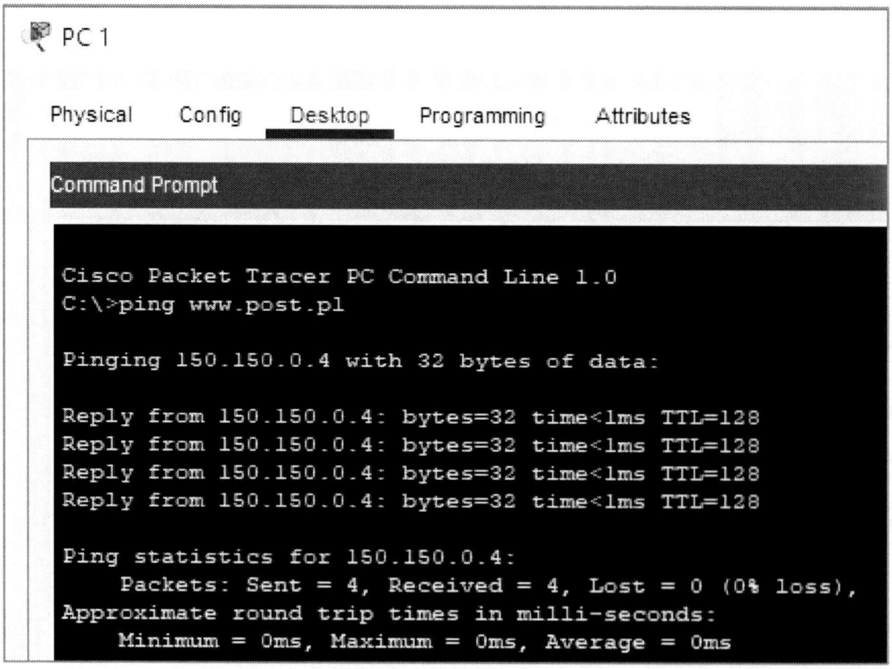

Figure 6.41 Verifying DNS operation via PING

The second option will be to enter the website via a browser using not the IP address but the name of the page. In our example, this will be typing the phrase: **www.itstart.com**

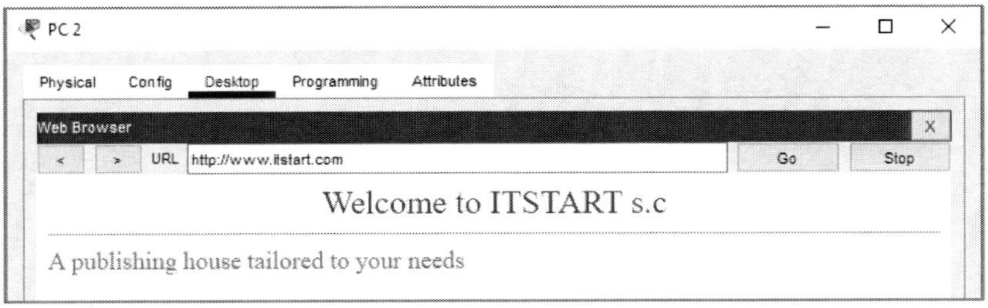

Figure 6.42 Correctly displayed web page, called by name

In a similar way, you can also check the operation of FTP services. Noteworthy, however, is the testing of mail. However, in the first place, the settings of each mail client must be changed. We delete the IP addresses in the **Incoming** and **Outgoing Mail Server** fields and enter the name of the mail server there, the same as entered in the record No. 2 in the DNS server.

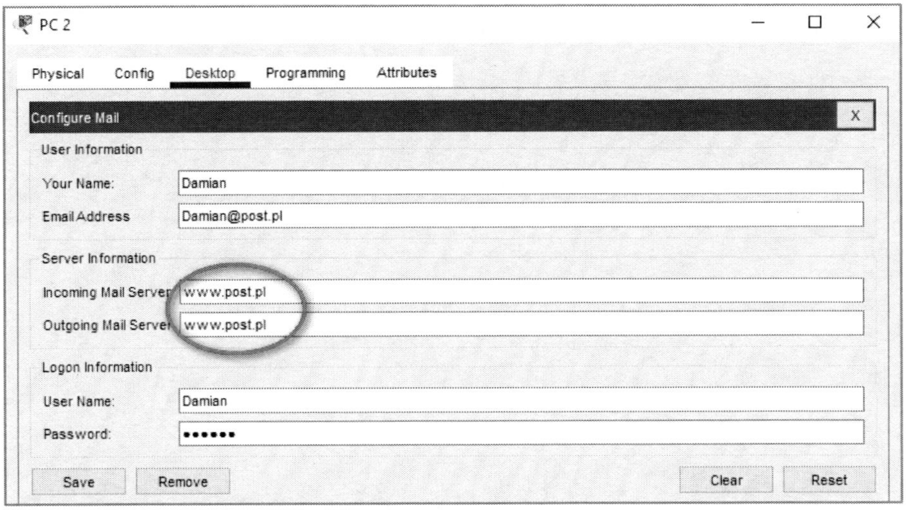

Figure 6.43 Typing the name of the incoming and outgoing server

Now all you have to do is compose a new message and send it. At the bottom of the window, a message will be displayed in which you will see information about the correct sending of the message, using not the IP address of the mail servers, but the names.

```
Sending mail to Marek@post.pl , with subject : Hello ..  Mail Server: www.post.pl
DNS resolving. Resolving name: www.post.pl by querying to DNS Server:
150.150.0.5 DNS resolved ip address: 150.150.0.4
Send Success.
```

Figure 6.44 Message about correctly sent mail

6.2.6 Firewall

Very often we deal with networks, with FIREWALLS, i.e. firewalls. Firewalls protect us either from unauthorized Internet traffic or from the possibility of potential intrusion on the server. In our example topology, we used four computers connected via a switch to a server running two HTTP and FTP services. By default, all devices (computers) can use these services. However, we will try to show how the FIREWALL on the server works and protects against unauthorized access from two computers.

Our assumption will be to configure the server in such a way that a computer with an IP address: **10.0.0.2** does not have access to the HTTP service, while a computer with an address of **10.0.0.4** does not have access to the FTP service. Other computers can use all services.

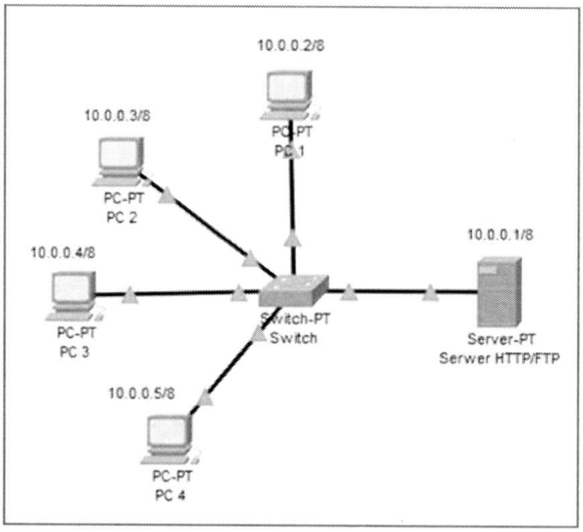

Figure 6.45 Topology to configure FIREWALL on the serve

First, go to the server settings, then to its desktop and find the FIREWALL tool, as shown in the figure below.

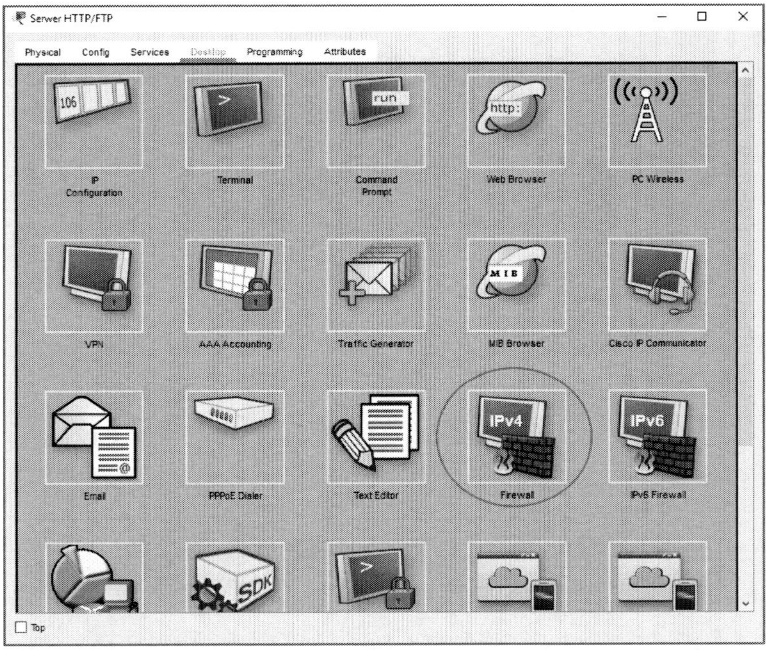

Figure 6.46 Enable the FIREWALL tool on the server

When you run the FIREWALL tool, the following window appears, in which you must first enable the service by switching the **On/Off** button to the **On** position in the Services field, as shown in the figure below.

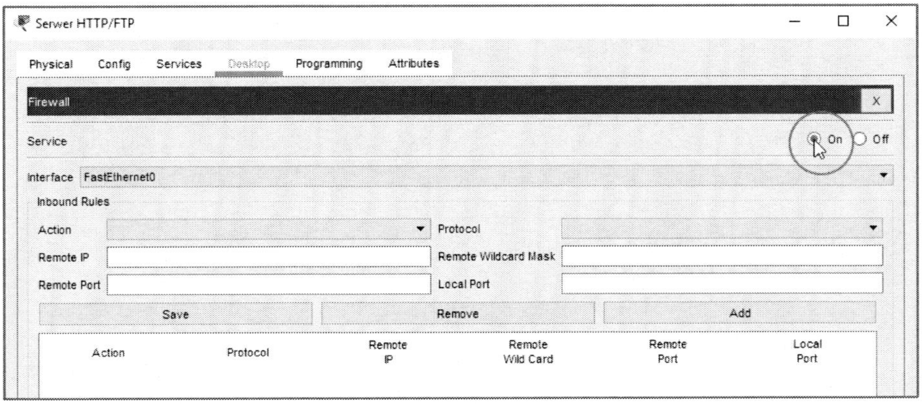

Figure 6.47 Enable the FIREWALL service on the server

Now you need to configure rules on the server that will cause the aforementioned filtration of network traffic. In the **Action** field, you can select two options: **Allow** or **Deny**.

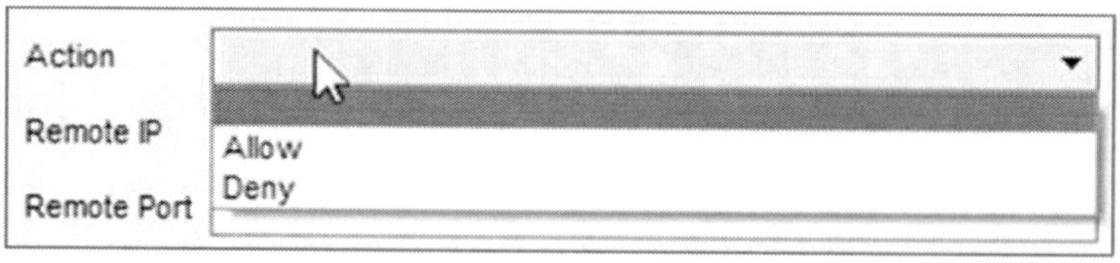

Figure 6.48 Action field: Allow and Deny

The next important field to configure the FIREWALL service is to determine for which protocol the defined rules will work. In this field, you can select one in several protocols:: **IP, ICMP, TCP, UDP.**

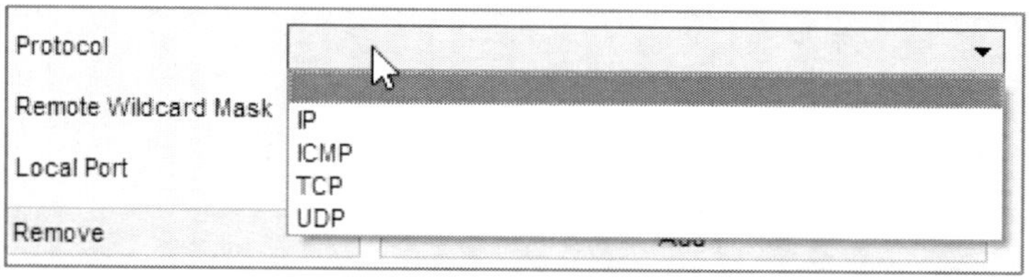

Figure 6.49 Protocols for which we want to define FIREWALL rules

IP addresses and inverted masks (so-called WILDCARD MASKS) remained to be configured, as well as port numbers intended to block or pass traffic, as shown in the next figure.

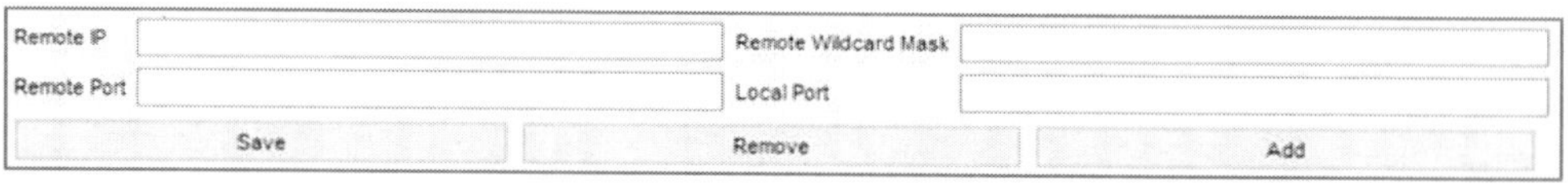

Figure 6.50 IP addresses and Wildcard Mask to define rules

Wildcard mask - a string of binary zeros and ones used to filter individual IP addresses or their groups. Zeros indicate the IP address bits to be matched, and the ones indicate the bits to ignore. For example, the inverse mask for **255.255.255.0** is **0.0.0.255**, which means matching the first **24** bits of the IP address. The inverse mask to the **255.0.0.0** mask is **0.255.255.255**, which means matching the first 8 bits of the IP address.

So let's start with the initial assumptions we made at the beginning in this chapter.

We define the first rule, for a computer 10.0.0.2, which we want to block from visiting a website located on the server with the address 10.0.0.1. To do this, in the **Action** field, select: **Deny**, then **TCP** protocol, specifying **Remote IP**, in which we type: 10.0.0.2 and **Remote Wildcard mask**: 0.0.0.0 (which is equivalent to the operation of the rule for only one computer as in the case of the /32 mask). Next, we need to determine from which ports it will not be possible to enter the server page: **Remote Port**: **ANY** (i.e. all) and which destination port to block: **Local Port**: 80 (because it is on this port that the HTTP service runs). Then we press the **Add** button to apply the rule. The full configuration of the first rule is shown in the figure below.

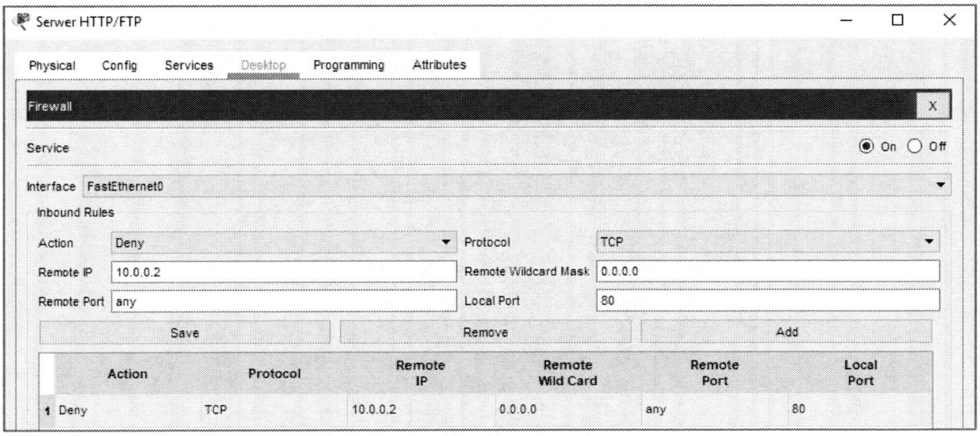

Figure 6.51 First Rule Configuration View

Now let's try from a computer with an IP address: 10.0.0.2, to enter the server's website. Open a web browser on the locked computer and enter the address 10.0.0.1 in it, which is the equivalent of the server's website. After a while, we receive the message: **Request Timeout,** which proves the correctness of the rule.

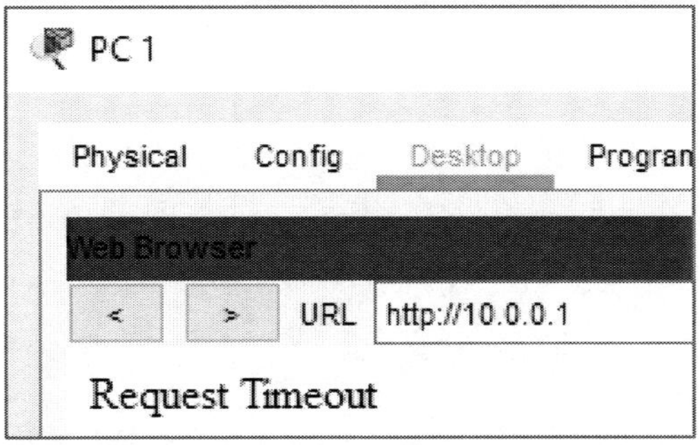

Figure 6.52 Web page not displayed due to the introduced FIREWALL rules

Now let's check if the same computer can send a typical PING to the server. As the figure below shows, PING does not occur, which indicates that the FIREWALL rules are not yet complete.

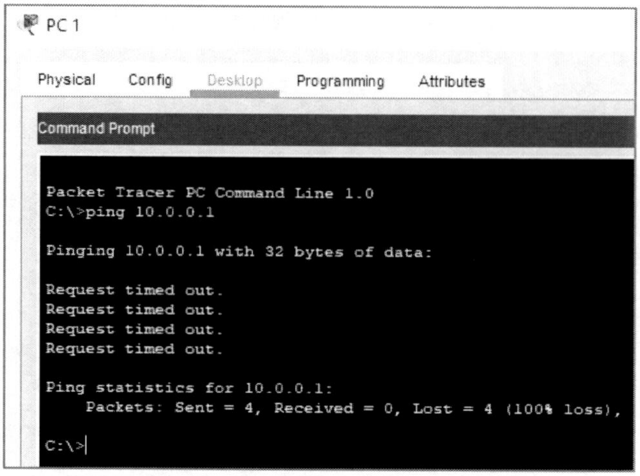

Figure 6.53 No response to PING after the applied FIREWALL rule

To restore the remaining traffic on PC1, go back to the server, to the FIREWALL tool, where you must now allow full IP traffic. To do this, we add a second rule according to the guidelines shown in the figure below:

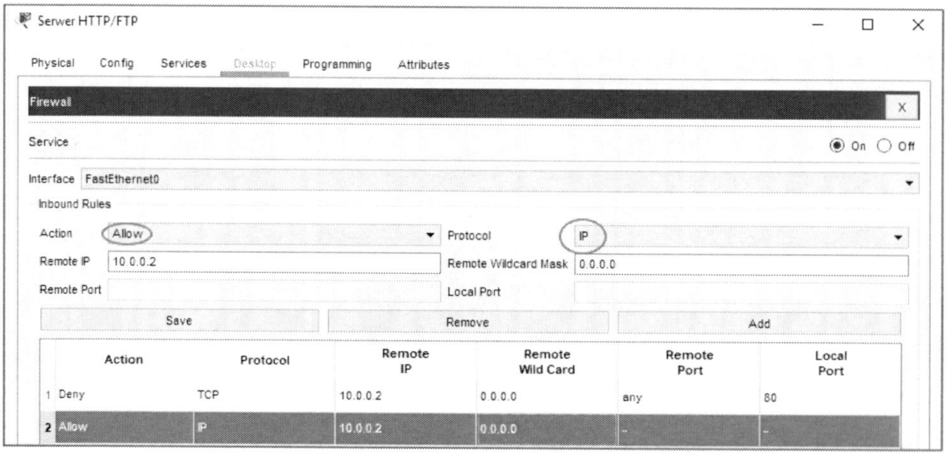

Figure 6.54 Apply an IP permission policy

After doing this, we open the command line on PC1 and try to send the PING to the server again, which this time is a complete success, as the figure below shows.

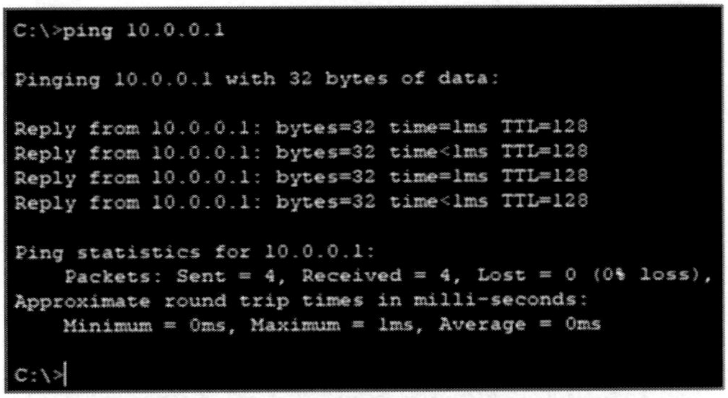

Figure 6.55 Response to PING after applying the FIREWALL rule

However, if we continue to try to open the page at 10.0.0.1 through the browser, it will end in failure, which confirms our assumptions.

Now we will define the next FIREWALL rule for PC3 with the IP address: 10.0.0.4. You want this computer to be denied access to the FTP service. As in the previous way, we define a prohibitive rule, as shown in the figure below. However, we must bear in mind that after its introduction, another rule must be added that will allow this computer to move in the IP protocol, as was the case with PC1.

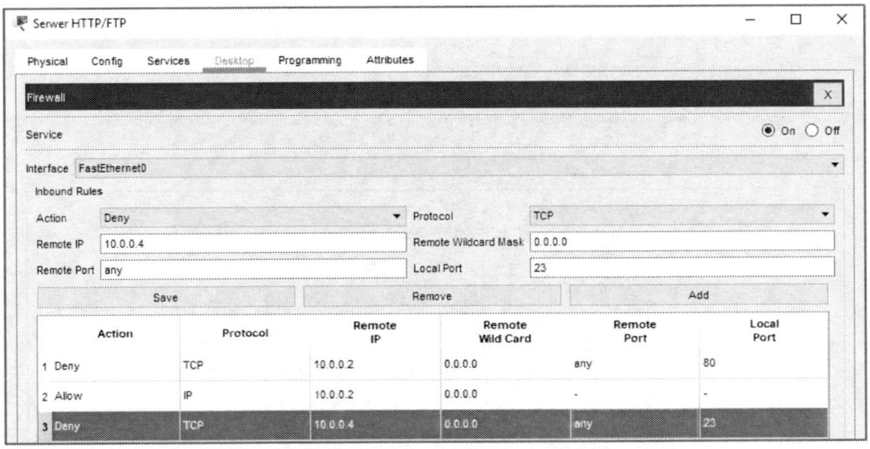

Figure 6.56 FIREWALL rule prohibiting ftp service

Let's check the operation of the rule: On PC3, open the command line and try to connect to the FTP server. Of course, this ends in failure, which once again confirms our assumptions.

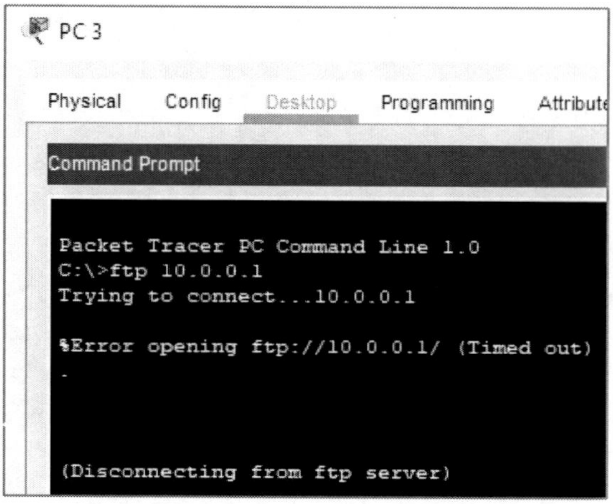

Figure 6.57 No PC3 connectivity with FTP, after entering the FIREWALL rule

To be sure, let's check whether PC1, which was supposed to be blocked from accessing only the HTTP service, can connect to the same FTP, which PC3 could not. As you can see in the next figure, PC1 does not have the slightest problems with connectivity to the FTP server.

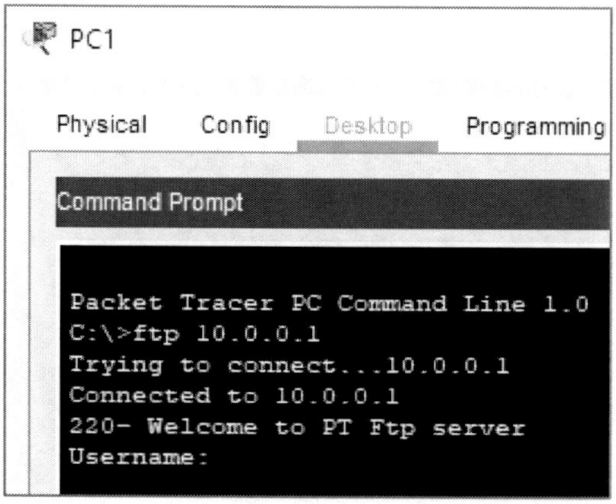

Figure 6.58 Correct connectivity of PC1 to the FTP server, after entering firewall rules

If we were to check the operation of the other computers that are not covered by any rules, it would turn out that none of them communicates with the server: (does not respond to PING and does not connect to any of the services). This does not indicate an error, but the lack of introducing additional but at the same time final rules on the FIREWALL for other computers.

This can be done in two ways. The first way is to add a separate rule for each of the other PCs (PC2, PC3, PC4) that allows the use of the IP protocol. However, it would be very inconvenient to define separate rules for each PC in large LANs. Therefore, we will also show a method that will allow this action to be implemented into one rule.

When creating entry data, we do not always have to refer to only one host, providing its unique IP address and typing 0.0.0.0 in the **Remote Wildcard Mask** field. Instead of a given IP address of the computer, we can enter the IP address of the network and in the **Remote Wildcard Mask** field specify for how many bits of the IP address the rule should apply. In this case, it is enough to enter the network address: 10.0.0.0 in the **remote IP** field and enter 0.255.255.255 in the **Remote Wildcard Mask** field, as shown in the figure below.

At this point, the remaining computers that were not covered by any FIREWALL rules so far were allowed full and unlimited network traffic.

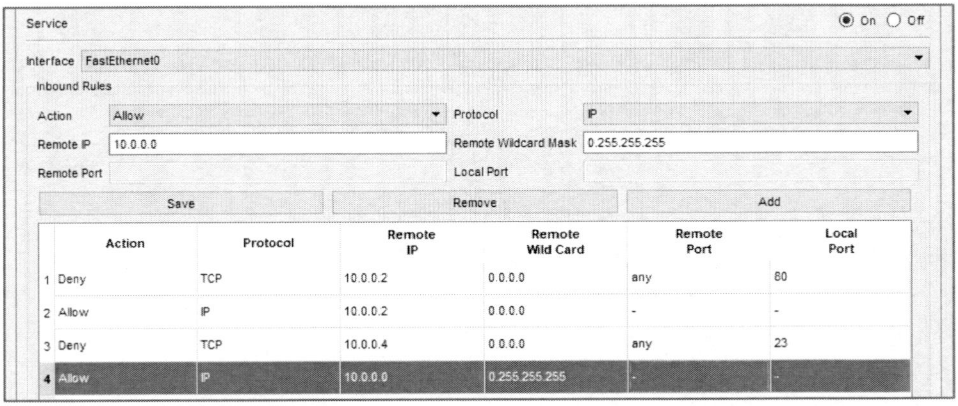

Figure 6.59 FIREWALL rule for a group of computers on a LAN

CHAPTER 7

SKILL EXERCISES – PART I

COMPUTER NETWORKS IN PACKET TRACER

FOR BEGINNERS

7 Skill Exercises – Part I

This chapter contains simple exercises designed for novice users, in order to consolidate the acquired theoretical and to check Your skills.

Note – Warning: Remember to periodically save the file state during exercises (keyboard shortcut CTRL+S)

7.1 Device-To-Device Connections

7.1.1 Connection of Devices According to the Scheme

Connect the devices together according to the diagram shown in the figure below. On some devices, you need to install new modules, because by default they are not built-in.

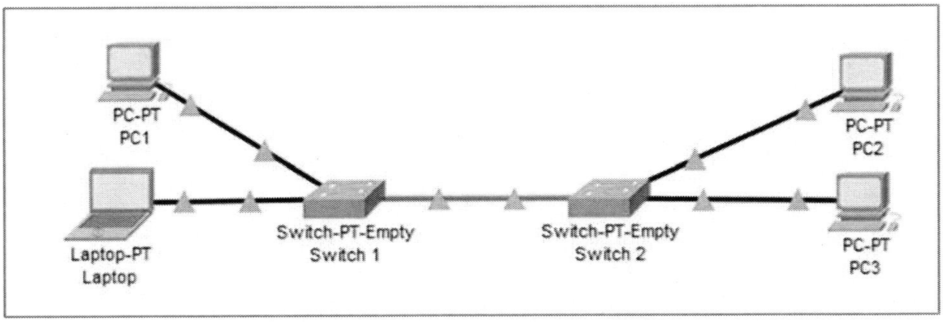

Figure 7.1 Exercise – Scheme Exercise 7.1.1.pkt

Solution:

- Check the installed network hardware on computers and switches.
- After finding that there are no modules on the switches, install two Fast Ethernet cards (1 for each computer) and one Fiber Fast Ethernet module for the connection between the switches.
- Make calls.
- Address computers (e.g. PC1:192.168.0.1/24, PC2:192.168.0.2/24)
- Perform a connection test with any tool (PING, simulation, etc.)

7.1.2 Connecting Devices to the Wi-Fi Router and Access Point

Connect laptops to a Wi-Fi router using a wireless medium and connect computers to Access-Point. There is to be a physical connection between the Access-Point and the Wi-Fi router. In Access Point for SSID is to be set on **PC**, and in router on **Laptop**.

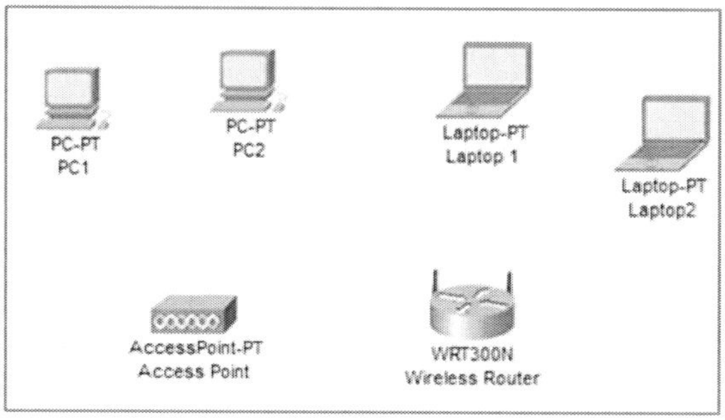

Figure 7.2 Exercise – Assumptions – Scheme Exercise 7.1.2.pkt

Solution:

- Check the type of network adapters installed in your computers.
- Replace the installed network adapters with the Linksys-WPC300N (wireless) adapters.
- Set the **SSID** parameter on the **PC** to the Access-Point and the **Laptop** parameter on the router.
- Set the same settings on computers and laptops respectively.
- Connect the Access-Point to the Wireless Router using a simple cable (to Ethernet port 1).
- On PC1 and PC2, set IP addresses from the same address pool from which laptops got the address dynamically.
- Perform a connection test with any tool (PING, simulation, etc.)

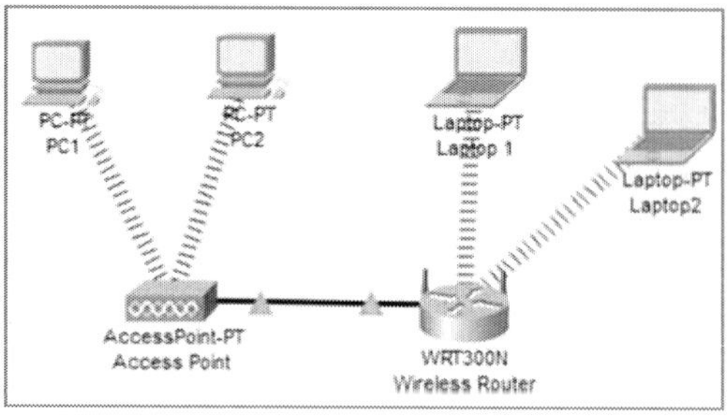

Figure 7.3 Exercise – Solution – Scheme Exercise 7.1.2.pkt

7.1.3 Connecting Computers That Are At Longer Distance Then 100 Meters

Connect computers that are separated from each other at a distance of about **225m - 280m**, in such a way that the signal strength is sufficient to carry out the transmission. Due to the low investment outlays, this should be done in an optimal way. It is also not possible to open the device cases, and thus it is not possible to make changes to the current network adapters.

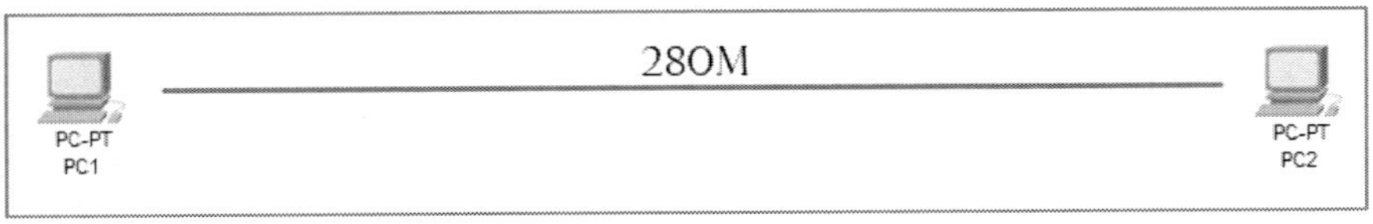

Figure 7.4 Exercise – Exercise 7.1.3-Assumptions.pkt

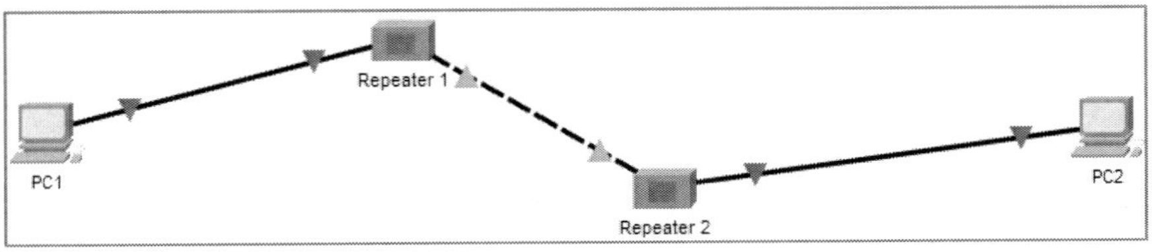

Figure 7.5 Exercise – Exercise 7.1.3-Assumptions.pkt

Solution:

- Check the type of network adapters installed in both computers (Ethernet adapters).
- According to the assumption of network standards in this standard, the maximum cable length is 100 m – so use repeaters.
- Use 2 repeaters.
- Connect the devices with appropriate wires – computers with repeaters using a simple cable, and the connection between repeaters with a patch cable.
- Address computers (e.g. PC1 – 172.16.0.1/24, PC2 – 172.16.0.2/24)
- Perform a connection test with any tool (PING, simulation, etc.)

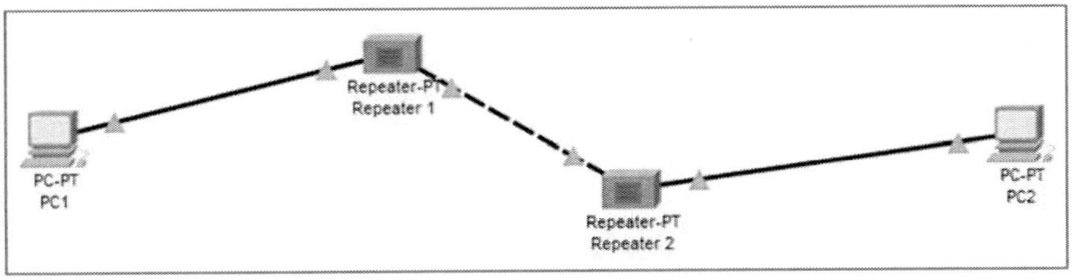

Figure 7.6 Exercise – Exercise 7.1.3-Solution.pkt

7.1.4 Using a HUB to Connect Devices Into a Single Local Network

Connect 5 computers into one LAN in such a way that all devices are in one network segment. Due to technical conditions, hardware changes cannot be made to computers. Be sure to use the simplest solution when doing the exercise.

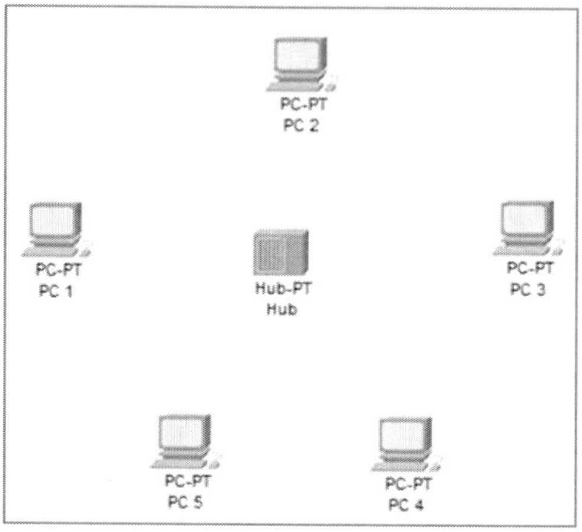

Figure 7.7 Exercise - The technical objectives - Scheme 7.1.4

Solution:

- Check the type of network adapters installed on all computers (a Fiber Gigabit Ethernet network adapter should be installed on PC4 and PC5 to make the task more difficult).
- Install the appropriate ports in the hub that are compatible with the network adapters of the computers.
- Connect devices to each other with cables.
- Address the devices so that they are all on the 10.0.0.0/8 network.
- Perform a connection test with any tool (PING, simulation, etc.)

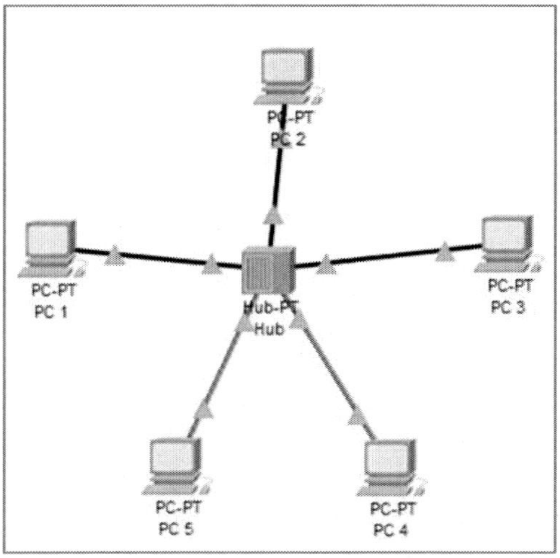

Figure 7.8 Exercise – Solution – Scheme Exercise 7.1.4.pkt

7.1.5 Using a Bridge to Limit Packet Collisions on a Local Network

In the local network shown in the figure, there are often packet collisions that we definitely do not want. To fix this, use a device called a **bridge** that divides the network into two collision domains.

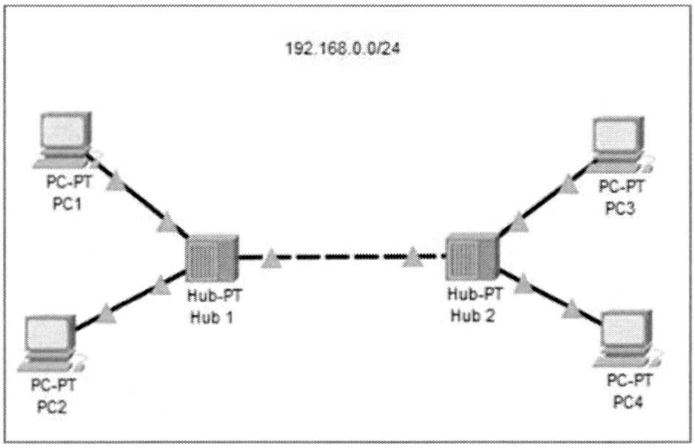

Figure 7.9 Exercise - The technical objectives

Solution:

- Search for a bridge in the device bar and insert it in the middle of the network – between two HUBs.
- Wait for the network to synchronize.
- Address devices so that they are on the 192.168.0.0/24 network

- Perform a connection test so that two devices simultaneously try to communicate with each other from two different parts of the network.

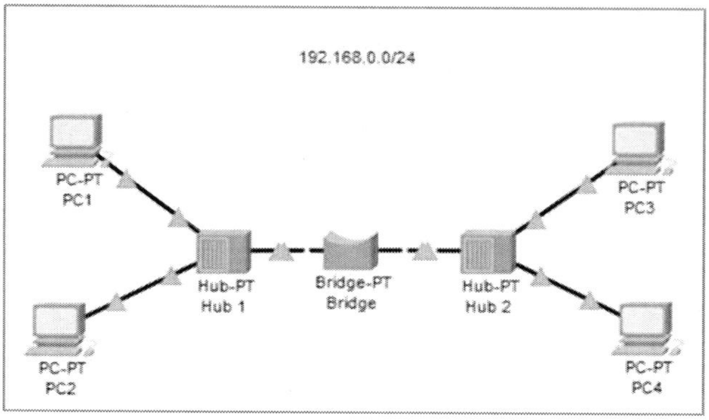

Figure 7.10 Exercise – Solution – Scheme Exercise 7.1.5.pkt

7.2 Configure Services on Servers

7.2.1 DNS and HTTP Configuration

You have to create a LAN working with two desktop computers and two servers connected to the switch. One server will serve as a DNS server with a **www.lan.xyz** entry that corresponds to the IP address of the other HTTP server. The addressing of this network is based on the address 20.0.0.0/24.

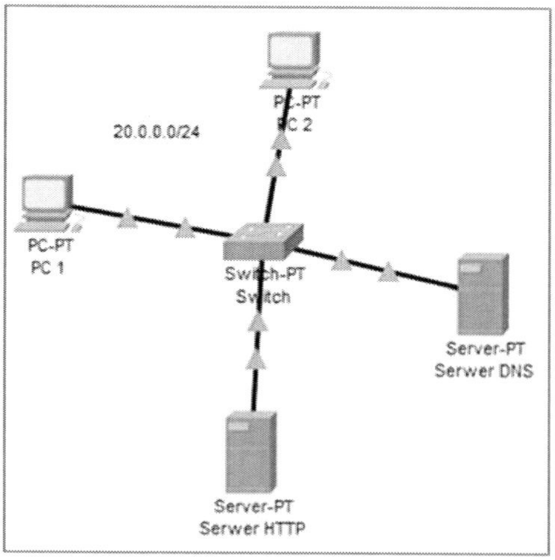

Figure 7.11 Exercise – The technical objectives – Scheme Exercise 7.2.1.pkt

Solution:

- Address the devices so that they are all on the 20.0.0.0/24 network.
- Configure the HTTP server by removing unnecessary files from the HTTP service and leaving index.html. In the finished index, change the HTML code so that your name and surname are displayed.
- Configure the DNS server so that dns contains an HTTP server entry under the name **www.lan.xyz.**
- Perform a DNS and HTTP test from one of the computers by typing the **www.lan.xyz** address in the browser.

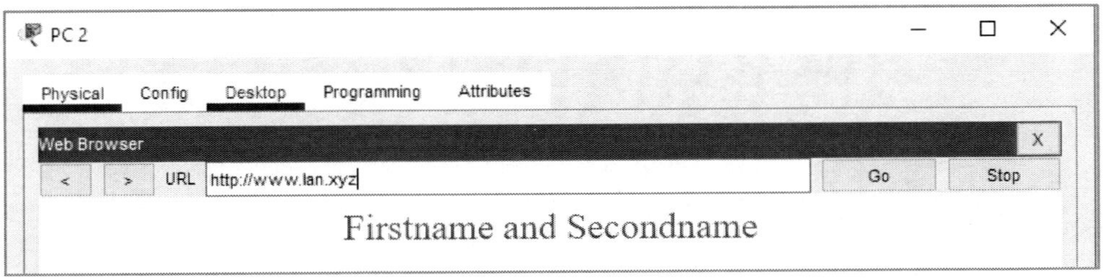

Figure 7.12 Exercise – Solution – www.lan.xyz - Exercise 7.2.1.pkt

7.2.2 Configuring DHCP and FTP

In this case, you have to create a network in which all end devices get addresses dynamically from the pool on the DHCP server (the address pool starts with 172.16.0.10, in the network 172.16.0.0/24) and have access to FTP server resources (address 172.16.0.1) by authorizing themselves as **user1** with the password **zaq1@WSX** .

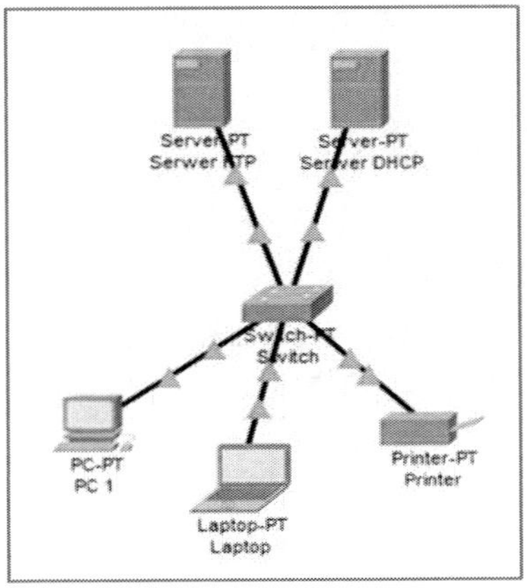

Figure 7.13 Exercise – The technical objectives

Solution:

- Address both servers statically (FTP server – 172.16.0.1/32, DHCP server – 172.16.0.2/32)
- Configure address pools on the DHCP server, which is available to a maximum of three users and starts at 172.16.0.10/24.
- On the FTP server, create **user1** with the password **zaq1@WSX**.
- Enable dynamic IP address on each of the three devices.
- Log in to the FTP server from your **Laptop**.

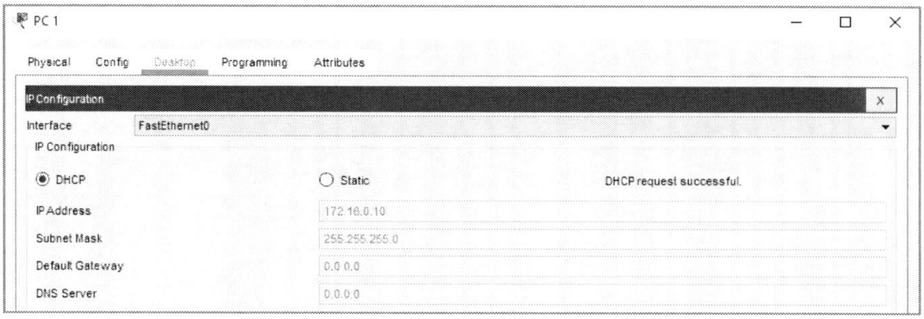

Figure 7.14 Exercise - Solution – part one

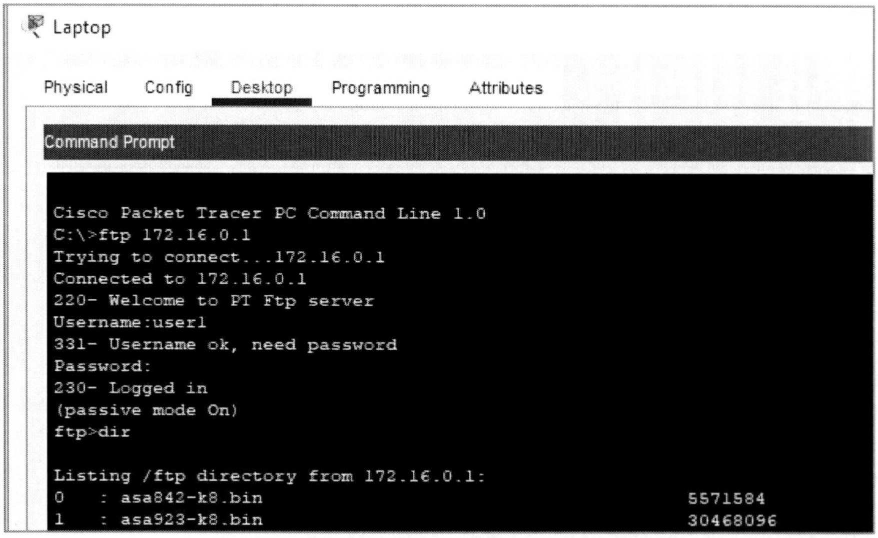

Figure 7.15 Exercise - Solution – part two

7.2.3 Mail Server Configuration (SMTP, POP3)

There are two laptops in the exercise – one is the **Boss** and the other is the **Employee**. They use the **email.com** server as their mail server. The domain name on the server is the same as its name, and the users are the names of the laptops (passwords the same). You have to configure the devices in such a way that both laptops can communicate with each other via mail. Finally, send an email called **TEST** from one to the other.

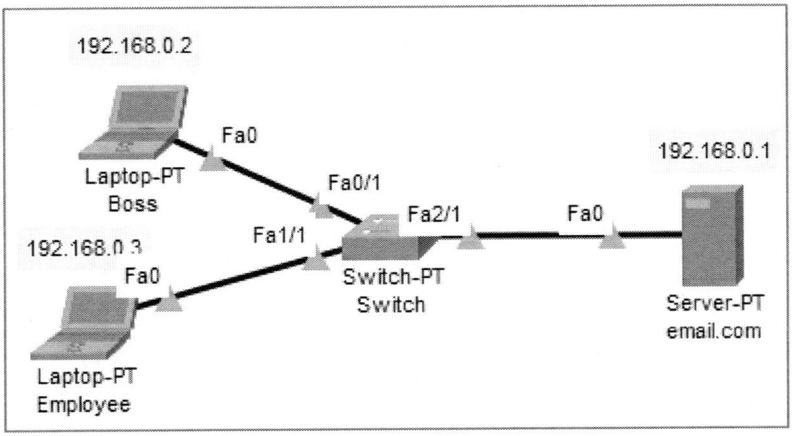

Figure 7.16 Exercise – The technical objectives – Scheme Exercise 7.2.3.pkt

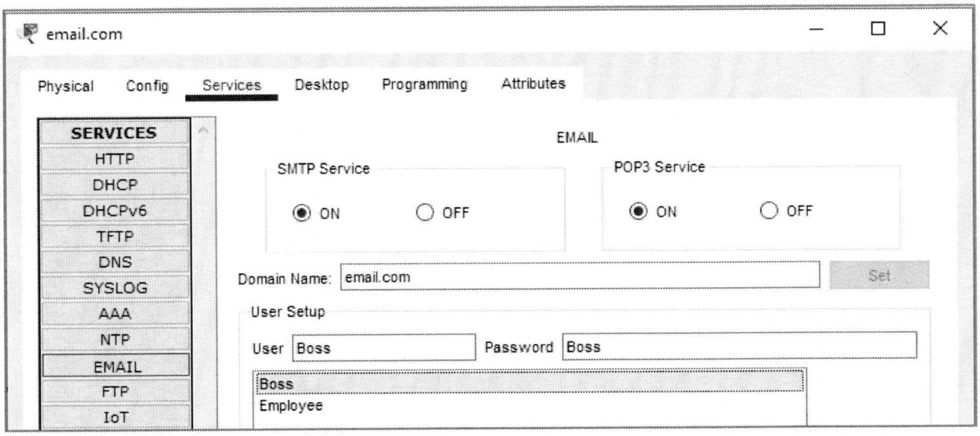

Figure 7.17 Exercise – Email configuration – Scheme Exercise 7.2.3.pkt

Solution:

- Address all devices in the right way.
- On the mail server, configure the domain name and two users.

- On both laptops, set the mail service based on device names and setting 192.168.0.1 as the mail address.
- Send an email with the title TEST from one laptop to another.

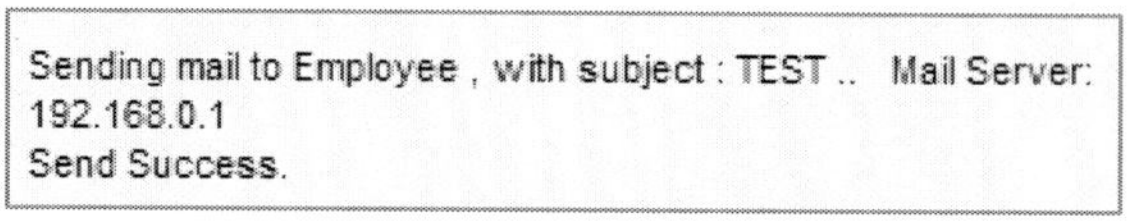

Figure 7.18 Exercise – sending e-mail

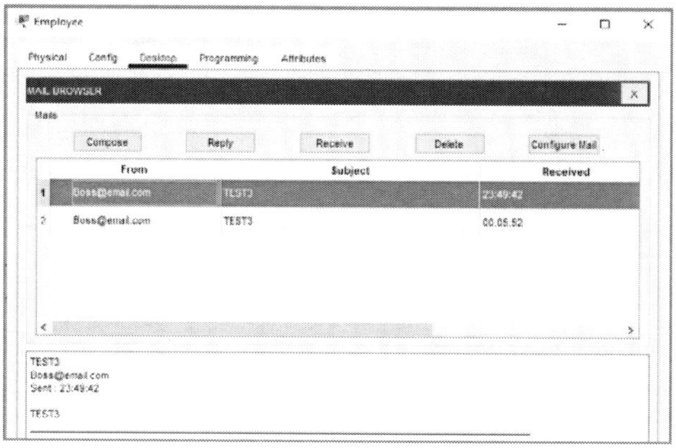

Figure 7.19 Exercise – receiving e-mail

CHAPTER 8

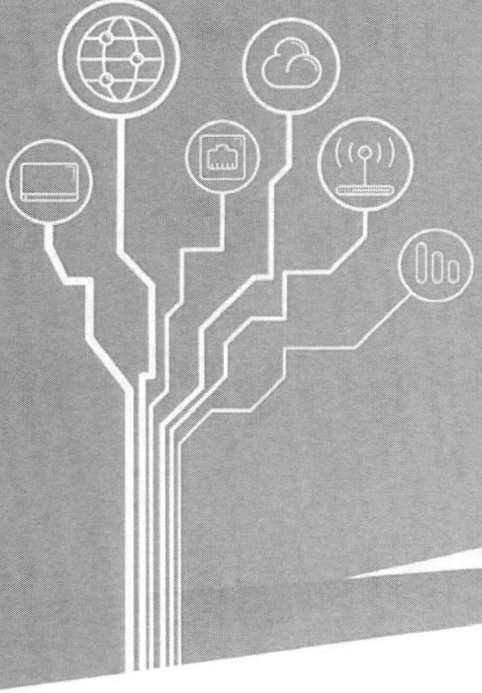

CONFIGURING CISCO ROUTERS

COMPUTER NETWORKS IN PACKET TRACER

FOR BEGINNERS

8 Configuring Cisco Routers

This chapter covers the basic theoretical and practical knowledge of configuring simulated routers in the Cisco Packet Tracer.

Note – Warning: Remember to periodically save the file state during exercises (keyboard shortcut CTRL+S)

8.1 Exploring the Equipment of Cisco Routers

At the beginning we will focus on the basic models of routers and their equipment that we will be able to install in them. We have twelve different types of routers from **829** to **4321** series. In addition to the standard routers, there are two more called **PT-Router** and **PT-Empty**, which can be modelled and reconfigured in any way.

Figure 8.1 Router models available in the Cisco Packet Tracer

Routers available in the program are equivalents of real models encountered in everyday life, they differ not only in physical appearance, but also in software, as well as equipment. Below we will discuss the most important types of routers available.

8.1.1 Series 1841

The first router, we will describe is the 1841 series router, usually dedicated to small and medium-sized businesses, in the CISCO IOS 12.4 software version. By default, it is equipped with two Fast Ethernet ports with a bandwidth of 10/100Mbps and two free WIC/HWIC slots for installing expansion cards.

Figure 8.2 Physical Appearance of Router 1841

The router has two free slots, to which it will be possible in the future to mount the following compatible modules:

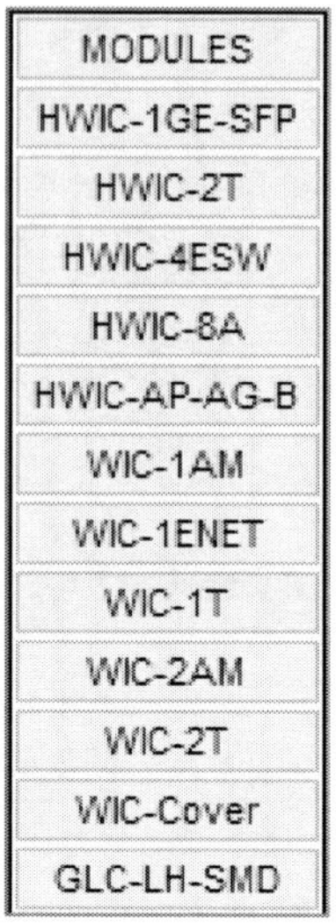

Figure 8.3 Router 1841 Optional Equipment

Below are the detailed parameters of the optional equipment of the 1841 series router:

-  **HWIC-1GE-SFP** – High-bandwidth network adapter for WAN connections,
- 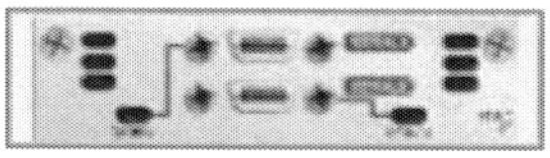 **HWIC-2T** - 2 serial interfaces for high-speed WAN connections,
-  **HWIC-4ESW** - 4 switch interfaces,
- 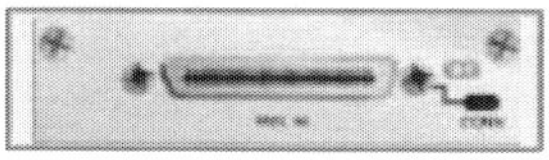 **HWIC-8A** - interface enabling connection of up to eight console connections in the EIA-232 standard,
-  **HWIC-AP-AG-B** - wireless interface, supporting single (802.11b/g) and dual-band (802.11a/b/g) bands,
-  **WIC-1AM** - 2 interfaces used for basic telephone service connections. One port can be used to connect to a standard telephone line, and the other to a regular analogue phone,

-  **WIC-1ENET** - a single Ethernet port with a bandwidth of 10Mbps for connecting LAN in the 10BASE-T standard,
-  **WIC-1T** - single serial port used for connections of remote locations or legacy network devices: SDLC hubs, alarm systems and devices operating via SONET,
-  **WIC-2AM** - two RJ-11 connectors used for basic telephone service connections, equipped with modem ports that can provide connections of various data,
- 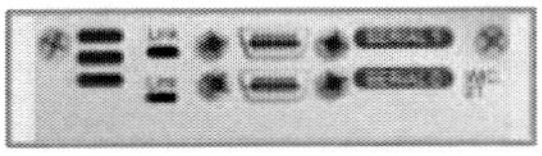 **WIC-2T** - Intelligent serial connector supporting a wide range of interfaces when using suitable transition cables. It can support various protocols such as: PPP, Frame Relay,
- 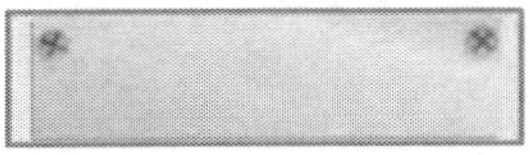 **WIC-Cover** - a cap to protect the router's internal electronic components and to ensure adequate airflow during cooling.
-  **GLC-LH-SMD** - allows you to set up a Gigabit Ethernet connection using single-mode fiber.

8.1.2 Series 1941

Another router available in the program is the 1941 series router, which, like its predecessor, is dedicated to small and medium-sized businesses, but has two gigabit Ethernet cards with a bandwidth of 1Gbps and IOS software version 15.1.

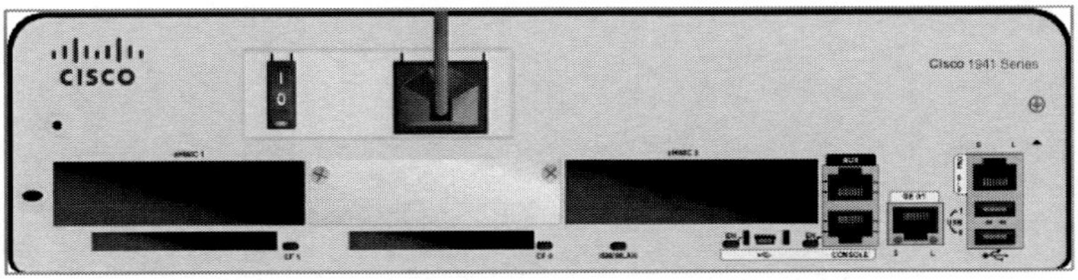

Figure 8.4 Physical appearance of the 1941 route

It has two free slots to which you can mount optional equipment, which is no longer as diverse as in the case of the 1841 series.

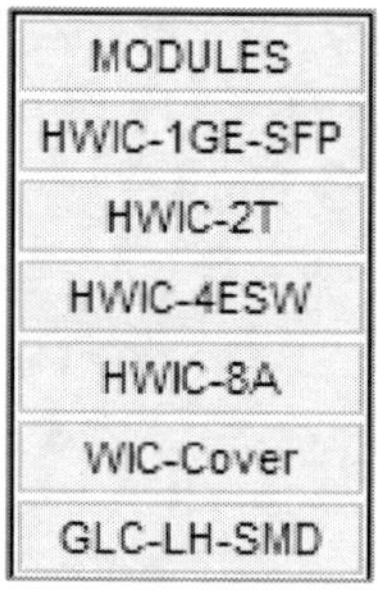

Figure 8.5 Optional Equipment for Router 1941

Due to the fact that the equipment coincides with the 1841 version, and is even much poorer, we will not describe it again.

8.1.3 Series 2620XM

Another router available in the program is the 2620XM series router, by default equipped with one Fast Ethernet port with a bandwidth of 10/100 Mbps. In addition, it has 3 free slots, to which you will be able to install very rich equipment.

Figure 8.6 Physical Appearance of the 2620XM Router

Unlike the 1800/1900 series, this type of router, in addition to two WIC/HWIC slots, can be additionally equipped with NM cards, which significantly expand its capabilities:

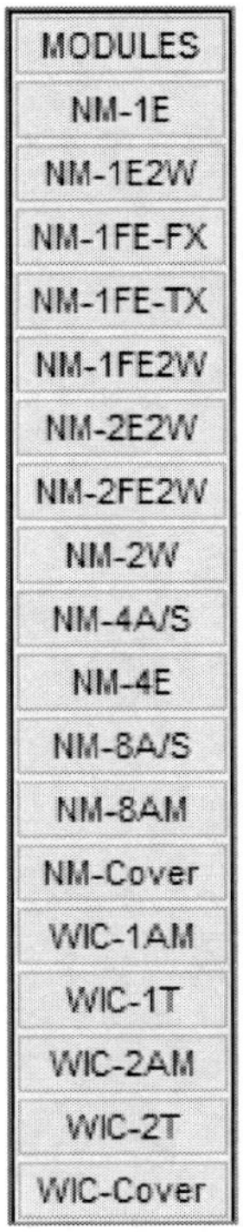

Figure 8.7 Optional equipment for the 2620XM

- 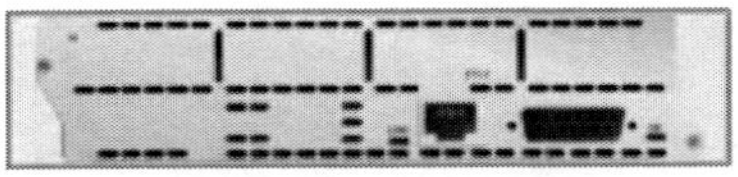 **NM-1E** - a single Ethernet port that can be used for both LAN applications and can support up to six PRI ISDN lines or 24 synchronous/asynchronous ports.
- 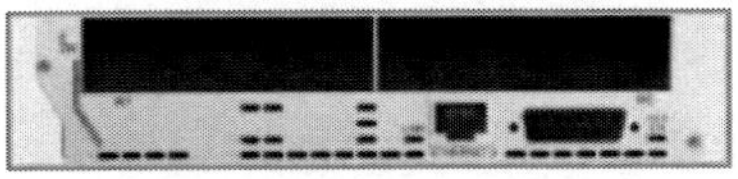 **NM-1E2W** - a single Ethernet port with the same application as the NM-1E, with the difference that it has two additional free WIC slots.
-  **NM-1FE-FX** - single Fast Ethernet port in fiber optic standard.
- 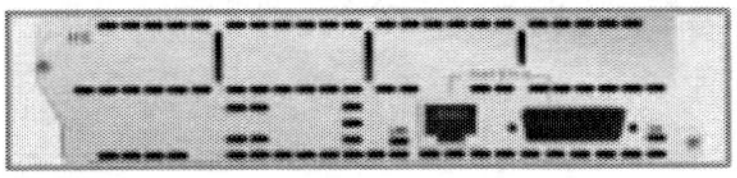 **NM-1FE-TX** - single Fast Ethernet port for use in typical LANs and VLANs.

-  **NM-1FE2W** - a single Fast Ethernet port with the same application as the NM-1FE-TX with the difference that it has two additional free WIC slots.
-  **NM-2E2W** - two Ethernet ports with two WIC slots.
-  **NM-2FE2W** - two Fast Ethernet ports and two blinded WIC slots.
-  **NM-2W** – two WIC slots.
- 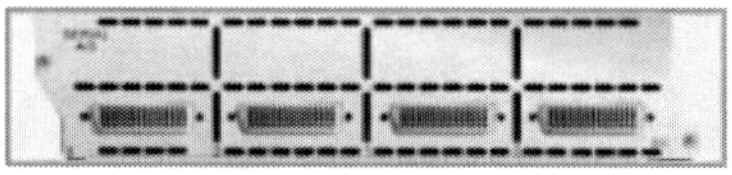 **NM-4A/S** - four asynchronous/synchronous serial modules. Each port can be configured individually in any synchronous or asynchronous mode.
-  **NM-4E** - 4 Ethernet ports.
- 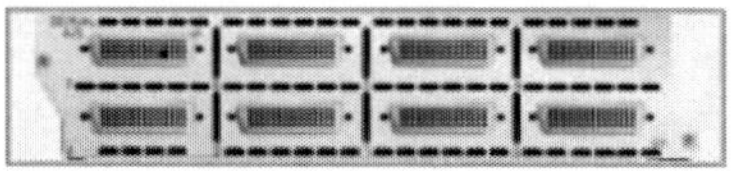 **NM-8A/S** - eight asynchronous/synchronous serial modules.
-  **NM-8AM** – network module providing 8 ports for low-bandwidth analogue telephone lines. The standard of the module sockets is RJ-11, dedicated to connections of integrated analogue modems of telephone lines operating on the public telephone network (PSTN) or private telephony systems.
-  **NM-Cover**.

The remaining WIC ports were already described in the case of the equipment of the **1841 router**.

8.1.4 Series 2621XM

Another router available in the program is the **2621XM** series router. By default, it is equipped with two Fast Ethernet ports with a bandwidth of 10/100 Mbps, It also has 3 free slots in which you can mount optional equipment. In principle, this router differs from the 2620XM only by the presence of an additional Fast Ethernet port.

Figure 8.8 Physical appearance of the 2621XM router

Two of the free slots can be equipped with WIC modules, while the third slot allows you to mount an NM card, so you can significantly expand the functionality of the router.

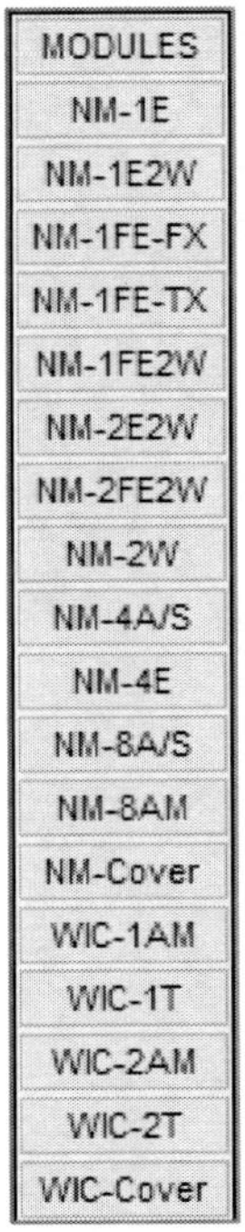

Figure 8.9 Optional Equipment for 2621XM Router

Due to the fact that the optional equipment coincides completely with the equipment of the router version of the **2620XM** version , we will not describe it again.

8.1.5 Series 2811

Another router available in the program is the **2811** series router. By default, it has two Fast Ethernet ports with a bandwidth of 10/100 Mbps, four WIC/HWIC slots for installing expansion cards and one slot for NM modules.

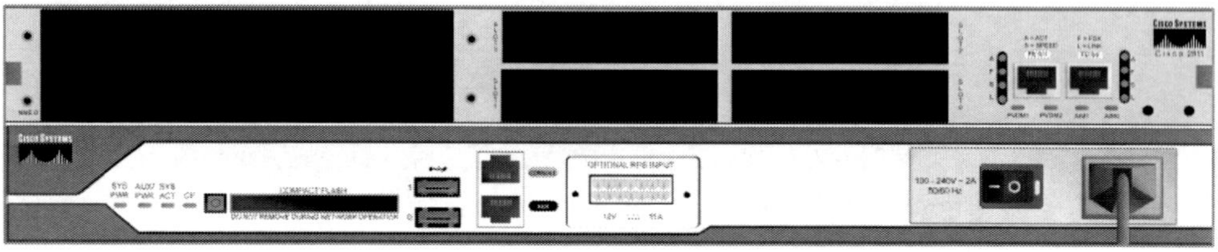

Figure 8.10 Physical appearance of Router 2811

Free router slots allow you to mount the following expansion cards:

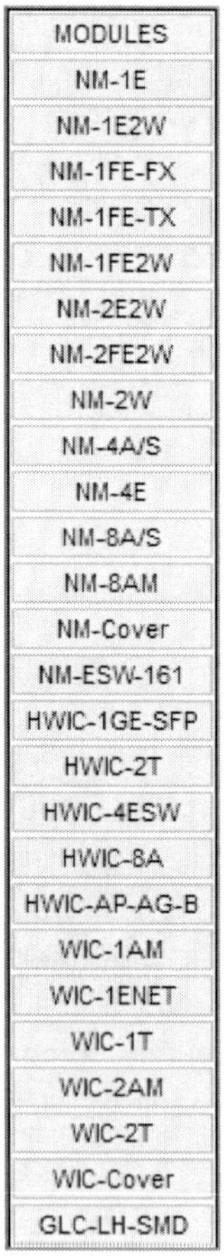

Figure 8.11 Optional equipment for router 2811

- 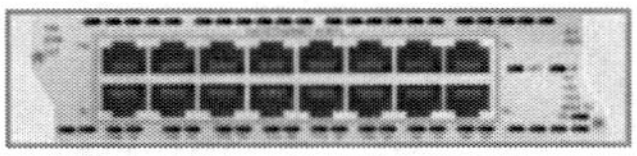 **NM-ESW-161** - provides 16 switch interfaces.

Other optional equipment has already been described in the case of the 1841 and 2620XM routers.

8.1.6 Series 2901

Another router available in the program is the **2901** series router. By default, it is equipped with two Gigabit Ethernet ports with a bandwidth of 10/100/1000 Mbps. It also has four slots for HWIC expansion cards.

Figure 8.12 Physical appearance of Router 2901

The optional equipment of the 2901 router includes:

MODULES
HWIC-1GE-SFP
HWIC-2T
HWIC-4ESW
HWIC-8A
WIC-Cover
GLC-LH-SMD

Figure 8.13 Optional Equipment for Router 2901

All these components have already been described in the case of the 1841 router.

8.1.7 Series 2911

Another router available in the program is the **2911XM** series router. By default, it has three Gigabit Ethernet ports with a bandwidth of 10/100/1000 Mbps, as well as 4 slots for HWIC expansion cards.

Figure 8.14 Physical appearance of Router 2911XM

Optional equipment on the 2911XM includes:

MODULES
HWIC-1GE-SFP
HWIC-2T
HWIC-4ESW
HWIC-8A
WIC-Cover
GLC-LH-SMD

Figure 8.15 Optional Equipment for 2911XM Router

This equipment coincides completely with the equipment of the 2901 series router, so we will not describe it again.

8.1.8 IR829 Router

Another router available in the program is the 800 series router. By default, it has three Gigabit Ethernet ports with a bandwidth of 10/100/1000 Mbps, as well as 4 slots for HWIC expansion cards.

The **IR829 (Industrial Integrated Services Router)** is a model of integrated industrial router that simulates an 800 series router, offering wireless and wired LAN connection, wireless 4G connection and fiber optic WAN connection.

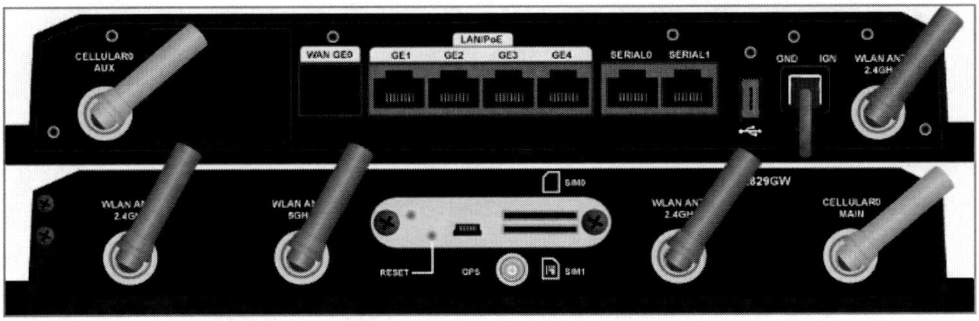

Figure 8.16 Physical appearance of IR829 router

Designed to work in harsh environments and to communicate with another AP access point or wireless controller of Internet omnipresent.

The router is equipped with:

- 1 Wireless Access Point (**wlan-ap0**)
- 1 GigaEthernet0 WLAN interface (**Wlan-GigabitEthernet0**)
- 2 x 4G LTE network interfaces (**Cellular0, Cellular1**)
- 4 Gigabit Ethernet LAN interfaces (**GigabitEthernet1 – 4**)
- 1 free GE0 WAN slot where only the **GLC-T** module can be installed.

The **GLC-T** module includes a single Gigabit Ethernet port and supports a Category 5 UTP cable up to 100 m long.

8.1.9 819IOX Router

The **Cisco 819IOX** (Integrated Services Router) is a model of router simulating the **C819HG-4G-IOX** router that supports M2M (Machine-to-Machine) applications and cellular network services.

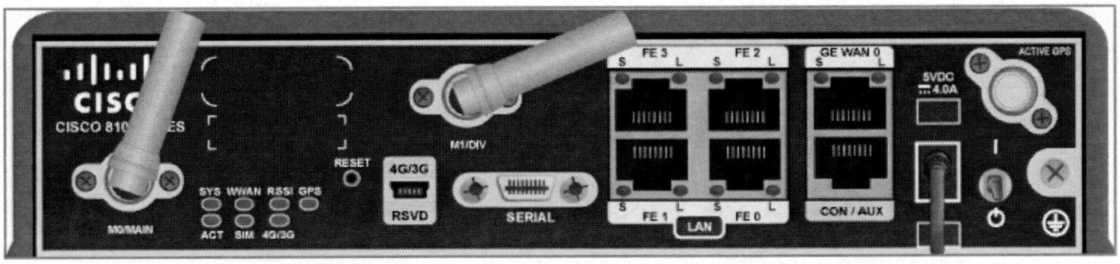

Figure 8.17 Physical appearance of the 819IOX router

8.1.10 CGR 1240 Router

The **CGR 1240** (Connected Grid Router) is a router model that simulates a 1000 series router. The main applications of this series of routers are: support for **FAN** (Field Area Network) distribution networks, integration of distributed solar farms, control of public lighting. It is shockproof and can be mounted on poles.

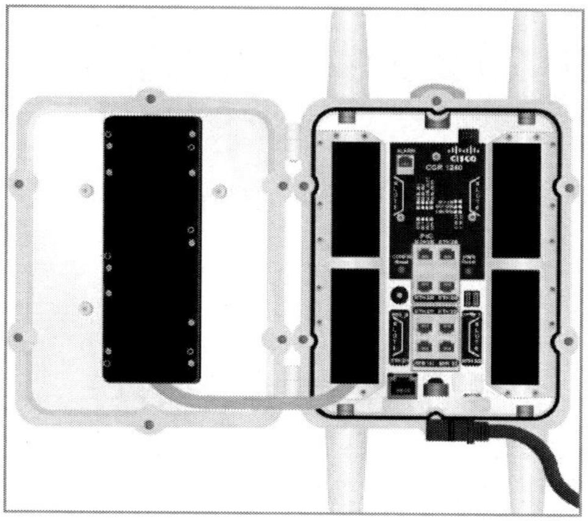

Figure 8.18 Physical appearance of the CGR 1240 router

The router is equipped with:

- 1 Gigabit Ethernet interface (**GigabitEthernet0/1**),
- 1 x 802.11 wireless (**Dot11Radio2/1**)
- 2 Giga Ethernet LAN interfaces (**GigaEthernet2/1 – 2/2**)
- 4 Fast Ethernet LAN interfaces (**FastEthernet2/3 – 2/6**)

8.1.11 ISR 4321 Router

The **ISR4321** router is mainly designed to offer advanced network services in small corporations. Its default total bitrate is 50 bps. By default, it has ports for management: USB and RJ-45, 2 Gigabit Ethernet ports with a bandwidth of 1000 Mbps for cable connection, as well as 2 slots for **NIM-ES2-4** or **NIM-2T** expansion cards.

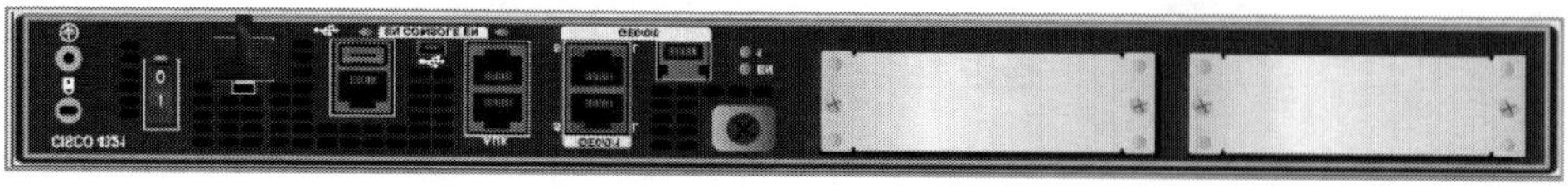

Figure 8.19 View of ISR4321 available in the program

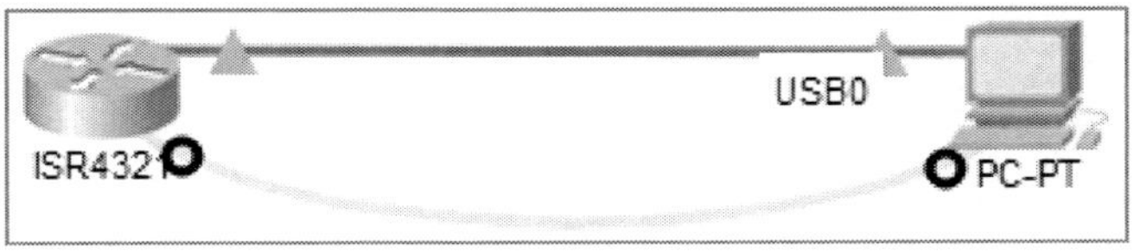

Figure 8.20 USB Console and Console ports on ISR4321

The router comes standard with:

- 1 USB console interface (**USB Console**)
- 1 RJ-45 console interface (**Console**)
- 2 **Gigabit Ethernet** LAN interfaces (GigabitEthernet0/0/0 – GigabitEthernet0/0/1)
- 2 free slots in which you can install only NIM-ES2-4 or NIM-2T modules **NIM-ES2-4** or **NIM-2T**

The **NIM-ES2-4** module has 4 Giga Ethernet ports for network switching.

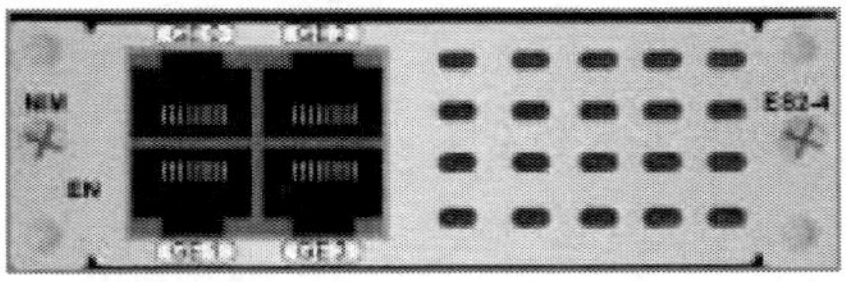

Figure 8.21 NIM-ES2-4 module

The **NIM-2T** module has 2 ports for serial synchronous communication.

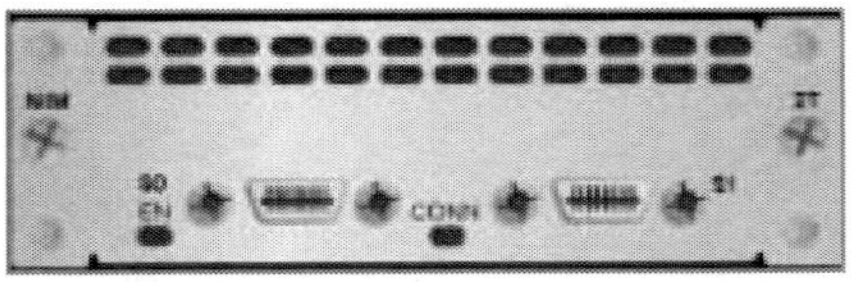

Figure 8.22 NIM-2T module

In addition, the **GLC-LH-SMD** or the **GLC-GE-100FX** can be inserted in place of the GigabitEthernet0/0/0 interface.

The **GLC-LH-SMD** module allows you to set up a Gigabit Ethernet connection using a single-mode fiber.

Figure 8.23 GLC-LH-SMD module

The **GLC-GE-100FX** allows you to set up a Gigabit Ethernet connection via multimode fiber for distances of up to 2 km.

Figure 8.24 GLC-GE-100FX module

8.1.12 819IOX Router

The **Cisco 819IOX** (Integrated Services Router) is a model of router simulating the **C819HG-4G-IOX** router that supports M2M (Machine-to-Machine) applications and cellular network services.

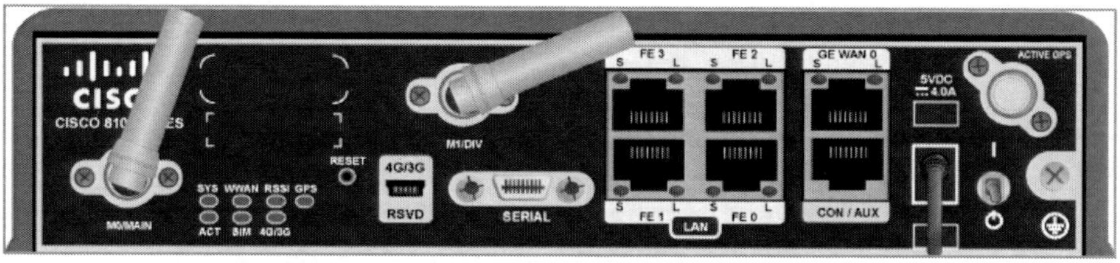

Figure 8.25 Physical appearance of the 819IOX router

The 819IOX comes standard with two antennas and non-replaceable antennas:

- 1 GigabitEthernet0 interface
- 4 FastEthernet0 interfaces – FastEthernet3
- 1 **Serial0** serial communication interface
- 1 **Ethernet1** interface
- 1 VirtualPortGroup0 port
- 1 **Cellular0** cellular network interface

8.1.13 819HGW Router

The **Cisco 819HGW** (Integrated Services Router) is a variant of the **C819** router model that supports M2M (Machine-to-Machine) applications and cellular network services.

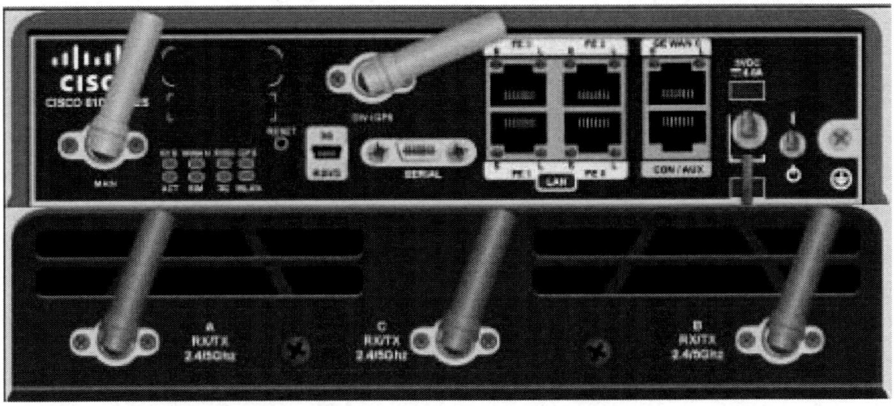

Figure 8.26 Physical appearance of the 819HGW router

The 819HGW comes standard with five antennas and non-replaceable antennas:

- 1 GigabitEthernet0 interface
- 4 FastEthernet0 interfaces – FastEthernet3
- 1 **Serial0** serial communication interface
- 1 Ethernet1 interface
- 1 Gigabit Ethernet Wlan-GigabitethernetO
- 1 **Cellular0** cellular network interface
- 1 internal module acting as an access point **wlan-ap0**

8.1.14 Series PT Router

The last router that we will discuss is the PT series router. We distinguish two such routers – it is a **PT-Router** and a **PT-Empty** router. The difference between them is only due to the fact that the former has already completed 6 slots for network cards, and the latter is completely empty - it has ten slots in the place of which we can mount the interface of our choice. The first one has two Fast Ethernet ports with a bandwidth of 10/100 Mbps using twisted pair cables, two Fast Ethernet ports with a bandwidth of 10/100 Mbps in the fiber standard and 2 serial interfaces for fast WAN connections.

Figure 8.27 Physical appearance of the PT-Empty router

In free slots we can install the following components:

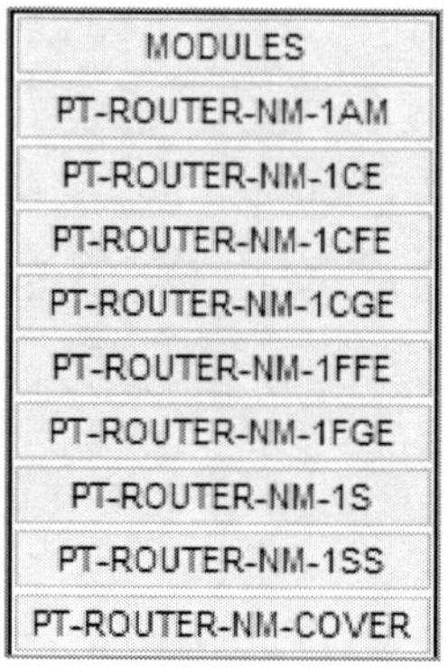

MODULES
PT-ROUTER-NM-1AM
PT-ROUTER-NM-1CE
PT-ROUTER-NM-1CFE
PT-ROUTER-NM-1CGE
PT-ROUTER-NM-1FFE
PT-ROUTER-NM-1FGE
PT-ROUTER-NM-1S
PT-ROUTER-NM-1SS
PT-ROUTER-NM-COVER

Figure 8.28 Optional equipment of the PT-Empty router

Below is a detailed description of the individual components:

PT-ROUTER-NM-1AM

Single connector type RJ-11,

PT-ROUTER-NM-1CE

Single Ethernet port with bandwidth 10/100 Mbps

PT-ROUTER-NM-1CFE

Single 10/100Mbps Fast Ethernet port

PT-ROUTER-NM-1CGE

Single Gigabit Ethernet port with 10/100/1000Mbps bandwidth

PT-ROUTER-NM-1FFE

Single 10/100Mbps Fast Ethernet port in fiber optic standard

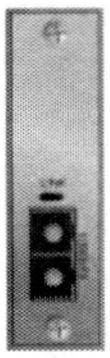

PT-ROUTER-NM-1FGE

Single 10/100/100Mbps Gigabit Ethernet port with fiber optic

PT-ROUTER-NM-1S

Single serial port used for connections remote locations or older network devices

PT-ROUTER-NM-1SS

Intelligent serial connector supporting a wide range of interfaces when using suitable adapter cables

8.2 Configure Cisco Routers Using the Graphical Interface

8.2.1 Interface Configuration

Router configurations in the Cisco Packet Tracer will start with configuration using the GUI, i.e. the graphical interface. Later we will go to the configuration using commands (CLI), which gives us much more possibilities, but before that we want to get to know our program as best as possible so we will see the pros and cons of using the graphical interface. First, let's create a simple topology consisting of one computer and one router (we will use a PT-Router).

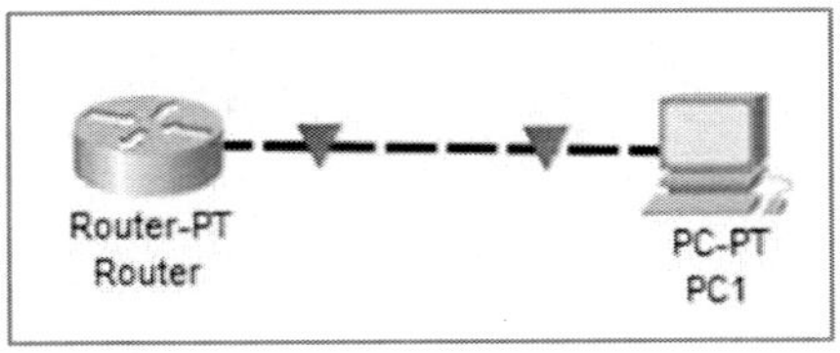

Figure 8.29 Basic topology for router configuration

For the connection to work properly, you must configure both devices. In this example, we will use a network with the address 200.200.200.0 and a network mask of

255.255.255.0. The configuration of computers has already been described in detail in the subsection **Basic configuration of devices**, so we will not describe it here.

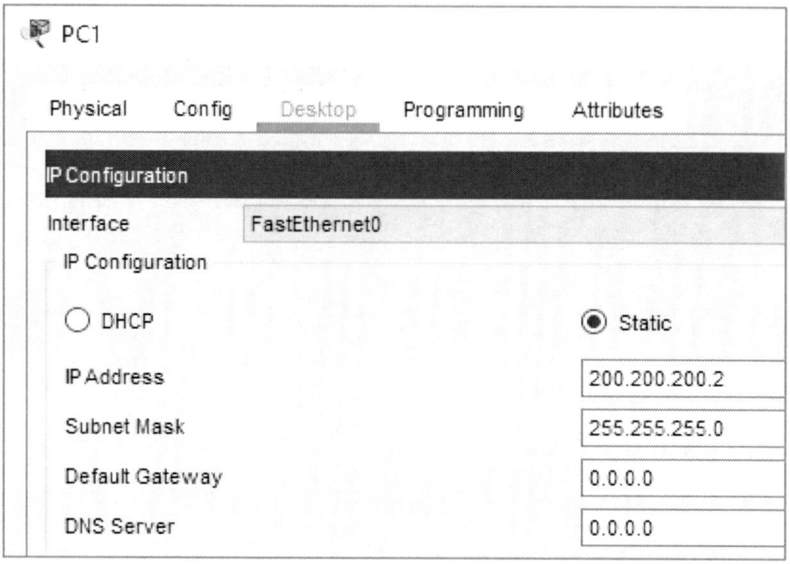

Figure 8.30 Addressing a computer

Now, in order for the connection to start working, you need to configure the interface of the router. To do this, click on the router, and then in the **Config** tab select the appropriate interface from the list - what interface has been connected can be determined in two ways. The first way is to remember which interface the cable is inserted into. The second way is shown in the figure below and consists in enabling the **Always Show Port Labels in Logical Workspace** option in **Options-Preferences** so that, as in the picture, you will be able to see device ports in a logical topology.

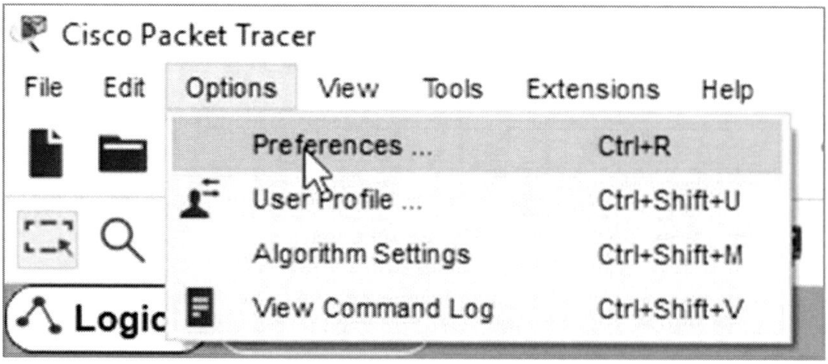

Figure 8.31 First step - displaying interfaces on the logical topology

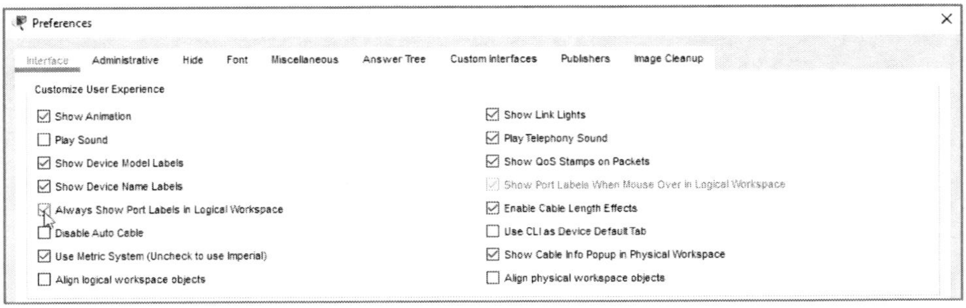

Figure 8.32 The second step - displaying the interfaces on the logical topology

Returning to the configuration of interfaces - in the **Config** tab in our case, we select the Fast Ethernet 0/0 interface (**Fa0/0**) and give it an IP address in accordance with previous assumptions.

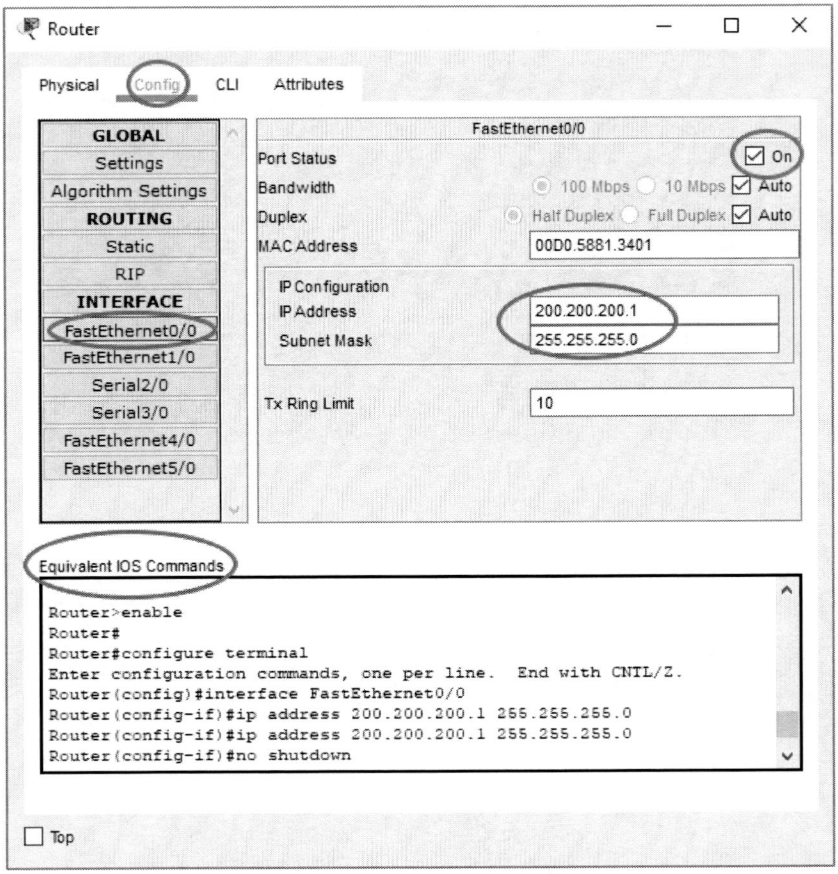

Figure 8.33 Router Interface Configuration - GUI

As we can see in the figure above, the configuration via GUI is similar to the configuration of other devices, e.g. PC, only in this case at the bottom we have an additional window that reflects what we do in the GUI only in the form of commands. If you want it now you can observe what the form of commands looks like, so it will be easier for you to configure routers later using the CLI.

Now to check if our configuration works correctly, first look at the LEDs - if both are green, it means that the ports are in the **Up** state. Next, PING PC1 to the configured router interface.

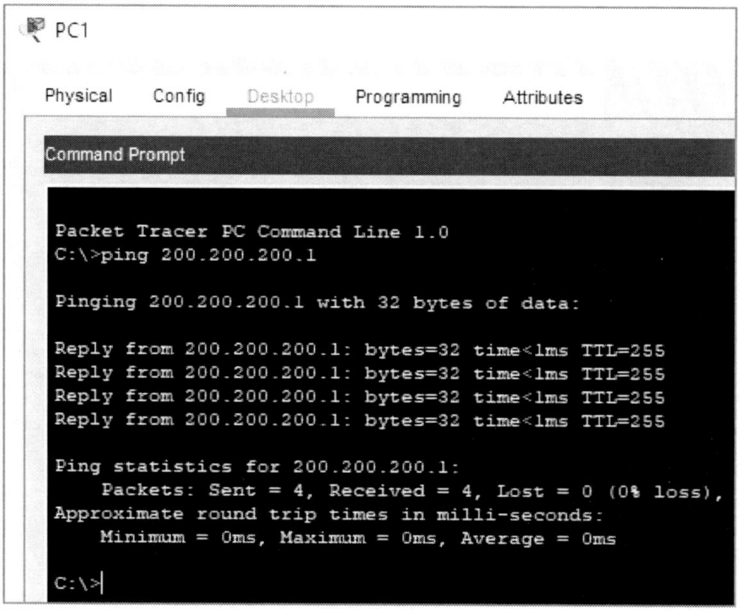

Figure 8.34 Successful PING from workstation to router interface

The connection is already configured and working. However, if we stop there and the router is turned off or restarted, its entire configuration will be lost. To prevent this, save the current configuration as a start-up configuration. Thanks to this, if the router is turned off or restarted, we will not lose its settings. To be able to save the configuration in the first place, we need to open the **Settings** window from the **Config** tab, as shown in the figure below.

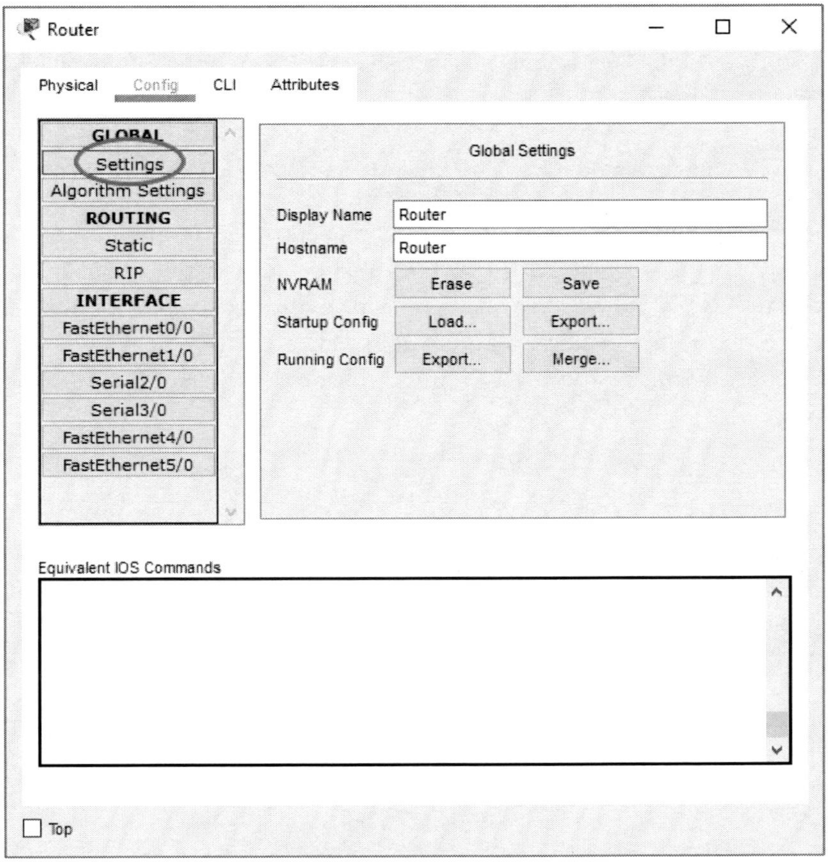

Figure 8.35 Settings tab in the router

As you can see, in addition to saving, we have several general options at our disposal here. Using the Display Name field, we can change the name of the device label displayed in our topology. The **Hostname** field allows us to change the name of the router under which it appears in IOS. It is very important to understand the important difference between Hostname and **Display Name** – **Hostnam**e is an actual parameter of a network device that is important in many configurations, for example in the PAP and CHAP authentication protocols. **Display Name** is just supporting text (the description shown below the device) in a logical topology.

Further options are already directly related to saving and loading configurations. To save the current configuration as a start-up configuration, click **Save**. The **Erase** button, in turn, allows us to reset the start-up configuration. Under the line separating the buttons there is an option that allows us to export (**Export**...) and import (**Load.../Merge**...) the configuration of the router from a text file on the computer disk.

Start-up Config refers to the start-up configuration, while **Running Config** refers to the current configuration. In our example, we need to click the **Save** button, saving the current configuration. Now the router configuration will no longer be lost.

8.2.2 GUI-Configurable Routing Protocols

As we probably know, the main task of routers is to carry out **routing**, i.e. to indicate the way for packets to the target host (network). Routers owe this functionality to various routing protocols – there are many of them and in this book we will discuss the most important of them, theoretically and practically. However, with the help of GUI we are able to configure only two types of routing - static routing and the simplest routing protocol, i.e. RIP.

8.2.2.1 Static Routing

Using static routing, we have to manually assign a packet route to each network we want to communicate with. This is a good solution for small networks and the only routing protocol that does not learn routes on its own. In order to present this way of routing, we will create the following topology consisting of 3 routers and 3 computers:

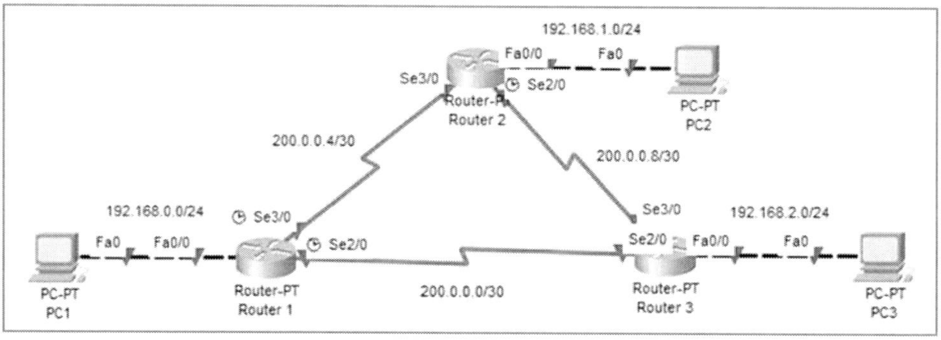

Figure 8.36 Test topology

As you can see, all connections are disabled and you need to use the knowledge described earlier to configure and run the interfaces. In this topology, there is a serial connection between the routers. When configuring them, we must remember to set the **Clock Rate** on the **DCE** device. Select this value from the drop-down list. If you do not know which device is DCE and which is DTE, just look at the connection with the **Always Show Port Labels in Logical Workspace** option enabled. When marking the interface of one of the routers, a clock icon will be shown – it is a DCE device.

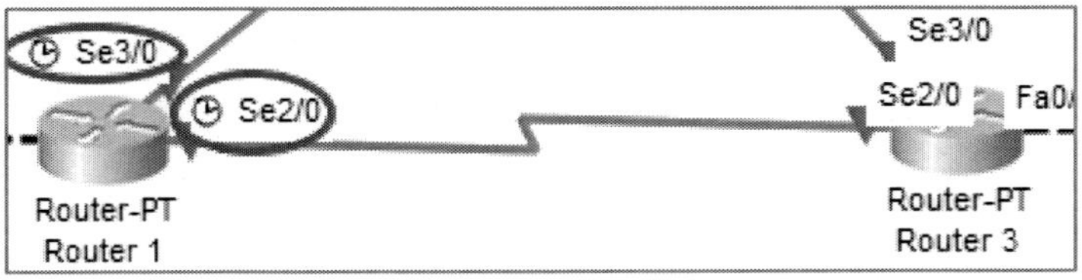

Figure 8.37 Specify a parent clock

A properly configured serial interface on a DCE device looks like this:

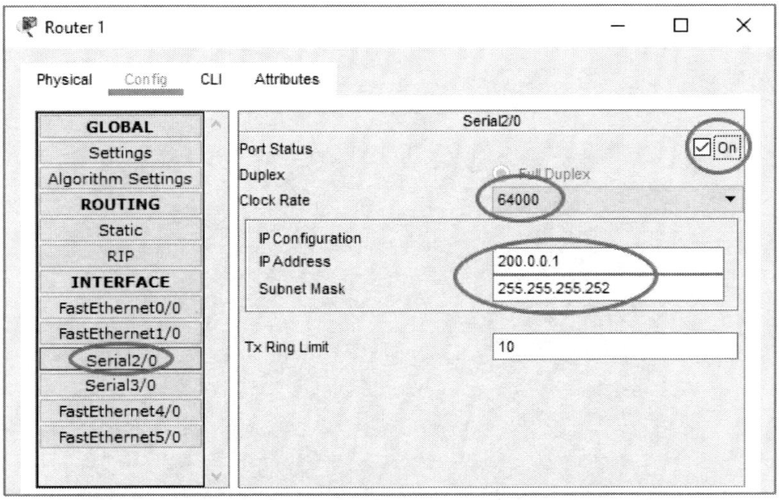

Figure 8.38 Properly configured DCE serial interface

In the case of the DTE interface, we do not simply change the Clock Rate value due to the fact that the other side of the link will negotiate this value. The next step after addressing each router interface is to address the end devices as we see in the figure below. In the case of connections to computers, we always give the first address from the pool - then we have more order in the network.

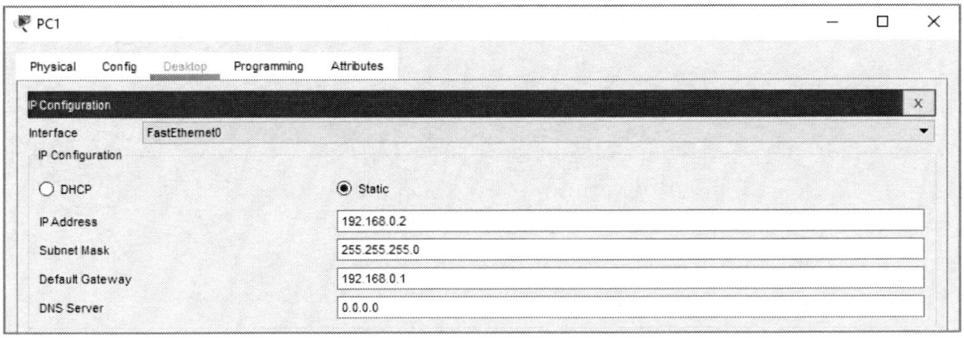

Figure 8.39 Correct configuration of the end device

As you can see, this time, we enter the address of the **Default Gateway**, that is, the default gateway. The default gateway is the nearest router on the network, thanks to which we will be able to communicate with other networks. It is not needed until we communicate with external networks (outside access from the local network).

After addressing the devices, we can test our network, how it works.

We will try to send a PING command from one of the devices first to the default gateway and then to another device.

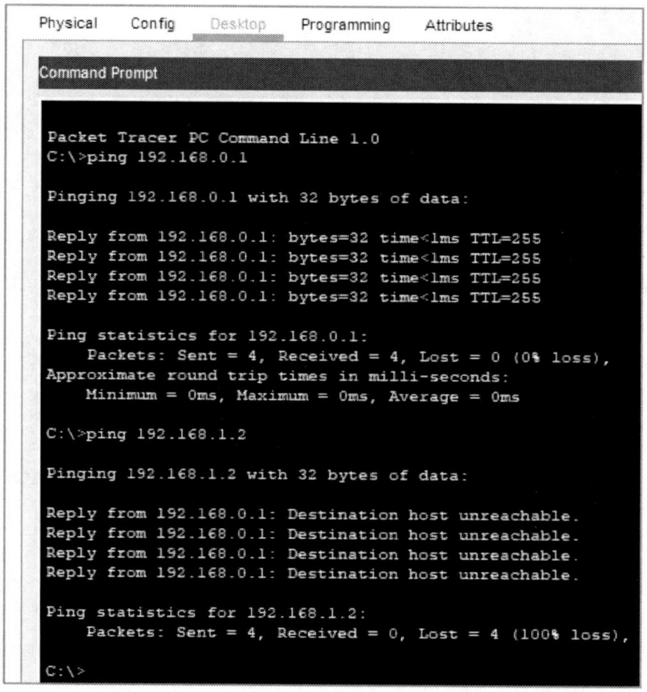

Figure 8.40 PING from workstation to default gateway and end device

PC1 has no problem communicating with the default gateway, due to the fact that it is in the same network.

When we try to communicate with a host on another network, a router without a configured routing protocol will not know where that network is located and returns a packet saying that the destination host is unavailable.

In order for our router to know where the target network is located, it should be indicated to it in the case of static routing.

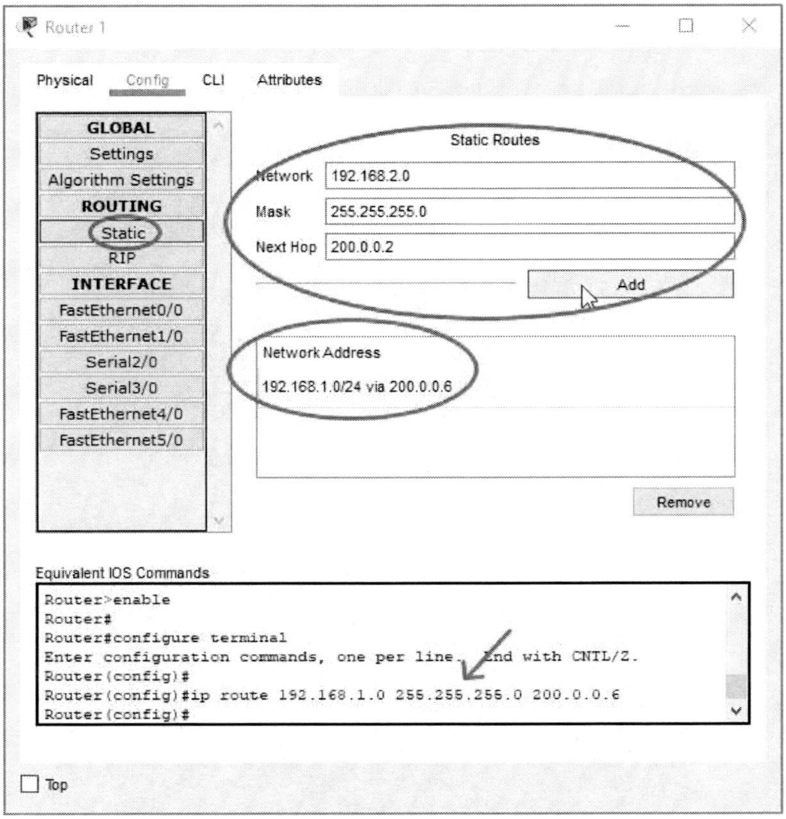

Figure 8.41 Static Routing Configuration - GUI

In tab [**Config→Routing→Static**], we can specify the target **network** together with the **mask** and the address of the **Next Hop**, i.e. the address of the router to which the packet is to jump to find the way to the target network. In our case, we have a network of 192.168.2.0, which is located "at the top" of our topology, so we direct packets to the address 200.0.0.2, which is the address of Router 2. Remember to always determine the way back and forth! Otherwise, routing will not work.

Now, after pinging other networks, everything works as it should.

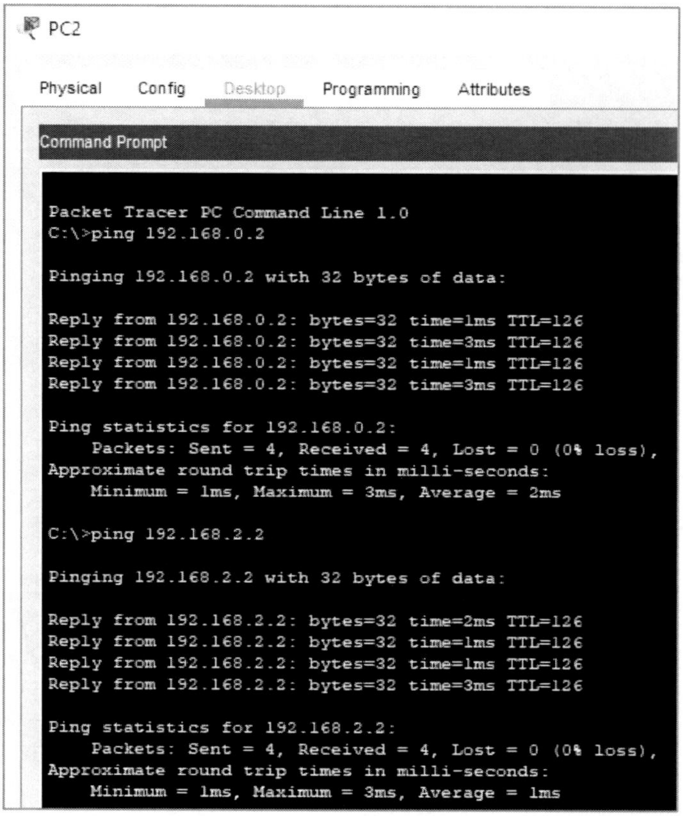

Figure 8.42 Correct PING to other networks - static routing

8.2.2.2 RIP Routing Protocol

Now that we have learned the **assumptions of routing protocols** and **how the router works**, we can move on to the first dynamic routing protocol - **RIP** (Routing Information Protocol).

Dynamic routing, which is one in which routers can exchange topology information with each other and complete their routing tables. This solution is much faster than manual configuration of all routes, and in the event of a failure of one of the links, routing will automatically redirect traffic to another (if available). Let's start with a slightly more elaborate topology:

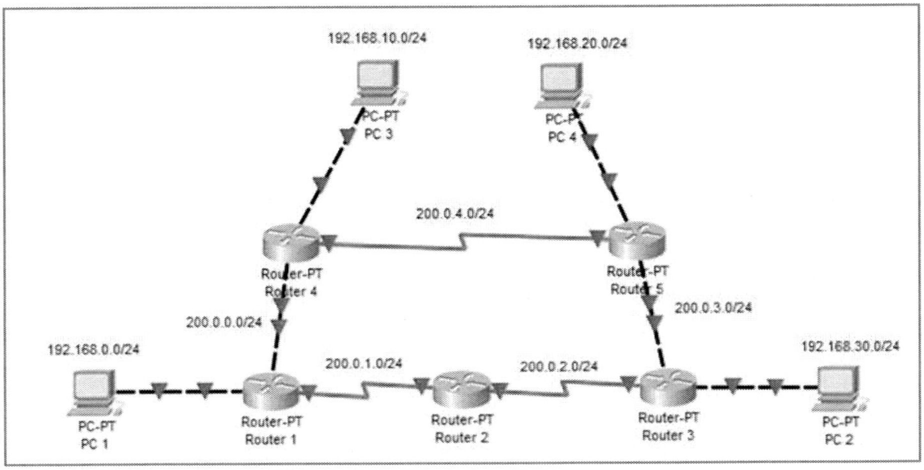

Figure 8.43 Topology with device addressing for RIP

In the above there are 5 routers and 9 networks. If we wanted to manually assign a route to each network, it would take a lot of time, but with RIP it is much simpler. All connections are disabled, so first we need to configure the computers and interfaces of the routers as described earlier.

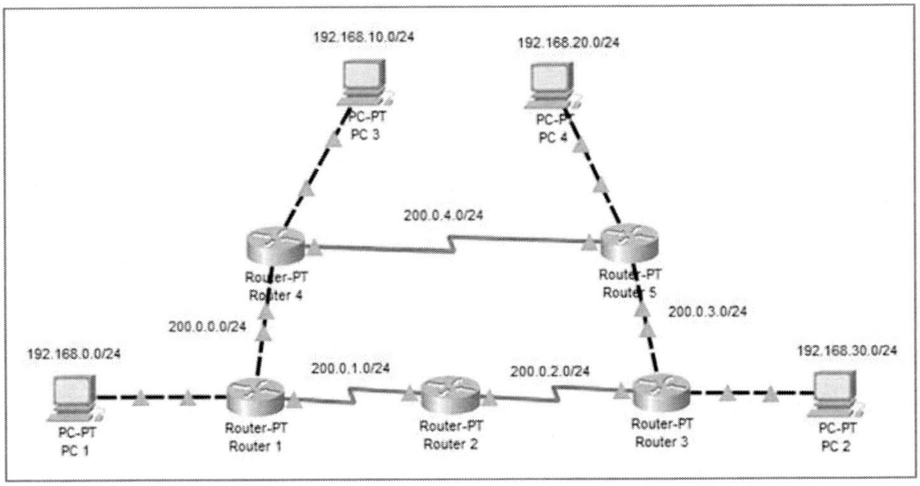

Figure 8.44 Topology after configuration

After correct configuration, all LEDs should be green, however, we can not communicate with remote networks.

Fire	Last Status	Source	Destination	Type	Color
	Successful	PC 1	Router 1	ICMP	
	Failed	PC 1	PC 3	ICMP	
	Failed	PC 1	PC 4	ICMP	

Figure 8.45 PING Command Results

We will now proceed to configure the RIP protocol. To do this, click on the router, enter the **Config** tab, and then select from the list on the left side of the **RIP**.

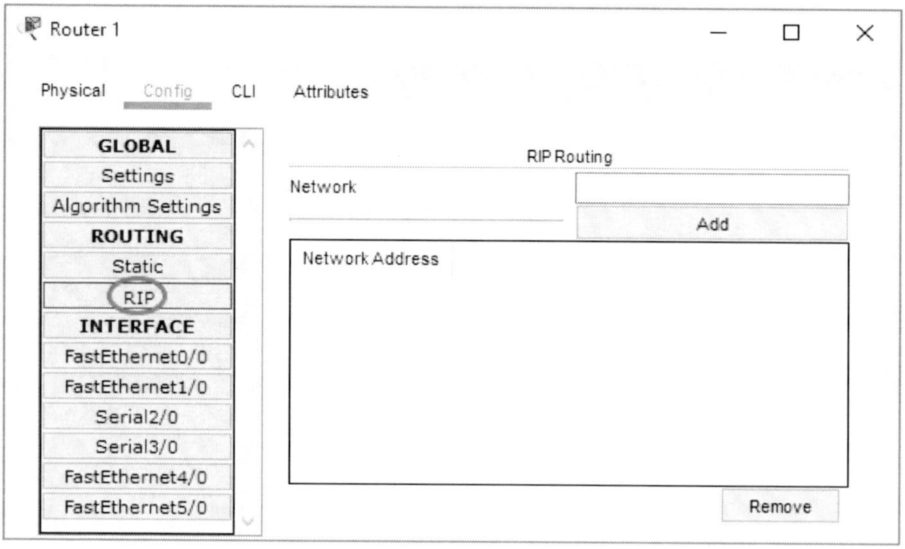

Figure 8.46 RIP tab

To configure the RIP protocol, we must enter in the **Network** field the address of each network that is connected directly to the router interface. For example, in the case of **Router 1**, these will be: 192.168.0.0, 200.0.0.0 and 200.0.1.0. Each entry is approved by the **Add** button, while using the **Remove** button we can delete already existing entries or possibly correct incorrect entries.

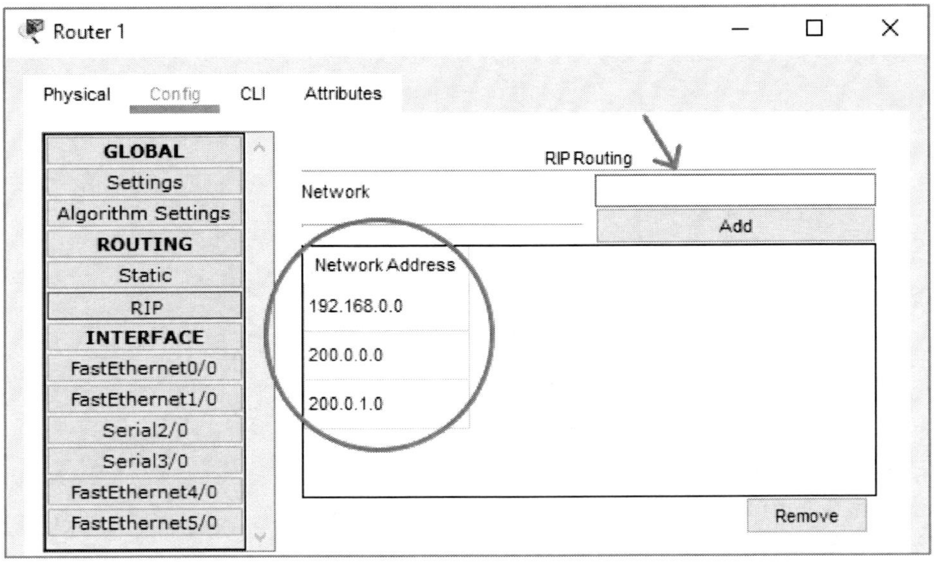

Figure 8.47 Properly configured protocol on Router 1

Similarly, other routers should be configured. Once you have configured them all, communication between all networks will be possible.

Fire	Last Status	Source	Destination	Type	Color
●	Successful	PC 1	PC 3	ICMP	
●	Successful	PC 1	PC 4	ICMP	
●	Successful	PC 1	PC 2	ICMP	

Figure 8.48 PING results after correct RIP configuration

As we can see, the routers themselves determined the route of the packets and delivered them to the destination. The RIP protocol uses the number of hops (routers) on a given route as a metric when choosing a route, always choosing a route with as few hops as possible. The route of packets can be checked in several ways, for example by using the **tracert** command or **graphical ping** in simulation mode. So let's check the packet route between PC1 and PC2 in the latter way.

Event List

Vis.	Time(sec)	Last Device	At Device	Type
	0.000	--	PC 1	ICMP
	0.001	PC 1	Router 1	ICMP
	0.002	Router 1	Router 2	ICMP
	0.003	Router 2	Router 3	ICMP
	0.004	Router 3	PC 2	ICMP
	0.005	PC 2	Router 3	ICMP
	0.006	Router 3	Router 2	ICMP
	0.007	Router 2	Router 1	ICMP
	0.008	Router 1	PC 1	ICMP

Figure 8.49 Package route between PC1 and PC2

As you can see, the packets pass through routers 1, 2 and 3. Now let's see what happens when we turn off **Router 2**.

Event List

Vis.	Time(sec)	Last Device	At Device	Type
	0.000	--	PC 1	ICMP
	0.001	PC 1	Router 1	ICMP
	0.002	Router 1	Router 4	ICMP
	0.003	Router 4	Router 5	ICMP
	0.004	Router 5	Router 3	ICMP
	0.005	Router 3	PC 2	ICMP
	0.006	PC 2	Router 3	ICMP
	0.007	Router 3	Router 5	ICMP
	0.008	Router 5	Router 4	ICMP
	0.009	Router 4	Router 1	ICMP
	0.010	Router 1	PC 1	ICMP

Figure 8.50 Package route between PC1 and PC2 after updating the routes

After a while, the routers updated the routing tables and set a new route. This time, the packets ran through routers 1, 4, 5 and 3, bypassing the disabled router 2. If we were using static routing, the administrator would have to manually update the routing tables. RIP did it automatically.

8.3 Configuring Cisco Routers in Cisco IOS

As we could see earlier, the **Config** tab located in the graphical interface for configuring the router does not have many options to configure, so it is recommended to configure routers in the Cisco IOS, i.e. using commands.

8.3.1 Basics

If you want to start configuring the router in a real environment, you will need to have any computer with a COM port (RS232), a console cable  and, of course, the router.

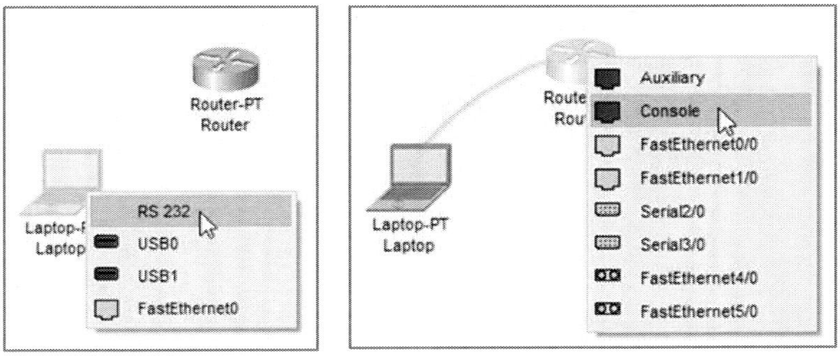

Figure 8.51 Steps to connect a computer to a router using a console cable

The correct connection of the computer to the router is shown in the figure below. However, it should be remembered that the console cable is used only for the configuration of the device.

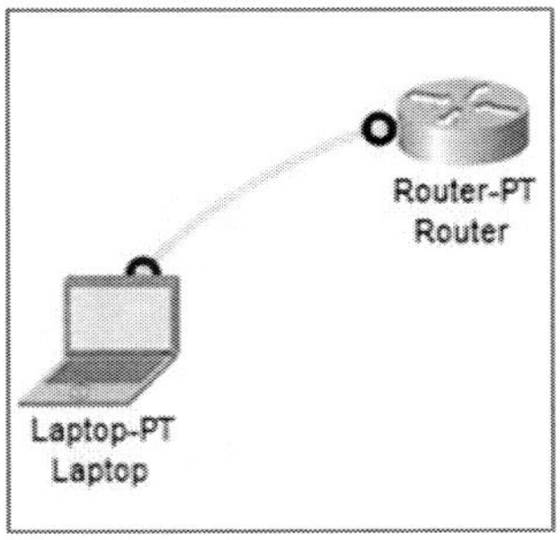

Figure 8.52 Correct console connection

Now it's time to try to connect to the router. For this we will need an application on the desktop of the computer called **Terminal**.

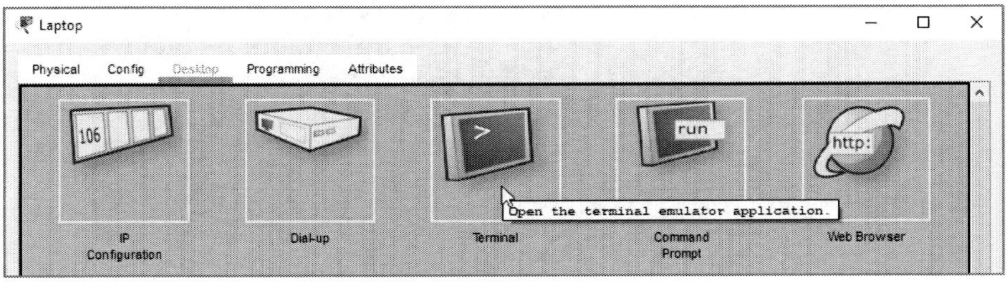

Figure 8.53 Terminal

After starting **Terminal**, a configuration window appears in which you should not change any parameters. Leaving, so the default settings, we click on the **OK** button, after which the connection to the router should take place.

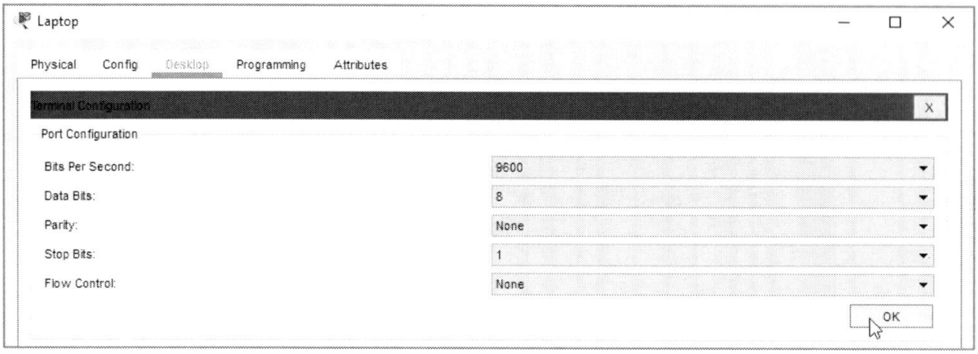

Figure 8.54 Terminal configuration window

After the correct connection, a window should appear, shown in the figure below. The last line of the console with the text: **Continue with configuration dialog? [yes/no]:** Indicating that the connection was correct and the router's operating system is waiting for the user to make a decision.

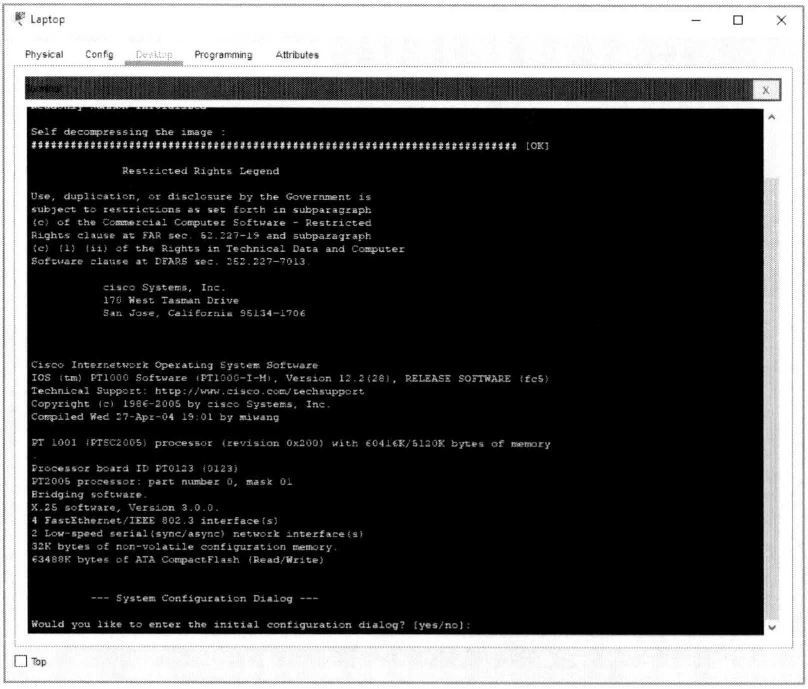

Figure 8.55 Log in to the router correctly

It may happen that when trying to connect to the router, the console window will be empty, which may mean that there is no connection between the devices, but the most common reason is a disabled router. On the other hand, when we have the terminal window open and the router has just been turned on, we can see the progress of extracting the system image, which can be seen in the figure below:

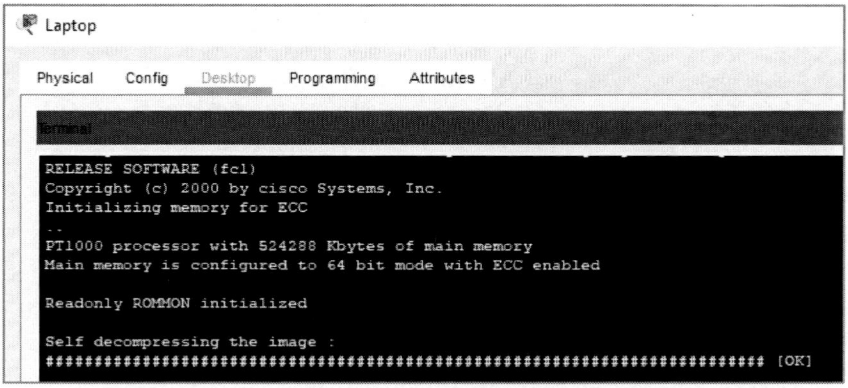

Figure 8.56 Extracting the system image by the router

Let's move on to the configuration of the router connected by a patch cable to the computer through the CLI console.

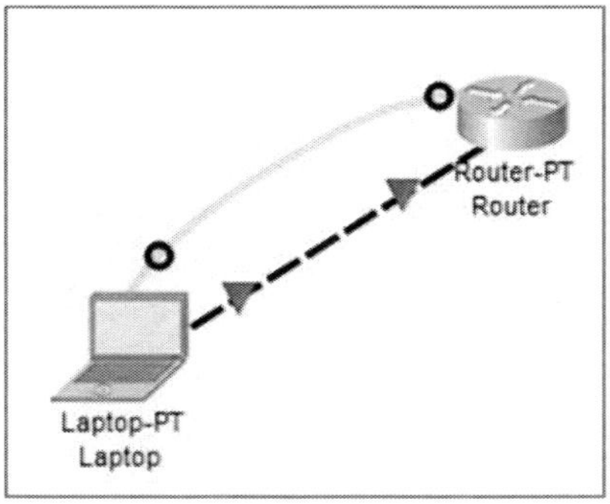

Figure 8.57 Computer connected via patch cable to the router

8.3.2 Wizard Mode

In the case of configuring routers from the IOS level, we have two options: through the wizard or without its use. In this chapter, we will discuss the wizard mode. If you want to start the wizard mode, you should answer the first question in the console: **Continue with configuration dialog? [yes/no],** answer **yes** and press **Enter**. After a while, the console window will change the content to the following form:

```
Would you like to enter the initial configuration dialog? [yes/no]: yes

At any point you may enter a question mark '?' for help.
Use ctrl-c to abort configuration dialog at any prompt.
Default settings are in square brackets '[]'.


Basic management setup configures only enough connectivity
for management of the system, extended setup will ask you
to configure each interface on the system

Would you like to enter basic management setup? [yes/no]:
```

Figure 8.58 Wizard mode selection - simple or advanced

8.3.2.1 Simple Wizard Mode

This is a wizard mode in which the simplest router settings are available for configuration without knowing any commands. To get to it, you need to answer the question: **Would you like to enter basic management setup?** answer **yes**.

After a while, another command will appear in the terminal window: **Enter host name [Router]**:p at which we have to give the name of our router

Note, however, that this time the hint that the device gives us is unambiguous, because in square brackets there is one word: **[Router],** and not as it was previously two: **[yes / no].** This means that it would be enough to press enter and the router would be given the default name, suggested in square brackets. However, in this configuration step, we can **enter** a different name, for example **Router123**, as shown in the figure below.

```
Enter host name [Router]: Router123
```

Figure 8.59 Naming a router - simple wizard

After confirming this step, you must enter three passwords, one in turn, which will protect against unauthorized access to the privileged mode of the router (the modes of operation of the router are described in the next chapters of the book).

```
The enable secret is a password used to protect access to
privileged EXEC and configuration modes. This password, after
entered, becomes encrypted in the configuration.
Enter enable secret: packettracer

The enable password is used when you do not specify an
enable secret password, with some older software versions, and
some boot images.
Enter enable password: tracer

The virtual terminal password is used to protect
access to the router over a network interface.
Enter virtual terminal password: tracer
```

Figure 8.60 Giving passwords to access the router - simple wizard

First, we are asked to enter the password for the privileged mode in general. Then we are asked again to enter the password for the privileged mode, which works in older versions of the software. The last password we are asked for is the virtual access password, which secures the router when someone tries to log in to it over the network (using protocols such as Telnet or SSH, which will be described later).

The next question concerns the **Simple Network Management Protocol** (SNMP), which allows the exchange of control information between network devices, but will not be described at the moment, so we answer this question **no**.

```
Configure SNMP Network Management? [no]:no
```

Figure 8.61 SNMP configuration question

After performing the above actions, the router displays the status of its interfaces, after which it asks us which interface we want to configure. in our case it will be **FastEthernet0/0**. Then the router asks if we want to configure the IP address on this interface - press **enter** or type **yes**. The next step is to assign any IP address to the interface, in our case, it can be **192.168.0.1** with a subnet mask of **255.255.255.0** (as the router tells us).

```
Current interface summary

Interface              IP-Address      OK? Method Status                Protocol

FastEthernet0/0        unassigned      YES manual administratively down down

FastEthernet1/0        unassigned      YES manual administratively down down

Serial2/0              unassigned      YES manual administratively down down

Serial3/0              unassigned      YES manual administratively down down

FastEthernet4/0        unassigned      YES manual administratively down down

FastEthernet5/0        unassigned      YES manual administratively down down

Enter interface name used to connect to the
management network from the above interface summary: FastEthernet0/0

Configuring interface FastEthernet0/0:
  Configure IP on this interface? [yes]: yes
    IP address for this interface: 192.168.0.1
    Subnet mask for this interface [255.255.255.0] : 255.255.255.0
```

Figure 8.62 Configuration of interfaces - simple wizard

Then the router will display the configuration and we will be able to finish the wizard by selecting one of the options **(Save this configuration to nvram and exit).**

```
interface FastEthernet0/0
 no shutdown
 ip address 192.168.0.1 255.255.255.0
!
interface FastEthernet1/0
 shutdown
 no ip address
!
interface Serial2/0
 shutdown
 no ip address
!
interface Serial3/0
 shutdown
 no ip address
!
interface FastEthernet4/0
 shutdown
 no ip address
!
interface FastEthernet5/0
 shutdown
 no ip address
!
end

[0] Go to the IOS command prompt without saving this config.
[1] Return back to the setup without saving this config.
[2] Save this configuration to nvram and exit.

Enter your selection [2]: 2
```

Figure 8.63 Completion of configuration - simple wizard

The first option allows us to go to the IOS level without saving the configuration displayed above. The second, in turn, allows us to return to the simple wizard also without saving the configuration. The last option saves the configuration to **startup-config**, i.e. the one that will be loaded after the router reset, and exits the configuration window.

We are interested in the latter option, which is why we choose it. Now it remains for us to address our Laptop and conduct a connection test using the **PING** command.

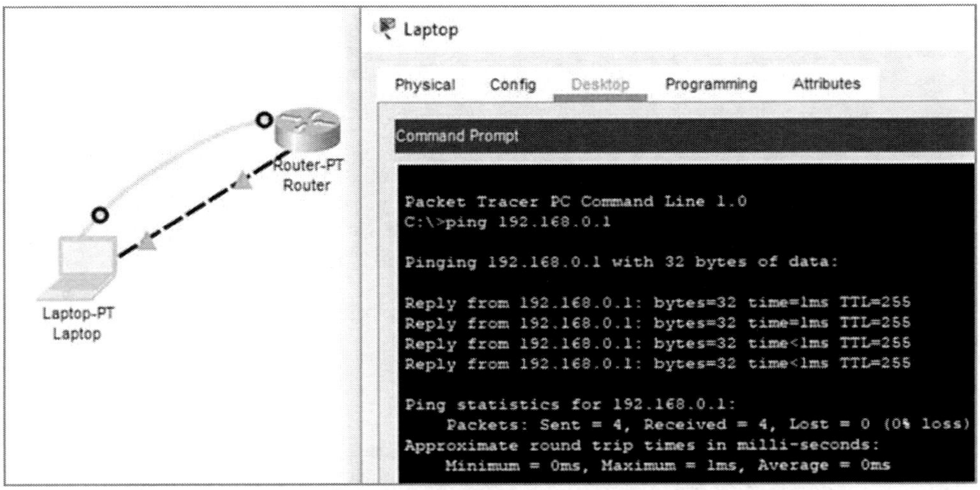

Figure 8.64 Test the connection between the laptop and the router

8.3.2.2 Advanced Wizard Mode

Advanced mode is not very different from simple mode. After the first start of the router, we will be asked if we want to enter the wizard mode (as we described in the previous subsection) and this time we also answer in the affirmative. The second question is the same as in discussing the previous mode, but now we answer negatively so that we go to the advanced wizard mode.

```
Would you like to enter the initial configuration dialog? [yes/no]: yes

At any point you may enter a question mark '?' for help.
Use ctrl-c to abort configuration dialog at any prompt.
Default settings are in square brackets '[]'.


Basic management setup configures only enough connectivity
for management of the system, extended setup will ask you
to configure each interface on the system

Would you like to enter basic management setup? [yes/no]: no
```

Figure 8.65 Enter the advanced wizard mode

First, we are asked if we want to display the current state of the interfaces - this is an option that better allows us to illustrate the current situation on the network. We answer in the affirmative.

```
First, would you like to see the current interface summary? [yes]:yes

Current interface summary

Interface              IP-Address      OK? Method Status                Protocol

FastEthernet0/0        unassigned      YES manual administratively down down

FastEthernet1/0        unassigned      YES manual administratively down down

Serial2/0              unassigned      YES manual administratively down down

Serial3/0              unassigned      YES manual administratively down down

FastEthernet4/0        unassigned      YES manual administratively down down

FastEthernet5/0        unassigned      YES manual administratively down down
```

Figure 8.66 Current status of interfaces - advanced wizard

The next steps are similar to those in a simple wizard, as we have already discussed them, we will configure them the same as before:

```
Configuring global parameters:

  Enter host name [Router]: Router123

  The enable secret is a password used to protect access to
  privileged EXEC and configuration modes. This password, after
  entered, becomes encrypted in the configuration.
  Enter enable secret: packettracer

  The enable password is used when you do not specify an
  enable secret password, with some older software versions, and
  some boot images.
  Enter enable password: packet

  The virtual terminal password is used to protect
  access to the router over a network interface.
  Enter virtual terminal password: packet
Configure SNMP Network Management? [no]:no
```

Figure 8.67 Router Name, Passwords and SNMP Configuration - Advanced Wizard

The next question is about the configuration of the interfaces, but this time we do not choose which interface specifically we want to configure, since we will be asked in turn about each. In our case, we will only configure **FastEthernet0/0** in the same way as before (**192.168.0.1/24**), and the rest of the interfaces will be omitted.

```
Configuring interface parameters:

Do you want to configure FastEthernet0/0  interface? [no]:yes
    IP address for this interface: 192.168.0.1
    Subnet mask for this interface [255.255.255.0] : 255.255.255.0
Do you want to configure FastEthernet1/0  interface? [no]:
Do you want to configure Serial2/0  interface? [no]:
Do you want to configure Serial3/0  interface? [no]:
Do you want to configure FastEthernet4/0  interface? [no]:
Do you want to configure FastEthernet5/0  interface? [no]:
```

Figure 8.68 Interface configuration - advanced wizard

Just like in the simple wizard, the last step is to view the current configuration and the same three steps. As before, we select the last option and save the configuration. Now let's address the computer and see if it can send PING to the FastEthernet0/0 interface of the router.

```
The following configuration command script was created:

!
hostname Router123
enable secret 5 $1$mERr$61KHCaWFNvLbPV6rOFt4P.
enable password packet
line vty 0 4
password packet
!
interface FastEthernet0/0
 no shutdown
 ip address 192.168.0.1 255.255.255.0
!
interface FastEthernet1/0
 shutdown
 no ip address
!
interface Serial2/0
 shutdown
 no ip address
!
interface Serial3/0
 shutdown
 no ip address
!
interface FastEthernet4/0
 shutdown
 no ip address
!
interface FastEthernet5/0
 shutdown
 no ip address
!
end

[0] Go to the IOS command prompt without saving this config.
[1] Return back to the setup without saving this config.
[2] Save this configuration to nvram and exit.

Enter your selection [2]: 2
```

Figure 8.69 Saving the current configuration - advanced wizard

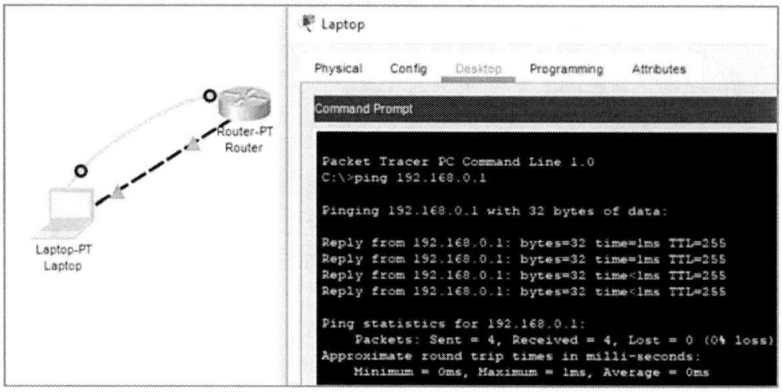

Figure 8.70 Test the connection between the laptop and the router

We have the same situation as before - the configuration is correct.

8.3.3 Basic Router Configuration Modes

The modes of working with the router in wizard mode described above allow only for its basic configuration, which does not satisfy us, due to the fact that the options that interest us are definitely more advanced. Therefore, we will now describe the individual steps leading to the configuration of the equipment using the manual method.

8.3.3.1 Console Mode Support

In this section we will describe how the so-called "modes of operation" can be used. Each of these modes will serve for something different. Most often, after switching on the router, the console screen will show the process of loading and decompressing the IOS image, and then the router will ask us if we want to use the wizard, the operation of which we described above. After answering the question in the negative, we will be transferred to the **user mode**, which is used for typical tasks related to checking the status of the router, but you can not make any changes in the configuration here. To easily recognize modes and distinguish them from each other, each mode has a different "prompt" after which the user will enter commands. In user mode, the prompt is: **Router>.** The following figure shows the basic modes of operation of the router and the commands for moving between them.

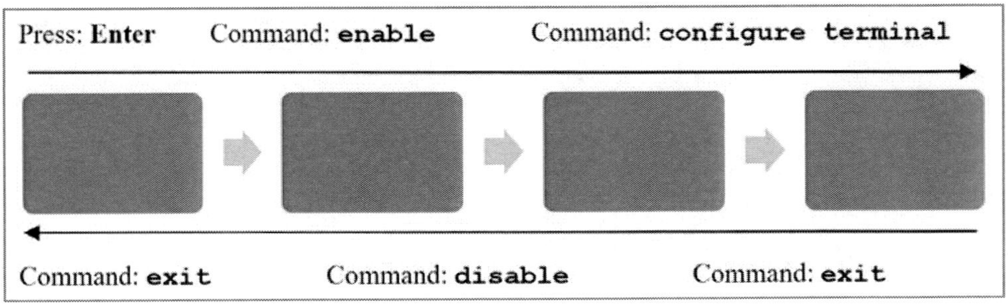

Figure 8.71 Navigating between basic router modes

According to the graph above, let's now try to move to the next mode of operation of the router – **Privileged Exec Mode**, a mode used both to display the status of the configuration of the hardware, memory, operating system, but also to issue simple diagnostic commands, e.g. **PING, TELNET, TRACERT**, etc. We enter this mode with the **enable** command, and the router's prompt changes to **Router#.**

The third mode, which is described in this subsection, is the **Global Configuration Mode**, used both to configure various elements of the router, and from this mode we will move to the next configuration modes, in which we will define almost all components of the equipment and its equipment. You can only enter the global configuration mode from privileged mode by typing the command: **configure terminal**, after which the router greets us with the **Router(config#)** prompt.

```
Router>enable
Router#configure terminal
Enter configuration commands, one per line.  End with CNTL/Z.
Router(config)#exit
Router#
%SYS-5-CONFIG_I: Configured from console by console

Router#disable
Router>exit
```

Figure 8.72 Navigating between basic router modes

```
Router con0 is now available




Press RETURN to get started.
```

Figure 8.73 Router splash screen

8.3.3.2 Using Help

Very often, when working with operating systems from the command line, administrators use help to check the syntax or application of a given command. The situation is also similar in the IOS system of CISCO routers. Therefore, we will now describe how we can use it. As we mentioned earlier, each of the router modes has a different use, which is why it will contain different commands that can be used in each of them separately.

To call up a list of commands available in a given mode, type a question mark: ?, and then press **Enter**.

```
Router>?
Exec commands:
  <1-99>      Session number to resume
  connect     Open a terminal connection
  disable     Turn off privileged commands
  disconnect  Disconnect an existing network connection
  enable      Turn on privileged commands
  exit        Exit from the EXEC
  logout      Exit from the EXEC
  ping        Send echo messages
  resume      Resume an active network connection
  show        Show running system information
  ssh         Open a secure shell client connection
  telnet      Open a telnet connection
  terminal    Set terminal line parameters
  traceroute  Trace route to destination
```

Figure 8.74 List of commands in user mode

We will not describe the meaning of all commands. We will show their application in specific situations. When we call in the same way help in privileged mode, sometimes we can notice that there are many more commands, and they may not even fit all in one console window, and at its bottom you may see the inscription: **--More--.** If you want to call further commands, you can best use two keys: **spacebar** – displays the next line, while the **Enter** key – displays another screen.

```
Router#?
Exec commands:
  <1-99>      Session number to resume
  auto        Exec level Automation
  clear       Reset functions
  clock       Manage the system clock
  configure   Enter configuration mode
  connect     Open a terminal connection
  copy        Copy from one file to another
  debug       Debugging functions (see also 'undebug')
  delete      Delete a file
  dir         List files on a filesystem
  disable     Turn off privileged commands
  disconnect  Disconnect an existing network connection
  enable      Turn on privileged commands
  erase       Erase a filesystem
  exit        Exit from the EXEC
  logout      Exit from the EXEC
  mkdir       Create new directory
  more        Display the contents of a file
  no          Disable debugging informations
  ping        Send echo messages
  reload      Halt and perform a cold restart
  resume      Resume an active network connection
  rmdir       Remove existing directory
  send        Send a message to other tty lines
  setup       Run the SETUP command facility
  show        Show running system information
  ssh         Open a secure shell client connection
  telnet      Open a telnet connection
  terminal    Set terminal line parameters
  traceroute  Trace route to destination
  undebug     Disable debugging functions (see also 'debug')
  write       Write running configuration to memory, network, or terminal
```

Figure 8.75 List of commands in privileged mode

Another very useful feature of the IOS system help is to suggest further syntax of more complex commands or their automatic completion. We will use for this purpose an example in which we deliberately simulate a certain error that very often happens when working with the command line. We will go to the privileged mode and try to call help for this mode by typing the command: **help**. After a while, it turns out that the console displays the message: **Translating "help"...domain server (255.255.255.255)** and we can not type anything. To avoid this inscription, press **Ctrl+Shift+6** and then release all key.

Please do not be afraid, after a while we will regain access to the router, and this is because there is no such command as **help** (calling help is possible only by using the sign: ?). At the moment of mistyped command, the router begins to search for the names of some host with the specified name or a computer with this address. When, of course, it does not find anything, it will display the second part of the message: **% Unknown command or computer name, or unable to find computer address**, and immediately returns to our control over the router.

```
Router#help
Translating "help"...domain server (255.255.255.255)
% Unknown command or computer name, or unable to find computer address

Router#
```

Figure 8.76 The result of typing an incorrect command

For those who are impatient, we provide a very useful keyboard shortcut that causes an immediate return to the command line level. This is **Ctrl+Shift+6**.

Let's assume that we now select the privileged mode and the clock command to show how else we can use the help and hints of the IOS system. Probably everyone knows what this command will be used for, and its name is also not alien to anyone, but let's assume a situation in which we forgot its name, we only know what letter it began with.

It is enough to write this letter and immediately after it press the question mark (?), as shown in the figure below. The router will then display all commands starting with the indicated letter and available in a given mode. Of course, you can enter the first few letters and press the question mark, but we must remember that there is no space between the questioner and the letters you type.

```
Router#c?
clear  clock  configure  connect  copy
Router#c
```

Figure 8.77 Display commands that begin with a letter

There may also be an event in which, after typing the correct command, you receive the error message: `% Incomplete command.`, which means that the entered command is not complete and most likely you need to finish its phrase.

```
Router#clock
% Incomplete command.
Router#
```

Figure 8.78 Enter an incomplete command

Therefore, if you want to check what is its further syntax, you should use the question mark again after entering an incomplete command. However, it should be separated by a space, as shown in the next figure. Then, on the next line, you will see a hint about the further syntax of the command and its explanation.

```
Router#clock ?
  set  Set the time and date
Router#clock
```

Figure 8.79 View further command syntax

With this method, acting in an analogous way, we can learn the full syntax of this basically simple but complex command, in which the time and date separators are important, as shown in the figure below.

```
Router#clock ?
  set  Set the time and date
Router#clock set ?
  hh:mm:ss  Current Time
Router#clock set 20:15:40 ?
  <1-31>  Day of the month
  MONTH   Month of the year
Router#clock set 20:15:40 9 ?
  MONTH  Month of the year
Router#clock set 20:15:40 9 december ?
  <1993-2035>  Year
Router#clock set 20:15:40 9 december 2019 ?
  <cr>
Router#clock set 20:15:40 9 december 2019
Router#
```

Figure 8.80 Type the full command after using help

Another important feature that makes life easier is using the **Tab** key to automatically complete typing commands from the keyboard. That is, when we type an incomplete command, for example **clo** and press the **Tab** key, it will be filled automatically for the user, obtaining the effect: **clock**.

It is also worth remembering that through the arrow keys ↑ ↓ you can view the history of entered commands and using these keys, you can call previously entered commands.

There may be a situation in which we make a mistake in the syntax of a command consisting of several members, as an example we use the command: **configure terminal** and intentionally simulate the so-called letter error, consisting in the fact that in the syntax of the second part of the command instead of the letter "**n**" we enter "**d**".

Then the router will point out that we made a mistake by displaying the message: **% Invalid input detected at '^' marker.** and the sign: ^ will indicate its location. This situation is shown in the figure below. This is very helpful, because sometimes it is difficult to notice the location of the error, and in this situation it is very easy.

```
Router#configure termidal
                     ^
% Invalid input detected at '^' marker.

Router#
```

Figure 8.81 Error message in command syntax

It is also worth knowing that working a little longer with the IOS system, and wanting to speed up the hardware configuration process a bit, administrators very often use shortcuts of known commands. Shortcuts are simply the first few letters of IOS commands that can be used at any time, but remember not to shorten the commands too much. That is, if we shorten the command to such an extent that the string we entered will be the equivalent of two or more commands, then the router will not know what command is in question and will return us an error message:% **Ambiguous command: "dis",** and an incomprehensible string will be marked in quotation marks. The use of shortcuts and a possible error message is shown in the next figure.

```
Router>en
Router#conf t
Enter configuration commands, one per line.  End with CNTL/Z.
Router(config)#ex
Router#
%SYS-5-CONFIG_I: Configured from console by console

Router#dis
% Ambiguous command: "dis"
Router#disa
Router>
```

Figure 8.82 Use shortcuts

8.3.3.3 View the Status of the Router

Before or during the configuration, and very often when solving various problems with routers, you will need to view the status of the device, preview the configuration, etc. For this purpose, we will use the **show** command, which we will now present.

This command is used in privileged mode, and its use is very rich. However, we will not present all its capabilities, we will only show what it is for, and its use will be known to everyone during everyday work with the router. In order to check the enormity of the possibilities of this command, let's call the help, the command **show**?, as shown in the figure below.

```
Router#show ?
  aaa              Show AAA values
  access-lists     List access lists
  arp              Arp table
  cdp              CDP information
  class-map        Show QoS Class Map
  clock            Display the system clock
  controllers      Interface controllers status
  crypto           Encryption module
  debugging        State of each debugging option
  dhcp             Dynamic Host Configuration Protocol status
  file             Show filesystem information
  flash:           display information about flash: file system
  flow             Flow information
  frame-relay      Frame-Relay information
  history          Display the session command history
  hosts            IP domain-name, lookup style, nameservers, and host table
  interfaces       Interface status and configuration
  ip               IP information
  line             TTY line information
  lldp             LLDP information
```

Figure 8.83 Help for the show command is displayed

The first of the commands of this type will be: **show version** – through it we can check the version of the IOS system, the location of the system image file and its name.

```
Router#show version
Cisco Internetwork Operating System Software
IOS (tm) PT1000 Software (PT1000-I-M), Version 12.2(28), RELEASE SOFTWARE (fc5)
Technical Support: http://www.cisco.com/techsupport
Copyright (c) 1986-2005 by cisco Systems, Inc.
Compiled Wed 27-Apr-04 19:01 by miwang
Image text-base: 0x8000808C, data-base: 0x80A1FECC

ROM: System Bootstrap, Version 12.1(3r)T2, RELEASE SOFTWARE (fc1)
Copyright (c) 2000 by cisco Systems, Inc.
ROM: PT1000 Software (PT1000-I-M), Version 12.2(28), RELEASE SOFTWARE (fc5)

System returned to ROM by reload
System image file is "flash:pt1000-i-mz.122-28.bin"

PT 1001 (PTSC2005) processor (revision 0x200) with 60416K/5120K bytes of memory
.
Processor board ID PT0123 (0123)
PT2005 processor: part number 0, mask 01
Bridging software.
X.25 software, Version 3.0.0.
4 FastEthernet/IEEE 802.3 interface(s)
2 Low-speed serial(sync/async) network interface(s)
32K bytes of non-volatile configuration memory.
63488K bytes of ATA CompactFlash (Read/Write)

Configuration register is 0x2102
```

Figure 8.84 Show version command

Another very useful command is **show ip interface brief**, a command with which we can display the status of all router interfaces and assigned IP addresses, as shown in the figure below.

```
Router#show ip interface brief
Interface              IP-Address      OK? Method Status                Protocol
FastEthernet0/0        unassigned      YES unset  administratively down down
FastEthernet1/0        unassigned      YES unset  administratively down down
Serial2/0              unassigned      YES unset  administratively down down
Serial3/0              unassigned      YES unset  administratively down down
FastEthernet4/0        unassigned      YES unset  administratively down down
FastEthernet5/0        unassigned      YES unset  administratively down down
Router#
```

Figure 8.85 Show ip interface brief command

The **show running-config** command is the most commonly used command by people who verify the configuration of the router or want to solve existing problems with the hardware configuration itself. However, we must remember that with its help, we display a temporary configuration, saved in RAM. To display the status of the configuration stored in non-volatile memory (NVRAM), we use **show startup-config** command.

```
Router#show running-config
Building configuration...

Current configuration : 686 bytes
!
version 12.2
no service timestamps log datetime msec
no service timestamps debug datetime msec
no service password-encryption
!
hostname Router
!
!
!
!
!
!
!
!
ip cef
no ipv6 cef
!
!
 --More--
```

Figure 8.86 Show running-config command

Through the **show flash** command, we can display information about the amount of occupied flash memory of the router, through all the files placed inside it.

```
Router#show flash

System flash directory:
File  Length   Name/status
  3   5571584  pt1000-i-mz.122-28.bin
  2   28282    sigdef-category.xml
  1   227537   sigdef-default.xml
[5827403 bytes used, 58188981 available, 64016384 total]
63488K bytes of processor board System flash (Read/Write)
```

Figure 8.87 Show flash command

Through the **show ip route** command, we can display the status of the routing array.

```
Router#show ip route
Codes: C - connected, S - static, I - IGRP, R - RIP, M - mobile, B - BGP
       D - EIGRP, EX - EIGRP external, O - OSPF, IA - OSPF inter area
       N1 - OSPF NSSA external type 1, N2 - OSPF NSSA external type 2
       E1 - OSPF external type 1, E2 - OSPF external type 2, E - EGP
       i - IS-IS, L1 - IS-IS level-1, L2 - IS-IS level-2, ia - IS-IS inter area
       * - candidate default, U - per-user static route, o - ODR
       P - periodic downloaded static route

Gateway of last resort is not set
```

Figure 8.88 Show ip route command

8.3.4 Configure Router Name, Passwords, and Message Of The Day (MOTD)

Another basic configuration step is to define the name of the router, which will make it easier to identify it in complex and extensive networks. The name of the router is configured in the global configuration mode, for this purpose it is not required to go to a specific configuration mode. If the name is not configured, IOS displays a prompt that precedes the default device name, **Router**.

We must remember that it is often not enough to place the description (**Display name**) of devices in the designed logical topology, although this action is very important. In addition to the above-mentioned fact, it is advisable to give the device a name (**Host name**) in the IOS system itself.

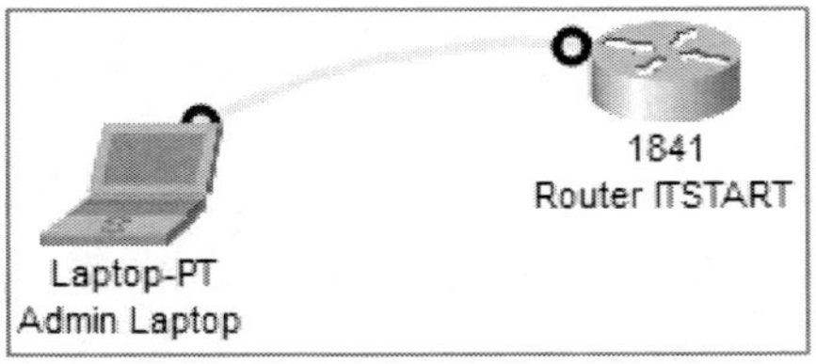

Figure 8.89 Display name in logical topology

If you want to enter a device name (**Host name**), use the command: hostname, and after the space you enter a new name. For example: **hostname ITSTART**. When you do this, the prompt changes as shown in the figure below.

```
Router>en
Router#conf t
Enter configuration commands, one per line.  End with CNTL/Z.
Router(config)#hostname ITSTART
ITSTART(config)#
```

Figure 8.90 Define a router name (Host name)

Each router should be properly protected against unauthorized access by third parties. For this purpose, passwords are used to protect both the entrance to the router from the console and virtual terminals (Telnet, SSH), as well as the transition from **user mode** to **privileged mode**. Describing the protection of the router with passwords will begin with the latter, because we will present two previous cases in the subsections devoted to the configuration of consoles and virtual terminals.

The password for the privileged mode, like the name of the device, is entered from the global configuration with the **enable password** command (then we enter the password, which will be saved in **running-config** in an explicit form) or **enable secret** (the password that we will give will be in encrypted form) and after the space we enter the password we are interested in (for example: "admin" and "admin1").

After the above actions have been performed correctly, we will check the correctness of our actions, so we will go to **privileged mode**, and then to **user mode** to re-enter **privileged mode**. We note that the router now requires us to enter the password that we have previously defined. As enable secret is safer, it will be the priority and we will have to give it.

```
ITSTART>en
ITSTART#conf t
Enter configuration commands, one per line.  End with CNTL/Z.
ITSTART(config)#enable password admin
ITSTART(config)#enable secret admin1
ITSTART(config)#exit
ITSTART#
%SYS-5-CONFIG_I: Configured from console by console

ITSTART#disable
ITSTART>en
Password:
ITSTART#
```

Figure 8.91 Define a privileged mode password

When you view the current configuration, you may notice that the first password is plaintext and the second is encrypted.

```
ITSTART#show running-config
Building configuration...

Current configuration : 625 bytes
!
version 12.4
no service timestamps log datetime msec
no service timestamps debug datetime msec
no service password-encryption
!
hostname ITSTART
!
!
!
enable secret 5 $1$mERr$7n6je7c9FKvO.o.40Rj1Q0
enable password admin
```

Figure 8.92 Unencrypted and encrypted passwords in the current configuration

To encrypt all passwords that exist on the router, execute the **service password-encryption** command presented below. When you view the current configuration again, you can see that both passwords are encrypted.

```
ITSTART(config)#service password-encryption
ITSTART(config)#exit
ITSTART#
%SYS-5-CONFIG_I: Configured from console by console

ITSTART#show run
Building configuration...

Current configuration : 631 bytes
!
version 12.4
no service timestamps log datetime msec
no service timestamps debug datetime msec
service password-encryption
!
hostname ITSTART
!
!
!
enable secret 5 $1$mERr$7n6je7c9FKvO.o.40Rj1Q0
enable password 7 0820484300017
```

Figure 8.93 Encrypt passwords on your router

Now we will present the possibility of displaying the welcome text on the console, i.e. a banner (the so-called Message of the day), which can be a greeting for users who will connect to the router. To do this, in the global configuration mode, execute the command: **banner motd** (and after a space press the character that will be the beginning for the text you are entering, similarly typing the same character a second time will mean the end of the text string). In the figure below we have an example configuration of the message of the day.

```
ITSTART(config)#banner motd #
Enter TEXT message.  End with the character '#'.
------------------------------------------
!            WELCOME TO ITSTART          !
------------------------------------------
#
```

Figure 8.94 Message Setup of the Day

In order to check whether the message will be displayed correctly after entering the router, type **exit**, **disable**, and **exit** again to see the message informing us about entering the router.

```
ITSTART#ex



ITSTART con0 is now available



Press RETURN to get started.
```

Figure 8.95 Router welcome window

We are now in the console window that informs us of the correct connection to the router. When you press **Enter**, a welcome message will be displayed.

```
------------------------------------------
!            WELCOME TO ITSTART          !
------------------------------------------
```

Figure 8.96 Message Of The Day (MOTD)

8.3.5 Other Modes of Operation of the Router

In order to start configuring CISCO routers, in addition to knowing the basic modes of operation previously learned, we need to know several new ones, with the help of which we will be able to fully set the basic parameters of the router. All the modes listed below are switched from the **global configuration** mode, which is the initial mode from which we must start working.

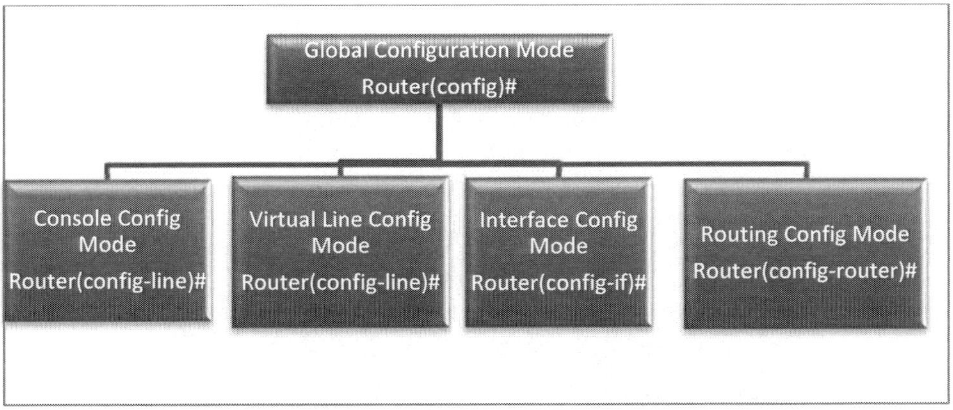

Figure 8.97 Other router modes

8.3.5.1 Console Port Configuration

Above we have described how to partially protect our router against unauthorized access. Now we will focus on how to configure and also secure access to the router from the console and virtual terminals. We go from the **global configuration mode** to the **console configuration mode** with the **line console 0** command, then enter the command: login, which will force the user authorization and define the password after the **password** command (in our case, let it be: **console**). Finally, finishing the configuration, we can leave the mode with the **exit** command.

```
ITSTART(config)#line console 0
ITSTART(config-line)#password console
ITSTART(config-line)#login
ITSTART(config-line)#exit
```

Figure 8.98 Console port configuration

Before we test the console port configured just now, and more precisely its protection via a password, we will show that in addition to the previously set so-called **message of the day**, you can set a **welcome message**, which will be additionally displayed when logging in to the router through this port. For this purpose, the **banner login** command is used, the text entry is done in the same way as in the case of the **banner motd** command. The whole procedure is illustrated in the figure below.

```
ITSTART(config)#banner login #
Enter TEXT message.  End with the character '#'.
Are You sure to login on the router ITSTART? #

ITSTART(config)#
```

Figure 8.99 Set up a welcome message

To check the correctness of our actions, let's go to the splash screen, then press **Enter** and after a while both messages will appear on the screen and two-step authorization is active as shown in the figure below.

```
-----------------------------------------
!            WELCOME TO ITSTART         !
-----------------------------------------


Are You sure to login on the router ITSTART?

User Access Verification

Password:
```

Figure 8.100 Message Of The Day and welcome message and user authorization

8.3.5.2 Configuration of Virtual Terminals (Telnet, SSH)

We have just learned how to configure and secure the entrance to the router from the console from the computer, which is most likely located near the router (most often in the same room). However, it rarely happens that our router would not be connected to any network, which is why it is possible to configure it remotely via LAN or even WAN.

We will use an example in which our router is configured to work in a LAN to which desktop computers are connected, as in the figure below.

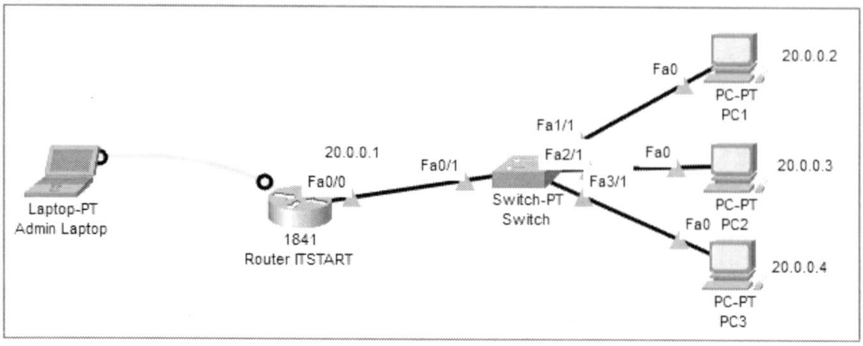

Figure 8.101 Topology for router configuration using a virtual terminal - Example 8.3.5.2a.pkt

Entering the virtual terminal configuration mode is very similar to the console, in the global configuration we enter **`line vty 0 4`** (the range between the first and second number is the number of channels that can be used by several people working remotely on the router at the same time – in our case, the range from 0 to 4 means 5 users at the same time). Then execute the **`login`** and **`password`** commands (in the same way as in the case of the console port), as shown in the figure below.

```
ITSTART(config)#line vty 0 4
ITSTART(config-line)#password virtualterminal
ITSTART(config-line)#login
ITSTART(config-line)#exit
ITSTART(config)#
```

Figure 8.102 Basic configuration of the virtual terminal

The maximum range of channels to configure can be 16 (that is, from 0 to 15). It should also be remembered that for different ranges we can define different passwords. We will not describe it, we leave it to the reader for their own exercises. However, we will now try to check the correctness of our previous actions, i.e. connect to the router remotely

We run the command line from any LAN computer, using the **Command Prompt** application, available on the computer's desktop. After starting the command line, type **telnet 20.0.0.1** (where the IP address is the address of the router interface). After a while, we get a connection to the router, we authorize ourselves according to the configured passwords. We can go into global configuration mode and start managing the router remotely.

```
C:\>telnet 20.0.0.1
Trying 20.0.0.1 ...Open
-------------------------------------------
!            WELCOME TO ITSTART           !
-------------------------------------------


Are You sure to login on the router ITSTART?

ITSTART>
```

Figure 8.103 Access to the router via Telnet protocol

It is also worth remembering that from the router itself you can also call a **TELNET** connection to another router. For this, we will now demonstrate a situation in which we log in from the computer to the intermediate router, and from it to the next router. An example of a topology is shown in the figure below. We assume that the **Internet Provider** router has been password protected with the password **'hardpassword'**.

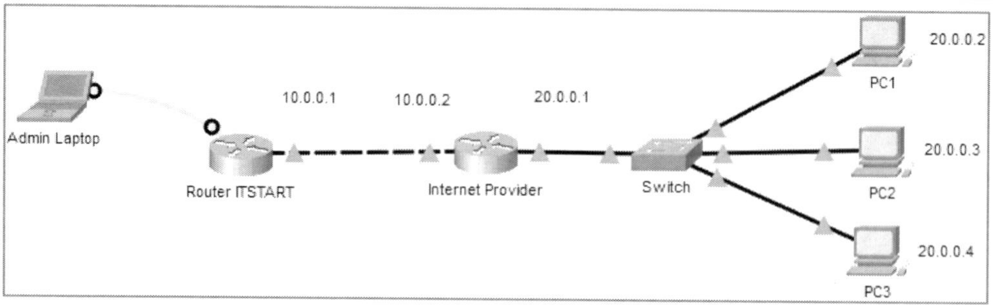

Figure 8.104 Topology to configure a telnet router from another router

First, we run the command line of any computer, and then connect to the **Internet Provider** router by executing **telnet 20.0.0.1**, and entering the **hardpassword** password. After correct authorization, we can execute the **telnet 10.0.0.1** command from user mode to connect to the ITSTART router. The whole procedure is shown in the figure below.

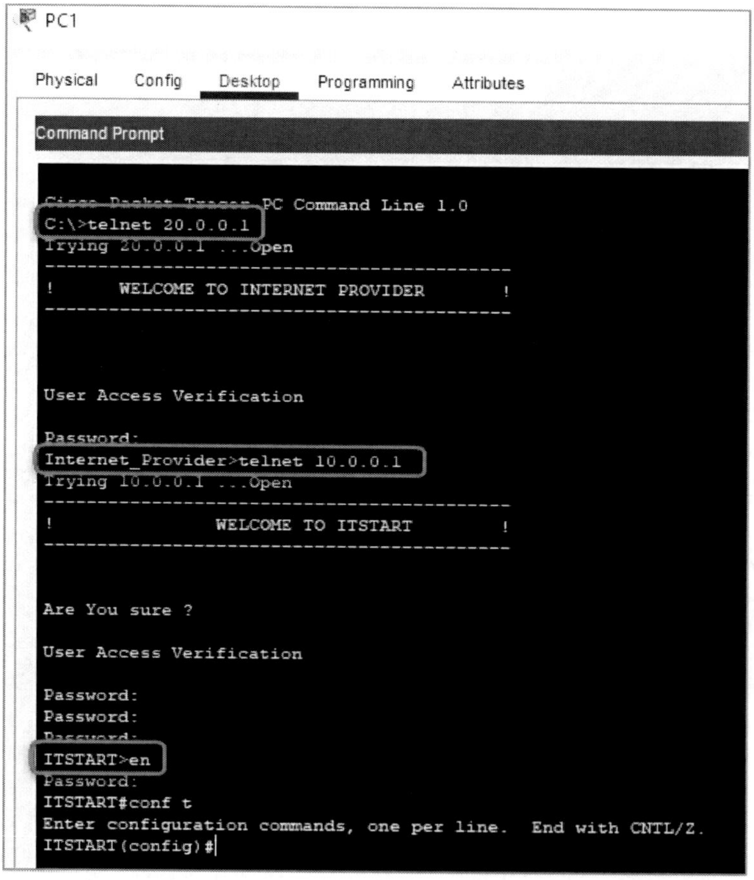

Figure 8.105 Indirect connection to the router via Telnet

Later in this section, you will describe the basic Telnet configuration of **SSH**. It is a much more secure cousin of the Telnet protocol. SSH uses only encrypted connections, and Telnet transmits all data as unencrypted.

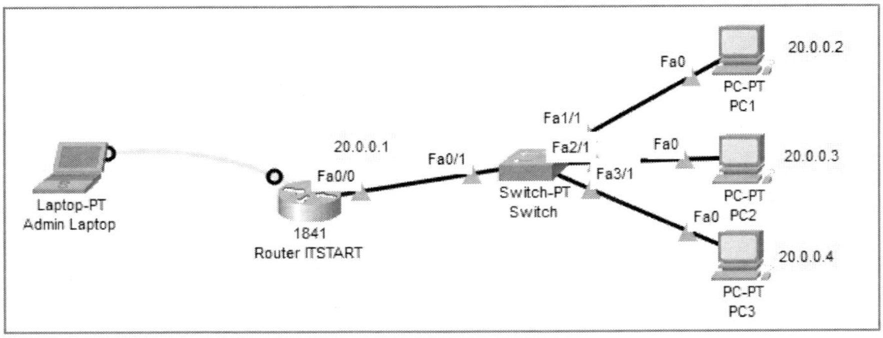

Figure 8.106 Topology for configuring SSH connections

To configure SSH access, on the router to which you want to have access, you must first create a user to whose account you will be able to log in. In our example, it will be **admin** with **admin**. Then we can choose on which channels we will connect the SSH protocol with the router (e.g. 5 and 6) and on them you need to specify two things: **login local** l or log in to the router you can only on the user created on this router and **transport input ssh** so that you can use the SSH protocol.

```
ITSTART(config)#username admin password admin
ITSTART(config)#line vty 5 6
ITSTART(config-line)#login local
ITSTART(config-line)#transport input ssh
ITSTART(config-line)#exit
ITSTART(config)#
```

Figure 8.107 Adaptation of the virtual terminal to SSH connections

The next step is to specify the domain name (**ip domain-name**) that is needed to identify the keys and generate this key pair, which will be used to encrypt the information sent between the user and the router. (details about connection encryption and network security are not included in the scope of the information described in this book.)

```
ITSTART(config)#ip domain-name itstart.com
ITSTART(config)#crypto key generate rsa general-keys modulus 1024
The name for the keys will be: ITSTART.itstart.com

% The key modulus size is 1024 bits
% Generating 1024 bit RSA keys, keys will be non-exportable...[OK]
*mar 1 1:38:56.459: %SSH-5-ENABLED: SSH 2 has been enabled
ITSTART(config)#
```

Figure 8.108 Domain name and RSA key generation

From this point on, you can connect to the router using an encrypted SSH connection. In order to connect to the router with the address 20.0.0.1 to the admin account, type the command **ssh -l admin 20.0.0.1**. in the **Command Prompt** command line. Successful connection and login to the router is shown in the figure below.

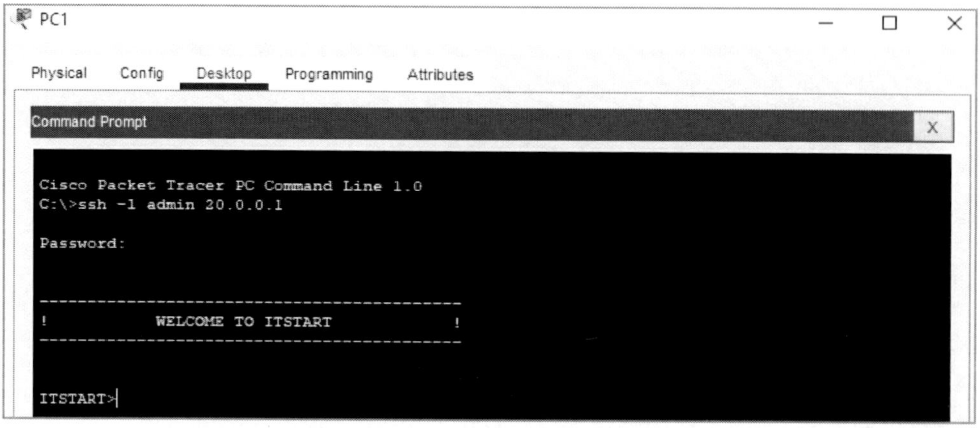

Figure 8.109 Successful SSH connection to router

8.3.5.3 Interface Configuration

One of the most important activities when setting up CISCO routers is the ability to prepare router interfaces for everyday work. Knowing the specifics of routers from the initial chapters of the book, we know that we can deal with interfaces: **Ethernet, Fast Ethernet, Gigabit Ethernet** (using copper or fiber optic media) or with serial interfaces. Let's start with the configuration of the **Ethernet** interface. For this purpose, we will connect the router with any computer with a **Fast Ethernet** interface in copper technology. A patch wire will be required for this type of connection.

After connecting the router to the computer with the appropriate cable, the topology should look as shown in the figure below. It is a good idea to determine the IP addressing in the topology at the beginning of the configuration.

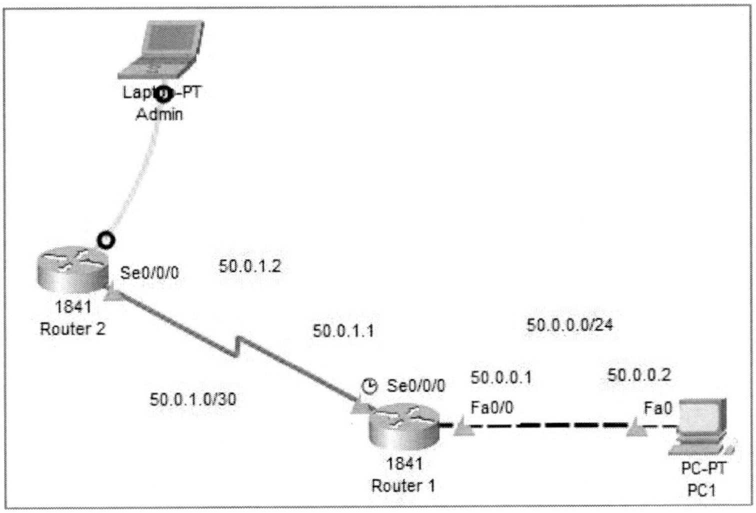

Figure 8.110 Topology for Configuring Fast Ethernet Interface

In the first place, we can set a static IP address on the computer, according to the figure above it will be 50.0.0.2/24. After performing the above action, the LEDs at the interfaces still remain red, because the connection is still not fully functional. To start connecting to the router, you must configure the interface on the router. The easiest way is to enable the **Always show port labels in Logical Workspace** option in Preferences to see which ports we have connected devices to.

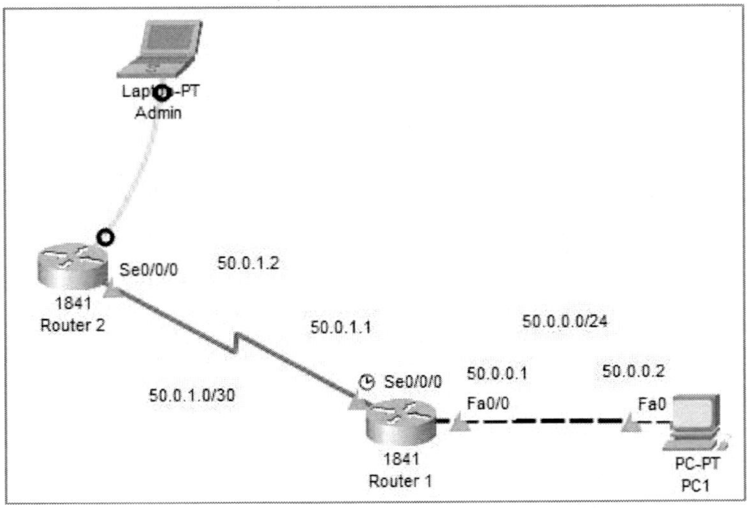

Figure 8.111 View of interface numbers in a logical topology

At this point, you can go to the IOS system of the router to make the necessary configuration changes. To do this, switch to **global configuration mode** to go from it to **Fast Ethernet** configuration mode.

```
ROUTER>en
ROUTER#conf t
Enter configuration commands, one per line.  End with CNTL/Z.
ROUTER(config)#interface ?
  Dialer             Dialer interface
  Dot11Radio         Dot11 interface
  Ethernet           IEEE 802.3
  FastEthernet       FastEthernet IEEE 802.3
  GigabitEthernet    GigabitEthernet IEEE 802.3z
  Loopback           Loopback interface
  Serial             Serial
  Tunnel             Tunnel interface
  Virtual-Template   Virtual Template interface
  Vlan               Catalyst Vlans
  range              interface range command
ROUTER(config)#interface fastethernet0/0
ROUTER(config-if)#?
  arp                 Set arp type (arpa, probe, snap) or timeout
  bandwidth           Set bandwidth informational parameter
  cdp                 CDP interface subcommands
  channel-group       Add this interface to an Etherchannel group
  crypto              Encryption/Decryption commands
  custom-queue-list   Assign a custom queue list to an interface
  delay               Specify interface throughput delay
  description         Interface specific description
  duplex              Configure duplex operation.
  exit                Exit from interface configuration mode
  fair-queue          Enable Fair Queuing on an Interface
  hold-queue          Set hold queue depth
  ip                  Interface Internet Protocol config commands
  ipv6                IPv6 interface subcommands
  lldp                LLDP interface subcommands
  mac-address         Manually set interface MAC address
```

Figure 8.112 Switch to interface configuration mode

Then you need to define the IP address, according to the previous assumptions, it will be **50.0.0.1/24**. To do this, type the command: ip address **50.0.0.1 255.255.255.0**, press **Enter** and in order to enable the network adapter, type ***:*** **no shutdown**. After a while, we notice that two messages are displayed on the screen:

```
%LINK-5-CHANGED: Interface FastEthernet0/0, changed
state to up.
%LINEPROTO-5-UPDOWN: Line protocol on Interface
FastEthernet0/0, changed state to up.
```

The messages mean that both the network adapter and the protocol itself have changed their state from "**down**" to "**up**", which means that the **Fast Ethernet** network adapter has been enabled and configured correctly.

```
ROUTER(config-if)#ip address 50.0.0.1 255.255.255.0
ROUTER(config-if)#no shutdown

ROUTER(config-if)#
%LINK-5-CHANGED: Interface FastEthernet0/0, changed state to up

%LINEPROTO-5-UPDOWN: Line protocol on Interface FastEthernet0/0, changed state to up

ROUTER(config-if)#
```

Figure 8.113 Address the interface and enable

As we can see in the diagram, the diodes lit up green and we are able to carry out the test with the PING command.

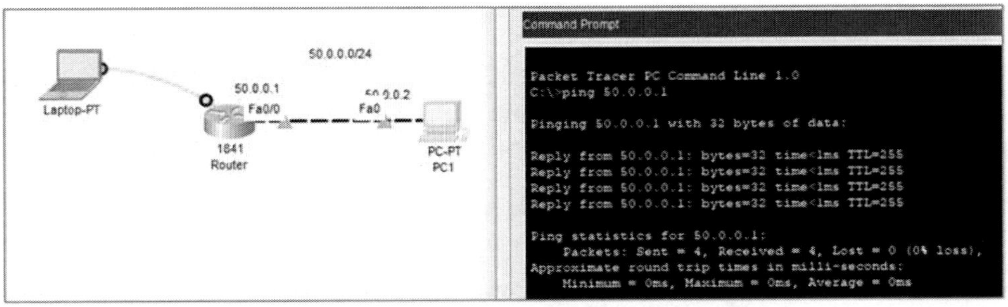

Figure 8.114 Correct configuration and PING test

You can also use the connection test on the other hand, which is to send ping from the router to the PC. To do this, enter privileged mode and type **ping 50.0.0.2**. As we note in the figure below, the packets have reached their destination 100%, however, the display of the PING response in IOS is slightly different than in the command line of the computer.

```
ROUTER#ping 50.0.0.2

Type escape sequence to abort.
Sending 5, 100-byte ICMP Echos to 50.0.0.2, timeout is 2 seconds:
!!!!!
Success rate is 100 percent (5/5), round-trip min/avg/max = 0/0/0 ms
```

Figure 8.115 PING command from router to computer

The configuration of the other Ethernet ports in CISCO routers is almost identical, so we will not discuss them in detail. The configuration of serial interfaces deserves a bit more attention, which we will present below.

Let's assume that we modernize our existing topology with another router (also in version 1841) which we connect to the second one via a serial cable. Note that none of the routers we have used has a suitable network card by default, which is why we need to install the appropriate equipment on their panels. First, turn off the devices, and then drag to the free slots one WIC-1T module for each device.

Figure 8.116 Serial module WIC-1T

Figure 8.117 Router 1841 with WIC-1T module installed

Then we select any of the wires: **Serial DCE**  or **Serial DTE** , after which we make a connection between the routers. An example of a topology is shown in the figure below.

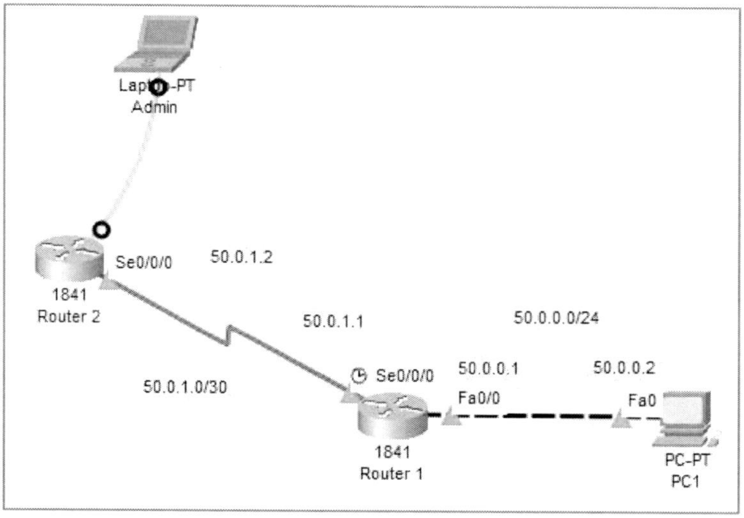

Figure 8.118 Topology for serial connection configuration

We can now proceed to the configuration. Differences in serial cabling can be noticed only in the fact that only with one device, there is a clock icon (in our case it is visible at the bottom router). Here it should be remembered that each serial cable has the same plugs on two sides, but marked in a different way: one of them is **DCE**, and the other **DTE**. The difference is that the router to which the **DCE** plug is connected will broadcast the so-called **Clock Rate**, and the second of them will adapt to this frequency. There will also be a small difference when configuring the DCE interface.

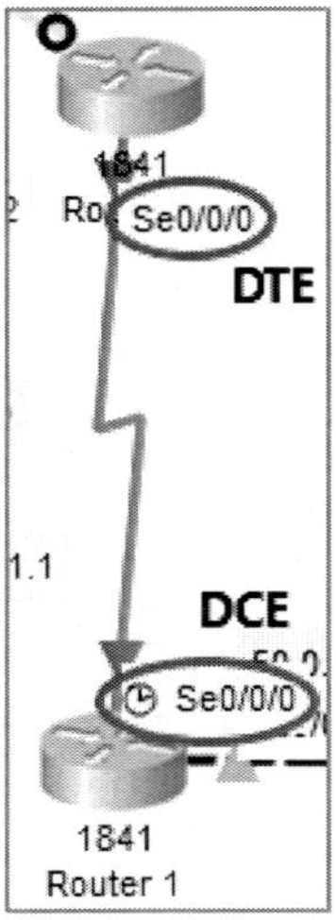

Figure 8.119 DTE and DCE serial interface

So, let's start with the configuration of the top router. After entering the **global configuration mode**, type the command: **interface serial 0/0/0** (to enter the serial **interface configuration mode**), then define its IP address and mask: ip address **ip address 50.0.1.2 255.255.255.252** and finally turn on the interface with the command: **no shutdown** (or using the abbreviation **no shut** as shown in the figure below).

However, we note that the interface has changed its state (it is still in the "**down**" state)

```
%LINK-5-CHANGED: Interface Serial0/0, changed state to down.
```

Only after configuring the serial interface in the second router will it change its state to "**up**". The last action that we have to do, but only on the router to which the **DCE** plug is inserted, is to set the previously mentioned **Clock Rate** parameter. For example, we will enter `clock rate 1000000`, which will be equivalent to a speed of 1 Mbps.

```
Router_2(config)#int se0/0/0
Router_2(config-if)#ip address 50.0.1.2 255.255.255.252
Router_2(config-if)#no shut

%LINK-5-CHANGED: Interface Serial0/0/0, changed state to down
Router_2(config-if)#
```

```
Router_1(config)#int se0/0/0
Router_1(config-if)#ip address 50.0.1.1 255.255.255.252
Router_1(config-if)#no shutdown

Router_1(config-if)#
%LINK-5-CHANGED: Interface Serial0/0/0, changed state to up

Router_1(config-if)#clock rate 1000000
Router_1(config-if)#exit
```

Figure 8.120 Configuration of serial interfaces

To check the correctness, we execute the **PING** command, for example from the top router to the bottom router. If the test passes correctly, it means that the configuration went without reservations.

```
Router_2#ping 50.0.1.1

Type escape sequence to abort.
Sending 5, 100-byte ICMP Echos to 50.0.1.1, timeout is 2 seconds:
!!!!!
Success rate is 100 percent (5/5), round-trip min/avg/max = 1/1/4 ms
```

Figure 8.121 PING command from top router to bottom router

When addressing routers, we must pay attention to one very important issue, namely remembering that on each interface of the router there is a different pool of IP addresses, or a different subnet, if a subnet is used. If we happen to have an error in such addressing of devices as shown in the figure below, then the router will display error messages in the configuration, which is shown in the next figure.

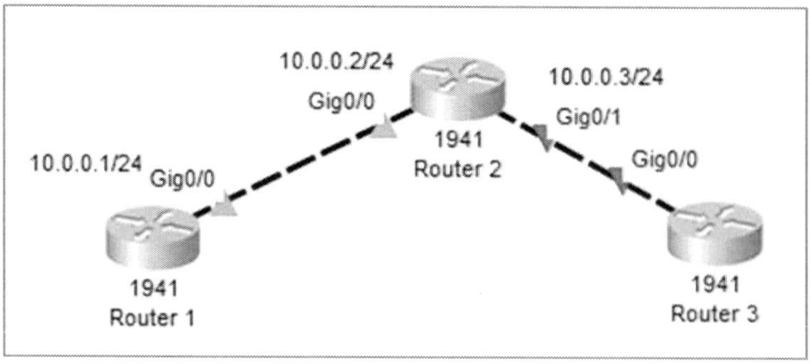

Figure 8.122 Logical topology with incorrect addressing

```
Router_2(config-if)#no shutdown
% 10.0.0.0 overlaps with GigabitEthernet0/0
GigabitEthernet0/1: incorrect IP address assignment
```

Figure 8.123 Consequences of poor addressing of interfaces

You have to reckon with the fact that sometimes the router will not display a message about the wrong addressing of the device and then the error is more complex because in the future with more complicated configurations it will be very difficult to find such a small error. Therefore, you need to be very careful when addressing devices.

8.3.5.4 Configuration of Sub-Interfaces

The use of so-called sub-interfaces is a feature of the CISCO device, which allows you to divide one physical interface into many logical (virtual) **sub-interfaces**. Sub-interfaces can be configured on CISCO routers in the same way as physical interfaces. This function is useful, for example, when configuring the so-called **router on a stick**. In this case, no IP address is configured on the physical interface. You only need to enable it, and set the IP addresses on the sub-interfaces as shown in the figure below.

```
Router(config)#int fa0/0
Router(config-if)#no shutdown

Router(config-if)#
%LINK-5-CHANGED: Interface FastEthernet0/0, changed state to up

Router(config-if)#exit
Router(config)#int fa0/0.10
Router(config-subif)#
%LINK-5-CHANGED: Interface FastEthernet0/0.10, changed state to up

Router(config-subif)#ip address 192.168.1.1 255.255.255.0

% Configuring IP routing on a LAN subinterface is only allowed if that
subinterface is already configured as part of an IEEE 802.10, IEEE 802.1Q,
or ISL vLAN.

Router(config-subif)#
```

Figure 8.124 Configure the sub-interface on the router

You switch to a sub-interface by using the command **interface <main interface>**.

In this example this is a command: **interface FastEthernet0/0.10** . When you enter the sub-interface configuration mode, the prompt changes to **Router(config-subif)#.**

However, when you try to address a sub-interface, you will receive a notification that the IP configuration is only available if you configure the sub-interface as part of the

IEEE802.10, **IEEE802.1Q**, or **VLAN** protocol. Currently, nothing comes of it, but it will be explained when describing the configuration of the switches.

8.3.6 DHCP Configuration

DHCP configuration is also possible on the router and is described in this section. Let's build a simple topology consisting of two routers, one switch, and three computers.

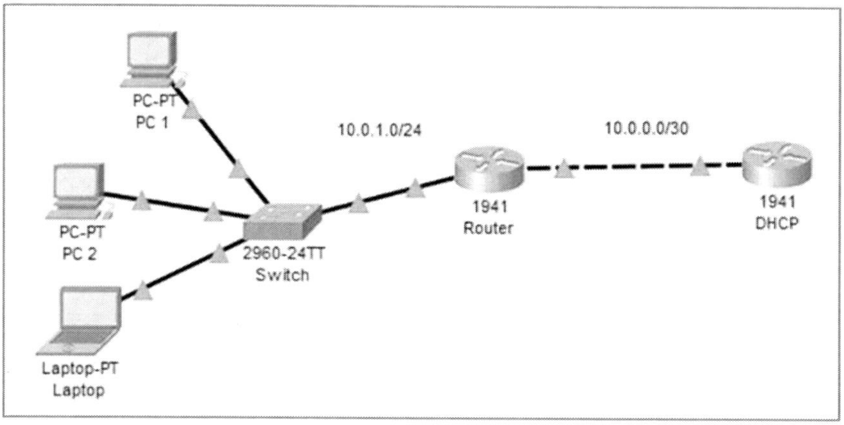

Figure 8.125 Topology for configuring DHCP on the router

In our example, we will configure the DHCP service on the **DHCP** router. We start by addressing the connection between the **Router** and **DHCP** devices. Next, let's address the second interface of the **Router** device, since this device will act as the default gateway for end users who retrieve IP addresses dynamically. Let's also use a simple command that will show the **DHCP** router where the 10.0.1.0 network is located. The **router** does not broadcast the networks to which it is connected, so the other router does not know anything about them. Routing protocols will be discussed later, but the **`ip route 10.0.1.0 255.255.255.0 gig0/0`** command, which defines a static route in the DHCP router, is needed to perform the task correctly.

```
DHCP(config)#ip route 10.0.1.0 255.255.255.0 gig0/0
```

Figure 8.126 Indication of the way to the network 10.0.1.0

The next step is to configure the address pool on the **DHCP** router that is available through the command shown below.

```
DHCP(config)#ip dhcp pool DHCP
DHCP(dhcp-config)#network 10.0.1.0 255.255.255.0
```

Figure 8.127 Define an address pool

The pool name is **DHCP** and the network whose addresses will be assigned dynamically is **10.0.1.0/24**. Now you need to specify the rest of the information for this DHCP pool, that is: default gateway, DNS server (optional, not applicable to this example, but we will show the command) and IP domain (also not applicable to this example, but we will show the command):

```
DHCP(dhcp-config)#default-router 10.0.1.1
DHCP(dhcp-config)#dns-server 10.0.1.254
DHCP(dhcp-config)#domain-name dhcp.com
```

Figure 8.128 Define the default gateway, DNS server, and domain

Now you need to configure IP addresses that should not be assigned automatically (e.g. to be reserved as statically reserved addresses for servers). In this command we provide a list of addresses (in our case it is a range from 10.0.1.10 to 10.0.1.20 inclusive):

```
DHCP(config)#ip dhcp excluded-address 10.0.1.10 10.0.1.20
```

Figure 8.129 Exclude addresses from the pool

If we now connected any device with a configured network adapter to dynamically receive an IP address, it would be assigned, provided that the router adapter is configured to the default gateway address of this pool. In this example, you notice that no end device is directly connected to the DHCP router that serves as the DHCP server. The **router** does not know what to do with it after receiving a **DHCP** query because it does not know where the DHCP server is located.

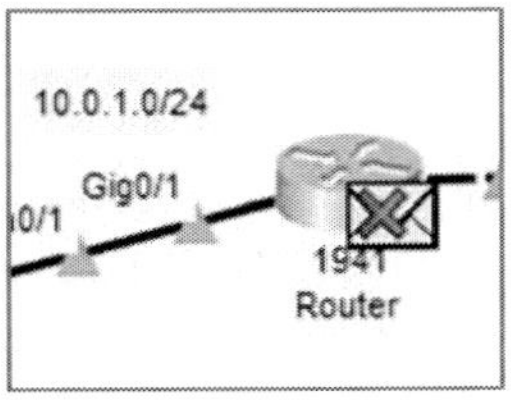

Figure 8.130 DHCP server information is missing

In order for the router to know where to send the **DHCP** query, a command indicating the address of the DHCP server should be configured on the interface where it receives DHCP queries.

```
Router(config)#int gig0/1
Router(config-if)#ip helper-address 10.0.0.2
```

Figure 8.131 Provide DHCP server information

From the **router**'s perspective, the **DHCP** server address is 10.0.0.2, which is why we provide this address. When we now try to ask for a dynamic IP address, the **router** will send this command further, i.e. to the address 10.0.0.2.

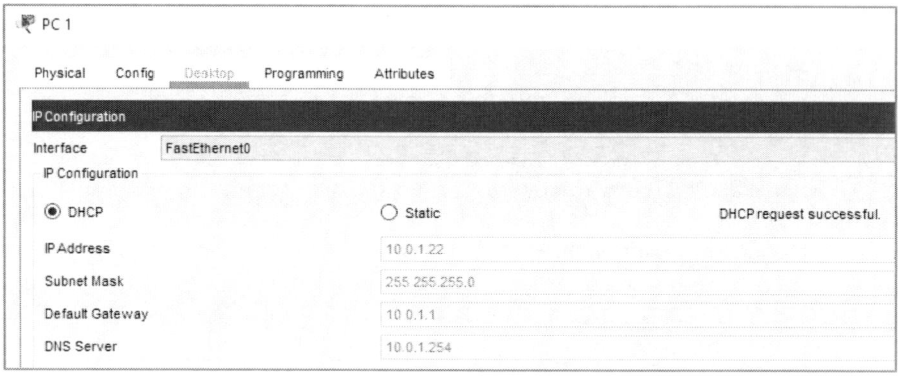

Figure 8.132 Positive result of a dynamic address query from the DHCP server

8.3.7 Static Routing Configuration

Static routing is a manual indication of the way to a different network on each router separately. Since this is not dynamic routing, if there is any change in the network, it will not be noted on any other router except the one on which the change occurred.

In this example, static routing will be configured manually and as in the case of configuration through the graphical interface it was possible to indicate only **Next hop** or the address of the next jump, so in this case you will be able to enter either **Next hop IP address** or the **output interface** from which the packets are to be routed.

An example of a static routing configuration will be discussed on the following topology, consisting of five routers through which PC1 and PC2 will send information to each other.

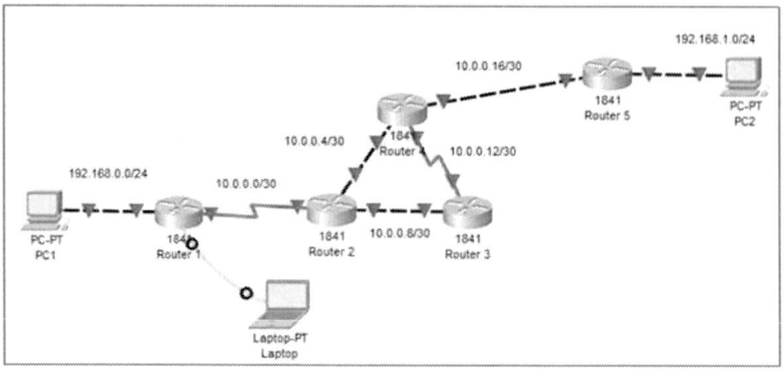

Figure 8.133 Topology for static routing configuration

In accordance with the assumptions and the topology designed by us, we will now configure the route with which the packets will be transmitted. Let's assume that network traffic starts from PC1 and leads along the shortest route, through routers: **Router1→Router2→Router4 → Router 5**, up to PC2. This route is marked in red in the figure below. Of course, before configuring static routing, we need to configure all interfaces, i.e. assign them IP addresses and enable them (or define the appropriate **Clock Rate** value). Static routing is configured in global configuration mode via the following command.

ip route [destination network address][target network mask][name of the output interface through which data or IP address of the intermediate router will be sent]

In the case of the way back (from PC2 to PC1) it will be the way through routers: **Router 5 → Router 4 → Router 3 → Router 2 → Router 1** as shown in the figure below in blue.

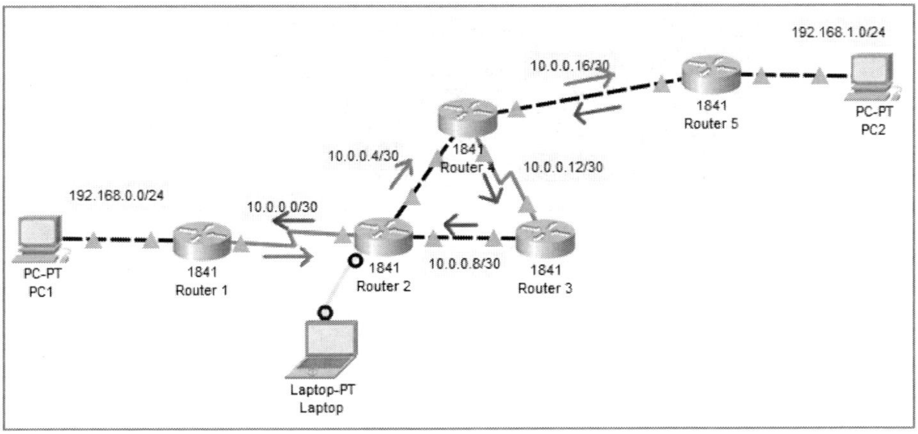

Figure 8.134 Direction of movement of packets

We start by configuring static routing on **Router1** and **Router2** as shown in the figures below.

```
Router_1(config)#ip route 192.168.1.0 255.255.255.0 se0/0/0
```

Figure 8.135 Static Routing Entry - Router 1

```
Router_2(config)#ip route 192.168.0.0 255.255.255.0 se0/0/0
Router_2(config)#ip route 192.168.1.0 255.255.255.0 fa0/1
```

Figure 8.136 Static Routing Entry - Router 2

```
Router_4(config)#ip route 192.168.0.0 255.255.255.0 se0/0/0
Router_4(config)#ip route 192.168.1.0 255.255.255.0 fa0/1
```

Figure 8.137 Static Routing Entry - Router 4

```
Router_5(config)#ip route 192.168.0.0 255.255.255.0 fa0/0
```

Figure 8.138 Static Routing Entry - Router 5

We do not need to configure two entries on **Router1** and **Router5**, because these routers know where their local networks are located. After PING checking the communication between computers, we should see on the simulation where the packets are going.

```
Command Prompt

Packet Tracer PC Command Line 1.0
C:\>ping 192.168.0.2

Pinging 192.168.0.2 with 32 bytes of data:

Reply from 192.168.0.2: bytes=32 time=1ms TTL=124
Reply from 192.168.0.2: bytes=32 time=5ms TTL=124
Reply from 192.168.0.2: bytes=32 time=12ms TTL=124
Reply from 192.168.0.2: bytes=32 time=13ms TTL=124

Ping statistics for 192.168.0.2:
    Packets: Sent = 4, Received = 4, Lost = 0 (0% loss),
Approximate round trip times in milli-seconds:
    Minimum = 1ms, Maximum = 13ms, Average = 7ms

C:\>
```

Figure 8.139 Positive PING from PC2 to PC1

Event List

Vis.	Time(sec)	Last Device	At Device	Type
	0.000	--	PC2	ICMP
	0.001	PC2	Router 5	ICMP
	0.002	Router 5	Router 4	ICMP
	0.003	Router 4	Router 3	ICMP
	0.004	Router 3	Router 2	ICMP
	0.005	Router 2	Router 1	ICMP
	0.006	Router 1	PC1	ICMP
	0.007	PC1	Router 1	ICMP
	0.008	Router 1	Router 2	ICMP
	0.009	Router 2	Router 4	ICMP
	0.010	Router 4	Router 5	ICMP
	0.011	Router 5	PC2	ICMP

Figure 8.140 The route of the packages

As we can conclude from the packet run, the configuration agrees with our assumption and in this way we have configured static routing. However, static routing is not the best idea for implementing network configuration, because it requires a very large amount of work from the network administrator and does not adapt to changes in the network and is prone to administrator errors. Dynamic routing protocols, on the other hand, when properly selected and configured, are characterized by greater flexibility.

In addition, one important piece of information. It is worth having one static entry on the router, which is called the default route or literally referred to as a phrase translated from English (**Gateway of last resort**). It is used when the packet does not find the destination network in the routing table.

```
Router_1(config)#ip route 0.0.0.0 0.0.0.0 se0/0/0
Router_1(config)#exit
Router_1#
%SYS-5-CONFIG_I: Configured from console by console

Router_1#show ip route
Codes: C - connected, S - static, I - IGRP, R - RIP, M - mobile, B - BGP
       D - EIGRP, EX - EIGRP external, O - OSPF, IA - OSPF inter area
       N1 - OSPF NSSA external type 1, N2 - OSPF NSSA external type 2
       E1 - OSPF external type 1, E2 - OSPF external type 2, E - EGP
       i - IS-IS, L1 - IS-IS level-1, L2 - IS-IS level-2, ia - IS-IS inter area
       * - candidate default, U - per-user static route, o - ODR
       P - periodic downloaded static route

Gateway of last resort is 0.0.0.0 to network 0.0.0.0

     10.0.0.0/30 is subnetted, 1 subnets
C       10.0.0.0 is directly connected, Serial0/0/0
C    192.168.0.0/24 is directly connected, FastEthernet0/0
S    192.168.1.0/24 is directly connected, Serial0/0/0
S*   0.0.0.0/0 is directly connected, Serial0/0/0
```

Figure 8.141 Gate of last chance - static entry

The last chance gateway determines to which interface or IP address (depending on which entry we make) all packets whose target network is not in the routing table entries of a given router will be directed. To execute this entry, use the command:

`ip route 0.0.0.0 0.0.0.0 <interface number>` or **`<IP address>`**

8.3.8 RIP Routing Protocol Configuration

The configuration of the interfaces on the routers alone is not enough for them to be able to transmit information from one network to another, for this purpose it will be necessary to configure one of the routing protocols. In our case, we will get to know the simplest one, i.e. RIP, and then EIGRP and OSPF. The following figure shows the topology that you will need to learn how to configure a routing protocol.

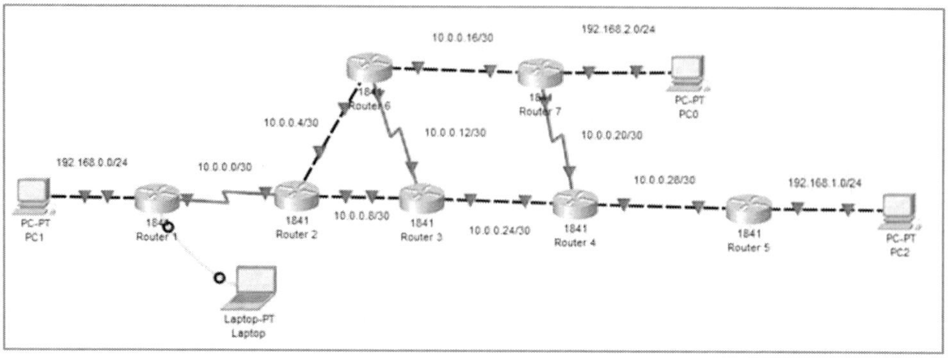

Figure 8.142 Topology for RIP routing protocol configuration

After completing the topology, you can proceed to configure the IP addresses of the router interfaces. After configuring IP addressing and enabling all interfaces, the LEDs should light up green, however, the network still does not work. To do this, we must inform each router about the network addresses bordering it. Each router borders three different networks, for example, **Router2** with networks: **10.0.0.0; 30.0.0.0**; and **40.0.0.0.**

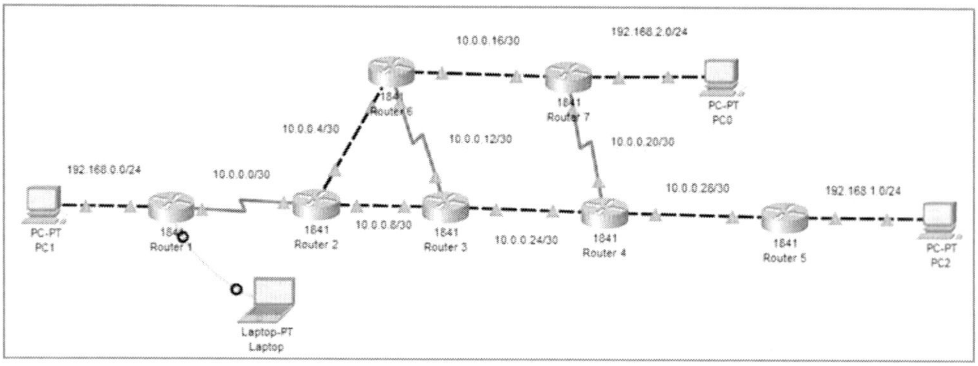

Figure 8.143 Initial configuration of interfaces before implementing RIP

To access the protocol configuration, from the global configuration, go to the RIP configuration level using the **RIP router** command, as shown in the figure below.

The first **version 2** command is a command that was not available in the GUI and that activates the second version of **RIP**. The difference between the first and second versions is that the first version only takes into account class addresses and could not be used in the above topology due to the fact that we have created different networks there that have non-class addresses and the router could not broadcast these individual networks. For example, Router 2, instead of broadcasting three networks: **10.0.0.0, 10.0.0.4** and **10.0.0.8**, would broadcast only one network: **10.0.0.0**, which would not allow the network to work properly. Therefore, it is recommended that you always use the second version of the RIP routing protocol (each subsequent newer version of the routing protocol already automatically distinguishes between network addresses).

The next **no auto-summary** command is a command that does not allow the router to sum up networks and broadcast rasterized networks. An example would also be Router 2, which instead of broadcasting networks **10.0.0.0, 10.0.0.4** and **10.0.0.8** would only announce that a **10.0.0.0** network is available through its interfaces. Further commands are already known and they apply to neighboring networks.

```
Router_1(config)#router rip
Router_1(config-router)#version 2
Router_1(config-router)#no auto-summary
Router_1(config-router)#network 192.168.0.0
Router_1(config-router)#network 10.0.0.0
Router_1(config-router)#exit
```

Figure 8.144 RIP Configuration - Router 1

```
Router_2(config)#router rip
Router_2(config-router)#version 2
Router_2(config-router)#no auto-summary
Router_2(config-router)#network 10.0.0.0
Router_2(config-router)#network 10.0.0.4
Router_2(config-router)#network 10.0.0.8
Router_2(config-router)#exit
```

Figure 8.145 RIP Configuration - Router 2

Similarly, we configure the remaining routers and after some time (you have to wait a while so that the routers have time to broadcast their networks) and check, for example, on **Router 4** what its routing table looks like.

```
Router_4#sh ip route
Codes: C - connected, S - static, I - IGRP, R - RIP, M - mobile, B - BGP
       D - EIGRP, EX - EIGRP external, O - OSPF, IA - OSPF inter area
       N1 - OSPF NSSA external type 1, N2 - OSPF NSSA external type 2
       E1 - OSPF external type 1, E2 - OSPF external type 2, E - EGP
       i - IS-IS, L1 - IS-IS level-1, L2 - IS-IS level-2, ia - IS-IS inter area
       * - candidate default, U - per-user static route, o - ODR
       P - periodic downloaded static route

Gateway of last resort is not set

     10.0.0.0/30 is subnetted, 8 subnets
R       10.0.0.0 [120/2] via 10.0.0.25, 00:00:04, FastEthernet0/0
R       10.0.0.4 [120/2] via 10.0.0.25, 00:00:04, FastEthernet0/0
R       10.0.0.8 [120/1] via 10.0.0.25, 00:00:04, FastEthernet0/0
R       10.0.0.12 [120/1] via 10.0.0.25, 00:00:04, FastEthernet0/0
R       10.0.0.16 [120/1] via 10.0.0.22, 00:00:17, Serial0/0/0
C       10.0.0.20 is directly connected, Serial0/0/0
C       10.0.0.24 is directly connected, FastEthernet0/0
C       10.0.0.28 is directly connected, FastEthernet0/1
R    192.168.0.0/24 [120/3] via 10.0.0.25, 00:00:04, FastEthernet0/0
R    192.168.1.0/24 [120/1] via 10.0.0.30, 00:00:28, FastEthernet0/1
R    192.168.2.0/24 [120/1] via 10.0.0.22, 00:00:17, Serial0/0/0
```

Figure 8.146 Routing Table - Router 2

All networks have been properly advertised and we can find a way to each network in our topology. Let's check which way the packets will travel between computers.

Event List

Vis.	Time(sec)	Last Device	At Device	Type
	0.000	--	PC1	ICMP
	0.001	PC1	Router 1	ICMP
	0.002	Router 1	Router 2	ICMP
	0.003	Router 2	Router 6	ICMP
	0.004	Router 6	Router 7	ICMP
	0.005	Router 7	PC0	ICMP
	0.006	PC0	Router 7	ICMP
	0.007	Router 7	Router 6	ICMP
	0.008	Router 6	Router 2	ICMP
	0.009	Router 2	Router 1	ICMP
	0.010	Router 1	PC1	ICMP

Figure 8.147 RIP - route from PC1 to PC0

Event List

Vis.	Time(sec)	Last Device	At Device	Type
	0.000	--	PC1	ICMP
	0.001	PC1	Router 1	ICMP
	0.002	Router 1	Router 2	ICMP
	0.003	Router 2	Router 3	ICMP
	0.004	Router 3	Router 4	ICMP
	0.005	Router 4	Router 5	ICMP
	0.006	Router 5	PC2	ICMP
	0.007	PC2	Router 5	ICMP
	0.008	Router 5	Router 4	ICMP
	0.009	Router 4	Router 3	ICMP
	0.010	Router 3	Router 2	ICMP
	0.011	Router 2	Router 1	ICMP
	0.012	Router 1	PC1	ICMP

Figure 8.148 RIP - RIP - route from PC1 to PC2

The RIP protocol works as it should - it chooses the route with the least number of jumps to the destination

8.3.9 EIGRP Routing Protocol Configuration

The second dynamic routing protocol is **EIGRP (Enhanced Interior Gateway Routing Protocol)** is a Cisco-designed, enhanced version of IGRP. This is the first routing protocol that works according to the link state, and not as in the case of RIP - using a distance vector. The difference is that EIGRP takes cost into account from source to goal – it has a more complicated metric. The most important thing you need to know now is that the metric consists of the bandwidth of links along the way and the delay that will be imposed on the packets. The advantage of this protocol is that EIGRP does not send periodic updates. Instead, it refreshes neighborhood relationships with nearby routers by sending small packets and sends partial updates when it detects changes in the network topology. Therefore, it consumes far less time and bandwidth than distance vector (RIP) protocols. The topology used to configure EIGRP will be similar to the previous one, but in this case we will increase the bandwidth of serial links (4Mbps).

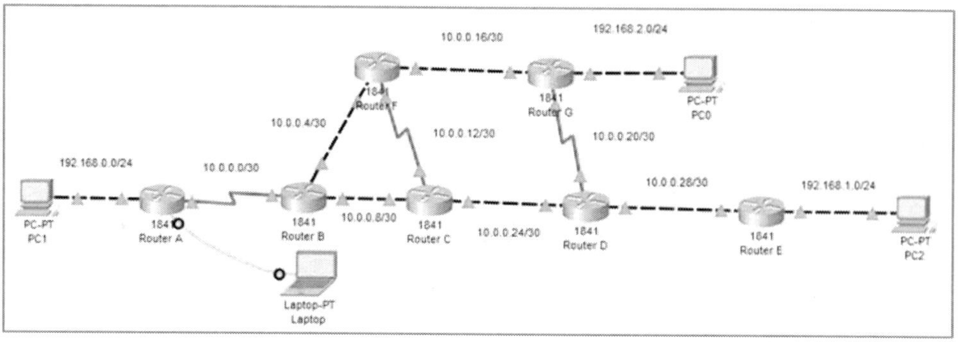

Figure 8.149 Topology for EIGRP routing protocol configuration

We start EIGRP protocol configurations in a similar way (provided that we have already addressed all interfaces) using the **`router eigrp <AS>`**, command, where we enter the autonomous system number instead. An autonomous system is a collection of devices that are under common administrative control, in which a consistent routing scheme is maintained. This protocol provides for the creation of from **1** to **65535** different autonomous systems connected to each other. In the example, it will be an autonomous system 1.

```
Router_A(config)#router eigrp 1
Router_A(config-router)#
```

Figure 8.150 Entry into EIGRP 1 configuration mode

In the case of EIGRP, we do not choose any version of this protocol, but we can immediately enter networks adjacent to the router. After specifying the network address, specify the inverted network mask as shown in the figure below.

```
Router_A(config)#router eigrp 1
Router_A(config-router)#network 192.168.0.0 0.0.0.255
Router_A(config-router)#network 10.0.0.0 0.0.0.3
Router_A(config-router)#no auto-summary
Router_A(config-router)#exit
```

Figure 8.151 Configuring EIGRP 1 on Router A

An additional command that can be used is **no auto-summary**, which we discussed earlier and it is worth using them so that no misunderstandings happen.

```
Router_B(config)#router eigrp 1
Router_B(config-router)#network 10.0.0.0 0.0.0.3
Router_B(config-router)#
%DUAL-5-NBRCHANGE: IP-EIGRP 1: Neighbor 10.0.0.1 (Serial0/0/0) is up: new adjacency

Router_B(config-router)#network 10.0.0.4 0.0.0.3
Router_B(config-router)#network 10.0.0.8 0.0.0.3
Router_B(config-router)#no auto-summary
```

Figure 8.152 Configuring EIGRP1 on Router B

After configuring the neighbouring router to the one we configured at the very beginning, we will get a notification **Neighbor 10.0.0.1 is up: new adjacency**. This is a message that the EIGRP on both routers has been properly configured and they could set up a connection with each other - exchange information about routes. Similarly, let's configure the other routers and try to display the routing tables on Router C.

```
Router_C#sh ip ro
Codes: C - connected, S - static, I - IGRP, R - RIP, M - mobile, B - BGP
       D - EIGRP, EX - EIGRP external, O - OSPF, IA - OSPF inter area
       N1 - OSPF NSSA external type 1, N2 - OSPF NSSA external type 2
       E1 - OSPF external type 1, E2 - OSPF external type 2, E - EGP
       i - IS-IS, L1 - IS-IS level-1, L2 - IS-IS level-2, ia - IS-IS inter area
       * - candidate default, U - per-user static route, o - ODR
       P - periodic downloaded static route

Gateway of last resort is not set

     10.0.0.0/30 is subnetted, 8 subnets
D       10.0.0.0 [90/20514560] via 10.0.0.9, 00:09:10, FastEthernet0/0
D       10.0.0.4 [90/30720] via 10.0.0.9, 00:09:10, FastEthernet0/0
C       10.0.0.8 is directly connected, FastEthernet0/0
C       10.0.0.12 is directly connected, Serial0/0/0
D       10.0.0.16 [90/33280] via 10.0.0.9, 00:01:10, FastEthernet0/0
D       10.0.0.20 [90/20514560] via 10.0.0.26, 00:06:16, FastEthernet0/1
C       10.0.0.24 is directly connected, FastEthernet0/1
D       10.0.0.28 [90/30720] via 10.0.0.26, 00:06:14, FastEthernet0/1
D    192.168.0.0/24 [90/20517120] via 10.0.0.9, 00:09:10, FastEthernet0/0
D    192.168.1.0/24 [90/33280] via 10.0.0.26, 00:02:40, FastEthernet0/1
D    192.168.2.0/24 [90/35840] via 10.0.0.9, 00:01:10, FastEthernet0/0
```

Figure 8.153 Routing Table - Router C

We see that all routes have been well advertised and the router has calculated the fastest route to each network. In square brackets in red is marked an example of a metric that the router calculated for a given network - the smaller the better the route to the destination.

Let's run the connection test again. Let's start with the command **PING** from PC1 to PC0, and then from PC1 to PC2.

Event List

Vis.	Time(sec)	Last Device	At Device	Type
	0.000	--	PC1	ICMP
	0.001	PC1	Router A	ICMP
	0.002	Router A	Router B	ICMP
	0.003	Router B	Router F	ICMP
	0.004	Router F	Router G	ICMP
	0.005	Router G	PC0	ICMP
	0.006	PC0	Router G	ICMP
	0.007	Router G	Router F	ICMP
	0.008	Router F	Router B	ICMP
	0.009	Router B	Router A	ICMP
	0.010	Router A	PC1	ICMP

Figure 8.154 PING from PC1 to PC0

Event List

Vis.	Time(sec)	Last Device	At Device	Type
	0.000	--	PC1	ICMP
	0.001	PC1	Router A	ICMP
	0.002	Router A	Router B	ICMP
	0.003	Router B	Router C	ICMP
	0.004	Router C	Router D	ICMP
	0.005	Router D	Router E	ICMP
	0.006	Router E	PC2	ICMP
	0.007	PC2	Router E	ICMP
	0.008	Router E	Router D	ICMP
	0.009	Router D	Router C	ICMP
	0.010	Router C	Router B	ICMP
	0.011	Router B	Router A	ICMP
	0.012	Router A	PC1	ICMP

Figure 8.155 PING from PC1 to PC2

8.3.10 OSPF Routing Protocol Configuration

OSPF (Open Shortest Path First) is the third and final dynamic routing protocol to be described. It is also a link state protocol, that is, it does not choose the path to the destination based on the smallest number of jumps but on the basis of complex mathematical calculations.

Routing using OSPF is based on autonomous systems (AS) in the same way as EIGRP, but with the difference that in the OSPF protocol autonomous systems are still divided into areas (so-called areas). The specificity of the OSPF algorithm and the amount of resources it consumes mean that the group should not have more than 50 routers in one area. In networks where there are regular link failures, frequent recalculations are necessary – in such networks small areas should

The maximum number of **AS** (i.e. the number of so-called **OSFP processes**) is 65535, and area numbers can be defined theoretically in the range from 0 to 4294967295.

We will start the configuration based on the same topology that you created in the previous section so that you can see the differences in the different routing protocols.

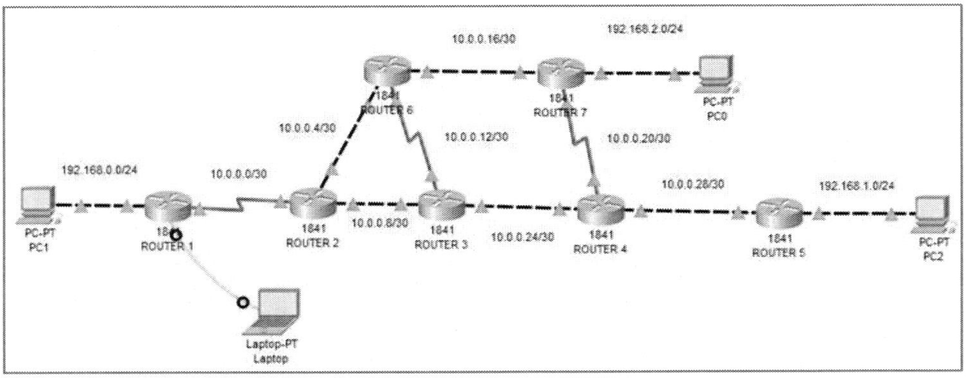

Figure 8.156 Topology for OSPF routing protocol configuration

After you configure IP addresses and interfaces, you must configure the routing protocol. Again, our autonomous **AS** system will be equal to **1**, and the area (which must be taken into account when entering neighbouring networks) will have the number **0**. In the case of **OSPF** configuration, it is worth giving each router its own **router-id** number, which facilitates communication between routers and building the OSPF database.

```
ROUTER_1(config)#router ospf 1
ROUTER_1(config-router)#router-id 1.1.1.1
ROUTER_1(config-router)#network 192.168.0.0 0.0.0.255 area 0
ROUTER_1(config-router)#network 10.0.0.0 0.0.0.3 area 0
ROUTER_1(config-router)#exit
```

Figure 8.157 Configuring OSPF1 - ROUTER 1

```
ROUTER_2(config)#router ospf 1
ROUTER_2(config-router)#router-id 2.2.2.2
ROUTER_2(config-router)#network 10.0.0.0 0.0.0.3 area 0
ROUTER_2(config-router)#network 10.0.0.4 0.0.0.3 area 0
ROUTER_2(config-router)#network 10.0.0.8 0.0.0.3 area 0
01:24:56: %OSPF-5-ADJCHG: Process 1, Nbr 1.1.1.1 on Serial0/0/0 from LOADING to FULL, Loading Done

ROUTER_2(config-router)#exit
```

Figure 8.158 Configuring OSPF1 - ROUTER 2

As in the case of EIGRP, OSPF displays a message stating that two routers have communicated with each other and replaced their routing tables and set up a connection, but in this case it is not the IP address of the neighbor router, but its **router-id.** After the analogous configuration of the rest of the network devices, we can go to the commands verifying the correctness of the configuration.

```
ROUTER_6#show ip ospf neighbor


Neighbor ID     Pri   State           Dead Time   Address         Interface
3.3.3.3           0   FULL/  -        00:00:39    10.0.0.13       Serial0/0/0
2.2.2.2           1   FULL/DR         00:00:30    10.0.0.5        FastEthernet0/0
7.7.7.7           1   FULL/BDR        00:00:37    10.0.0.18       FastEthernet0/1
```

Figure 8.159 Command `show ip ospf neighbor`

The command to verify the correctness of the configuration is **show ip ospf neighbor**, which shows us neighbouring routers that are also involved in broadcasting routes using the OSPF protocol. In the first column (**Neighbor ID**) there are IDs of routers that have been assigned by us (if we did not give it, the router would choose the **router-id**, which would usually be equal to the smallest IP address on its interfaces).

The third column (**State**) shows the current status of the neighbouring router. The inscription FULL means that the router has finished the initial communication, has exchanged networks and is ready to work. In the fourth column (**Dead Time**) there is a time left to exchange subsequent packets, which will be counted down every 1 second. If this time passes and these packets are not exchanged between the two neighbours, the connection will cease to exist and the routers will no longer be able to communicate with each other using **OSPF**. The last two items refer to the nearest IP addresses and interfaces from which adjacent routers are accessible.

```
ROUTER_6#sh ip route
Codes: C - connected, S - static, I - IGRP, R - RIP, M - mobile, B - BGP
       D - EIGRP, EX - EIGRP external, O - OSPF, IA - OSPF inter area
       N1 - OSPF NSSA external type 1, N2 - OSPF NSSA external type 2
       E1 - OSPF external type 1, E2 - OSPF external type 2, E - EGP
       i - IS-IS, L1 - IS-IS level-1, L2 - IS-IS level-2, ia - IS-IS inter area
       * - candidate default, U - per-user static route, o - ODR
       P - periodic downloaded static route

Gateway of last resort is not set

     10.0.0.0/30 is subnetted, 8 subnets
O       10.0.0.0 [110/65] via 10.0.0.5, 00:11:26, FastEthernet0/0
C       10.0.0.4 is directly connected, FastEthernet0/0
O       10.0.0.8 [110/2] via 10.0.0.5, 00:11:26, FastEthernet0/0
C       10.0.0.12 is directly connected, Serial0/0/0
C       10.0.0.16 is directly connected, FastEthernet0/1
O       10.0.0.20 [110/65] via 10.0.0.18, 00:10:39, FastEthernet0/1
O       10.0.0.24 [110/3] via 10.0.0.5, 00:11:26, FastEthernet0/0
O       10.0.0.28 [110/4] via 10.0.0.5, 00:11:04, FastEthernet0/0
O    192.168.0.0/24 [110/66] via 10.0.0.5, 00:11:26, FastEthernet0/0
O    192.168.1.0/24 [110/5] via 10.0.0.5, 00:11:04, FastEthernet0/0
O    192.168.2.0/24 [110/2] via 10.0.0.18, 00:10:39, FastEthernet0/1
```

Figure 8.160 Command `show ip route` - OSPF

The **show ip route** command displays the current routing table of the router. The designation for routes obtained through the OSPF protocol is the letter **O** placed in the first column. In square brackets, a pair of values [**administrative distance/metric**] is placed. The administrative distance for OSPF is always 110 as standard, while the metric is calculated using a special algorithm and its value depends on the current state of the entire network. You can now perform the test using the PING command from PC1 to PC0 and from PC1 to PC2.

Event List

Vis.	Time(sec)	Last Device	At Device	Type
	0.000	--	PC1	ICMP
	0.001	PC1	ROUTER 1	ICMP
	0.002	ROUTER 1	ROUTER 2	ICMP
	0.003	ROUTER 2	ROUTER 6	ICMP
	0.004	ROUTER 6	ROUTER 7	ICMP
	0.005	ROUTER 7	PC0	ICMP
	0.006	PC0	ROUTER 7	ICMP
	0.007	ROUTER 7	ROUTER 6	ICMP
	0.008	ROUTER 6	ROUTER 2	ICMP
	0.009	ROUTER 2	ROUTER 1	ICMP
	0.010	ROUTER 1	PC1	ICMP

Figure 8.161 PING from PC1 to PC0

Event List

Vis.	Time(sec)	Last Device	At Device	Type
	0.000	--	PC1	ICMP
	0.001	PC1	ROUTER 1	ICMP
	0.002	ROUTER 1	ROUTER 2	ICMP
	0.003	ROUTER 2	ROUTER 3	ICMP
	0.004	ROUTER 3	ROUTER 4	ICMP
	0.005	ROUTER 4	ROUTER 5	ICMP
	0.006	ROUTER 5	PC2	ICMP
	0.007	PC2	ROUTER 5	ICMP
	0.008	ROUTER 5	ROUTER 4	ICMP
	0.009	ROUTER 4	ROUTER 3	ICMP
	0.010	ROUTER 3	ROUTER 2	ICMP
	0.011	ROUTER 2	ROUTER 1	ICMP
	0.012	ROUTER 1	PC1	ICMP

Figure 8.162 PING from PC1 to PC2

Based on the test performed, the route chosen by the **OSPF** protocol is the route going from the source (PC1) to the destination (PC0), through routers: **ROUTER1, ROUTER2, ROUTER6, ROUTER7**, but if the network changes parameters such as link bitrate, overstatement or underestimation of the contractual cost of the link, then the route set by **OSPF** may be different.

Final remark. OSPF is widely used in WANs, but RIP is not. On the other hand, the RIP protocol, due to its limitations (the maximum number of jumps is 15, it heavily loads network resources and routers, and thus slows down the operation of the network) can be optionally used in very small local networks and most often, only for educational purposes (its advantage is the simplicity of configuration).

8.3.11 Local Definition of Router Names

When the network is working properly, i.e. the IP addresses of the devices have been properly configured and the routing protocol has been selected and configured, and all devices can communicate via IP addresses, we will describe how to introduce the possibility of communicating via names instead of IP addresses. Assumed that the devices are connected as follows, as shown in the figure below.

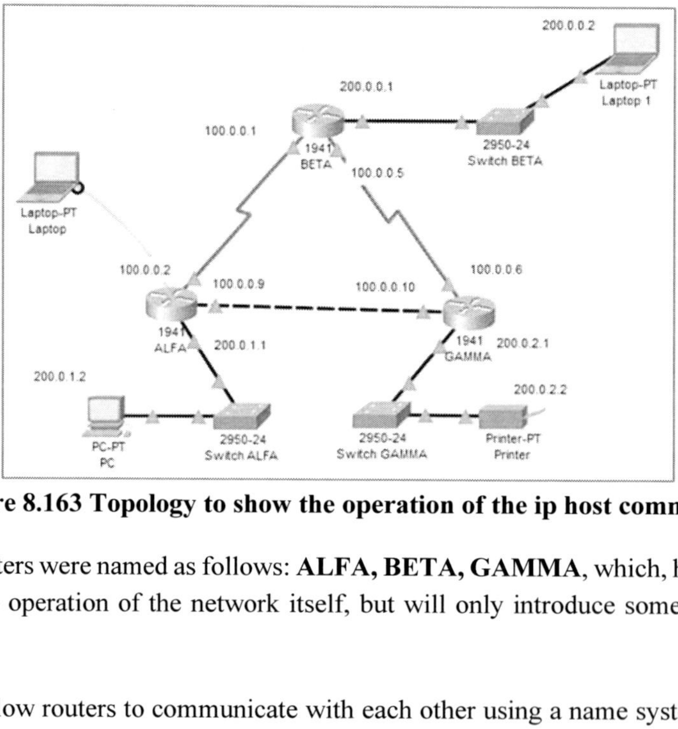

Figure 8.163 Topology to show the operation of the ip host command

The three routers were named as follows: **ALFA, BETA, GAMMA**, which, however, will not affect the operation of the network itself, but will only introduce some order in the topology.

In order to allow routers to communicate with each other using a name system, enter the names of the routers and all their IP addresses assigned to the interfaces into the configuration. You can not forget to enter this type of information also about neighbouring routers.

For each router, enter three configuration lines in global configuration mode, starting with the ***ip host*** command, then specifying its name and all IP addresses that are assigned to the router, as shown in the following drawings.

```
ALFA(config)#ip host ALFA 100.0.0.2 100.0.0.9 200.0.1.1
ALFA(config)#ip host GAMMA 100.0.0.6 100.0.0.10 200.0.2.1
ALFA(config)#ip host BETA 100.0.0.1 100.0.0.5 200.0.0.1
```

Figure 8.164 ALFA router configuration - ip host

```
BETA(config)#ip host ALFA 100.0.0.2 100.0.0.9 200.0.1.1
BETA(config)#ip host BETA 100.0.0.1 100.0.0.5 200.0.0.1
BETA(config)#ip host GAMMA 100.0.0.10 100.0.0.6 200.0.2.1
```

Figure 8.165 BETA router configuration - ip host

```
GAMMA(config)#ip host ALFA 100.0.0.2 100.0.0.9 200.0.1.1
GAMMA(config)#ip host GAMMA 100.0.0.10 100.0.0.6 200.0.2.1
GAMMA(config)#ip host BETA 100.0.0.1 100.0.0.5 200.0.0.1
```

Figure 8.166 GAMMA router configuration - ip host

In order to test the performed configuration, you need to PING the **ALFA** router to the **BETA** router (this should be done from the privileged mode), but instead of the IP address of the destination host, you must specify its name – in this case it will be: **ping BETA**. After a while, we will receive a response confirming the success of PING packet delivery, as shown in the figure below.

```
ALFA#ping BETA

Type escape sequence to abort.
Sending 5, 100-byte ICMP Echos to 100.0.0.1, timeout is 2 seconds:
!!!!!
Success rate is 100 percent (5/5), round-trip min/avg/max = 1/1/1 ms
```

Figure 8.167 Attempt to send PING from ALFA router to BETA router

In the event that the **IP HOST** configuration went incorrectly, then when you try to refer to the destination host by its name, you receive the following message, shown in the following figure.

```
ALFA#ping beta
Translating "beta"...domain server (255.255.255.255)
```

Figure 8.168 No response to the PING command using the host name

8.3.12 Save the Current Configuration

When working with hardware (real and simulated in the Cisco Packet Tracer), experience teaches us how easy it is to lose configurations that took us many minutes and sometimes many hours to create, all you need to do is turn off the power of the device, or other events such as hanging or failure of the Cisco Packet Tracer program. Therefore, at the beginning of each chapter there is a warning informing that during the performance of exercises or control tasks / project / periodically save the state of the file (keyboard shortcut **Ctrl + S**).

This section describes how you can protect your router configuration from accidental power off. By default, the configuration is saved in RAM, which is volatile memory. Therefore, it is worth remembering about the possibility of saving it in **NVRAM** (***non-volatile random-access memory***), which is a non-volatile memory.

Once the device is fully configured and has passed the necessary performance tests, we can proceed to save the configuration. For this purpose, we will use the topology, which is illustrated in the figure below.

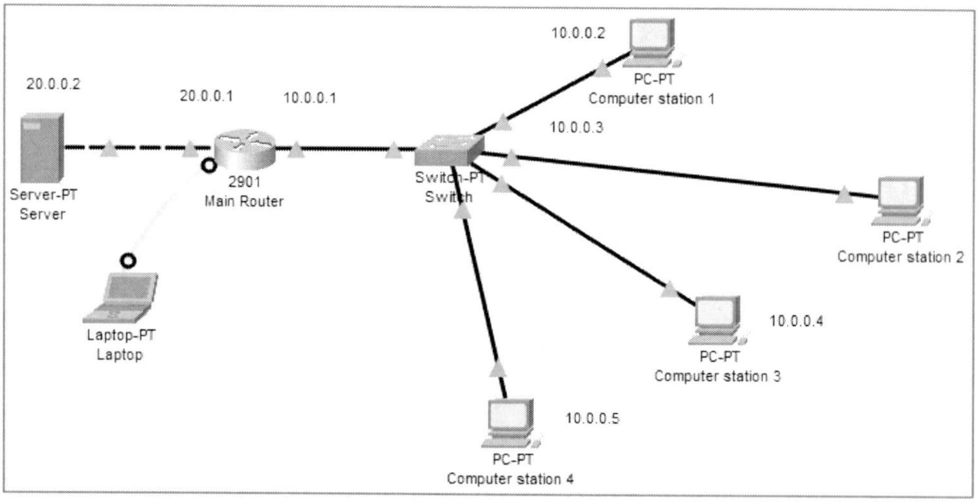

Figure 8.169 Sample topology showing how to save the current configuration

The contents of the current configuration are displayed through the command: **show running-config,** which must be typed in privileged mode. A fragment of the router configuration from the described topology is shown in the figure below.

```
Main_Router#sh run
Building configuration...

Current configuration : 684 bytes
!
version 15.1
no service timestamps log datetime msec
no service timestamps debug datetime msec
no service password-encryption
!
hostname Main_Router
!
!
!
enable secret 5 $1$mERr$hx5rVt7rPNoS4wqbXKX7m0
!
!
!
!
!
!
ip cef
no ipv6 cef
 --More--
```

Figure 8.170 Fragment running-config

This configuration is not saved permanently, it is valid as long as the device is turned on, i.e. until the power is turned off in the device. Therefore, the configuration should be stored in **NVRAM** non-volatile memory.

To check what has been saved in the **NVRAM** memory of the router, just run the command: **show startup-config** (also in privileged mode). When we have a router in which nothing has ever been saved in NVRAM before or its contents have been cleared, then the router will display a message:

```
Main_Router#show startup-config
startup-config is not present
Main_Router#
```

Figure 8.171 Effect of trying to display a non-existent config

If you want to copy the current configuration to the startup configuration, just execute the command (in privileged mode): **`copy running-config startup-config`**, after pressing the **Enter** key, you will be asked in which file it should be saved. By default, this is the **`startup-config`** file, which is confirmed again by pressing the **Enter** key. The following message will then be displayed:

```
Main_Router#copy running-config startup-config
Destination filename [startup-config]?
Building configuration...
[OK]
Main_Router#
```

Figure 8.172 Copy the current configuration to the startup configuration

Note for Advanced Cisco Packet Tracer Users.

In most routers, instead of the **`copy running-config startup-config`** command, you can use another command, e.g. **`write`** or shortcut **`w`**, but **this remark does not apply to real CISCO devices**. On the other hand, in multilayer switches or ASA devices, instead of the **`copy running-config startup-config`** command, you can use the **write memory** command or the shortcut ***`w m`***.. The above method allows you to significantly shorten the time of testing and performing device configuration.

After you copy the current configuration to the startup configuration, you can turn off the power to the router because the configuration has been properly secured. In the event that incorrect information has been saved in the startup configuration and it is required to delete it, you can delete the startup configuration at any time using the command: **`erase startup-config`**. After entering the command, it is required to confirm the decision using the **Enter** key.

```
Main_Router#erase startup-config
Erasing the nvram filesystem will remove all configuration files! Continue? [confirm]
[OK]
Erase of nvram: complete
%SYS-7-NV_BLOCK_INIT: Initialized the geometry of nvram
Main_Router#
```

Figure 8.173 Delete a startup configuration

8.3.13 Securing Your Configuration

Often, when working with CISCO devices, it happens that you need to test some new configuration or implement other settings. You do not need to perform many manual configurations, but you can use the configuration that we previously saved on the Trivial File Transfer Protocol (**TFTP**) server. **TFTP** is a simple protocol used to transfer files that cannot display directories or authenticate users, and its only purpose is to transfer files to or from a computer. TFTP is a simplified version of FTP service.

A TFTP transmission begins with a request to read or write a file, which also requests a connection. The file is sent in blocks from 0 to 512 bytes in length. A data packet of less than 512 bytes indicates the end of the transfer.

To illustrate this possibility, we will use the topology shown in the figure below.

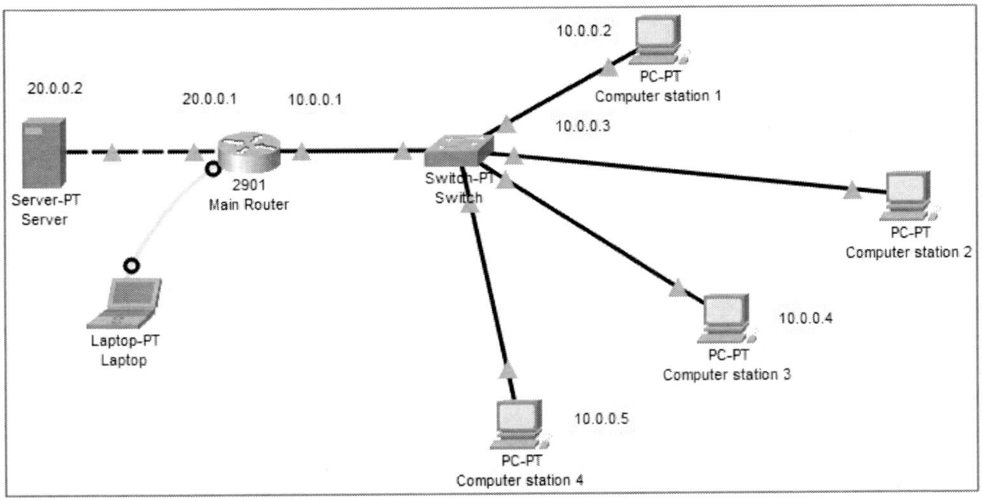

Figure 8.174 Topology for device configuration security

The **LAN (20.0.0.0)** that is connected to the router hosts a server on which you can configure the TFTP service, which will be used to store the router configuration.

To do this, go to the server, open the **Services** tab, and then enter the **TFTP** section. Due to the fact that the TFTP service is a simplified version of FTP, you do not need to configure anything here, you just need to make sure that it is attached, as shown in the figure below. In the **File** window, there are already files that are on the server, these are images of IOS systems that will not bother us. Therefore, after switching on the service, we can leave the server configuration and return to the router.

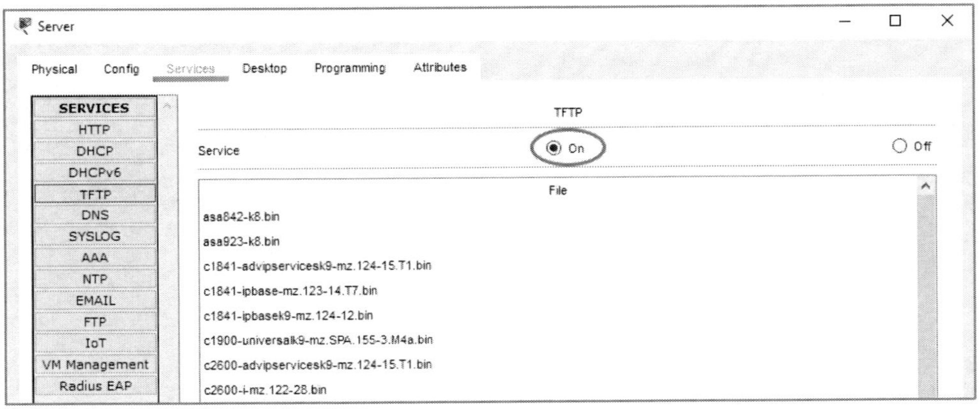

Figure 8.175 Configure the TFTP service on the server

Copying the configuration to the TFTP server is done in privileged mode using the **`copy running-config tftp`** command. After some time, you will be asked for the server address. This is the IP address of the TFTP server. In our case, it will be **`20.0.0.2`**. The next question concerns the name under which the file should be stored on the TFTP server. The router suggests the name **`Main_router-confg`**, if we agree to it, press **Enter** or type a new file name. After the configuration is saved correctly, you should see the message as in the figure below.

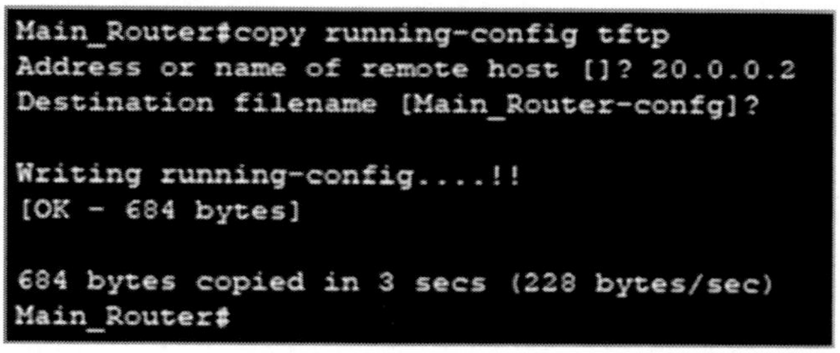

Figure 8.176 Successful attempt to copy the configuration to the server

You can check if the file with the saved configuration exists on the TFTP server.

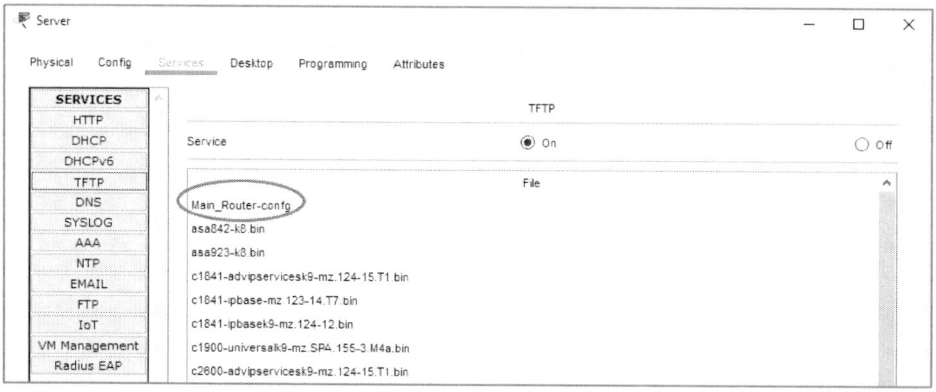

Figure 8.177 Copied file on TFTP server

How can i restore a saved configuration, i.e. copy it from the **TFTP** server to the startup configuration? To do this, execute the **`copy tftp startup-config`** command. You will be asked for the server address and file name to copy.

```
Main_Router#copy tftp startup-config
Address or name of remote host []? 20.0.0.2
Source filename []? Main_Router-confg
Destination filename [startup-config]?

Accessing tftp://20.0.0.2/Main_Router-confg...
Loading Main_Router-confg from 20.0.0.2: !
[OK - 684 bytes]

684 bytes copied in 0 secs
```

Figure 8.178 Steps to copy a configuration from a TFTP server to a startup configuration

CHAPTER 9

CONFIGURING CISCO SWITCHES

COMPUTER NETWORKS IN PACKET TRACER

FOR BEGINNERS

9 Configuring Cisco Switches

The chapter covers basic theoretical and practical knowledge of configuring simulated switches in the Cisco Packet Tracer.

Note – Warning: Remember to periodically save the file state during exercises (keyboard shortcut CTRL+S)

9.1 Exploring the Equipment of Cisco Switches

Another type of devices available in the program are **switches**. We have at our disposal three basic switches that are equivalent to real models from the **2950** to **2960** series, models called **PT-Switch** and **PT-Empty**, which can be modified in any way, as well as third layer switches **3560**, **3650** and **IE 2000**.

Figure 9.1 Switch models available in the Cisco Packet Tracer

Unlike routers, each of which had the ability to install optional modules, in the case of switches, only **PT** models allow the replacement of modules. Other devices do not allow you to change their equipment.

9.1.1 Switch 2950

The first switch we will discuss is the 2950 series switch. It is a manageable device dedicated to small and medium-sized networks. It has 24 Fast Ethernet interfaces with a bandwidth of 10/100 Mbps.

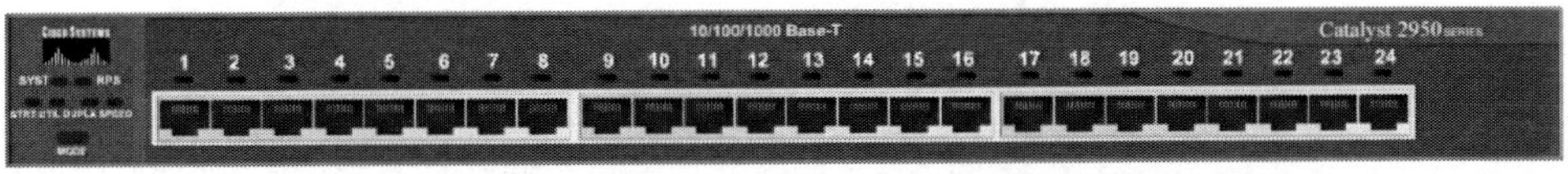

Figure 9.2 Physical appearance of the 2950 series switch

The 2950 Series Switch does not support any optional equipment.

9.1.2 Switch 2950T

Another switch available in the program is the 2950T series switch. This switch is a managed device dedicated to a medium-sized network. It has 24 Fast Ethernet interfaces with a bandwidth of 10/100 Mbps, as well as two Gigabit Ethernet interfaces with a bandwidth of 10/100/1000 Mbps.

Figure 9.3 Physical appearance of the 2950T series switch

The 2950T Series Switch does not support any optional equipment.

9.1.3 Switch 2960

Another switch available in the program is the 2960 series model. It is a manageable device dedicated to medium-sized networks. It has 24 Fast Ethernet interfaces with a bandwidth of 10/100 Mbps, as well as two Gigabit Ethernet interfaces with a bandwidth of 10/100/1000 Mbps similar to the switch version 2950.

Figure 9.4 Physical appearance of the 2960 series switch

The 2960 Series Switch does not support any optional equipment.

9.1.4 PT-Switch and PT-Empty Switch

The next switches available in the program are the two PT series switches, which are devices only found in the PT program, but allow you to create many different hardware configurations. They have ten slots, in the place of which we can mount the selected interface. When adding this switch to the topology, there are two versions to choose from: **PT-Switch** and **PT-Empty**. These switches also have power switches.

The first of them by default has four Fast Ethernet ports with a bandwidth of 10/100 Mbps, using twisted pair cables and two Fast Ethernet interfaces with a bandwidth of 10/100 Mbps in the fiber optic standard and two free slots. The second is a completely empty version, without mounted modules.

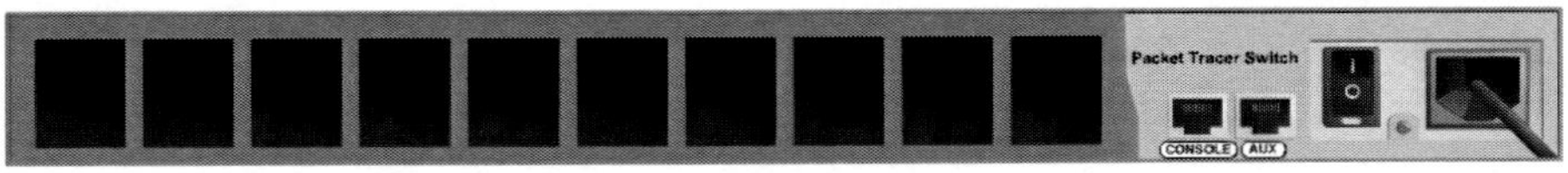

Figure 9.5 Physical appearance of the PT-Empty switch

In free slots we can install the following components:

MODULES
PT-SWITCH-NM-1CE
PT-SWITCH-NM-1CFE
PT-SWITCH-NM-1CGE
PT-SWITCH-NM-1FFE
PT-SWITCH-NM-1FGE
PT-SWITCH-NM-COVER

Figure 9.6 PT Switch Optional Equipment

Below is a detailed description of the individual components:

-  **PT-SWITCH-NM-1CE** - a single Ethernet port with a bandwidth of 10 Mbps,
-  **PT-SWITCH-NM-1CFE** - single Fast Ethernet port with a bandwidth of 10/100 Mbps,
-  **PT-SWITCH-NM-1CGE** - single Gigabit Ethernet port with 10/100/1000 Mbps bandwidth,
-  **PT-SWITCH-NM-1FFE** - single Fast Ethernet port with a bandwidth of 10/100 Mbps in the fiber optic standard,

-  **PT-SWITCH-NM-1FGE** - a single 10/100/1000 Mbps Gigabit Ethernet port in fiber optic standard.
-  **PT-SWITCH-NM-COVER** - module for protecting the inside of the switch

9.1.5 Series 3560

Another switch available in the program is the 3560 series switch. It is a so-called multi-layer switch, which means that it has wider possibilities compared to other switches, because it works not only in the second ISO / OSI layer, but also in the third layer (in the same as routers). It has 24 Fast Ethernet interfaces with a bandwidth of 10/100 Mbps, as well as two Gigabit Ethernet interfaces with a bandwidth of 10/100/1000 Mbps.

Figure 9.7 Physical appearance of the 3560 series switch

The 3560 Series Switch does not support any optional equipment.

9.1.6 Series IE 2000

The **IE 2000** (*Industrial Ethernet 2000 Series*) switch is an industrial switch that simulates a 2000 series switch model. The switch is running IOS **IE2000 Software (IE2000-UNIVERSALK9-M), version 15.2(1)EY**. The switch meets the requirements of industrial networks for speed of convergence and security.

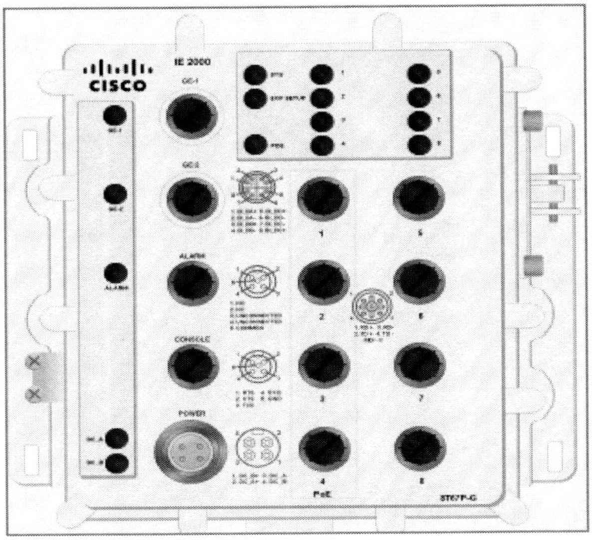

Figure 9.8 Physical appearance of the IE 2000 series switch

The switch has 8 Fast Ethernet interfaces and 2 Gigabit Ehternet interfaces. Supports Resilient Ethernet Protocol (**REP**).

9.2 Configure Cisco Switches Using the Graphical Interface

9.2.1 Interface Configuration

At the beginning we will create a simple topology consisting of four computers and one switch.

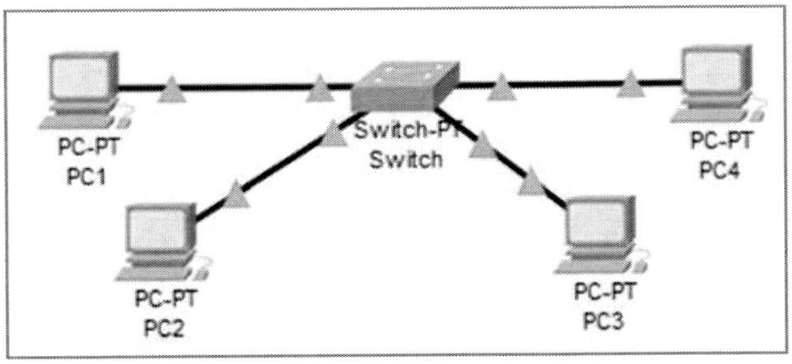

Figure 9.9 Topology for switch configuration

As we already know, when we address these computers now (for example, so that they are in the network 192.168.0.0/24), they will be able to communicate with each other without any problem as shown in the figure below – despite the fact that the configuration of the switch remained the default.

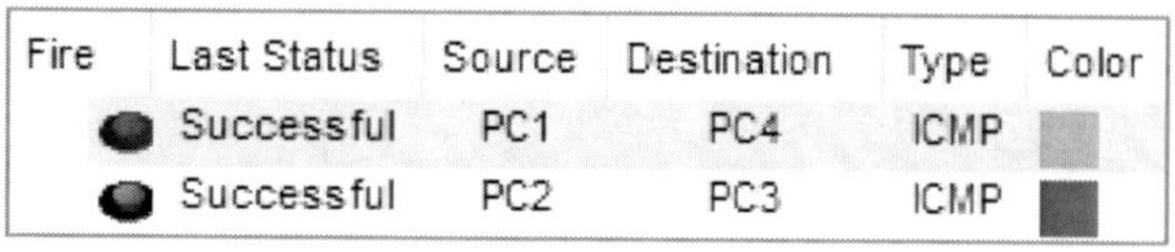

Fire	Last Status	Source	Destination	Type	Color
	Successful	PC1	PC4	ICMP	
	Successful	PC2	PC3	ICMP	

Figure 9.10 PING between devices

Now that we are sure that with the default configuration our network works seamlessly, we can go to the **Config** tab on the switch and see what options the configuration offers us using the GUI.

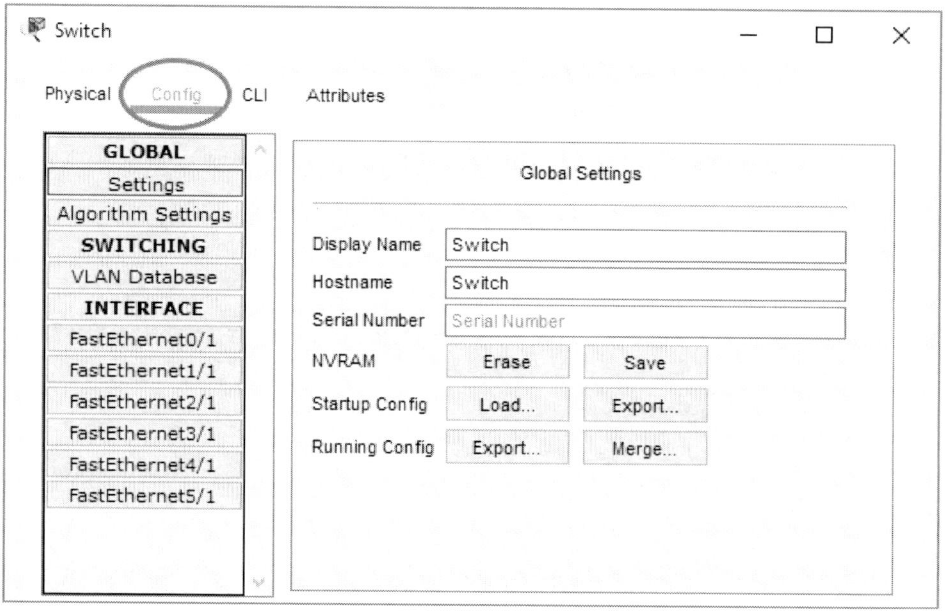

Figure 9.11 Switch Config tab

As you can see, we do not have too many options to choose from - configuration of basic settings such as the name of the switch or saving the current configuration, then there is **Algorithm Settings** - not the option we are interested in, **VLAN database** and configuration of the interfaces themselves. Let's take a look at the interface configuration at the beginning.

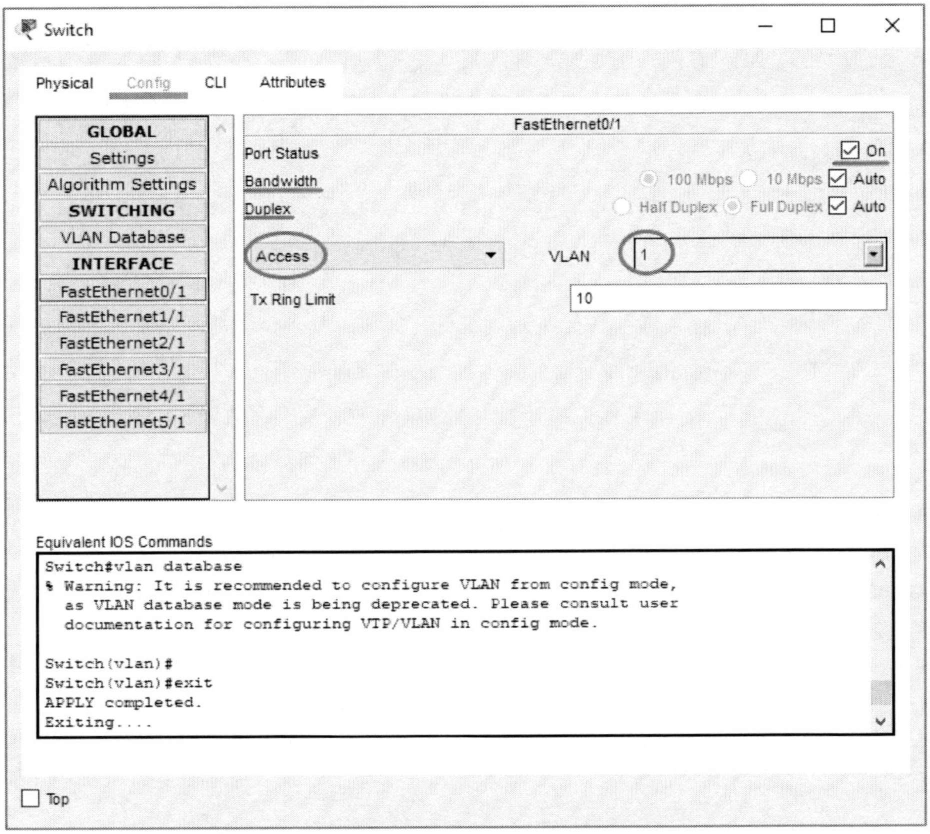

Figure 9.12 Switch Interface Configuration - GUI

We have at our disposal enabling / disabling the interface, with what bandwidth a given port works, what duplex it supports and what VLAN belongs to and in what mode the port is located (we have a choice of **Access** or **Trunk** mode, as in the figure below).

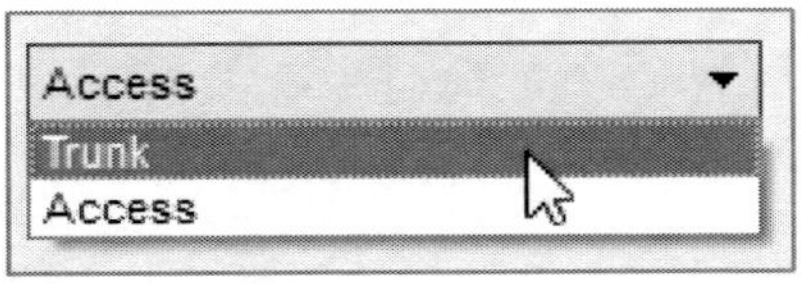

Figure 9.13 Selecting the port mode

The difference in the operation of these modes is described below:

- **Access** - if the port is in this mode, the switch usually accepts all untagged frames from this port and gives them a predefined tag - depends on which VLAN the port is located in. If data is to be sent to a port that is in this mode, the tag is removed. Most often, access mode is used on ports to which end users are attached, e.g. desktops, laptops, printers.

- **Trunk** - a port through which information from all VLANs can be sent by default. In this port pass frames that are tamed and usually ports of this type connect two switches, or a switch to the router.

Tagging frames involves adding an additional field (VLAN tag) containing the VLAN number to them. In this example, the ports work in the default Access mode.

9.2.2 Configuring Virtual LANs (VLANs)

What is a **VLAN** (Virtual LAN) and how do I configure it? This is one of the most useful functions of switches that we can configure, so it is worth getting to know this issue and mastering it as much as possible.

As the name suggests, these are LANs, but separated from each other virtually, not physically. For example – in a residential building we have many LANs, as a standard each apartment is a separate LAN, and in the case of VLANs we can virtually divide one apartment into smaller LANs that cannot communicate with each other without the participation of a router.

To illustrate the division of LANs into VLANs, we will use the same topology that was presented a moment ago, but we will divide it in the diagram into two separate VLANs: **VLAN10** and **VLAN20**.

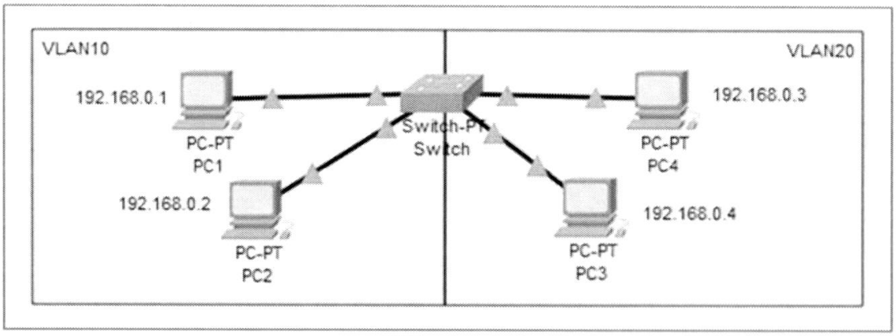

Figure 9.14 Topology for VLAN configuration (Example 9.2.2a.pkt)

Now you need to configure VLANs on the switch. In the **Config** tab, go to the **VLAN Database**. There we need to add two VLANs that interest us: number **10** and number **20** with the names **VLAN10** and **VLAN20**. respectively.

VLAN number 1 is the default VLAN and includes all ports before the switch is configured.

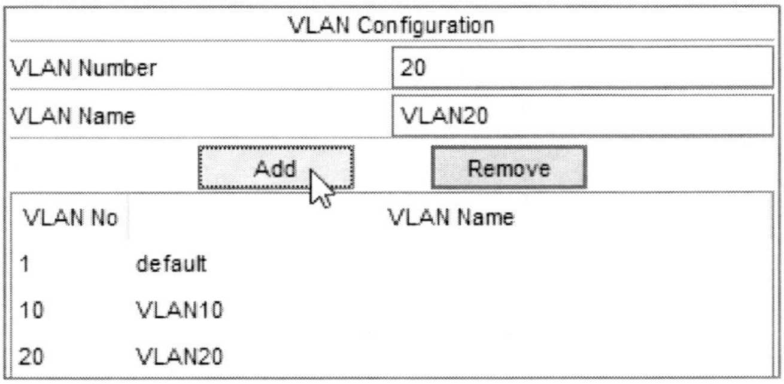

Figure 9.15 Adding new VLANs using the GUI

The next and last step is to configure the ports in such a way that they work in Access mode and belong to the appropriate VLANs.

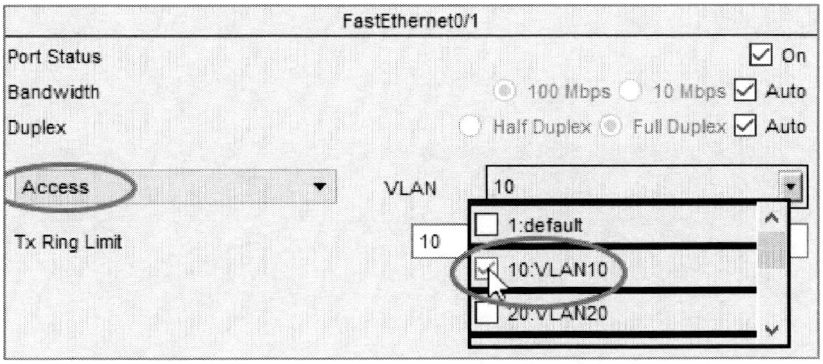

Figure 9.16 Assigning VLAN to the appropriate interface - VLAN10

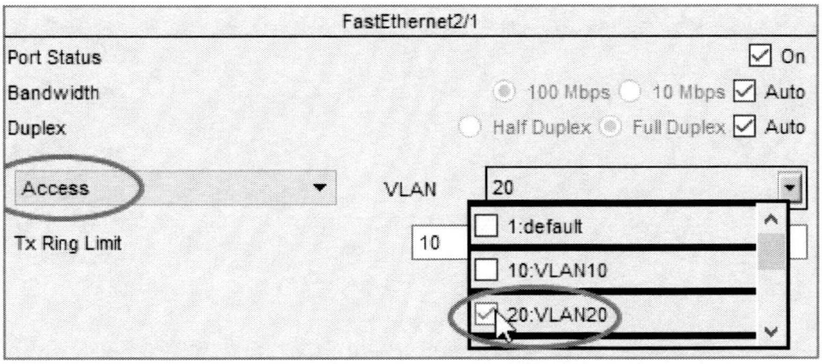

Figure 9.17 Assigning VLAN to the appropriate interface - VLAN20

Similarly, we assign the other two interfaces to the respective ports. We can now test whether we are able to communicate in the area of one VLAN and whether we are able to connect to a computer located in another VLAN.

Fire	Last Status	Source	Destination	Type	Color
	Successful	PC1	PC2	ICMP	
	Failed	PC1	PC3	ICMP	
	Successful	PC4	PC3	ICMP	
	Failed	PC4	PC2	ICMP	

Figure 9.18 Test of communication in VLAN and between VLANs

As we might have expected - communication in the area of one VLAN is possible as if nothing has changed since the previous attempt, but communication between VLANs is blocked.

To illustrate how the port that is in **Trunk** mode works, we will add to our topology one more switch, connected to the first via optical fiber, and two additional computers located in **VLAN10** and **VLAN30**.

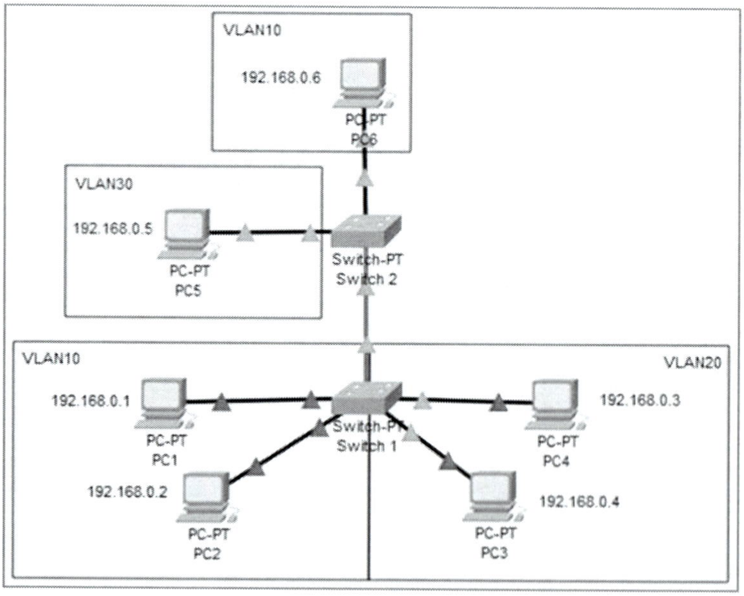

Figure 9.19 Topology with two switches to configure trunk connection (Example 9.2.2b.pkt)

After properly addressing two additional computers, we will configure the **Trunk** connection on the Switch **1**.

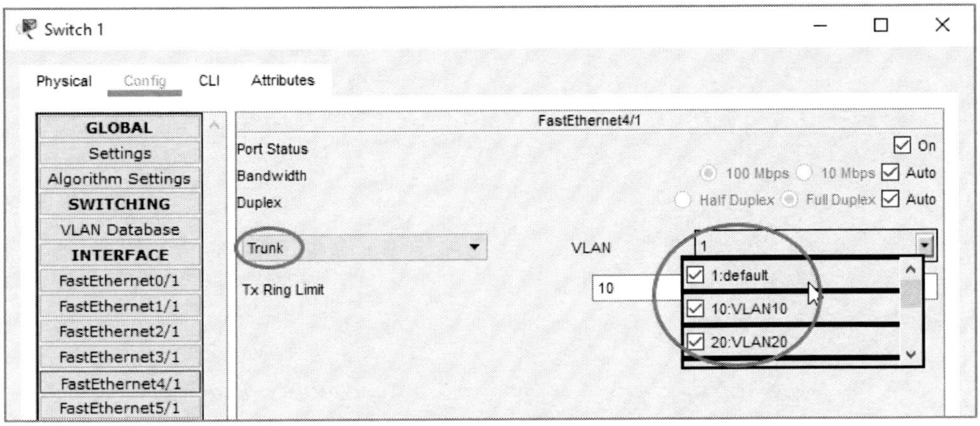

Figure 9.20 Trunk - Switch Connection Configuration 1

When you select **trunk** on the appropriate interface, all existing VLANs on the switch are automatically assigned to this port. We proceed to the configuration of **Switch 2**. We first create a database of VLANs - **VLAN10** and **VLAN30**, and then assign them to ports operating in **Access** mode.

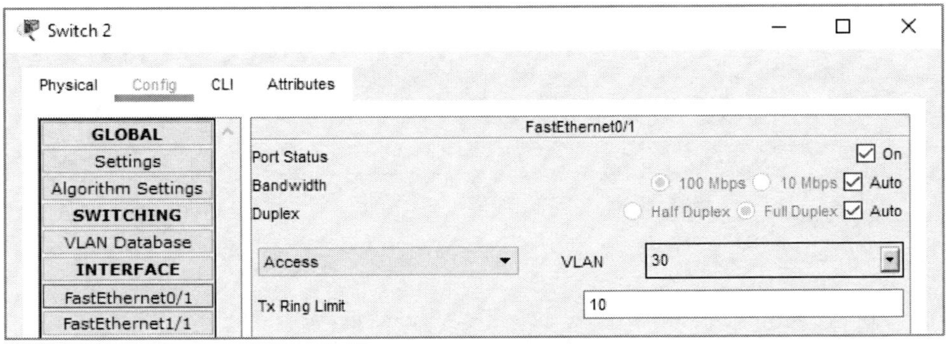

Figure 9.21 Port assignment to the corresponding VLAN - VLAN30

The second port leading to PC6, but assigned to VLAN10, should look similar. Now let's deal with the connection to The **Switch 1**. Let's set this port as a **Trunk** port and try to achieve communication between PC6 and PC1.

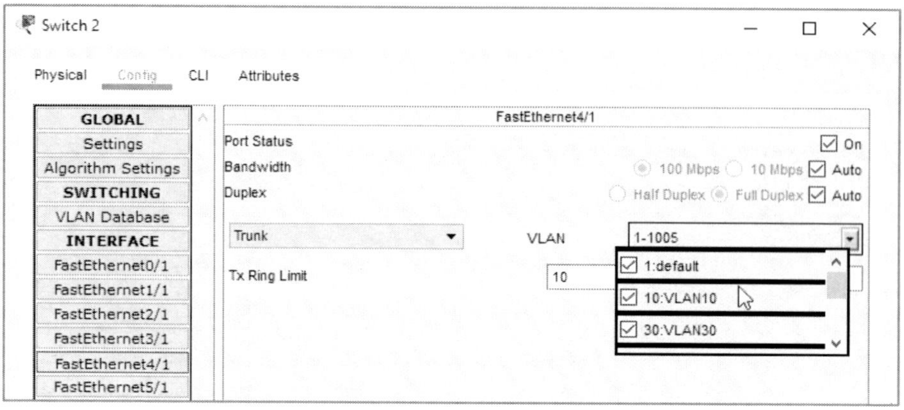

Figure 9.22 Trunk Connection Configuration - Switch 2

Fire	Last Status	Source	Destination	Type	Color
●	Successful	PC6	PC1	ICMP	■

Figure 9.23 Communication between PC6 and PC1

Everything works as it should, but when we try to communicate between VLANs again, we will not achieve a positive result, because we have not configured any router that would allow it.

Fire	Last Status	Source	Destination	Type	Color
●	Failed	PC6	PC4	ICMP	■
●	Failed	PC6	PC5	ICMP	■

Figure 9.24 Communication between VLANs

9.2.3 Enabling Communication Between VLANs

To enable communication between different virtual networks that have been created on switches, you need to add a router to our topology and connect it to one of the switches, for example the **Switch 2**, and configure the router with a function that we have already discussed – the so-called sub-interfaces. If we did not do this, we would have to create one connection between the switch and the router for each existing VLAN, which is neither practical nor simpler.

The topology that we will use to show how routing between VLANs works will look similar to the previous ones, but we will attach the router to the **Switch 2** and change the network addressing. Now each VLAN will have its own part of the **192.168.0.0/16** network due to the fact that you have to specify different default gateways on computers.

The first available network address will be the default gateway address, e.g. for the **192.168.10.0/24** network it will be **192.168.10.1.**

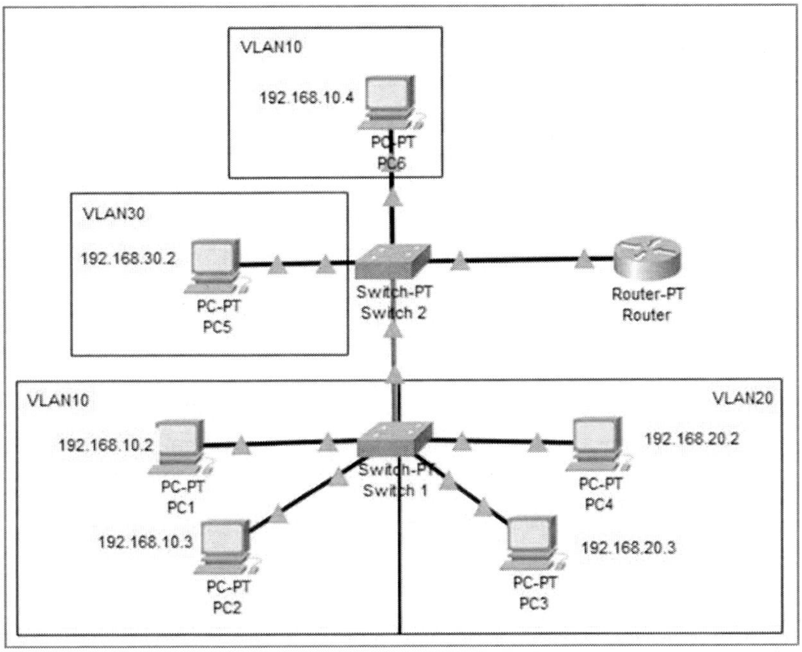

Figure 9.25 Topology for configuring Router on a stick (Example 9.2.3.pkt)

The first step to configure routing between virtual networks is to configure the switches themselves – you need to agree on **vlan databases** so that both switches have the same VLANs. This will be needed later due to the fact that on **trunk** links on both sides must be configured permission to move the same VLANs.

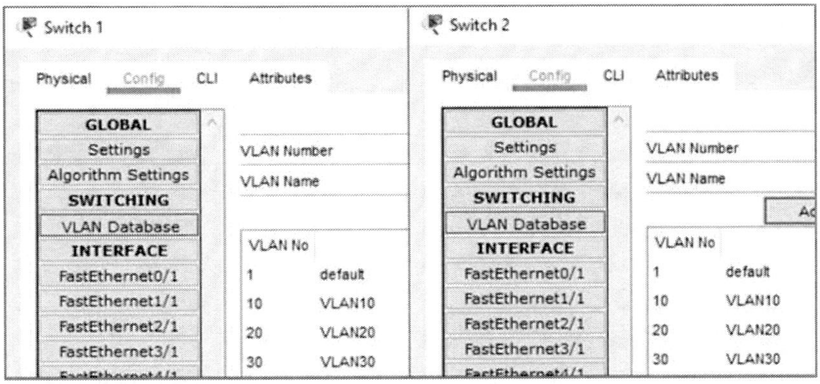

Figure 9.26 VLAN Database - Switch 1 and Switch 2

When the VLAN base agrees on both switches, **Trunk** connections should also be allowed to move the same VLANs from two sides (on **Switch 1** and on **Switch 2**). It's time to switch to Switch 2 and set up one more **Trunk** connection – between the switch and the router.

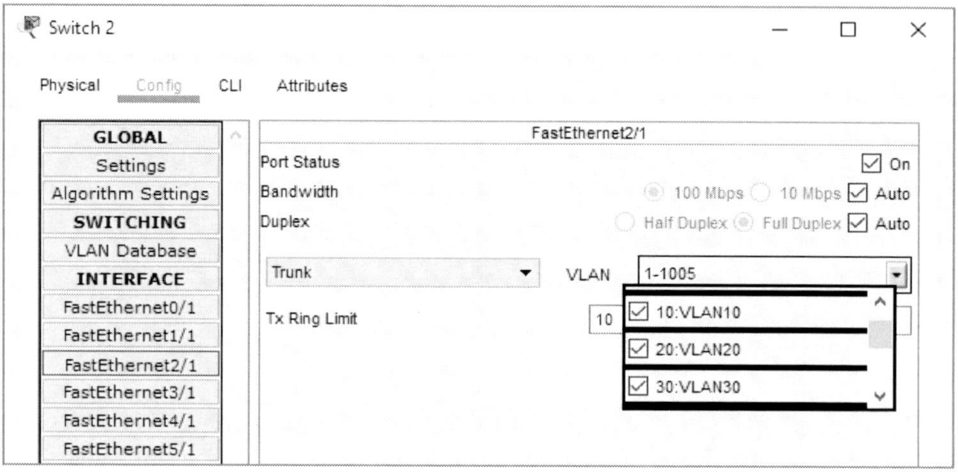

Figure 9.27 Setting up another Trunk - Switch 2 connection

We can now configure the Interface of the Fa0/0 router using commands to create three sub-interfaces – one for each existing VLAN. The next step is to execute the appropriate command on each **encapsulation dotlq <VLAN number >** (thanks to which the router will know how to mark, i.e. tag each frame from a given sub-interface) and assign the appropriate IP addresses for each sub-interface as shown in the figure below.

```
Router(config)#int fa0/0
Router(config-if)#no shutdown
Router(config-if)#exit
Router(config)#int fa0/0.10
Router(config-subif)#encapsulation dotlq 10
Router(config-subif)#ip address 192.168.10.1 255.255.255.0
Router(config-subif)#exit
Router(config)#int fa0/0.20
Router(config-subif)#encapsulation dotlq 20
Router(config-subif)#ip address 192.168.20.1 255.255.255.0
Router(config-subif)#exit
Router(config)#int fa0/0.30
Router(config-subif)#encapsulation dotlq 30
Router(config-subif)#ip address 192.168.30.1 255.255.255.0
Router(config-subif)#exit
```

Figure 9.28 Configuring Router-on-a-stick

It remained for us to carry out tests of communication between VLANs. Through the configuration process, we could already understand how the idea of **Router on a stick** works, in which the router is the default gateway for each VLAN and it is he who performs routing between VLANs. Until this router is included in the network, VLANs cannot communicate with each other.

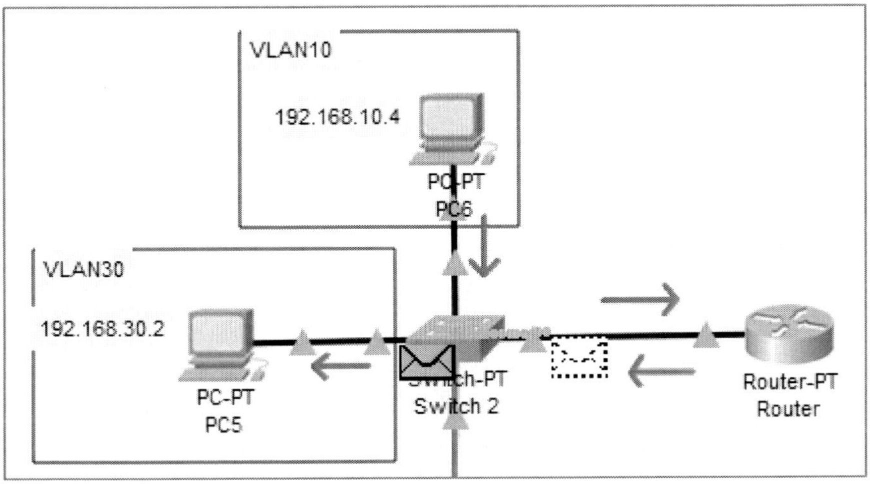

Figure 9.29 Traffic from VLAN10 to VLAN30

The figure above shows how the communication between VLANs looks like. Using the PING commands, you can confirm the path traveled by the packet, which is shown in the figure below.

Event List

Vis.	Time(sec)	Last Device	At Device	Type
	0.000	--	PC6	ICMP
	0.001	PC6	Switch 2	ICMP
	0.002	Switch 2	Router	ICMP
	0.003	Router	Switch 2	ICMP
	0.004	Switch 2	PC5	ICMP
	0.005	PC5	Switch 2	ICMP
	0.006	Switch 2	Router	ICMP
	0.007	Router	Switch 2	ICMP
	0.008	Switch 2	PC6	ICMP

Figure 9.30 PING between VLAN10 and VLAN30

0.006	--	PC4	ICMP
0.007	PC4	Switch 1	ICMP
0.008	Switch 1	Switch 2	ICMP
0.009	Switch 2	Router	ICMP
0.010	Router	Switch 2	ICMP
0.011	Switch 2	PC6	ICMP
0.012	PC6	Switch 2	ICMP
0.013	Switch 2	Router	ICMP
0.014	Router	Switch 2	ICMP
0.015	Switch 2	Switch 1	ICMP
0.016	Switch 1	PC4	ICMP

Figure 9.31 PING between VLAN20 and VLAN10

9.3 Configuring Cisco Switches in the IOS

9.3.1 Basic Information

In order to start configuring the switch in a real environment, you will need to have any computer with a COM port (**RS232**), a **console** cable and, of course, the switch itself. We connect the computer to the switch in the same way as in the case of a router, so we will not describe it here again.

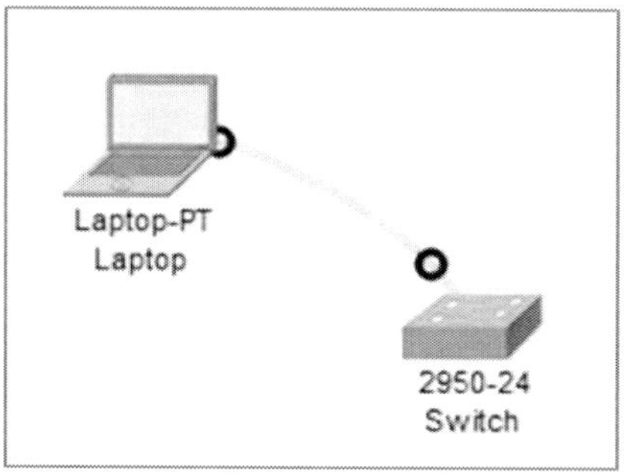

Figure 9.32 Correct console connection

The connection to the switch is established in the same way as in the case of a router, using the **Terminal** application. In the configuration window that appears after starting **Terminal**, do not change any parameters and click **OK**.

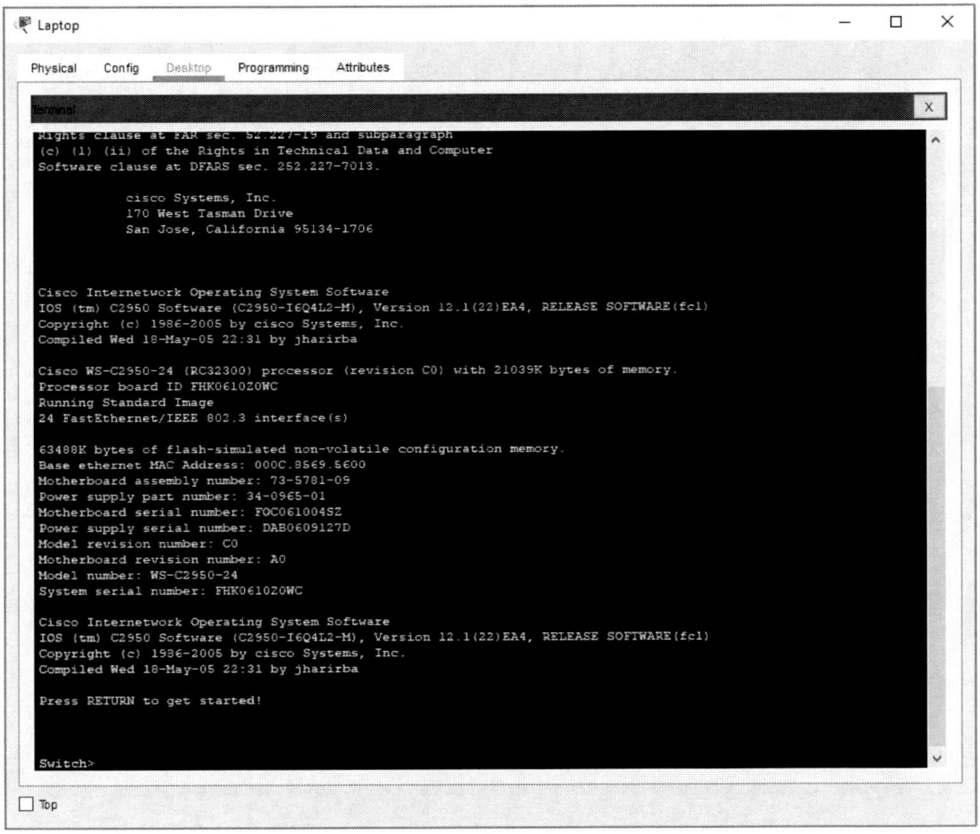

Figure 9.33 Correctly log into the switch

9.3.2 Basic Switch Configuration Modes

Unlike routers, switches do not have a wizard mode, so they must be configured only manually. Basic functions such as navigating the console, using help, and even checking the status of the device look analogous to routers, so they will not be described again.

9.3.3 Interface Configuration

The configuration of a given interface is analogous to the configuration of the interface in a router. First, we go into the global configuration mode, and then using the interface command **interface <type><number>** we configure the interface.

You can change the port bandwidth using the command **speed <bandwidth of Mb/s>**.

```
Switch>en
Switch#conf t
Enter configuration commands, one per line.  End with CNTL/Z.
Switch(config)#int fa0/1
Switch(config-if)#speed 10
```

Figure 9.34 Change interface bandwidth

Another interface parameter that we can configure is duplex mode. The mode is set with the command **duplex <mode>**, where the available modes are: **full, half** and **auto**.

```
Switch(config)#int fa0/1
Switch(config-if)#duplex auto
```

Figure 9.35 Changing the duplex mode of the interface

Another option is to configure the interface to use VLANs. If the interface is to be in **Access** mode and only one VLAN is to belong to it, we use the **`switchport mode access`** command to set the interface mode to **`access`**, and then assign the interface to a specific VLAN with the switchport access VLAN command **`switchport access vlan [number]`**. On the other hand, if the interface is to work in **trunk** mode, instead of the two previous commands, enter **`switchport mode trunk`**. How to use these commands is described in the chapter on VLAN configuration.

To assign **VLANs** to the **Trunk** port we use the switchport trunk allowed vlan command **`switchport trunk allowed vlan [all or VLAN number]`**,, of course the default option is **all.**

```
Switch(config)#int fa0/1
Switch(config-if)#switchport mode access
Switch(config-if)#switchport access vlan 10
Switch(config-if)#exit
Switch(config)#int fa0/2
Switch(config-if)#switchport mode trunk
Switch(config-if)#switchport trunk allowed vlan all
Switch(config-if)#exit
```

Figure 9.36 Changing the mode of operation of ports and assigning VLANs

9.3.4 VLAN Configuration

We will start by creating the following topology, on the example of which we will configure VLANs:

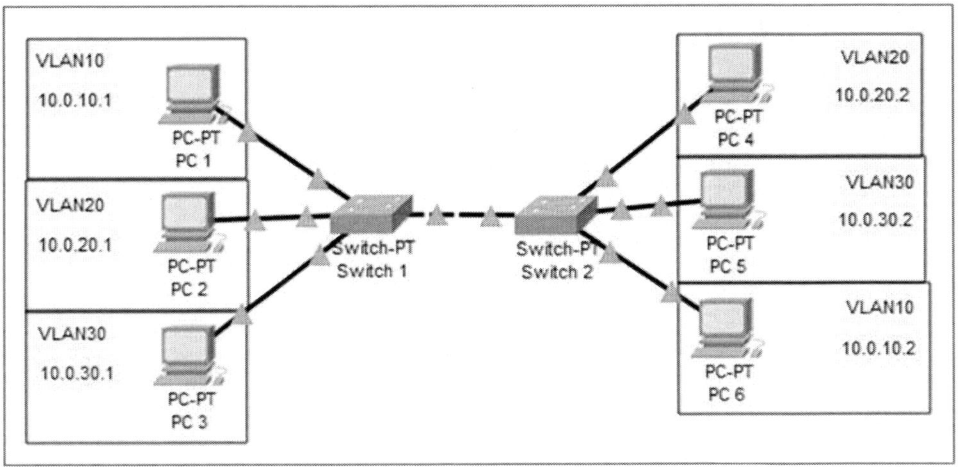

Figure 9.37 Topology for switch configuration (Example 9.3.4.pkt)

As you can see, the topology predicts the existence of three VLANs – VLAN 10, VLAN 20 and VLAN 30. So we'll start by creating them on the switches. To create a VLAN, we must first enter the **global configuration** mode and use the command with the syntax: **`vlan [number]`**.. We can then name the virtual network by using the **`name`** command. We return to the **global configuration** mode with the **`exit`** command, and then create the second necessary VLAN and the third. Repeat on the second switch as well.

```
Switch_1(config)#vlan 10
Switch_1(config-vlan)#name VLAN10
Switch_1(config-vlan)#exit
Switch_1(config)#vlan 20
Switch_1(config-vlan)#name VLAN20
Switch_1(config-vlan)#exit
Switch_1(config)#vlan 30
Switch_1(config-vlan)#name VLAN30
Switch_1(config-vlan)#exit
```

Figure 9.38 Create VLANs on the switch

If we do not give VLAN a name, it will get the default name, in the above case it would be VLAN0010. VLANs can also be deleted, we do this by typing the command **`no vlan [number]`** in the **global configuration** mode. Now let's check if the corresponding VLANs have been created correctly. To do this, we need to enter **privileged mode** and then use the **`show vlan`** command.

```
Switch_1#show vlan

VLAN Name                             Status    Ports
---- -------------------------------- --------- -------------------------------
1    default                          active    Fa0/1, Fa1/1, Fa2/1, Fa3/1
                                                Fa4/1, Fa5/1
10   VLAN10                           active
20   VLAN20                           active
30   VLAN30                           active
1002 fddi-default                     active
1003 token-ring-default               active
1004 fddinet-default                  active
1005 trnet-default                    active

VLAN Type  SAID       MTU   Parent RingNo BridgeNo Stp  BrdgMode Trans1 Trans2
---- ----- ---------- ----- ------ ------ -------- ---- -------- ------ ------
1    enet  100001     1500  -      -      -        -    -        0      0
10   enet  100010     1500  -      -      -        -    -        0      0
20   enet  100020     1500  -      -      -        -    -        0      0
30   enet  100030     1500  -      -      -        -    -        0      0
1002 fddi  101002     1500  -      -      -        -    -        0      0
1003 tr    101003     1500  -      -      -        -    -        0      0
1004 fdnet 101004     1500  -      -      -        ieee -        0      0
1005 trnet 101005     1500  -      -      -        ibm  -        0      0

VLAN Type  SAID       MTU   Parent RingNo BridgeNo Stp  BrdgMode Trans1 Trans2
---- ----- ---------- ----- ------ ------ -------- ---- -------- ------ ------

Remote SPAN VLANs
------------------------------------------------------------------------------

Primary Secondary Type              Ports
------- --------- ----------------- ------------------------------------------
```

Figure 9.39 Show vlan command on a switch

We can find here information about VLANs that were created on the switch and what ports are assigned to the VLAN data. We will start by assigning those interfaces that connect computers to the switch. So we enter the **global configuration** mode, and then the interface, in the way already described above. These interfaces belong to individual VLANs and connect to end devices, so they will work in **Access** mode.

```
Switch_1(config)#int fa1/1
Switch_1(config-if)#switchport mode access
Switch_1(config-if)#switchport access vlan 10
Switch_1(config-if)#exit
Switch_1(config)#int fa2/1
Switch_1(config-if)#switchport mode access
Switch_1(config-if)#switchport access vlan 20
Switch_1(config-if)#exit
Switch_1(config)#int fa3/1
Switch_1(config-if)#switchport mode access
Switch_1(config-if)#switchport access vlan 30
Switch_1(config-if)#exit
```

Figure 9.40 Changing the operating modes on the switch interfaces

Similarly, it should look on the second switch with the corresponding change of interfaces. Next, proceed to change the operating mode of the interface, connecting both switches. It connects two network devices and will transmit data from several VLANs, so it will work in **Trunk** mode.

```
Switch_1(config)#int fa0/1
Switch_1(config-if)#switchport mode trunk

Switch_1(config-if)#
%LINEPROTO-5-UPDOWN: Line protocol on Interface FastEthernet0/1, changed state to down

%LINEPROTO-5-UPDOWN: Line protocol on Interface FastEthernet0/1, changed state to up

Switch_1(config-if)#switchport trunk allowed vlan all
```

Figure 9.41 Change the interface mode to Trunk

To perform connection tests between once whether computers in the same VLANs can communicate with each other.

Fire	Last Status	Source	Destination	Type	Color
●	Successful	PC 1	PC 6	ICMP	
●	Successful	PC 2	PC 4	ICMP	
●	Successful	PC 3	PC 5	ICMP	

Figure 9.42 PING between VLANs

9.3.5 Configuration of Virtual Terminals (Telnet, SSH)

In the case of switches, as for routers, they can be configured remotely from LAN or even VAN via virtual terminals such as **Telnet** or **SSH**. Now let's create the following topology.

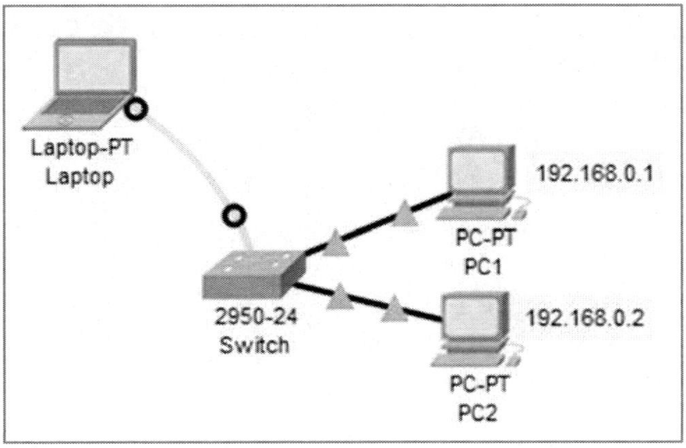

Figure 9.43 Topology to configure remote configuration

To configure a switch to connect to it via Telnet or SSH, you must first give it an IP address so that it is visible on the network. Configure the **VLAN1** interface and give it an IP address, e.g. **192.168.0.254/24**.

```
Switch(config)#interface vlan 1
Switch(config-if)#ip address 192.168.0.254 255.255.255.0
Switch(config-if)#no shutdown

Switch(config-if)#
%LINK-5-CHANGED: Interface Vlan1, changed state to up

%LINEPROTO-5-UPDOWN: Line protocol on Interface Vlan1, changed state to up

Switch(config-if)#exit
```

Figure 9.44 Giving an IP address for VLAN 1

After such a configuration, computers in the topology will be able to communicate with the switch, e.g. using the PING command, however, if we try to connect to it using Telnet, we will receive the message `Connection to 192.168.0.254 closed by foreign host`, as you can see in the figure below.

```
Command Prompt

Packet Tracer PC Command Line 1.0
C:\>ping 192.168.0.254

Pinging 192.168.0.254 with 32 bytes of data:

Request timed out.
Reply from 192.168.0.254: bytes=32 time<1ms TTL=255
Reply from 192.168.0.254: bytes=32 time<1ms TTL=255
Reply from 192.168.0.254: bytes=32 time<1ms TTL=255

Ping statistics for 192.168.0.254:
    Packets: Sent = 4, Received = 3, Lost = 1 (25% loss)
Approximate round trip times in milli-seconds:
    Minimum = 0ms, Maximum = 0ms, Average = 0ms

C:\>telnet 192.168.0.254
Trying 192.168.0.254 ...Open

[Connection to 192.168.0.254 closed by foreign host]
C:\>
```

Figure 9.45 Attempt to communicate with a switch

To connect to the switch, we must enable the ability to remotely connect via Telnet, as well as enable authorization by setting a password. We do it in the same way as on a router.

```
Switch(config-if)#exit
Switch(config)#line vty 0 4
Switch(config-line)#password switch
Switch(config-line)#login
Switch(config-line)#exit
```

Figure 9.46 Activating switch access using virtual terminals

Now we are able to connect to the switch using the **Telnet** protocol:

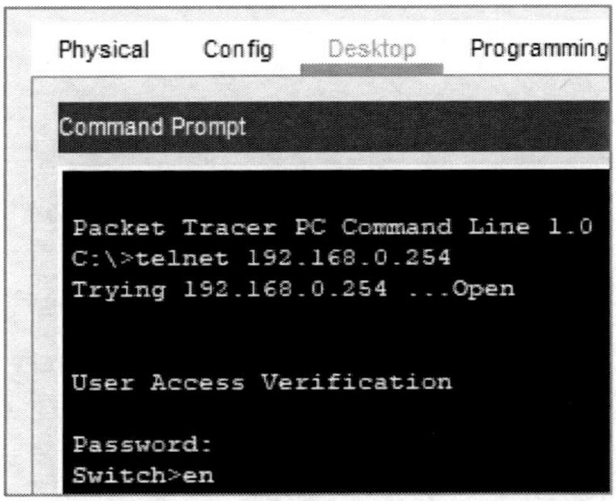

Figure 9.47 Positive attempt to access the switch using the Telnet protocol

Once we have access via Telnet, we can configure a more secure connection – a connection using the **SSH** protocol. To do this, you need to rename the **switch** (due to the fact that Switch is the default name of the switch and SSH is a secured protocol, so it does not allow default values for names, among other things). After that, configure the IP domain and generate RSA keys, which are already described in the section on configuring SSH access to the router.

```
Switch1(config)#ip domain-name switch.com
Switch1(config)#hostname Switch1
Switch1(config)#ip domain-name switch.com
Switch1(config)#crypto key generate rsa general-keys modulus 1024
The name for the keys will be: Switch1.switch.com

% The key modulus size is 1024 bits
% Generating 1024 bit RSA keys, keys will be non-exportable...[OK]
*mar 1 0:22:27.693: %SSH-5-ENABLED: SSH 1.99 has been enabled
```

Figure 9.48 Configure SSH switch access

You must also create a user (login and password) to which you will be able to log in.

```
Switch1(config)#username admin password admin
```

Figure 9.49 Create a user on a switch

Next, you need to perform permission on the switch for SSH connections.

```
Switch1(config)#line vty 0 4
Switch1(config-line)#transport input ssh
Switch1(config-line)#exit
```

Figure 9.50 Permission for internal SSH connections

Now you need to perform a login test (access using SSH) from the computer to the switch.

```
Command Prompt

Packet Tracer PC Command Line 1.0
C:\>telnet 192.168.0.254
Trying 192.168.0.254 ...Open


User Access Verification

Password:
Switch>en
% No password set.
Switch>

[Connection to 192.168.0.254 closed by foreign host]
C:\>ssh -l admin 192.168.0.254

Password:

Password:



Switch1>en
```

Figure 9.51 SSH access to the switch

9.3.6 REP Protocol

Cisco RESILIENT Ethernet Protocol (**Cisco REP**) is a Cisco protocol used in networks known as **Carrier Ethernet**. Carrier Ethernet is a technology used to build large WAN structures based on the Ethernet standard. This technology allows **ISR** providers and operators to build large-area, multi-branch corporate networks to provide standardized services. The primary goals of Carrier Ethernet are standardization, scalability, management, reliability, and quality of service.

The main features of the REP protocol are:

- the protocol is owned by Cisco,
- it is mainly used in Metro Ethernet networks based on ring topology,
- it allows you to prevent the formation of a second layer loop,
- it is faster than the STP protocol, it can provide short network convergence times (about 50 mS – 150 mS).

9.3.6.1 Purpose of REP

The main purpose of REP is to prevent Layer 2 loops in physical and logical topologies of the following types:

- point-to-point,
- star,
- bus,
- ring.

9.3.6.2 Basic Concepts of REP

REP segment – a chain of ports connected to each other and marked (configured) with one and the same identifier, the so-called **segment ID**. The ID segment is an integer from 1 d o1024.

A **REP edge switch** is a switch located at the edge of a REP segment. Edge port of the REP segment (edge port) – a **port of the edge switch**, located inside the REP segment.

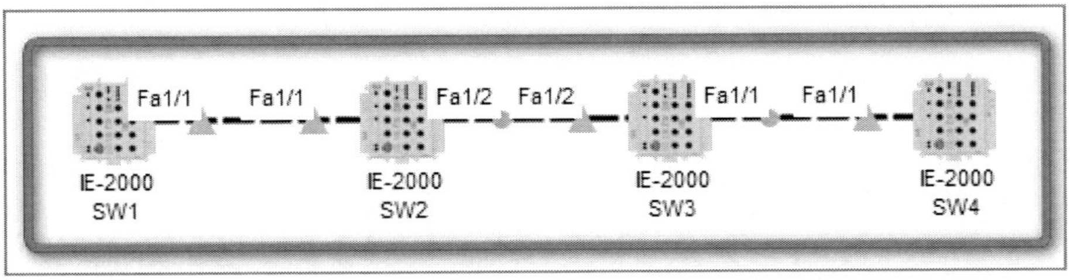

Figure 9.52 An example of a REP segment in a point-to-point topology.

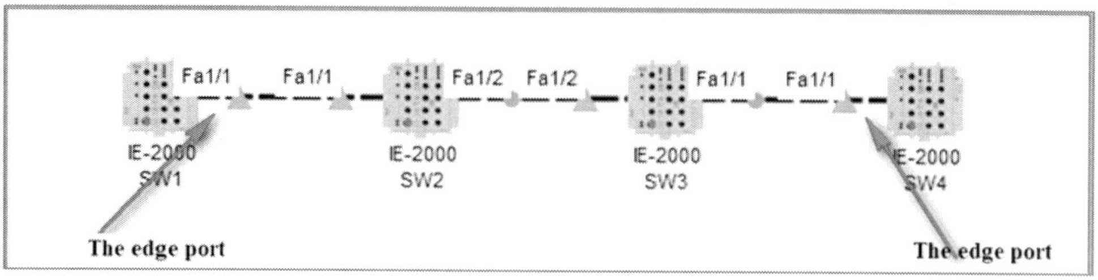

Figure 9.53 An example of a REP segment in a point-to-point topology.

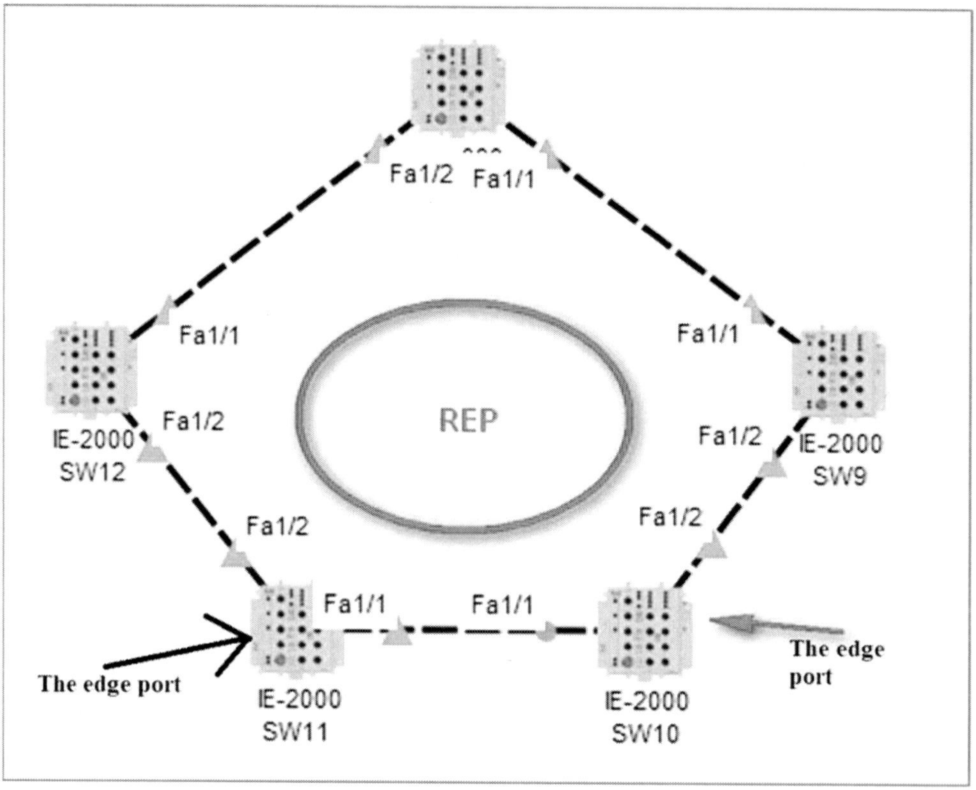

Figure 9.54 Sample REP segment in Ring topology

Setting up a REP segment is very simple. On each of the ports inside the **REP** segment, use the following commands:

```
SW1 (config-if)# sw mod trunk
SW1 (config-if)# rep segment N
```

where **N** is an integer **between 1 and 1024**, denoting the segment ID. On each switch, execute the following commands.

```
en
conf t
interface fa1/1
sw mod trunk
rep segment 1
interface fa1/2
sw mod trunk
rep segment 1
```

CHAPTER 10

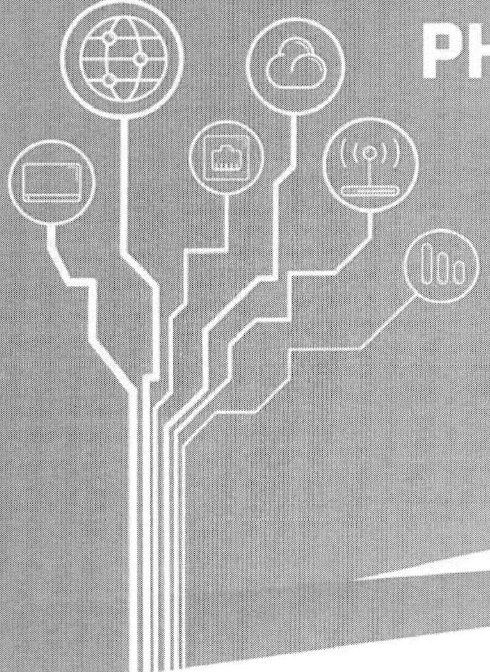

PHYSICAL TOPOLOGY IN THE CISCO PACKET TRACER

10 Physical Topology in the Cisco Packet Tracer

This chapter covers basic working knowledge of configuring a simulated physical topology in the Cisco Packet Tracer.

Note – Warning: Remember to periodically save the file state during exercises (keyboard shortcut CTRL+S)

Physical topologies are used to illustrate how network equipment has been deployed in rooms, buildings, housing estates, etc. It shows the actual wiring process, taking into account, among others, such factors as: distance between devices, wireless network coverage or length of cables connecting given devices. Before you describe physical topologies in detail, you must create a logical topology, along with a description of the buildings. In this example, this is the following logical topology, which will be used further as the basis for creating a physical topology.

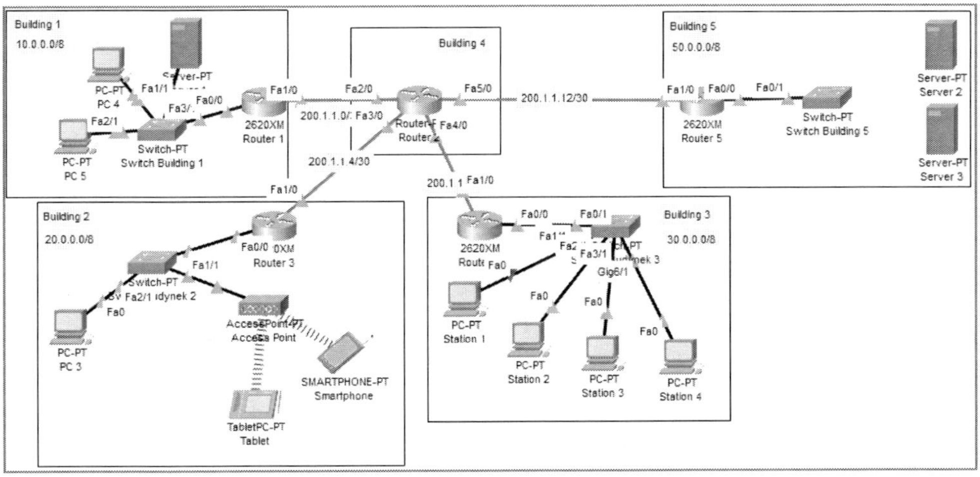

Figure 10.1 Example logical topology

The assumptions necessary to create a **physical** topology are:

- Buildings 1 to 4 are located in city A, while building 5 is located in city B.
- Connections between buildings will use optical fibres.

To create a physical topology, start by switching the program to Physical mode.

To do this, click the icon in the upper-left corner of the workspace. In the same place, you can return to logical topology design mode at any time. You can also use the keyboard shortcuts **Shift + P** for physical topology and **Shift + L** for logical topology.

Figure 10.2 Switch to physical view

When you switch to **Physical** mode, the physical topology design mode appears. We have four types of locations at our disposal where we can place devices. These are: **Intercity** (the largest area, covering the entire working area), **City** (city), **Building** (building), **Wiring Closet** (rack cabinet with equipment, i.e. e.g. the main distribution point or intermediate distribution point).

It is not a tool for advanced structural network designers, but it is suitable for teaching the basics of network design, for example, for creating basic network designs (mainly for educational purposes). An example of a physical network project is described in a separate chapter. Physical devices form a kind of hierarchy – the main area contains cities, cities contain buildings, buildings contain devices, etc. However, it is not necessary to accept this hierarchy as binding, it is possible to place a given device, for example, directly in the city.

By default, each topology contains one city, one building in it, and as many stations in the building as needed to accommodate all the equipment.

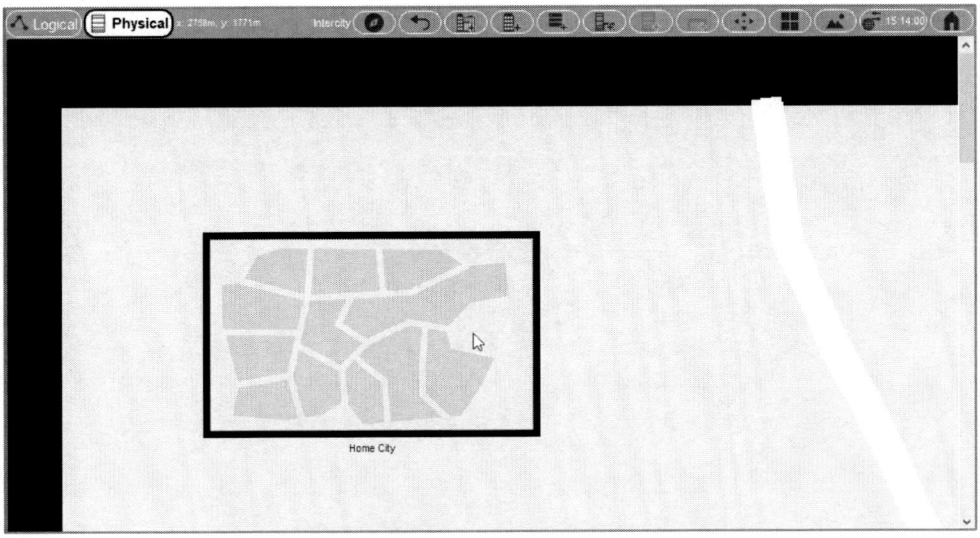

Figure 10.3 Program window in Physical mode

You can zoom in and out of the physical topology view as you see fit using the magnifying glass icons in the top bar. In physical topology, you can move in two ways. The first is to click the mouse on the location of the object in question, which can be opened. To return one level higher, use the **Back** button on the navigation bar at the top.

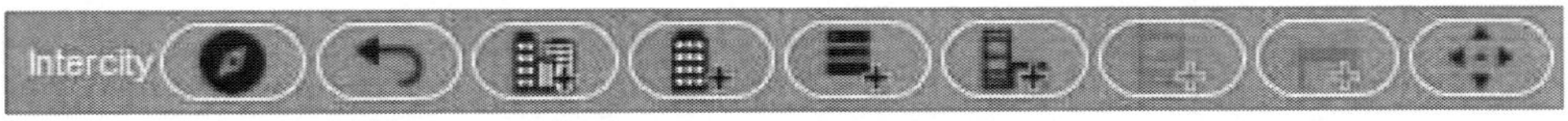

Figure 10.4 Navigation bar

The navigation bar shows the name of the location that is currently open. The second way to navigate the physical topology is to click the **NAVIGATION** button. A list of all existing locations opens.

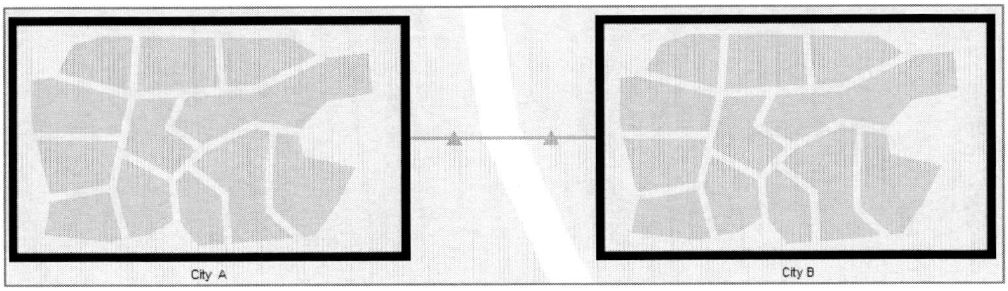

Figure 10.5 Intercity locations

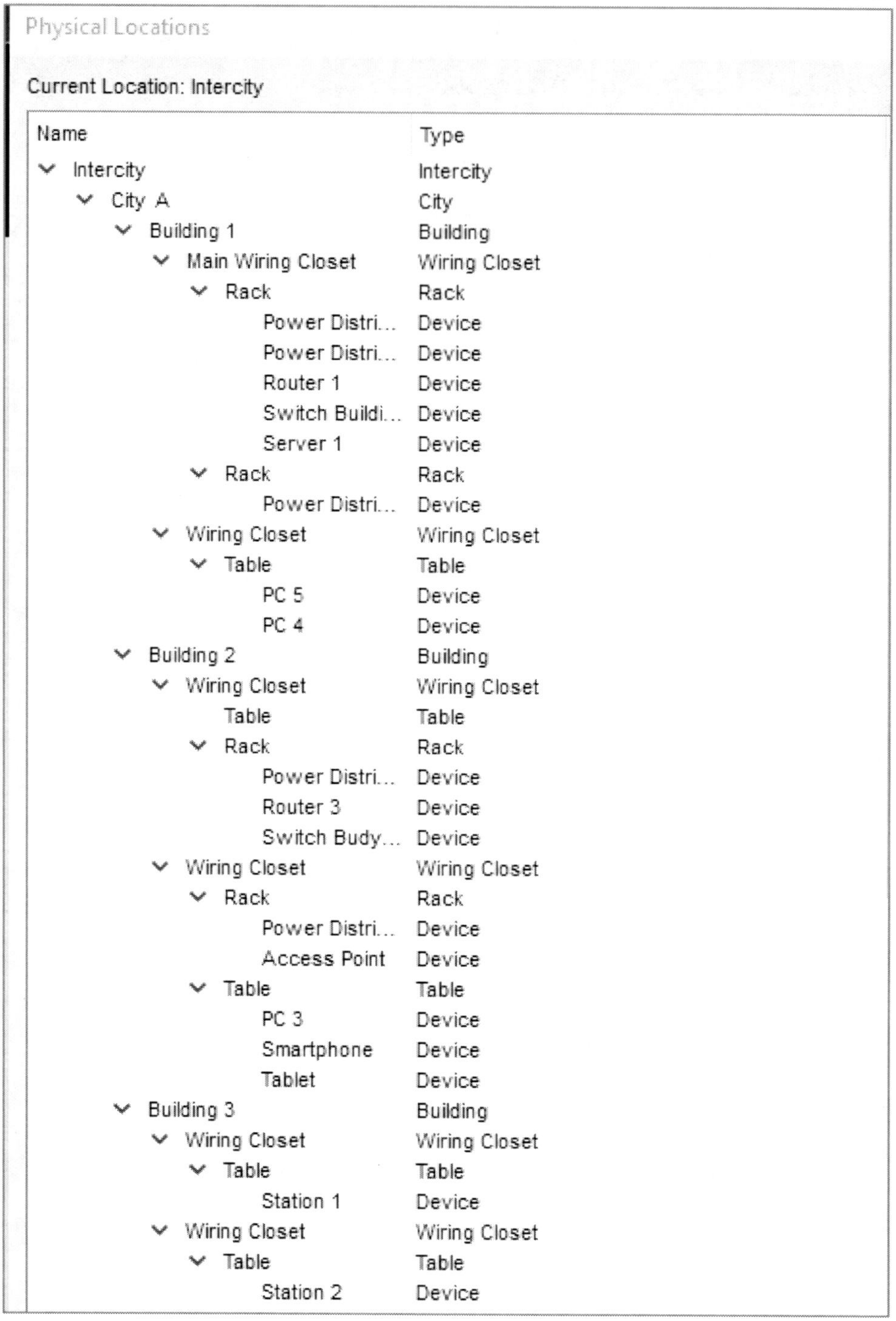

Figure 10.6 Window with a list of existing locations

The list is presented in the form of a table. On the left there are the names of the locations along with their location in the hierarchy. We can also collapse specific fragments. On the right, however, you can see the types of locations – **City**, **Building**, **Device**, Wardrobe (**Wiring Closet**). To move to any of them, click on it, and then on the **Jump to Selected Location** button.

The appearance of the stations with the equipment is significantly different from the view of the city or building, because it shows the physical appearance of the equipment, along with such elements as diodes and interfaces. The equipment can be located in rack cabinets (devices such as routers, switches, access points or servers) or on tables (devices such as computers, laptops or tablets).

Each station can contain a maximum of three cabinets or tables, which means that the number of devices it can accommodate is limited.

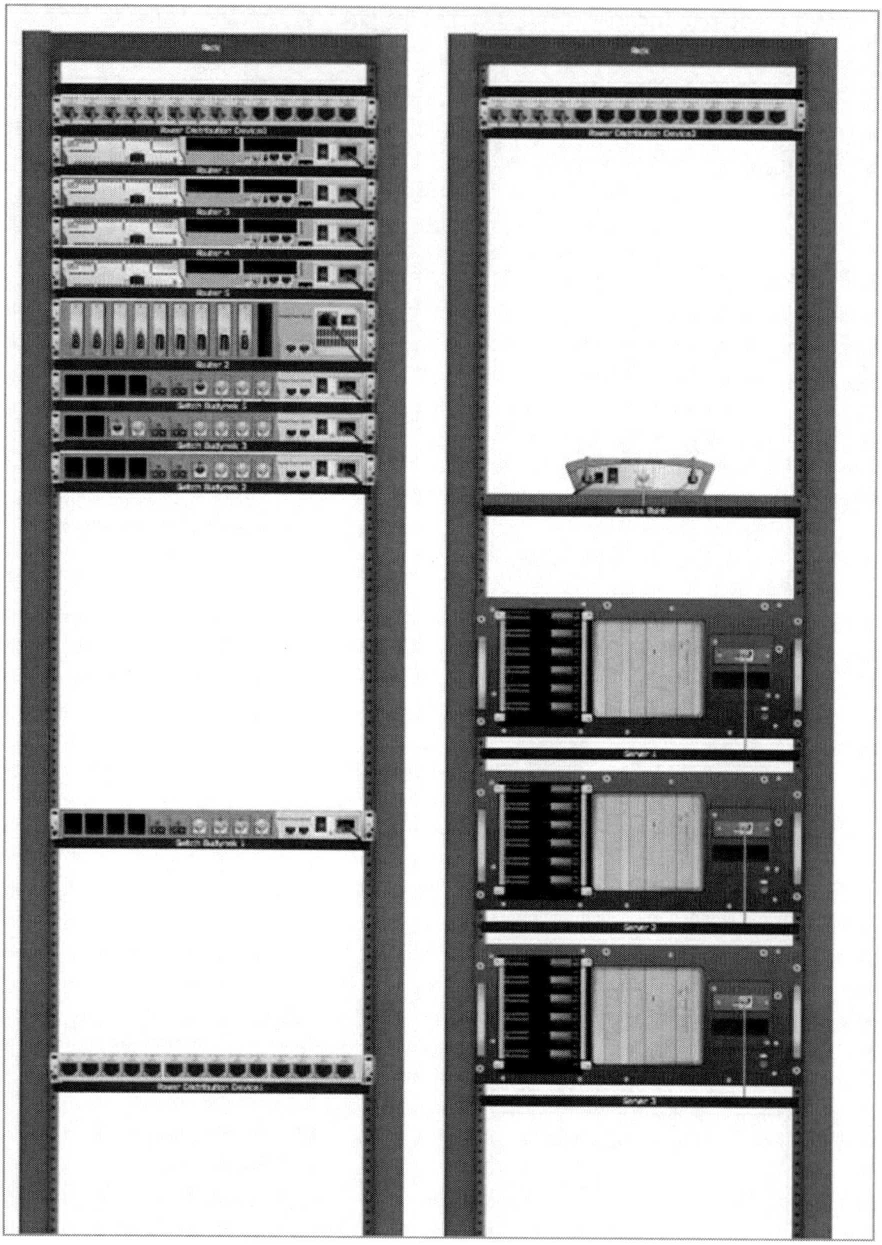

Figure 10.7 The appearance of rack cabinets with devices

We begin to create a physical topology. It provides for two cities – city A and city B. One city is always created by default, its name should be changed to **"City A".** To do this, click on its old name, and then type a new one. If this is successful, enable options **Options → Preferences → Interface → Show Device Name Labels** (Ctrl+R) in PT.

Then, add another city to the workspace. To add a site, use the buttons at the top of the workspace.

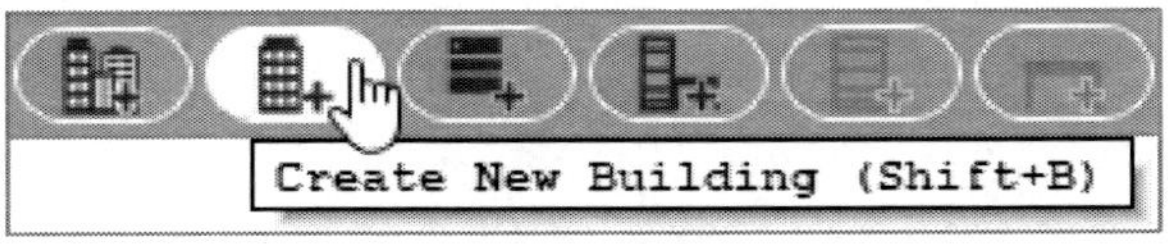

Figure 10.8 Buttons for adding city, buildings

The **New City** button adds a new city, **new Building** a new building, and **New Closet** adds a new station with equipment. In this case, click New City, and then the new city should appear in the workspace. By default, new objects appear in the upper-left corner of the area, so drag them to a different location so that cities don't obscure each other. Then, as in the case of the first city, change its name.

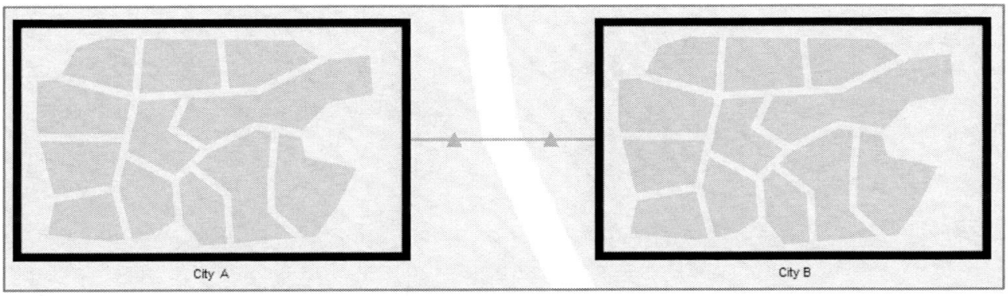

Figure 10.9 Two Cities in the Cisco Packet Tracer

Next, you need to create all the buildings you need. To do this, the location **City A** should be opened. A total of four buildings will be located in this city. Since the first, one default building is already in this city, you should add only three buildings (Building 2, 3, 4) in a manner analogous to adding cities using the **New Building** button, and then rename them to:

Building 1, **Building 2**, **Building 3**, **Building 4**.

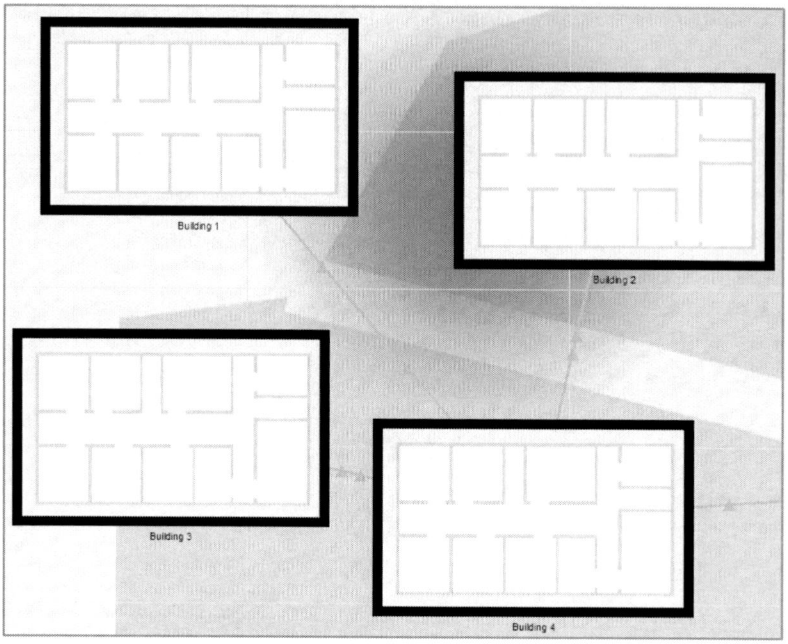

Figure 10.10 Created buildings

The next step is to create equipment stations in the buildings. Positions with equipment are created in the same way as cities or buildings. Enter the building where the appropriate cabinets are to be created (installed) (using the **New Closet** button).

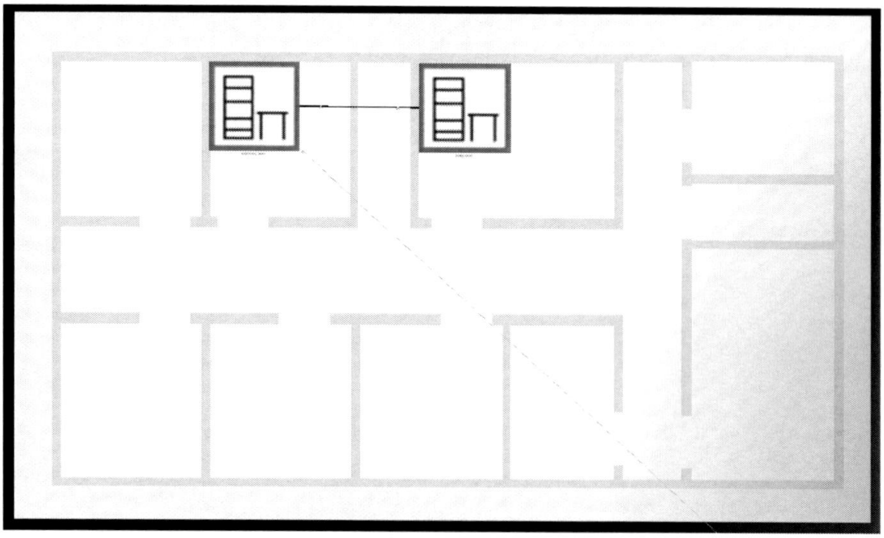

Figure 10.11 For example, arranged desks and rack cabinets

All cities, buildings, and positions (except for one named **Intercity**, which includes all newly added devices by default) can be removed by clicking the cross symbol in the toolbar and then on the object that needs to be removed. After creating the stations in the same way in other buildings, you can proceed to the next stage, i.e. placing devices in the topology.

10.1 Arranging Devices

To move a device to a location, you must first open its current location by any means. Then click the **Move Object** button, click on the device you want to move, and select its new location from the list. The device will be moved. In the same way, you can also move positions, buildings, and cities (but keep in mind that you can't move a larger object to a smaller object, such as a city to a building).

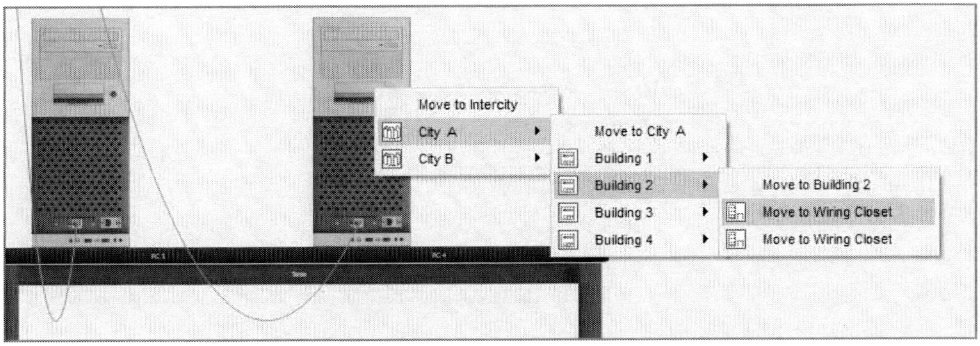

Figure 10.12 Changing the position of the device

10.2 Physical Cable Lengths and Distances

In physical topologies, the actual distance between devices is taken into account (measured as the length of the physical cable in meters or feet). The unit of measurement of length is set using the **Options → Preferences → Interface → Use Metric System**.

The length of the cable can be checked by guiding the mouse cursor over the cable. The actual distance between the devices determines whether communication will be possible. For connection by UTP or STP copper wire, the maximum distance is 100 m, with a longer connection, the devices will not be able to communicate. If devices more than 100 m apart are combined with each other, a device must be placed between them to amplify the signal, e.g. a repeater, which will amplify the signal, or, as in the case of our topology, use optical fibres.

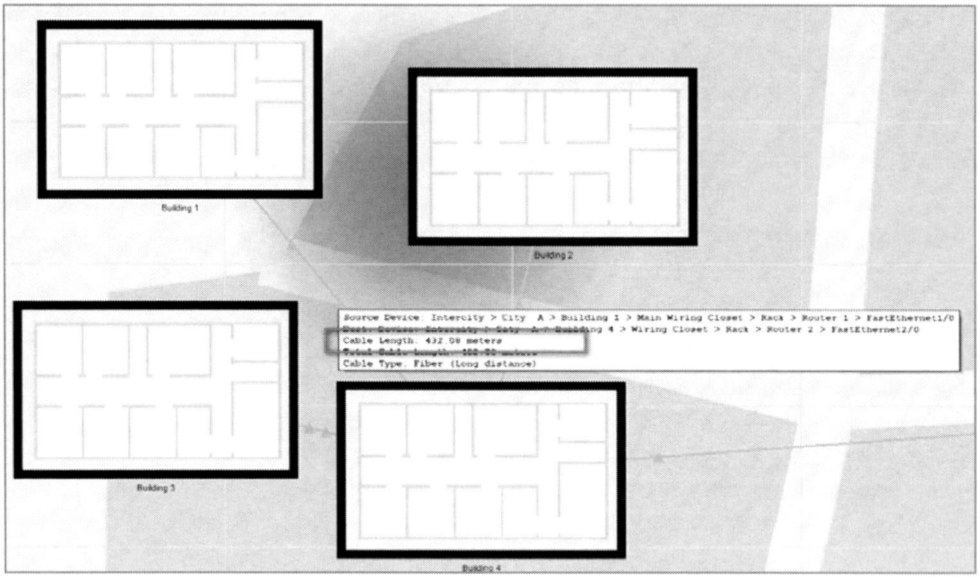

Figure 10.13 Checking the length of the cable

Distance is also important in wireless networks. The range of the wireless network is marked with a circle as in the picture below. Only devices inside the circle are within the network coverage.

To make it easier to orient yourself in distances, you can enable the coordinate grid. To do this, click on the **Grid** button in the bar above the workspace. In the window that appears, you can select the appropriate grids to decide in which areas (**Intercity, City, Building**) the grid should be turned on, as well as the distances to be measured (in meters). **Grid-X** refers to the horizontal axis, while **Grid-Y** refers to the vertical axis. You can also choose the colour of the drawn grid.

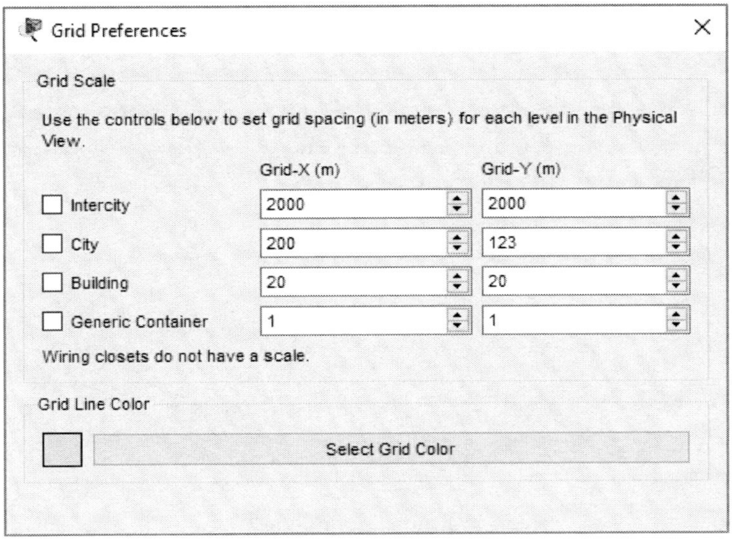

Figure 10.14 Grid tab

This example enables a grid in cities that measures 200 meters horizontally and 100 meters vertically.

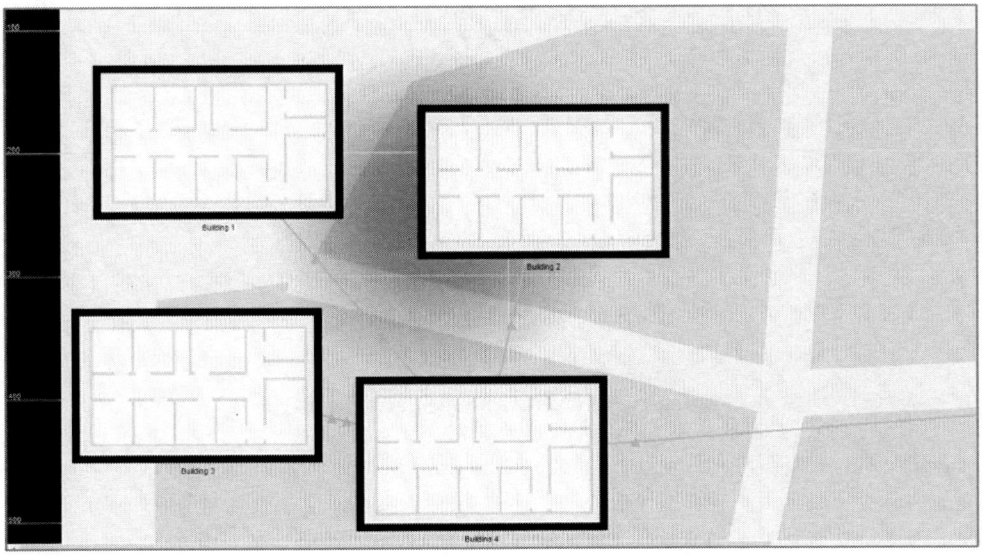

Figure 10.15 Distance grid and cities

10.3 Cable Management

The program allows us in physical topologies to have more control over the course of wiring. The first thing we can do is to create bend points (**Bend Points**), which are the points through which a given cable will pass.

Figure 10.16 Create a point

To create such a point, click the left mouse button on the cable, and then select **Create Bend Point.** The point you create is in the form of a red dot. Then we can freely drag the created point to get the desired effect. However, it should be remembered that the way the cable is routed affects its length.

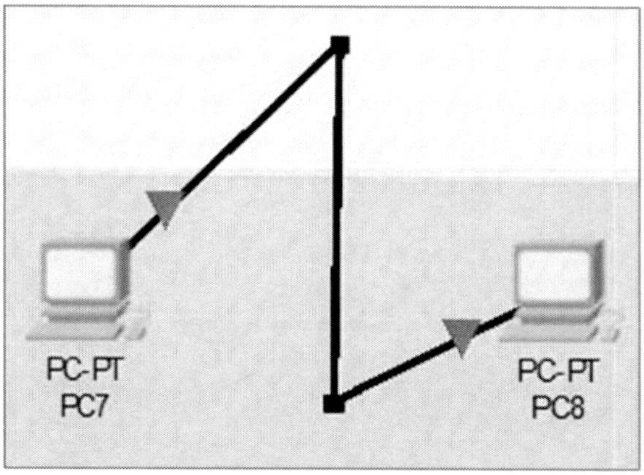

Figure 10.17 Cable guided using BendPoint

Another function present in the program is the grouping of cables. Several grouped cables are routed together as if they were a single cable. To group several cables, you must first create **Bend Points** on them in the places where you want to group them. Then you just need to drag the point of one cable to the point of another. In this way, we will create **Group Point**, which is a point that groups cables. The red dot will change to a yellow square.

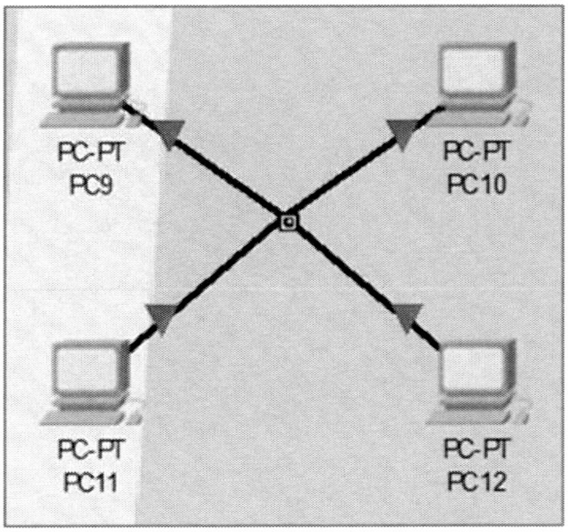

Figure 10.18 Created Group Point

In order for several cables to be routed as a single cable, they must be grouped at least two points.

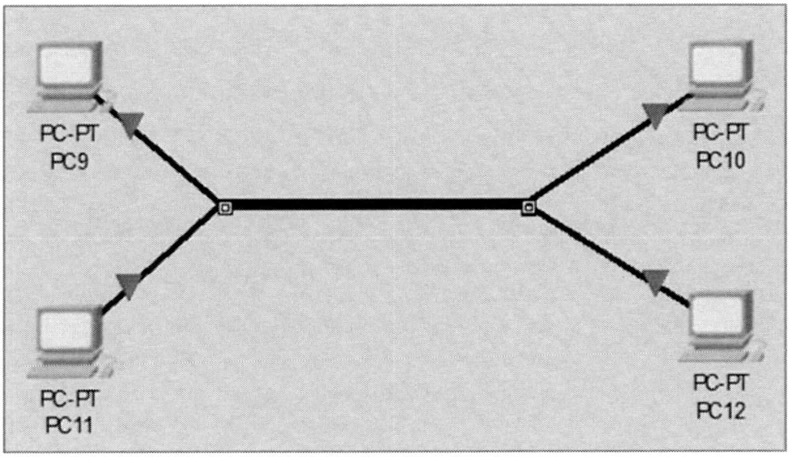

Figure 10.19 Several cables routed as a single

In addition, you can change the colour of the cables. To do this, click on the cable with the left mouse button, and then select the **Color Cable** option. In the window that appears, select the colour of the cable.

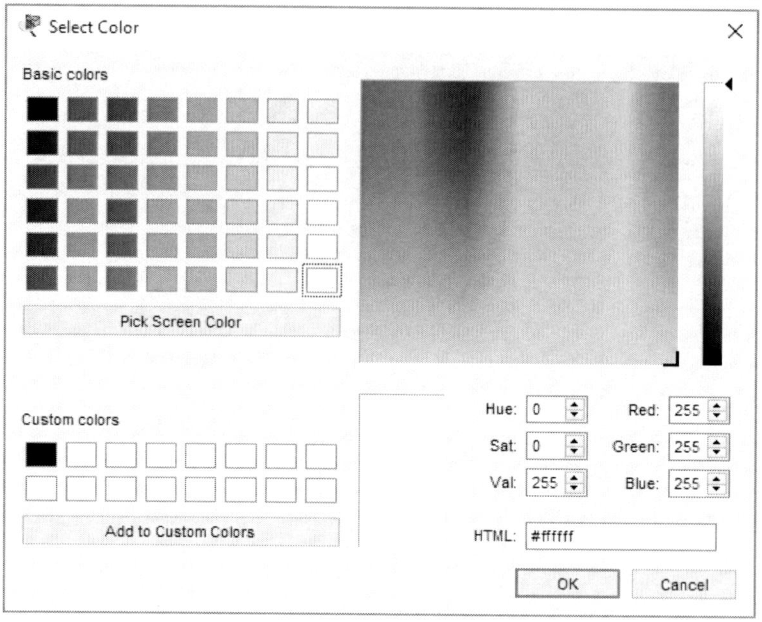

Figure 10.20 Cable colouring panel

The acres of available colours is very similar to the colours used in MS-Paint. You can change the colour of all individual cables, but you cannot change the colour of cable groups.

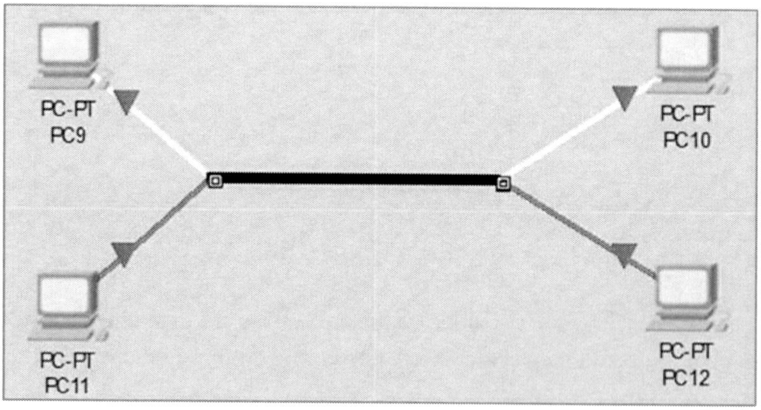

Figure 10.21 Coloured cables

CHAPTER 11

SKILL EXERCISES – PART II

COMPUTER NETWORKS IN PACKET TRACER

FOR BEGINNERS

11 Skill Exercises – Part II

This chapter contains checking exercises for beginners users, testing their skills.

Note – Warning: Remember to periodically save the file state during exercises (keyboard shortcut CTRL+S)

11.1 Configure Devices Using the Graphical Interface

11.1.1 Interface configuration, static routing

Create the topology shown in the figure below, and then use the graphical interface to configure the routers so that **NETWORK 1** can communicate with **NETWORK 2**. Use static routing.

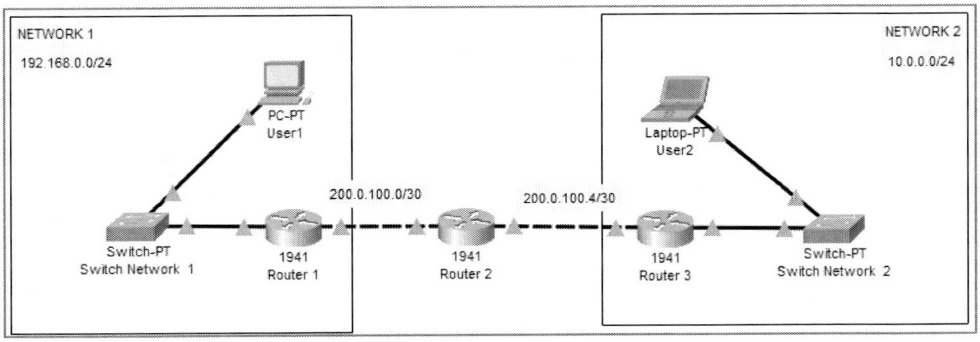

Figure 11.1 Exercise's topology

Solution:

- Create a topology as in the picture, connect the devices to each other using appropriate cables - if the device does not have the appropriate module, add it.
- Address and enable interfaces as in the diagram **(Config tab → [appropriate interface]).**
- PING connectivity to the two default gateways within **NETWORK 1** and then within **NETWORK 2.**
- Configure static routing in both directions **(Config tab → Static).**
- Use the tracert command to verify that **NETWORK 1** can communicate with **NETWORK 2.**

11.1.2 Switch Modes, VLANs Configuration

Start by creating a topology as in the figure below. Address the end devices in the right way and create a database of three VLANs on both VLAN10, VLAN20 and VLAN30 switches. Assign these VLANs in such a way that only devices from a given VLAN can communicate with each other.

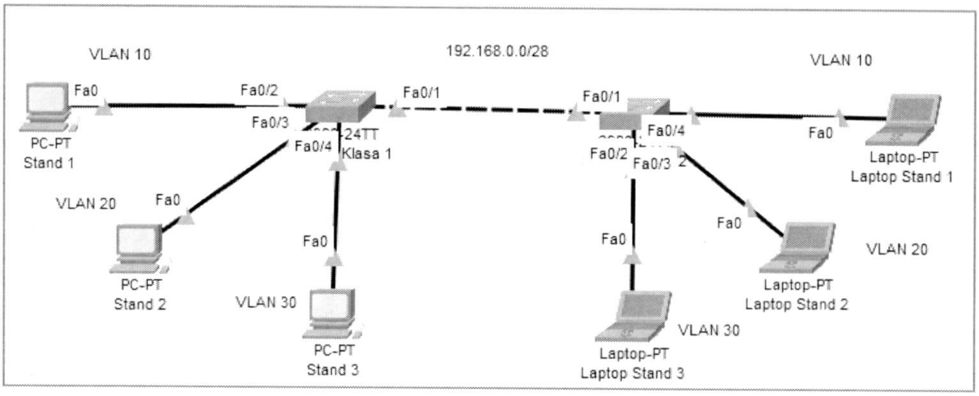

Figure 11.2 Exercise's topology

Solution:

- Create a topology as in the picture, connect the devices to each other using the appropriate cables.
- Address the end devices so that they are on the main network (192.168.0.0/28).
- Create a VLAN database on both switches so that the names and numbers match (VLAN10, VLAN20 and VLAN30).
- On the **Class 1** switch on the appropriate ports, change the operating modes and assign the appropriate VLANs.
- Repeat the same action on the **Class 2** switch.
- Using the PING command, test communications within one VLAN, e.g. from **Stand 1** to **Laptop Stand 1**, and then test communication from VLAN10 to VLAN20 (it should fail).

11.2 Routing Protocols, Remote Management

11.2.1 RIPv2 and Configuration Using Telnet, Local Name Definition

Create a topology consisting of four routers and several end devices and two switches, as shown below. Use fiber optic connections between routers **Split, Makarska, Dubrovnik**. Then address the devices according to the topology scheme. Each router is to be distinguished by other routers by its name (local definition of names). Also configure the dynamic routing protocol – RIP v2, so that **Zagreb** can exchange information with **Dubrovnik**, in which **Laptop Admin** is to have access to the configuration of each router using the Telnet protocol (password is the name of the router, e.g. "**dubrovnik**" for the **Dubrovnik** router).

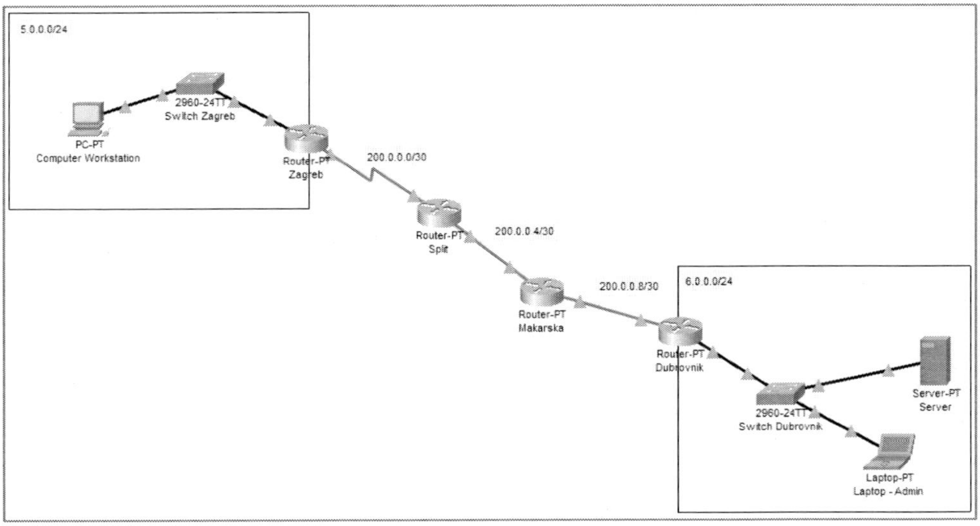

Figure 11.3 Exercise topology

Solution:

- Create a topology as in the picture, connect the devices to each other using the appropriate cables.
- Address and enable the interfaces of network devices and end devices according to the scheme.
- Configure local name definitions on routers.
- Configure the Dynamic Routing Protocol - RIPv2 on each router, and then test the connection between **Server** and **Computer Workstation**.

- Set the configuration of the routers so that they can be accessed remotely using the Telnet protocol and then check if there is access from **Laptop Admin** to **Zagreb**.

11.2.2 RIPv2 and Configuration Using Telnet, Local Name Definition

In the figure below, there is a topology that must be created and configured in such a way that the OSPF dynamic routing protocol (**AS 10**) operates on the network, and each router in addition to its own ID in OSPF is to be accessible via a virtual Telnet terminal. On the **SERVER HTTP** device, create a web page that displays your name in green, you want every user of the network to have access to this page.

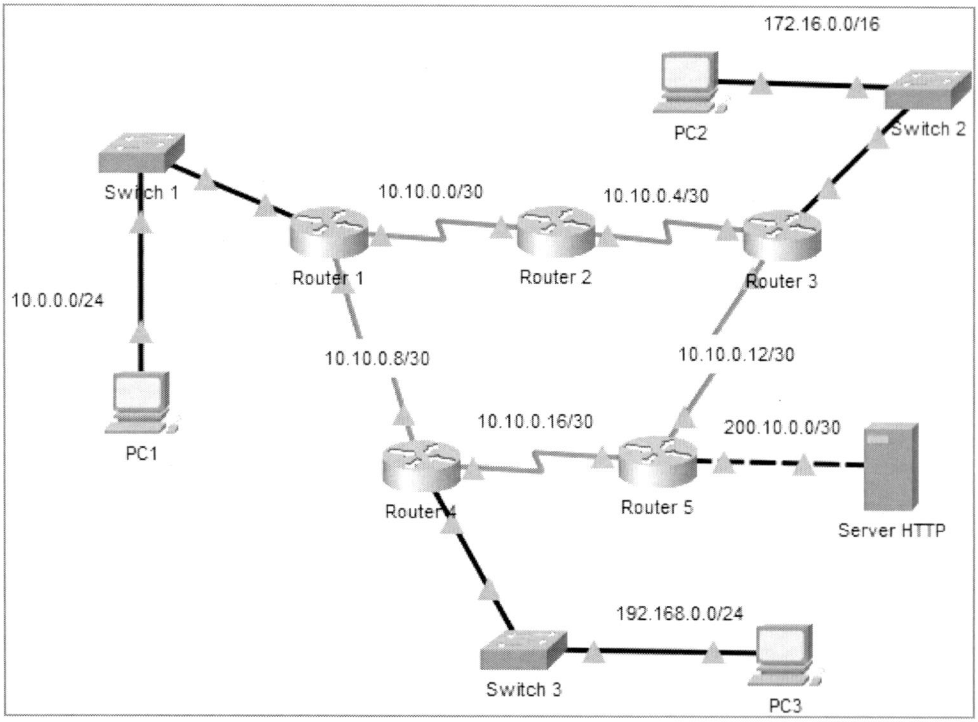

Figure 11.4 Exercise topology

Solution:

- Create a topology as in the picture, connect the devices to each other using the appropriate cables.
- Address and enable the interfaces of network devices and endpoints according to the topology scheme.

- Configure the OSPF dynamic routing protocol with an AS number of **10** and a area of **0**. Each router is to have a unique defined identifier.
- Set the routers so that they can be configured remotely using telnet and then try to access **Router 2** from **PC3**.
- Configure index.html on the **HTTP Server** device as intended.
- Try to access the website with the address **200.10.0.2** from **PC1**.
- Test the connectivity between **PC3** and **PC2** with the **tracert** command.

11.2.3 EIGRP and Configuration via SSH, HTTP and DNS

The required topology is shown in the figure below. Address it correctly and enable network interfaces according to the schema and configure the Dynamic Routing Protocol (EIGRP) (**AS 5**). Also configure the routers in such a way that they can be accessed using the **SSH** protocol. An IP domain is **eigrp.com**. The SSH protocol is to be available on two channels: 0 and 1. When you have completed these steps, edit the HTML page on the **HTTP Server** so that the page displays any inscription in the middle. This page is to be available at **www.anyname.com** .

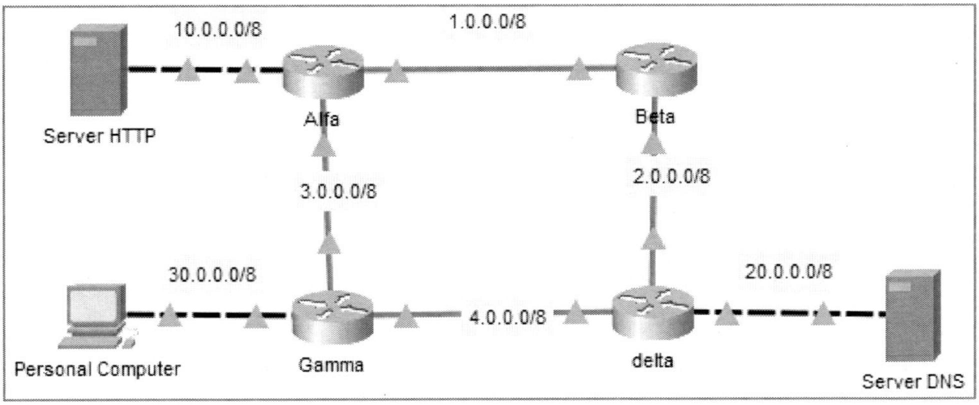

Figure 11.5 Exercise topology

Solution:

- Create a topology as in the picture, connect the devices to each other using the appropriate cables.
- Address and enable the interfaces of network devices and endpoints according to the topology scheme.
- Configure the EIGRP dynamic routing protocol with an AS number of 5.

- Position the routers so that they can be configured remotely using the SSH protocol. Create an admin account with admin password, use **modulus 1024** and **eigrp.com** domain. Set the privileged mode password to **enable**.
- Configure index.html on the **HTTP Server** as intended.
- Add an entry on the DNS server so that the **HTTP Server** is available under the **www.anyname.com.**
- Test the connection by using the PING command between **Personal Computer** and **Server DNS**.
- Try displaying the **www.anyname.com** from Personal Computer page.

11.3 VLANs, Router on a Stick, Remote Management

11.3.1 Switch Modes, VLAN Configuration

Create a topology that consists of three offices connected to each other by three switches. You have to configure the switches in the right way so that the end devices can only communicate within their offices.

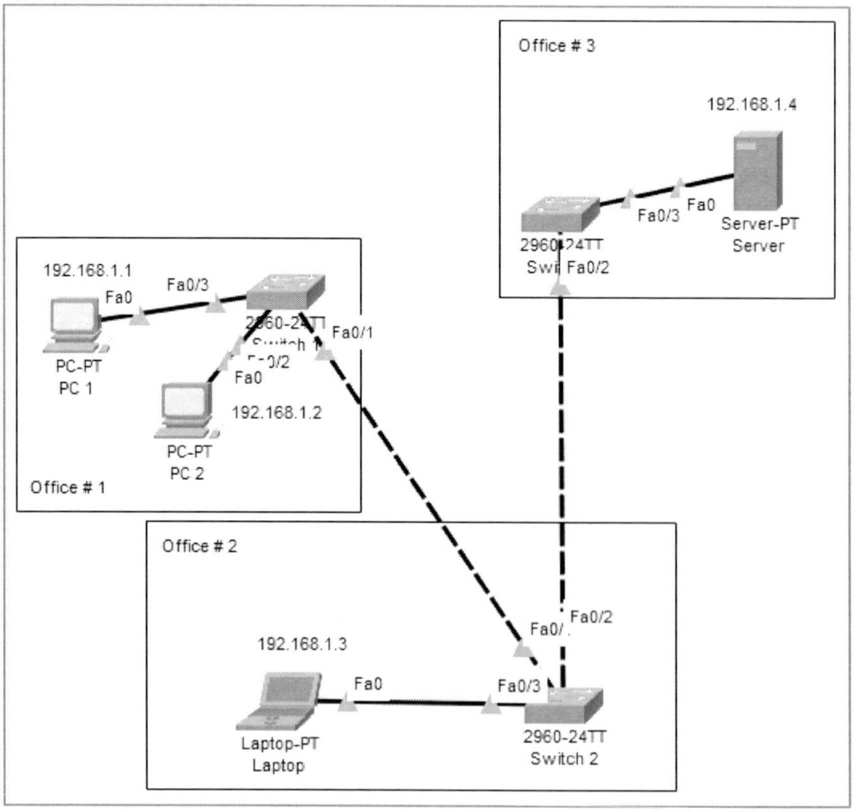

Figure 11.6 Exercise topology

Solution:

- Create a topology as in the picture, connect the devices to each other using the appropriate cables.
- Address endpoint interfaces according to the topology scheme.
- Configure the switches correctly, configure the VLAN database: three VLANs on each switch vlan10 - **OFFICE1**, vlan20 - **OFFICE2**, vlan30 - **OFFICE3**.
- Change the modes of operation of the ports on the switches accordingly so that they match the assumptions.
- Check if you can communicate between offices – the result should be negative.

11.3.2 VLAN Configuration, Routing Between VLANs

In a logical topology, there should be four switches and one router in this exercise. Create a VLAN database that will include: **VLAN11**, **VLAN22** and **VLAN33**. According to the topology scheme, assign VLANs to ports and configure the router in such a way that VLANs can communicate with each other. There is an additional emergency connection between **Switch 1** and **Switch 2**.

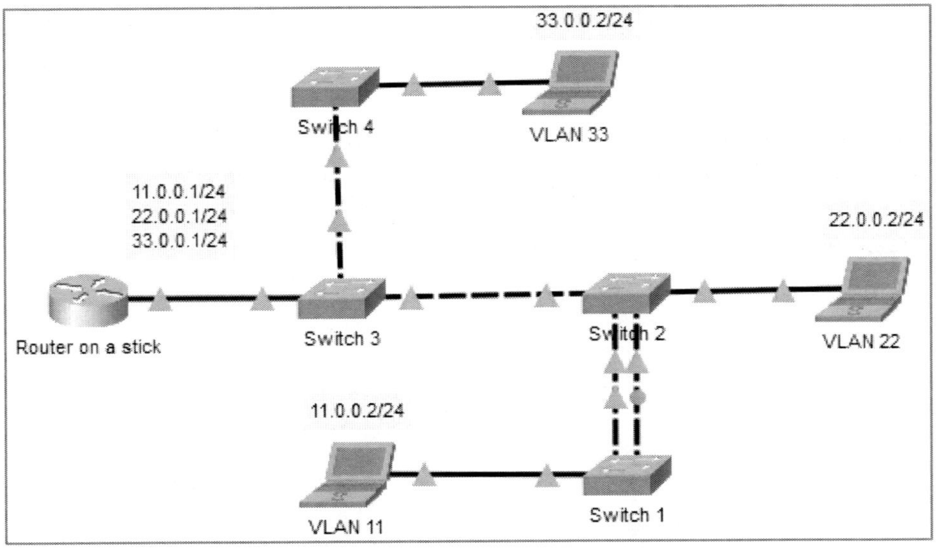

Figure 11.7 Exercise topology

Solution:

- Create a logical topology as in the figure, connect the devices to each other using the appropriate cables.
- Address endpoint interfaces according to the schema.
- Go to the switches and configure the VLAN database - three VLANs on each switch: 11 - **VLAN11,** 22 - **VLAN22**, 33 - **VLAN33**.
- Change the modes of operation of the ports on the switches accordingly so that they match the assumptions.
- Check if you can communicate between VLANs – the result should be negative.
- Configure the router interface and sub-interfaces to route traffic between VLANs.
- Try to send an ICMP packet between **VLAN11** and **VLAN33.**
- The result should be positive.

11.3.3 Remote Switch Management

Build a simple topology that includes one wireless router, two switches, and one **Admin** mobile device. Configure the switches so that the **S1** is configurable remotely using Telnet. The password is **zaq1**, the login account is **admin**, and the privileged mode password is **@WSX.**

In turn, the **S2** switch is to be remotely accessible using the **SSHv2** protocol – logging in is to be performed only to the **admin** user account with the **admin** password, while access to the privileged mode is to be protected by a **qwerty** password. An IP domain is a **switch.com** .

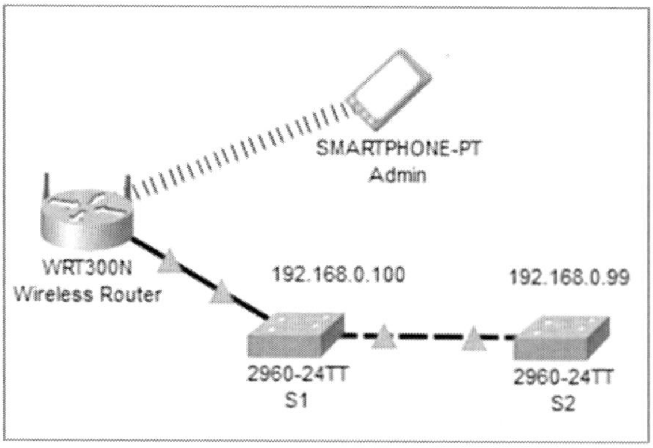

Figure 11.8 Exercise's topology

Solution:

- Create a topology according to the drawing, connect the devices to each other using the appropriate cables.
- Address the interfaces of network devices according to the topology drawing.
- Make sure that the **Admin** computer gets a dynamic IP address.
- Configure **S1** so that network access can be possible using a virtual terminal and **Telnet**. Use the **admin** user, the password for privileged mode **@WSX**, and the password for the **zaq1** terminal.
- Configure **S2** so that network access can be possible using a virtual terminal and the **SSHv2** protocol. Use the **admin** user, the privileged mode password **qwerty**, and the IP domain **switch.com**.
- Perform an access check using **Telnet** from the **Admin** smartphone to **S1** and using **SSH** to **S2**.

11.3.4 Protocol REP in Switches

Perform REP configuration in the following point-to-point topology.

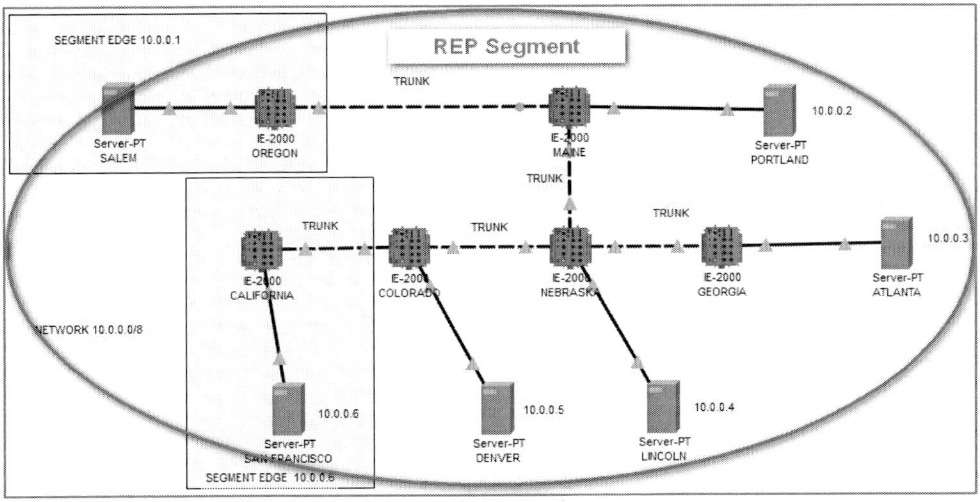

Figure 11.9 REP Segment Topology

Solution:

- Create a topology according to the figure shown.

- Configure addressing of SALEM, PORTLAND, SAN FRANCISCO, DENVER, LINCOLN, ATLANTA, computers in the local network (next addresses: 10.0.0.1/8, 10.0.0.2/8, 10.0.0.3/8, 10.0.0.4/8, 10.0.0.5/8, 10.0.0.6/8)
- Make connections of SALEM, PORTLAND, SAN FRANCISCO, DENVER, LINCOLN, ATLANTA computers with appropriate switches: OREGON, MAINE, CALIFORNIA, COLORADO, NEBRASKA, GEORGIA, using Fast Ethernet 1/1 interfaces.
- Connect the switches to each other using patch cables in TRUNK mode:
- Fa1/2 LINCOLN - Fa1/2 ATLANTA
- Gi1/1 OREGON - Gi1/1 MAINE
- Gi1/2 MAINE - Gi1/2 NEBRASKA
- Gi1/1 NEBRASKA - Gi1/1 COLORADO
- Gi1/2 COLORADO - Gi1/2 CALIFORNIA
- Configure the **REP** segment **number 1** in each switch using the commands:

interface <interface name>

switchport mode trunk

rep segment 1

CHAPTER 12

WORKING WITH LARGE TOPOLOGIES

COMPUTER NETWORKS IN PACKET TRACER

FOR BEGINNERS

12 Working with Large Topologies

This chapter describes the use of clouds and the basics of Multiuser mode and is intended for intermediate users.

Note – Warning: Remember to periodically save the file state during exercises (keyboard shortcut CTRL+S)

12.1 Introduction to Device Grouping

What is the use of device grouping? Very often, the person responsible for the design of the network, before implementing it into practical operation, creates a network model using simulation programs.

When creating complex networks that contain multiple subnets, each with a different purpose and a different area of operation, network design becomes increasingly complex. Therefore, it becomes very useful for the network designer to be able to divide the network into subnets also in a graphical form.

The main purpose of grouping devices when creating more complex networks is the need to group them so that the final logical scheme of the network with a high degree of complexity contains fewer graphic elements depicted on the screen. Device grouping (according to the original Cisco Systems **Clustering devices** nomenclature) does not affect the logical configuration of the network (addressing) and its functioning.

The original English name in the Cisco Packet Tracer for grouped devices (as originally named by Cisco Systems) is **Cluster**. The book uses the name **Cloud,** because according to the subjective opinion of the authors, this Polish equivalent most closely matches the icon representing a group of devices.

The Cisco Packet Tracer also allows you to move individual devices or their groups between clouds and create a hierarchical structure of clouds (sub cloud in the clouds).

12.2 Device Grouping – Description of Tool Buttons

At the top of the Cisco Packet Tracer is the main menu and the toolbar. On the left (under the toolbar) is a switch between the logical and physical modes of the network. In order to perform the basic operations described in this subsection, we will set this switch to **Logical** mode.

Figure 12.1 Logical topology area

In the **Logical** view, the blue bar contains the following buttons: **[Root]**, **Go back one level, New Cluster, Move Object, Set Tiled Background, Environment.** To perform actions related to clouds, we will use the following buttons.

Figure 12.2 Buttons in logical topology view

After starting the program in the logical topology view, all devices are placed at the main level (**[Root]**). To familiarize yourself with the program's capabilities regarding the grouping of devices in the clouds, we will follow the steps described in the next subsection.

12.3 Device Grouping – Step-By-Step Algorithm

We start by creating a simple network, consisting of a router, a switch and five computers.

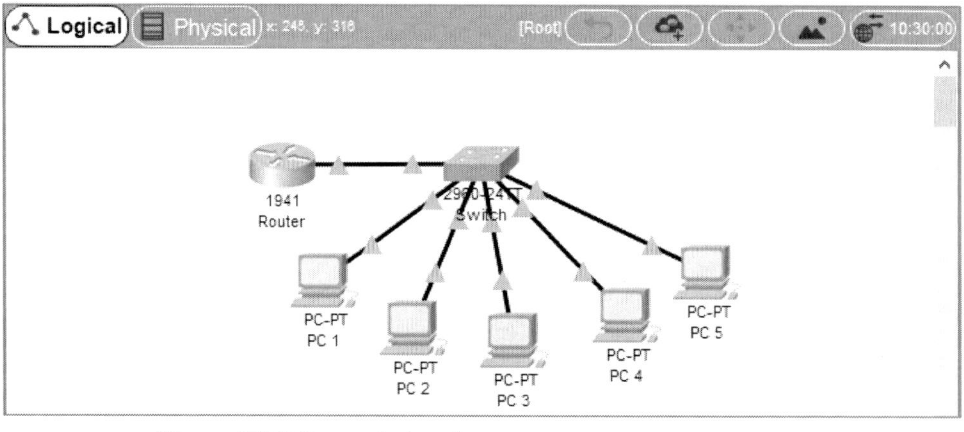

Figure 12.3 Example topology

To group devices into one graphic object, select a group of devices (using the **Select** tool).

Figure 12.4 Selecting tool, located at the top left

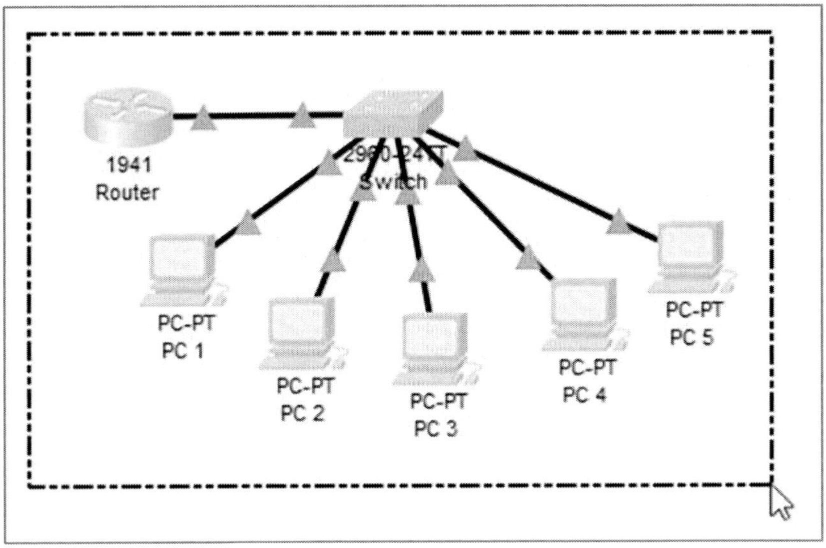

Figure 12.5 Devices selected with the Select tool

After selecting the device group, click the **New Cluster** button.

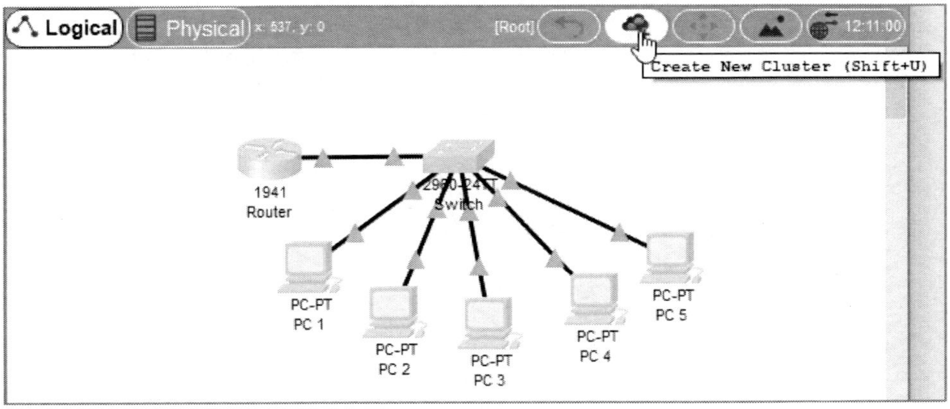

Figure 12.6 Create a new cloud

We have created a new graphic object. In the area of logical topology, a cloud called **Cluster0** appeared. We did a simple grouping of devices in the cloud.

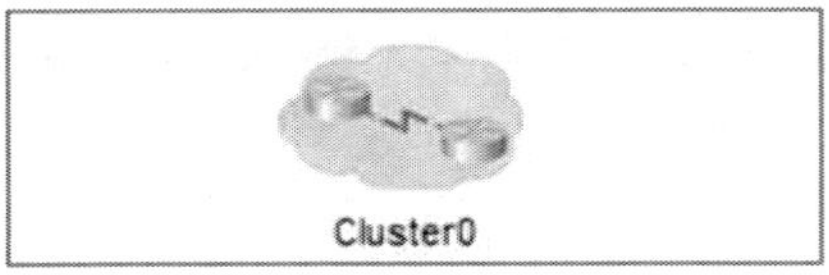

Figure 12.7 A new cloud called Cluster0

To enter the cloud, we click on the cloud with the left mouse button.

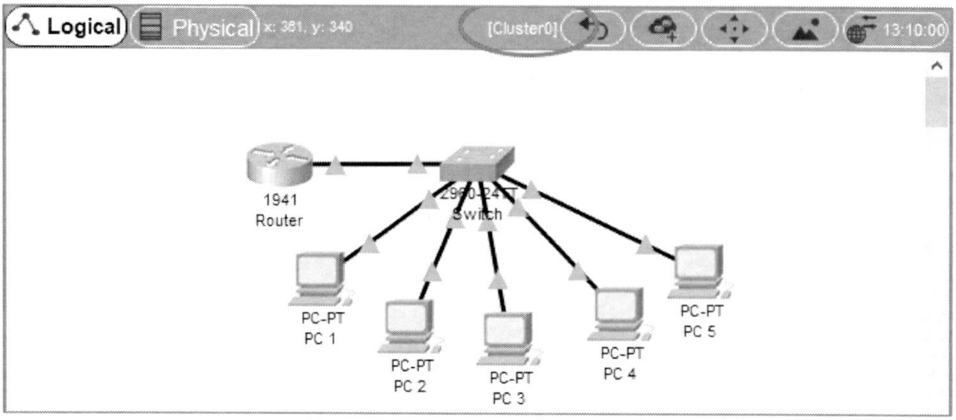

Figure 12.8 Cluster0 cloud content view

To exit the cloud, use the **Back** button. In this way, the main logical topology level is returned.

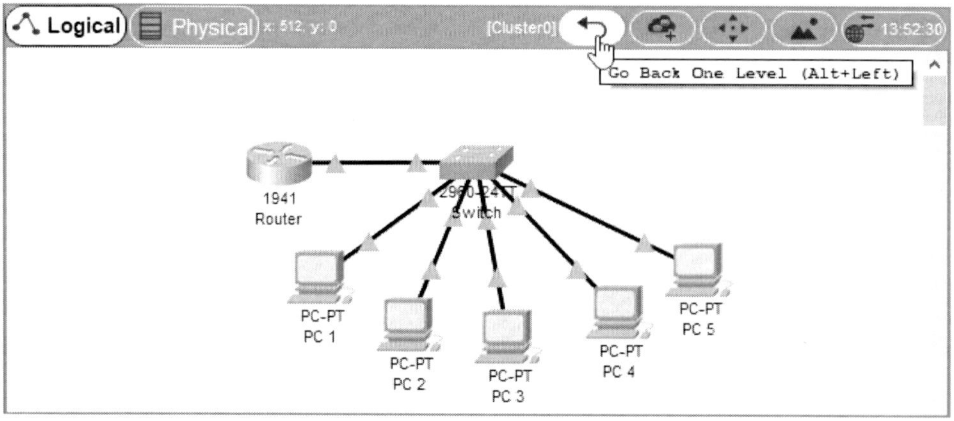

Figure 12.9 Exiting the Cluster0 cloud

12.4 Move a Single Device From the Cloud to the Root Level

In the example below, we will continue cloud operations, that is, we will move the router from the **Cluster0** cloud to the main topology level. To move the router out of the cloud, click **Move Object**, and then select the router.

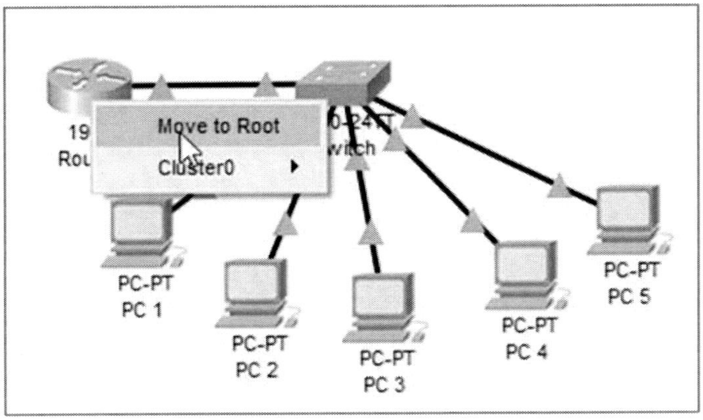

Figure 12.10 Select a Cluster0 cloud router

To move the router to the **Root** level, we select the **Move to Root** option. The router will be removed from the cloud, while the cable connection will remain, as shown in the figure below. After exiting the cloud, the router will appear at the main level.

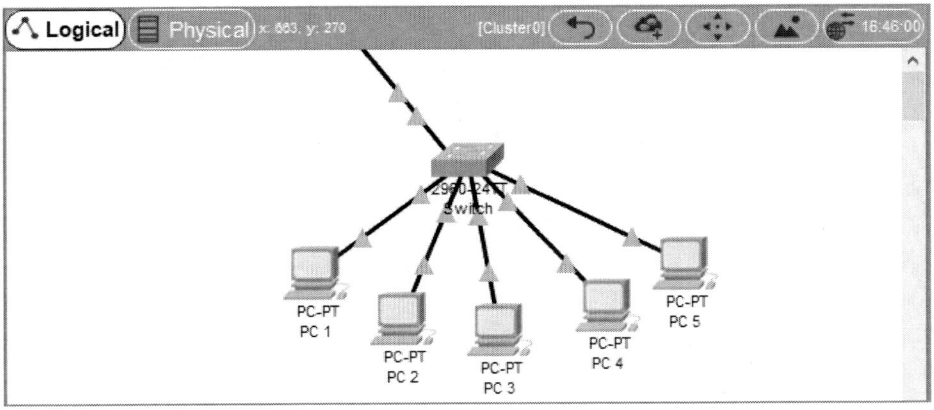

Figure 12.11 Cluster0 Cloud Topology

At the main level, a router will appear and as you can see in the figure, the router is located outside the **Cluster0** cloud.

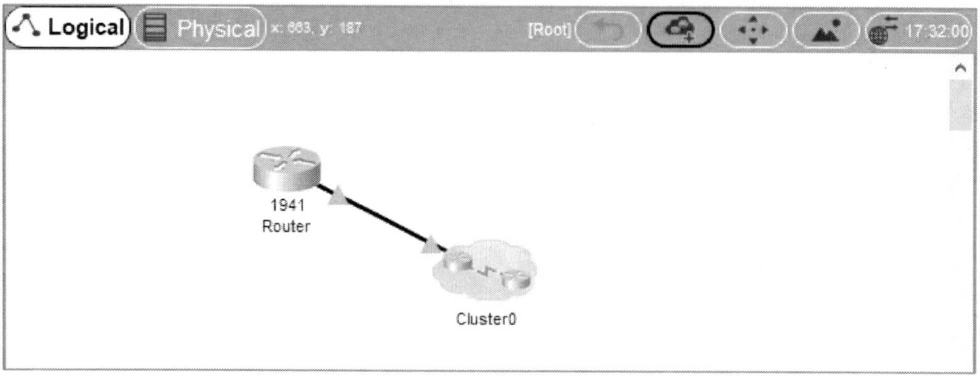

Figure 12.12 Root level topology

12.5 Move a Single Device from the Root Level to the Cloud

In the following example, we will move the router from the main topology to the **Cluster0** cloud. To move the router from the **Root** level to the cloud called **Cluster0**, we must first click the **Move Object** button, and then select the router.

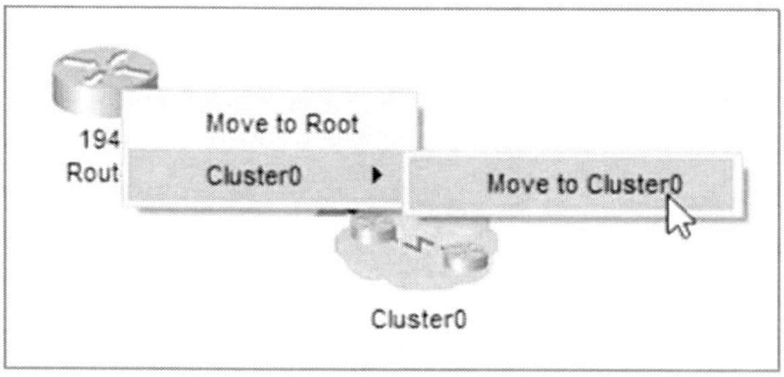

Figure 12.13 Root level topology before moving the router

After performing this option, we will notice that the router will disappear from the main level, but will appear at the **Cluster0** cloud level. To check this, we need to go to the **Cluster0** cloud.

To go to the cloud we click on it. The contents of the **Cluster0** cloud will appear, where you can see that the router is still properly connected to the other devices. The **Cluster0** cloud topology is shown in the figure.

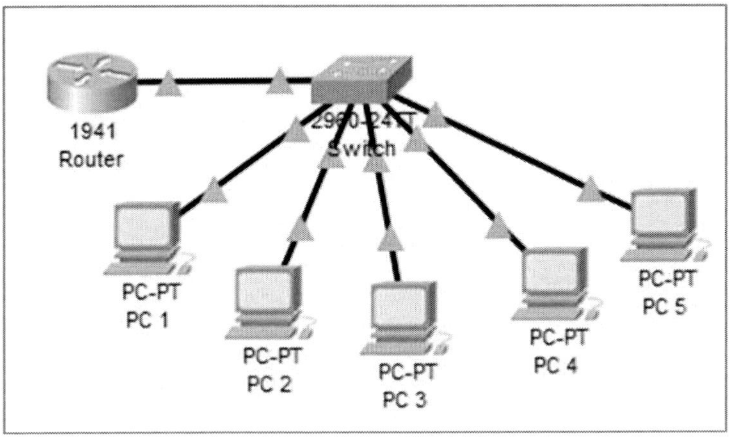

Figure 12.14 Cloud-level topology after router transfer

12.6 Purpose of the Set Tiled Background Button

In the Cisco Packet Tracer, you can change the icons that represent devices and configure the topology background. The example shown in this section is provided for informational purposes only.

To take advantage of this capability, you must first create icon files that represent devices and backgrounds. They should be created using any external program that can save images in PNG or JPG format. The recommended resolution for an icon file is: **45 pixels x 31 pixels. Note: Higher resolutions will be automatically scaled to lower resolutions**.

Use the **Set Tiled Background** button on the blue bar to configure the background image for the current logical topology. To change the default background of the logical topology, click the **Set Tiled Background** button.

Figure 12.15 Set Tiled Background button

At the bottom of the window, set the **Display Tiled Background Image** option. Then we select the background image file using the **Browse** button.

Figure 12.16 Select a file for the background and set background display options

An example of how the logical topology looks like as bellow showed, when you change the default values of **Background Image.**

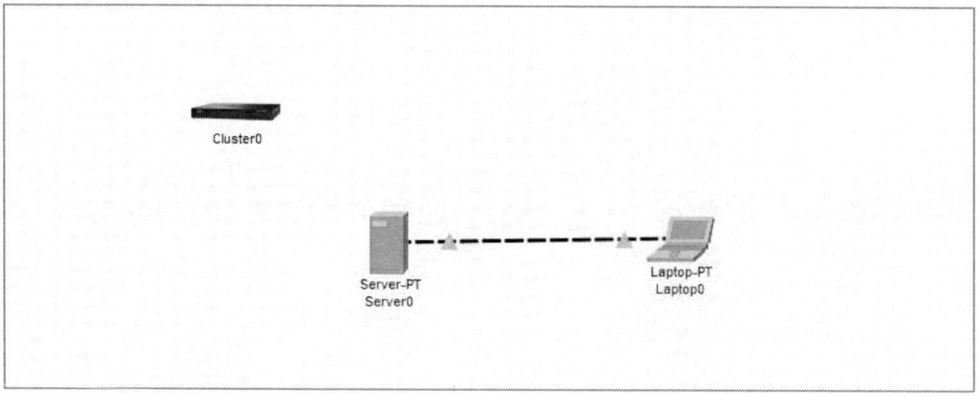

Figure 12.17 Topology after background change

The second example of the logical topology in the **Cluster0** cloud after changing the default values of **Background Image** and **Cluster Icon.**

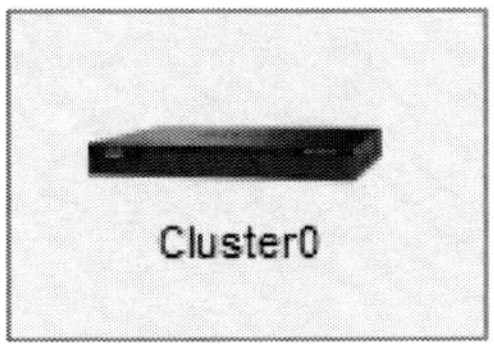

Figure 12.18 Cluster icon after changing the icon

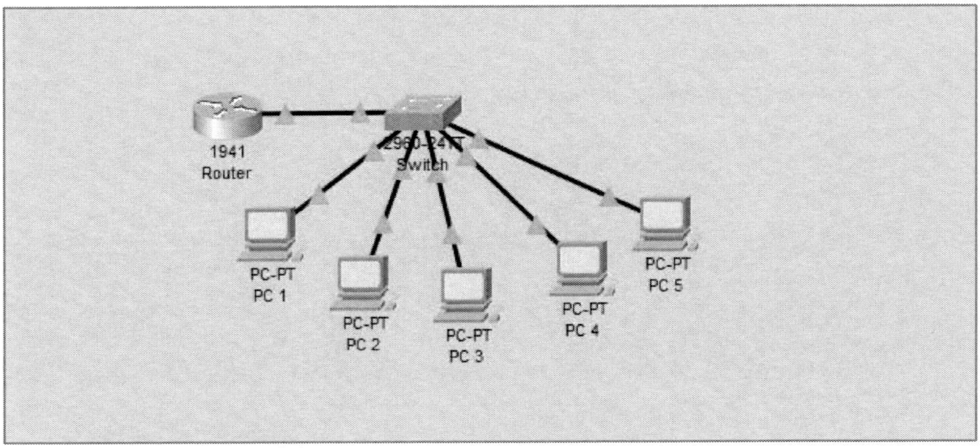

Figure 12.19 Example Topology after background change for Cluster0

12.7 Rename a Cloud

Changing the name of the cloud can be freely carried out provided that the names of the clouds differ from each other. This operation is very simple, because you only need to click on the name under the cloud symbol and edit the appropriate text.

Remember, however, that it is a good habit to use cloud names according to their purpose or area of application, e.g. **"Internet", "ISP", "Cellular network", "ALABAMA".** It is not recommended to leave the default generated names of type "Cluster0", because in the case of more complex networks, they will not inform us about the nature of a given subnet.

12.8 Multiuser Mode

Multiuser, i.e. communication with many users, allows you to create point-to-point (peer) connections between many Cisco Packet Tracer instances. What is an instance? An instance is the launch of a given application (in this case the Cisco Packet Tracer) as a separate process in an operating system, e.g. Windows.

By enabling communication between the Cisco Packet Tracer instances, the door opens to new types of tasks and variety of work in groups. Communication between different Packet Tracer stations is via TCP and uses port **38000** by default. The default password is **cisco.**

To start working in two different instances, first run the Cisco Packet Tracer in two windows and execute the two basic networks. In the first one there will be a computer and a router, and in the second one there will be a router and a laptop. The devices are addressed as shown in the diagram below.

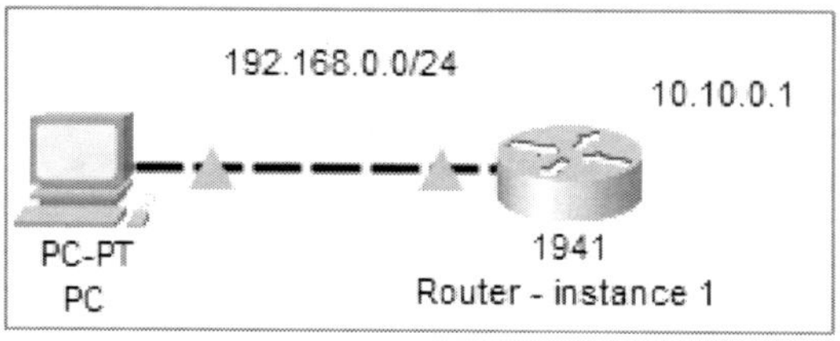

Figure 12.20 Topology to configure Mutliuser - instance 1

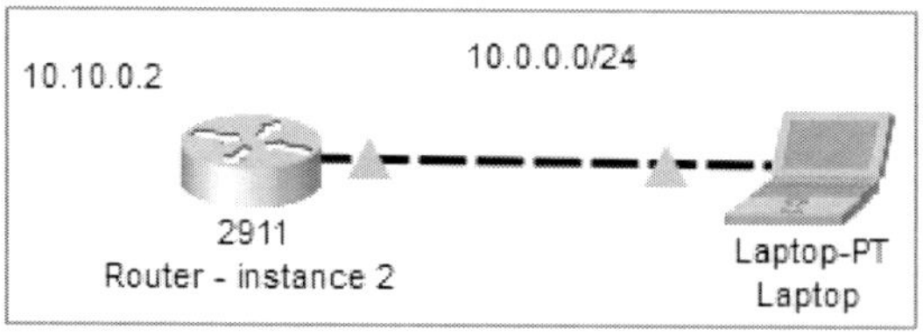

Figure 12.21 Topology to configure multiuser - instance 2

After configuring two networks in two separate instances, select the **Extensions →Multiuser →Port Visibility** tab in the tabs at the top of the program to set which ports are visible in the second instance of the program. On both instances, select one port of the Router.

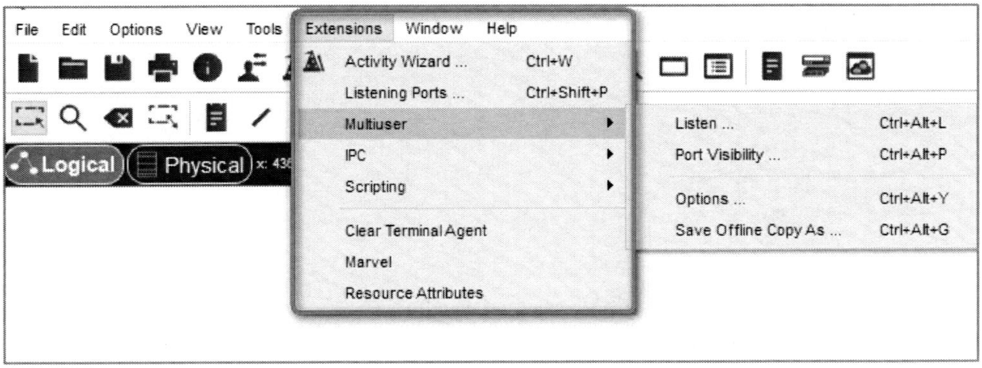

Figure 12.22 Multiuser configuration options

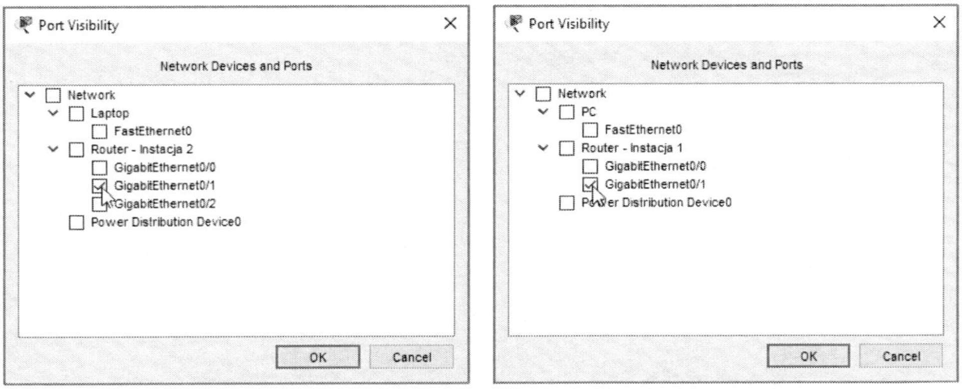

Figure 12.23 Enable port visibility in another instance

Once you know which ports will be visible in another instance, set a default password (**cisco**) for connections and change the listening so that all connections are activated as shown in the figure below.

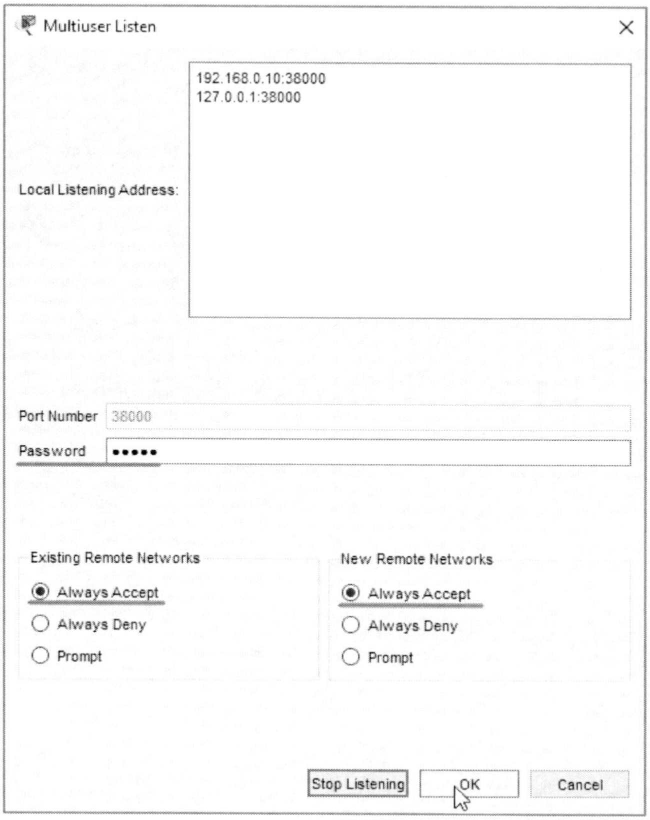

Figure 12.24 Change your password and listening options

This should be done in the same way in the case of the second instance. Now you need to add a new device to one of our instances (no matter which one you choose - in our example it is **Instance 1**). This device is called **Remote Network** and is named as **Multiuser**.

Figure 12.25 Remote Network device

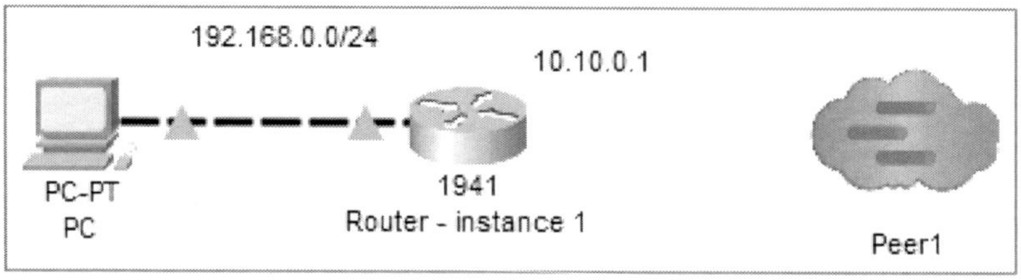

Figure 12.26 Appearance of the topology when you add a new device

According to which port we have chosen before, in order to be visible, you should pull the connection to **Peer1** and choose to create a new connection.

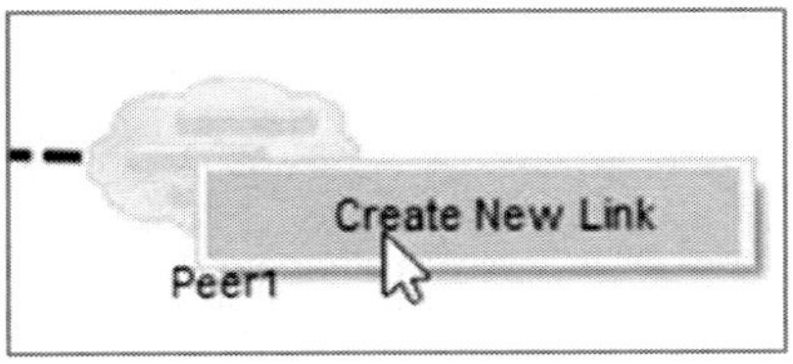

Figure 12.27 Connection to Peer1

We are left with the configuration of the **Peer1** cloud so that it connects to the second instance, which is enabled at all times. Select the **Outgoing** connection type and enter the appropriate password that you have previously set.

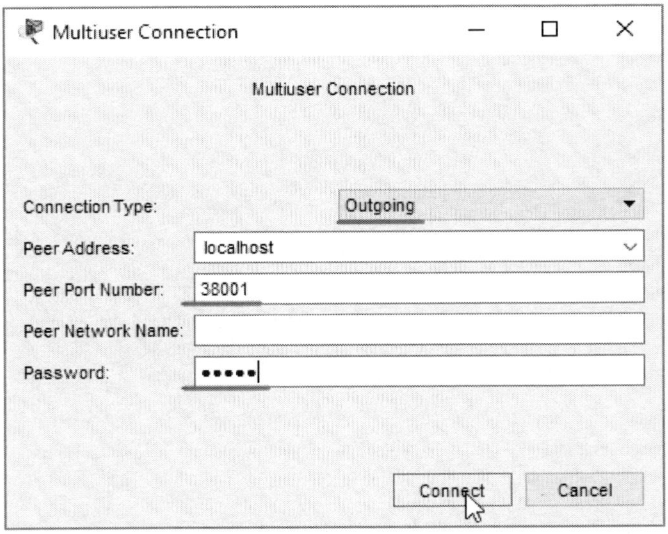

Figure 12.28 Connection to the second instance

If everything is well configured, then after clicking the **Connect** button, a new device with a yellowish colour should appear in **Instance 2 (number two).**

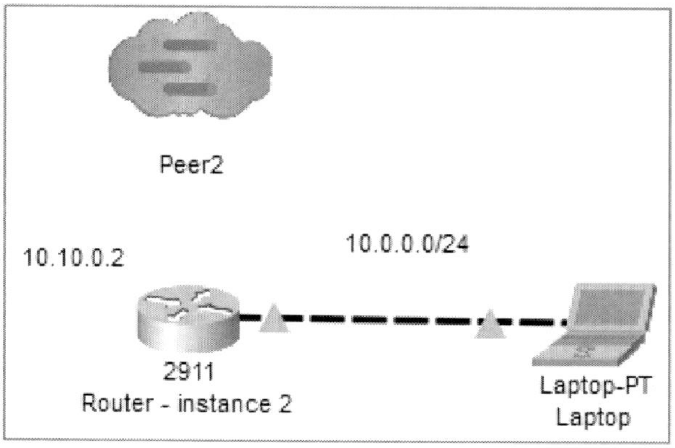

Figure 12.29 New cloud Peer2 in Instance 2

We select the patch cable and from the appropriate interface **Router - Instance 2** we connect to the router, which is located in another instance.

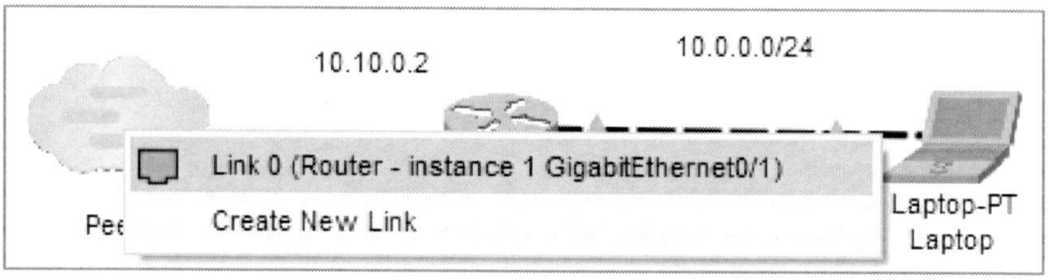

Figure 12.30 Connect to a router in another instance

To test our connection, we will address the interfaces between the routers so that they are in the 10.10.0.0/30 network and on each router we will configure the simplest dynamic routing protocol – **RIPv2**.

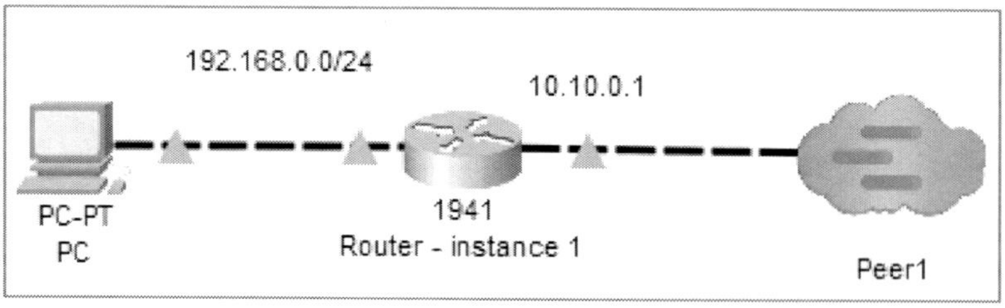

Figure 12.31 Instance 1 - ready example

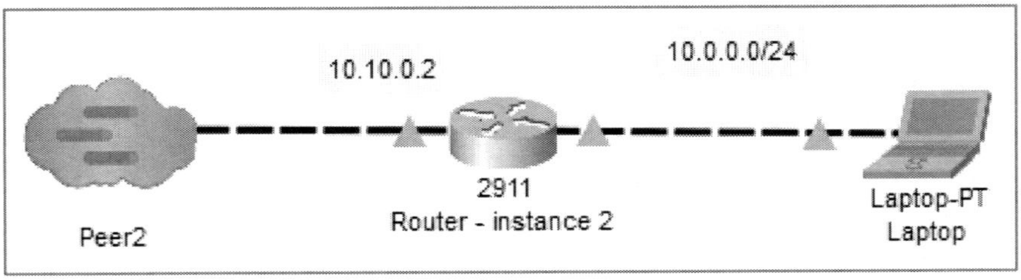

Figure 12.32 Instance 2 - ready example

After conducting a simple PING command from PC to Laptop, we get a positive result, which proves that our network between instances works in the correct way.

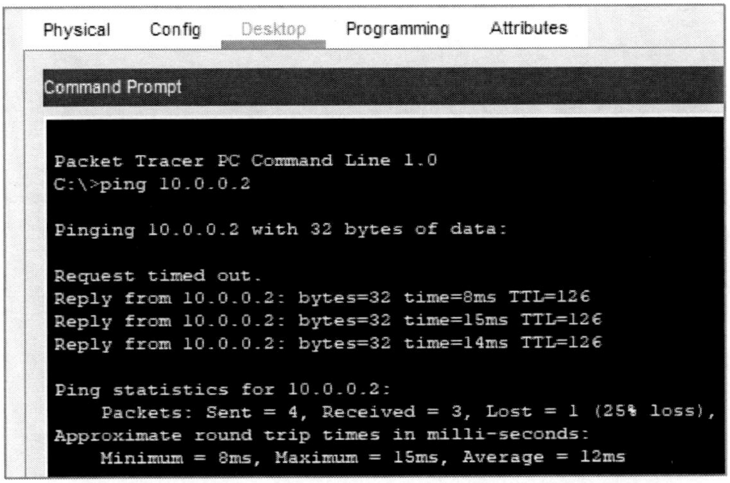

Figure 12.33 Successful PING from PC to Laptop

This is just a simple example to show you how to configure the simplest connection between instances. Of course, the possibilities are endless and you can use this function in a very interesting way, so we encourage you to experiment.

CHAPTER 13

DHCP PROTOCOL FOR IPV4

COMPUTER NETWORKS IN PACKET TRACER

FOR BEGINNERS

13 DHCP Protocol for IPV4

This chapter describes DHCP for IPv4.

Note – Warning: Remember to periodically save the file state during exercises (keyboard shortcut CTRL+S)

13.1 Introduction to DHCP

13.1.1 DHCP Basics

The DHCP service is very widely used in large networks that we encounter every day. This chapter describes this topic in more detail compared to what has already been written in the previous sections. For the record and consolidation, we'll discuss what DHCP is all about from the beginning:

Unlike static IP configuration of network devices, Dynamic Host Configuration Protocol (DHCP) provides dynamic configuration for network devices (hosts). Network device after receiving the following information:

- IP address
- Netmask
- Default gateway
- and optional DNS server address

can communicate with other devices. Dynamic host configuration requires that there be **at least one** properly functioning **DHCP server** on the network.

A DHCP server can be a computer with a network operating system installed (e.g., Linux, Windows Server, or another) or any router running a DHCP service (e.g., a Cisco or other router, MikroTik, a wireless ISR router). The most important configuration information obtained from the DHCP server is:

- Assigned host IP address,
- Assigned host subnet mask,
- Assigned default gateway address,
- DNS server address
- Lease time, i.e. the time for which a given configuration applies to us

The principle of the DHCP service (the dynamic process of obtaining configuration data from a DHCP server) consists of four phases, shown in the following figure.

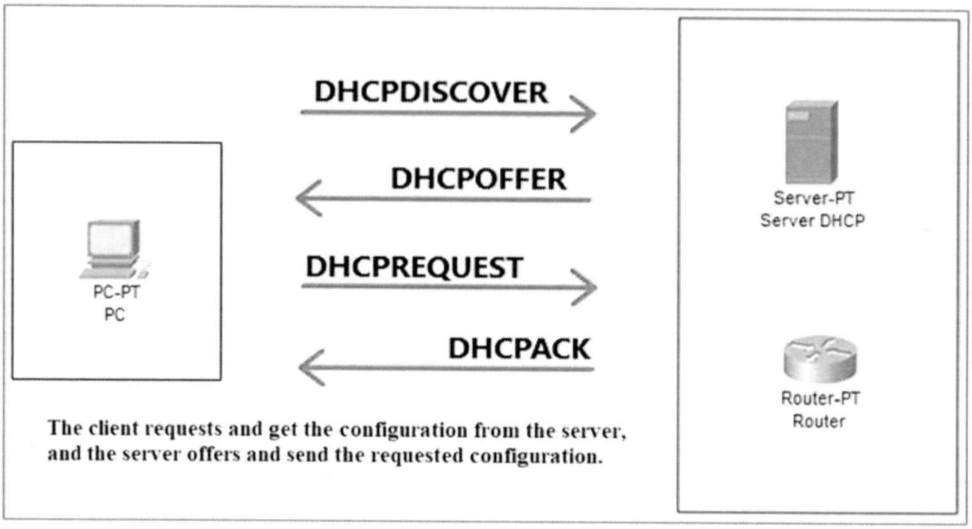

Figure 13.1 How the DHCP service (process) works

13.1.2 DHCP Phases

Phase 1: Searching for a DHCP server

The client (**PC**) sends a **DHCPDISCOVER** message to the entire network to get feedback on whether a DHCP server exists on the network. In general, there can be three situations:

- there is no DHCP server on the network, or the network is corrupted and the client does not have access to the DHCP server,
- There are multiple DHCP servers on the network,
- there is only one DHCP server on the network.

Let's answer the following question: **What happens if a client does not have access to DHCP?** If for any reason the client cannot receive a response from the DHCP server, by default it receives a random IP address from the **169.254.0.0/16** subnet. In this case, the customer will receive an address from the range of:

169.254.1.0/16 – 169.254.254.255/16

The above address range is intentionally designed to avoid accidental conflicts with other host addresses on the network. This range is officially recognized as a reserved pool of part of the Class B addresses, only for DHCP failure to obtain dynamic IP (see **RFC 3927**). Examples illustrating this situation can be found in the figures below.

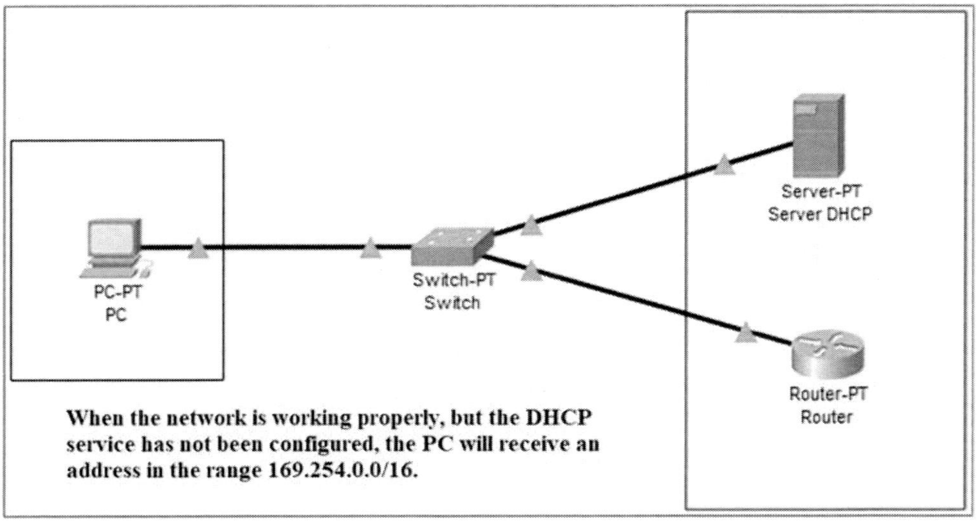

Figure 13.2 The network is working properly and there is no DHCP server configured

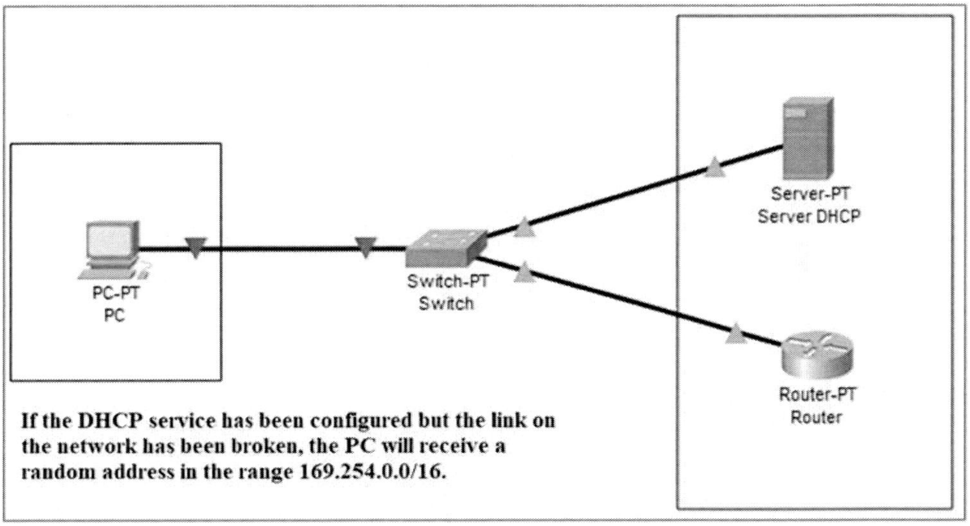

Figure 13.3 The network is corrupted and there is no access to the DHCP server

Let's answer the next question: **What happens when we have multiple DHCP servers on our network?**

If we have multiple DHCP servers in the network offering IP address configuration, the client will choose the offer that will be **the first** to be received from any DHCP server (i.e. the client will choose the DHCP server that **first** reported). The remaining servers will not be supported. Below we see a situation in which there are two running DHCP servers on the network (for example, one of them offers configuration on the **192.168.0./24** subnet, and the other on the **10.0.0.0/8** subnet).

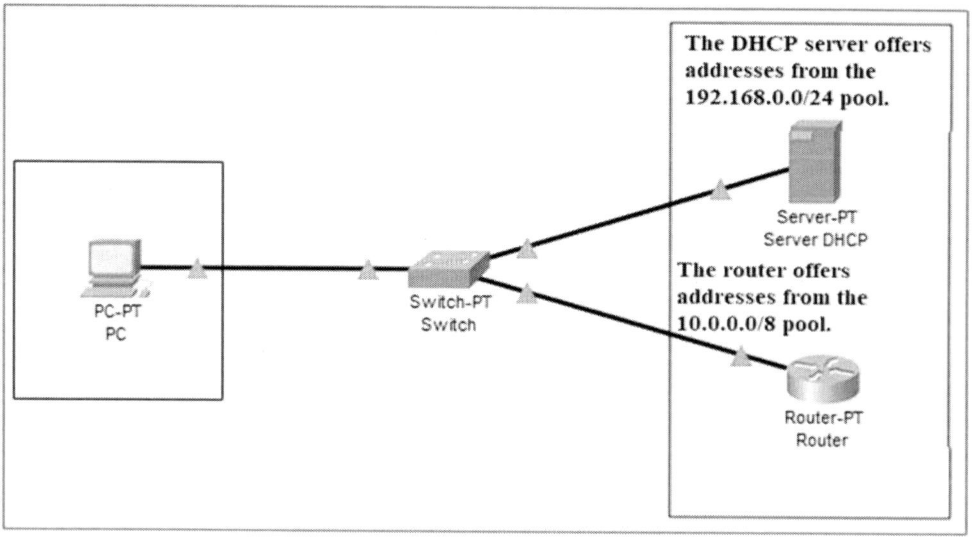

Figure 13.4 The network is working properly and contains two DHCP servers

In the presented example, a PC can get the following configuration:

```
IP Address......................: 10.0.0.2
Subnet Mask.....................: 255.255.255.0
Default Gateway.................: 10.0.0.1
DNS Server......................: 10.0.0.1
```

Figure 13.5 PC configuration obtained with Router

or configuration:

```
IP Address......................: 192.168.0.6
Subnet Mask.....................: 255.255.255.0
Default Gateway.................: 192.168.0.1
DNS Server......................: 192.168.0.254
```

Figure 13.6 PC Configuration obtained from DHCP Server

Next, let's answer the next question.

What happens if we have one DHCP server on the network?

If we have only one DHCP server in the network, this is the simplest situation, because the offered configuration of IP addresses will always be sent from only one server. After completing Phase 1, the DHCP server found responds to the client with a message containing an addressing offer (the server moves to perform Phase 2).

Phase 2: Send a DHCP server proposal to all DHCP clients

The DHCP server sends a **DHCPOFFER** message to all DHCP clients (DHCP hosts) containing the proposed address parameters. The main transmitted parameters are contained in the DHCPOFFER message fields:

- YIADDR (ang. *your IP address*) – the proposed IP address of the host,
- Subnet Mask – subnet mask,
- Source Address – source address (IP address of the DHCP server),
- Destination Address – broadcast destination address (255.255.255.255),

In this way, clients receive information about which server reported first (**Source Address**) and which address it offers to the client (**YIADDR**).

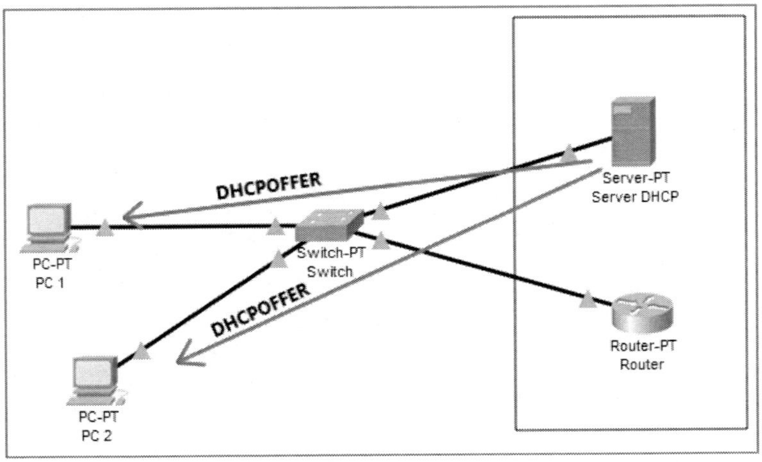

Figure 13.7 Send a DHCPOFFER response from the DHCP Server

Phase 3: Send a request for approval of a proposal to the DHCP server

The DHCP server waits for **DHCPREQUEST** messages from clients. The rule applies **"the customer who confirmed the offer first is the first"**. For example, **PC 1**. **PC 1** sends a **DHCPREQUEST** message to the DHCP server requesting that the offered address configuration be assigned.

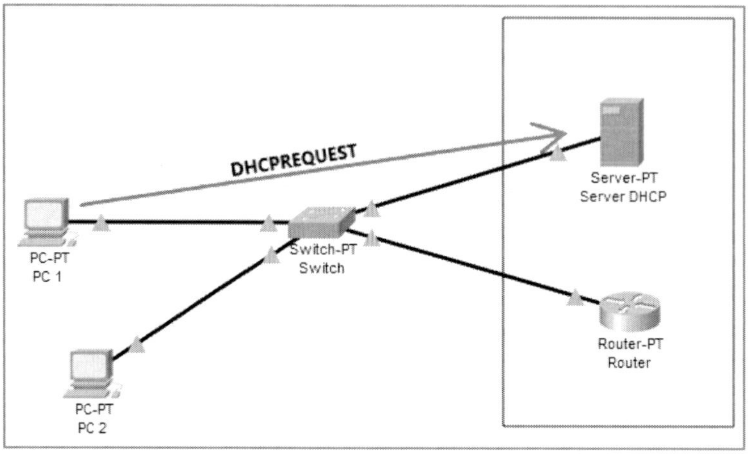

Figure 13.8 Send a DHCPREQUEST request to the DHCP server

Phase 4: DHCP server approval of the addressing proposal

After completing Phase 3, the DHCP server sends a **DHCPACK** message confirming the DHCP client's request and assigns address parameters (and their validity time, i.e. **lease time**). The default lease time varies and depends on the operating system that offers DHCP. The process of dynamically configuring client addressing is completed.

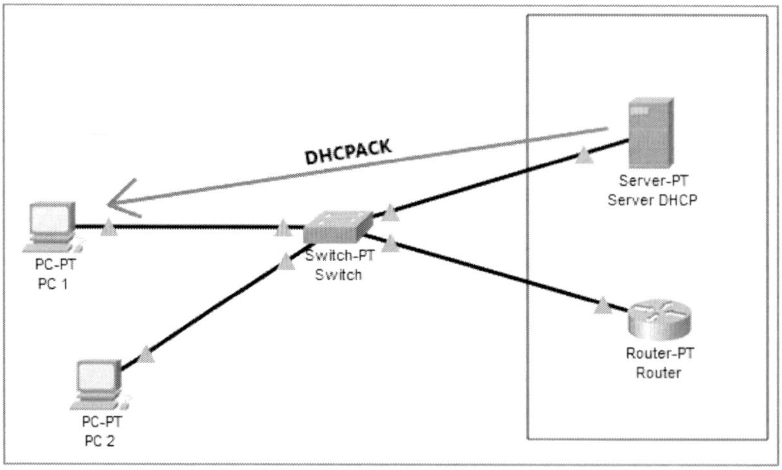

Figure 13.9 Send DHCPACK confirmation to DHCP client - Configuration completes

PC 1 has been assigned an address configuration and is therefore ready to communicate with the network.

13.2 Configuring DHCP on the Server

Before configuring the DHCP server service, we will configure its server network adapter, i.e. we will assign the following address data to it:

- IP address of the server,
- subnet mask,
- default gateway (optional)

As it has often been reworked, we will let go of showing how to do it and go straight to the configuration of the service.

13.2.1 Configuring the DHCP Server Service

Setting up DHCP on the server is very easy. To do this, activate the DHCP service and enter the appropriate values into the following fields in the **Services → DHCP**:

- Pool Name – name of the IP address pool,
- Default Gateway – default gateway address,
- DNS Server – the address of the default DNS server,
- Start IP Address – the initial (first) address in the IP address pool,
- Subnet Mask – subnet mask,
- Maximum number of Users – the maximum number of IP addresses in the pool.

To configure DHCP on the server, follow these steps:

Step 1. We choose a service

Select **DHCP Server**, go to the Services tab, and then select the **DHCP** service.

Step 2. We activate the DHCP service

Select the **On** option for DHCP.

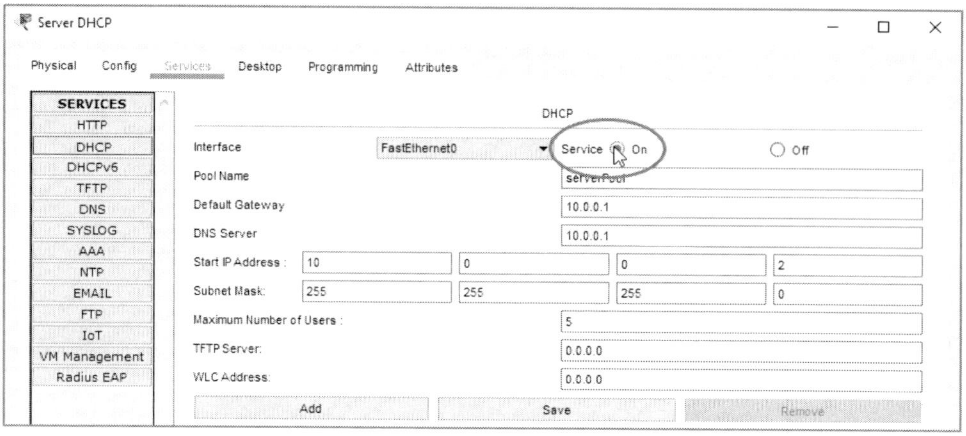

Figure 13.10 Activate DHCP on the server

Step 3. Configure DHCP service parameters

We fill in the appropriate fields for the service:

- Pool Name – name of the IP address pool,
- Default Gateway – default gateway address,
- DNS Server – the address of the default DNS server,
- Start IP Address – the initial (first) address in the IP address pool,
- Subnet Mask – subnet mask,
- Maximum number of Users – the maximum number of IP addresses in the pool,

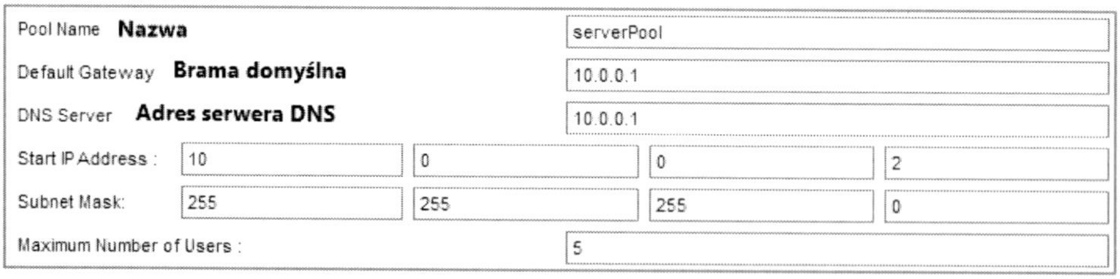

Figure 13.11 Configure DHCP parameters on the server

Step 4. We approve DHCP parameters

To confirm and save DHCP parameters, click **save**.

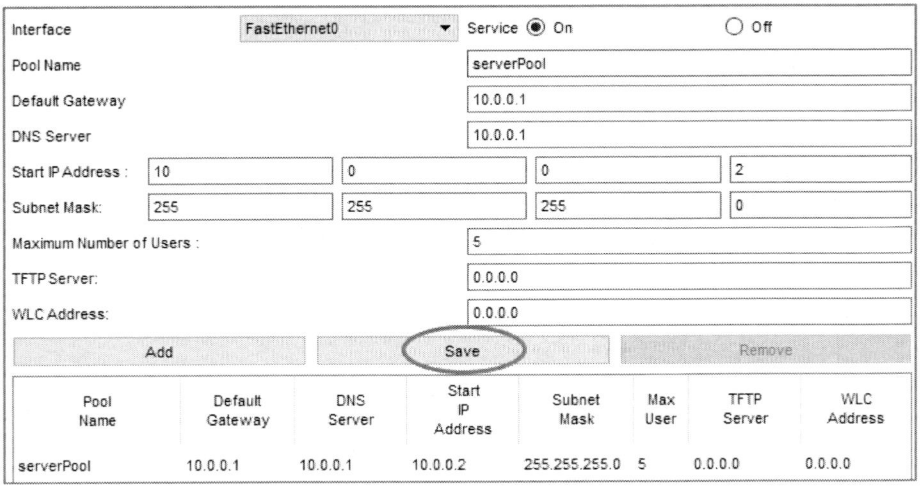

Figure 13.12 Saving DHCP parameters to the server

Step 5. We check the operation of the DHCP service

PC1, PC2, PC3 received IPv4 configuration from Server1. We can check this without using the command line or configuration windows. To check the current configuration of IP addresses for a given device, we move the mouse pointer to the appropriate computer icon. A small information frame in grey will be displayed, which will show us the configuration data of a given computer: the current IP address, subnet prefix, DNS server address.

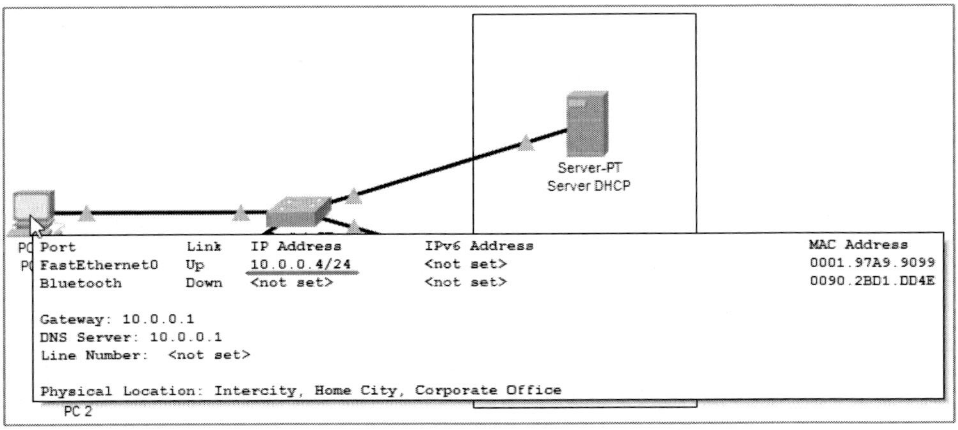

Figure 13.13 Check IPv4 addresses on PC1

We can also check whether the computers are communicating with the server. We use the single envelope symbol and ping from **PC 1** and **PC 2** to the **DHCP Server.**

Fire	Last Status	Source	Destination	Type	Color
	Successful	PC 1	Server DHCP	ICMP	
	Successful	PC 2	Server DHCP	ICMP	
	Successful	Server DHCP	PC 1	ICMP	

Figure 13.14 Check the communication of computers with the server

13.2.2 Erasing DHCP on the Server

The term "Erasing DHCP on the server" is understood to mean disabling the DHCP service or deleting the address pool in the DHCP service.

13.2.3 Disabling DHCP on the Server

Select a DHCP server. In the **Services→DHCP** tab, select the **Off** option.

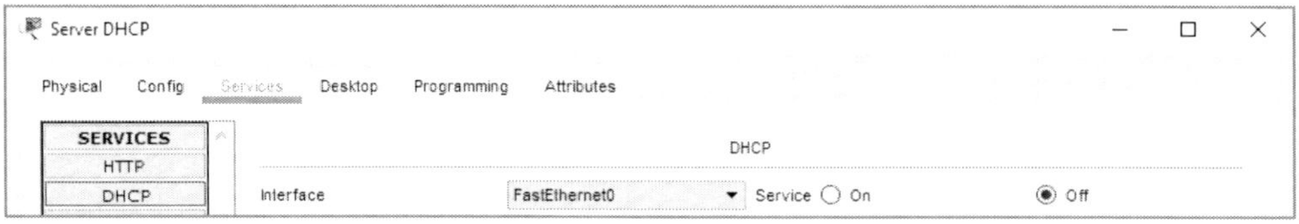

Figure 13.15 DHCP server is disabled

13.2.4 Deleting DHCP Address Pool on the Server

You can only remove an address pool from the DHCP server service if you have more than one pool. When we have only one pool defined, it must remain (it cannot be deleted). Suppose you have two address pools defined:

- serverPool (5 addresses in subnet 10.0.0.0/24) – pool one, default,
- secondPool (50 addresses on the 192.168.1.0/24 subnet) – second pool.

Pool Name	Default Gateway	DNS Server	Start IP Address	Subnet Mask	Max User
secondPool	192.168.1.1	192.168.1.2	192.168.1.10	255.255.255.0	50
serverPool	10.0.0.1	10.0.0.1	10.0.0.2	255.255.255.0	5

Figure 13.16 Defined DHCP address pools

To delete the pool called **secondPool**, go to the **Services→DHCP** tab, select the **secondPool** pool, and then click the **Remove** button.

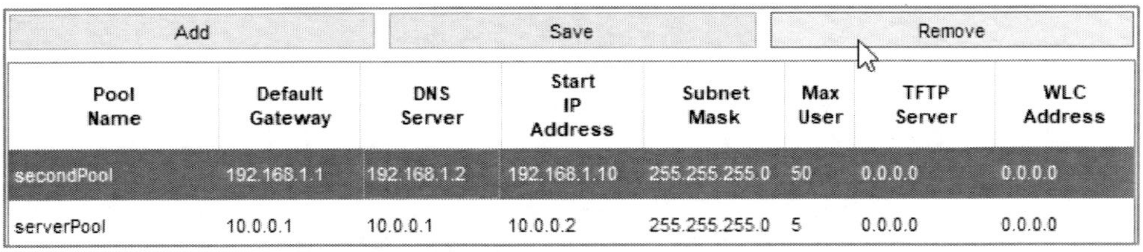

Pool Name	Default Gateway	DNS Server	Start IP Address	Subnet Mask	Max User	TFTP Server	WLC Address
secondPool	192.168.1.1	192.168.1.2	192.168.1.10	255.255.255.0	50	0.0.0.0	0.0.0.0
serverPool	10.0.0.1	10.0.0.1	10.0.0.2	255.255.255.0	5	0.0.0.0	0.0.0.0

Figure 13.17 Delete a DHCP address pool

Pool Name	Default Gateway	DNS Server	Start IP Address	Subnet Mask	Max User	TFTP Server	WLC Address
serverPool	10.0.0.1	10.0.0.1	10.0.0.2	255.255.255.0	5	0.0.0.0	0.0.0.0

Figure 13.18 DHCP address pool has been removed

13.3 Configuring DHCP on Your Router

In this example, we will configure the DHCP service as intended in the following table.

DHCP server address	192.168.0.1
DHCP pool name	PULA
IP address range in the pool	192.168.0.10-192.168.0.100/24
Default Gateway address	192.168.0.1
DNS Server address	10.0.0.1
Computer addresses (DHCP clients)	assigned automatically

Table 13.1 DHCP configuration data

We will use the above configuration data for the topology shown in the figure.

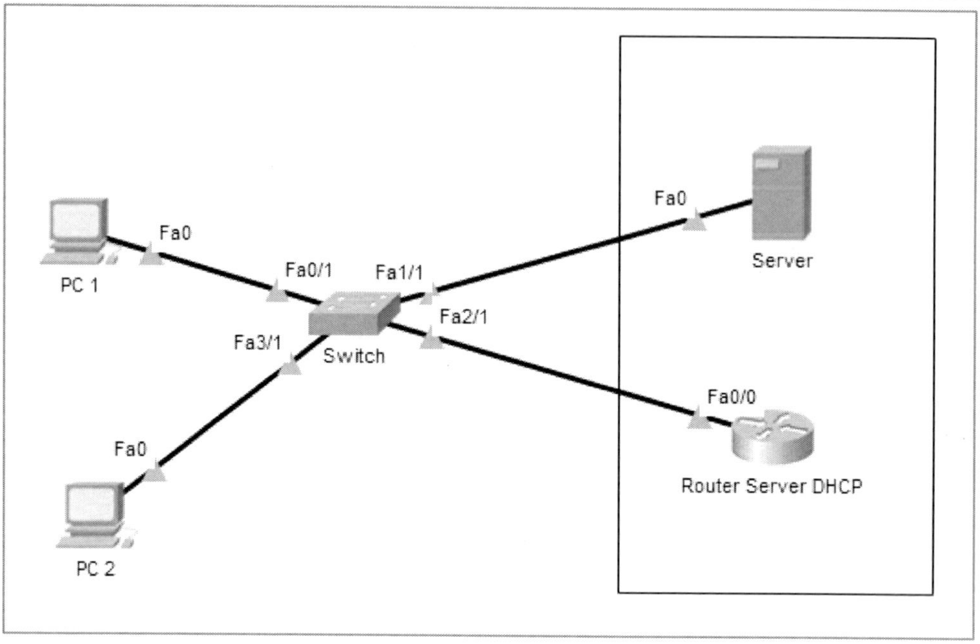

Figure 13.19 Network topology with DHCP server router and DHCP clients

Before configuring the DHCP service on the router, we need to make sure that the configurations of the router interfaces have been performed correctly. The interface should have the address 192.168.0.1 with a subnet mask /24.

If the configurations of the router interfaces are correct, then we proceed to the configuration of the DHCP server router.

Configuration of the **Router (DHCP server)** will be performed in the following stages:

- configuring the Fa0/0 interface (default gateway) of the DHCP server,
- configure the address pool on the router,
- displaying an array of assigned addresses,
- checking the operation of the service and the communication of computers with the router.

Configuring the Router Interface (DHCP Server)

We perform the configuration of the default gateway (Fa0/0 interface) of the Router router using the CLI command line.

We go to the global configuration mode and address the interface in the appropriate way and enable it.

```
Router>en
Router#conf t
Enter configuration commands, one per line.  End with CNTL/Z.
Router(config)#int fa0/0
Router(config-if)#ip address 192.168.0.1 255.255.255.0
Router(config-if)#no shutdown
Router(config-if)#exit
```

Figure 13.20 Configure the Router's Fa0/0 interface as the default gateway

13.3.1 Configure the Router (DHCP Server) Address Pool

After configuring the default gateway, we proceed to the proper configuration of the DHCP service on the router.

Practical note: after each change of DHCP configuration, we must renew the addressing lease on computers (DHCP clients) using the **ipconfig /renew command.**

```
C:\>ipconfig /renew

   IP Address......................: 10.0.0.3
   Subnet Mask.....................: 255.255.255.0
   Default Gateway.................: 10.0.0.1
   DNS Server......................: 10.0.0.1
```

Figure 13.21 Renew your addressing lease on PC1

Our first task will be to inform the router that its own address cannot be assigned to computers (DHCP clients).

If we do not do this, there may be an address conflict on the network (so-called *duplicate IP addresses* may occur on the network).

To do this, use the **ip dhcp excluded-address** command in the router's global configuration mode to indicate to the router a range of addresses that will not be allocated to DHCP clients.

In our case, the command will have the following form:

```
Router(config)#ip dhcp excluded-address 192.168.0.1
```

Figure 13.22 Router line with a command to exclude one address from the DHCP pool

Now we move from the global configuration mode to the address pool configuration mode on the DHCP router-server. The command used for this is **ip dhcp pool <name>**

```
Router(config)#ip dhcp pool PULA
Router(dhcp-config)#
```

Figure 13.23 Router line after entering DHCP pool configuration mode

Now we can configure the DHCP pool (according to the data at the beginning of this subsection). For this purpose, we will use the following commands, described below:

default-router <IP address> - specify the default gateway

dns-server <IP address> - DNS server determination

network <IP address> <netmask> - the network from which addresses will be assigned

```
Router(config)#ip dhcp pool PULA
Router(dhcp-config)#default-router 192.168.0.1
Router(dhcp-config)#dns-server 10.0.0.1
Router(dhcp-config)#network 192.168.0.0 255.255.255.0
Router(dhcp-config)#exit
```

Figure 13.24 Router line with commands to configure the DHCP pool.

We use the **show running-config** command to check the DHCP configuration.

```
Router#sh running-config
Building configuration...

Current configuration : 878 bytes
!
version 12.2
no service timestamps log datetime msec
no service timestamps debug datetime msec
no service password-encryption
!
hostname Router
!
!
!
!
ip dhcp excluded-address 192.168.0.1
!
ip dhcp pool PULA
 network 192.168.0.0 255.255.255.0
 default-router 192.168.0.1
 dns-server 10.0.0.1
```

Figure 13.25 A portion of the configuration of the current router with DHCP configuration commands.

13.3.2 Viewing the Assigned IP Address Array in DHCP

To display the array of assigned IP addresses on the router (DHCP server), we execute, in privileged mode, the command **show `ip dhcp binding`.**

```
Router#show ip dhcp binding
IP address          Client-ID/                  Lease expiration          Type
                    Hardware address
192.168.0.2         0001.97A9.9099              --                        Automatic
192.168.0.3         00E0.F993.D793              --                        Automatic
```

Figure 13.26 An array of assigned IP addresses by DHCP.

The following displayed columns contain the following information:

- **IP address -** assigned IPv4 address to the end device,
- **Client ID/Hardware address -** MAC address of the device's network card,
- **Lease expiration -** IP address lease validity (unspecified here – the Cisco Packet Tracer does not support this option),
- **Type -** how to assign an IPv4 address to the end device.

13.3.3 Verifying the DHCP Service Is Working on the Router

After completing the configuration of the router, we check whether the computers have received the correct addressing. The best and surest way is to renew the IP lease on all computers using the **`ipconfig /renew`**.

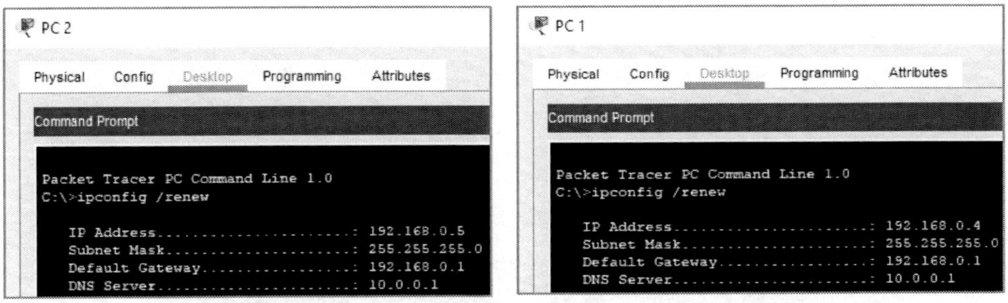

Figure 13.27 Renewed addressing lease on PC1 and PC2.

Next, we can check the communication of computers with the router. To do this, we will use the **`ping`** command or the symbol of a single envelope. As you can see in the figure, the ping response is correct.

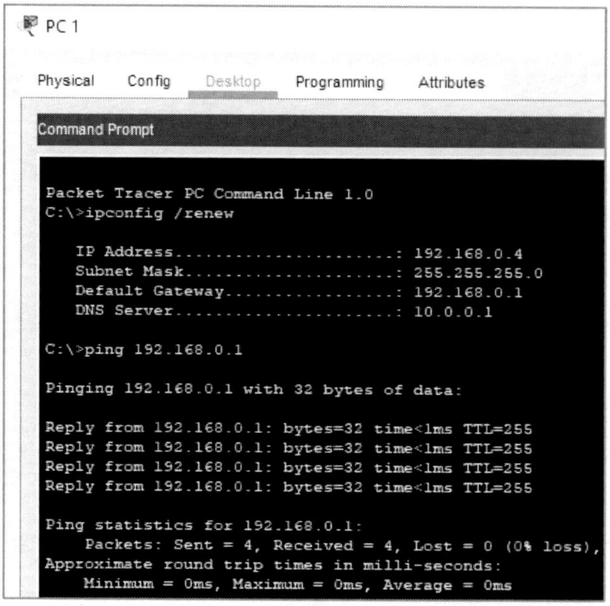

Figure 13.28 Example of checking communication between PC 1 and a router with the address 10.0.0.1

We can also check the communication between computers, for example, between **PC 1** and **PC 2**.

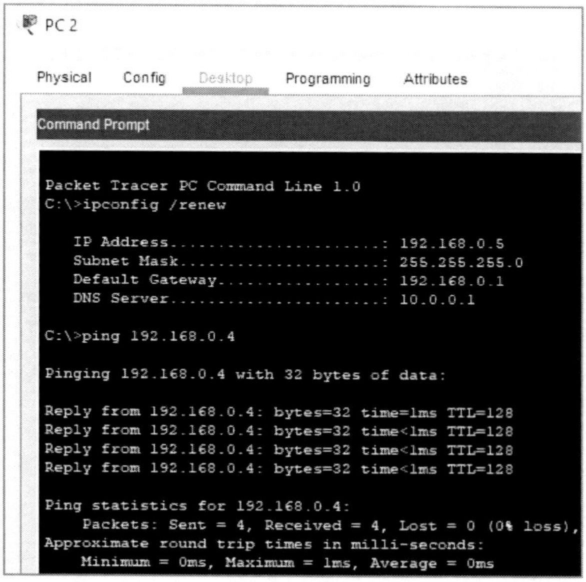

Figure 13.29 Example of checking communication between PC1 and PC2

13.3.4 Deleting the DHCP Configuration on the Router (DHCP Server)

In order to remove the current DHCP configuration on the server (Server2 router), we will use the previously learned commands and the keyword no, adding it at the beginning of the configuration commands:

```
Router(config)#no ip dhcp pool PULA
Router(config)#no ip dhcp excluded-address 192.168.0.1
```

Figure 13.30 Commands that remove the current DHCP configuration from the Server2 router.

13.3.5 Deleting DHCP Configurations on Computers (DHCP Clients)

To remove the current DHCP configuration on clients (PC1, PC2), we will use the **ipconfig** command with the **/release** option. The command must be executed on all computers.

```
C:\>ipconfig /release

   IP Address......................: 0.0.0.0
   Subnet Mask.....................: 0.0.0.0
   Default Gateway.................: 0.0.0.0
   DNS Server......................: 0.0.0.0
```

Figure 13.31 Command to remove the current DHCP configuration from PC 1

13.4 DHCP on a Network with Multiple Routers

When dealing with networks composed of many routers, it becomes a bit more difficult to configure DHCP. By default, each router divides the network into separate **broadcast domains** and therefore they cannot forward DHCP messages between routers. However, this is possible provided that we configure the so-called **intermediary routers** to forward DHCP requests (**broadcast messages**) to the correct DHCP server.

We will apply the topology shown in the figure below.

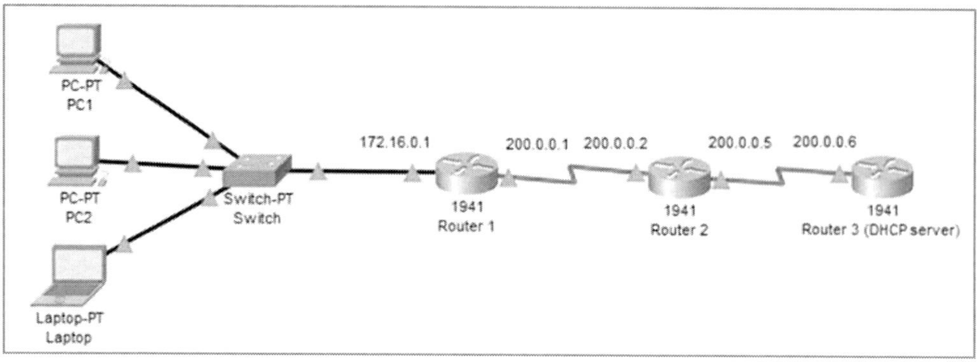

Figure 13.32 Network topology with multiple intermediary routers

We assume that the routers have been configured correctly - they have been addressed as in the diagram and the RIPv2 routing protocol between connections has been configured. In this example, we will configure DHCP on a network consisting of multiple intermediary routers and a router acting as a DHCP server, as intended in the following table.

DHCP Parameter	***Parameter value***
Router (DHCP server) Name	**Router3**
DHCP server address	**200.0.0.6**
DHCP pool name	**PULA**
IP address range in pool	**172.16.0.11-172.16.0.100**
Default Gateway address	**172.16.0.1**
DNS server address	**No configured**
Computer addresses (DHCP clients)	**assigned automatically**

Table 13.2 DHCP Configuration Parameters

Configuration of a network consisting of multiple intermediary routers and a router that acts as a DHCP server will be performed in three steps.

13.4.1 Set Up an Intermediary Router

To configure an intermediary router, we select the nearest router connected to the subnet of computers. In this example, the intermediary router closest to the subnet of PC1, PC2, and Laptop is Router1.

To configure it for the role of message forwarding to the DHCP service running on router Router3, we need to execute the command

ip helper-address <adres serwera DHCP>

and we perform them on the interface to which queries for a dynamic IP address come.

```
Router1(config)#int gig0/0
Router1(config-if)#ip helper-address 200.0.0.6
Router1(config-if)#exit
```

Figure 13.33 Router1 router line with commands to configure DHCP server address

Router1 can now forward DHCP messages from computers to routers with the address **200.0.0.6.** Similarly, **Router2** should be configured.

13.4.2 Start DHCP and Configure the Address Pool

In order to start and configure the address pool **DHCP_Server** of the router **Router3**, we need to set the following parameters

```
Router3(DHCP_Server)(config)#ip dhcp pool PULA
Router3(DHCP_Server)(dhcp-config)#default-router 172.16.0.1
Router3(DHCP_Server)(dhcp-config)#network 172.16.0.0 255.255.255.0
Router3(DHCP_Server)(dhcp-config)#exit
Router3(DHCP_Server)(config)#ip dhcp excluded-address 172.16.0.1 172.16.0.10
```

Figure 13.34 Router3 router line with DHCP Server configuration commands

After configuring the address pool of the R3 main router, we can check what addresses have been assigned to the computers. Computers PC1... PC4 obtained IPv4 addresses using the automatic DHCP service.

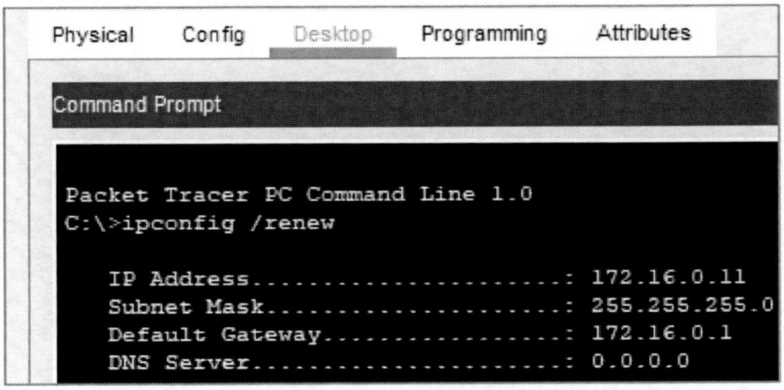

Figure 13.35 Obtained IP address on Laptop

13.4.3 Check the Array of Assigned IP Addresses on the Router

To display the array of assigned IP addresses on the router (**DHCP server**), we use (in privileged mode) on the router the command

`show ip dhcp binding`

```
Router3(DHCP_Server)#sh ip dhcp binding
IP address       Client-ID/              Lease expiration        Type
                 Hardware address
172.16.0.11      0001.6432.EAE0           --                     Automatic
172.16.0.12      0001.4375.6DDD           --                     Automatic
172.16.0.13      000D.BD7D.4B8A           --                     Automatic
```

Figure 13.36 Current router table with DHCP address quotas

13.5 Configuring DHCP on the Wireless Router

13.5.1 Configuring DHCP on the WRT300N

In this example, we will configure DHCP on the **ISRWRT300N** wireless router, as intended in the following table.

Manufacturer	Linksys
Router Model	WRT300N
DHCP Server Address	192.168.0.1
IP address range in pool	192.168.0.11 – 192.168.0.14
Default gateway address	192.168.0.1
DNS server address	10.0.0.6
computer addresses (DHCP clients)	automatically assigned
How addresses are assigned	randomly

Table 13.3 Configuring Wireless DHCP on the WRT300N

We will use the above configuration data for the topology shown in the figure.

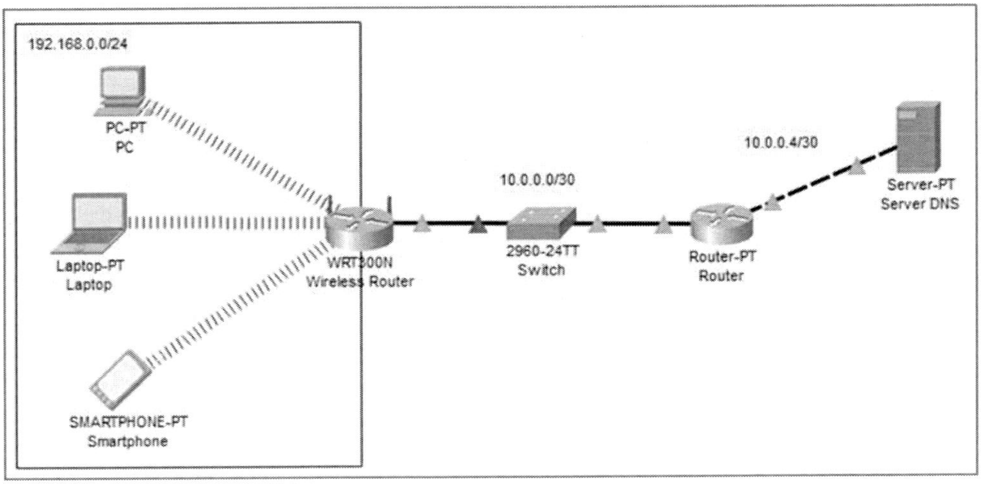

Figure 13.37 Network topology with WRT300N router and wireless clients

In the local wireless network we will place three devices equipped with Wi-Fi network adapters (DHCP clients): **PC, Laptop and Smartphone**, and the **WRT300N** wireless router acting as a DHCP server and default gateway. In addition, we will connect the **Internet** interface of the **WRT300N** router, with an external cable network consisting of a switch: **Switch0**, router **R1** and **DNS** server with the address 10.0.0.6.

If you want to configure DHCP so that endpoints are randomly assigned IP addresses from a specific address pool on the 192.168.0.0/24 subnet, follow these steps:

Step 1. Connect Laptop (ADMIN) to WRT300N

We connect the **Laptop (ADMIN)** to **Ethernet port 1** of the **WRT300N** router, using an Ethernet cable (simple).

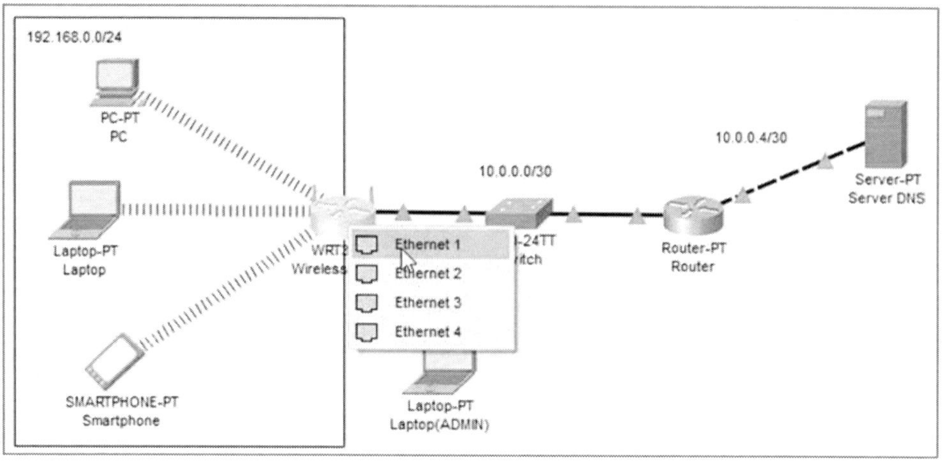

Figure 13.38 Connecting Laptop (ADMIN) to WRT300N to configure the router

Step 2. Configure Laptop (ADMIN)

We configure a static IP address and subnet mask for the Ethernet **Laptop(ADMIN)** network adapter (any address except 192.168.0.1, since it is the default configuration address of the WRT300N router). Configuration can be done using the **IP Configuration** applet in the **Desktop** tab.

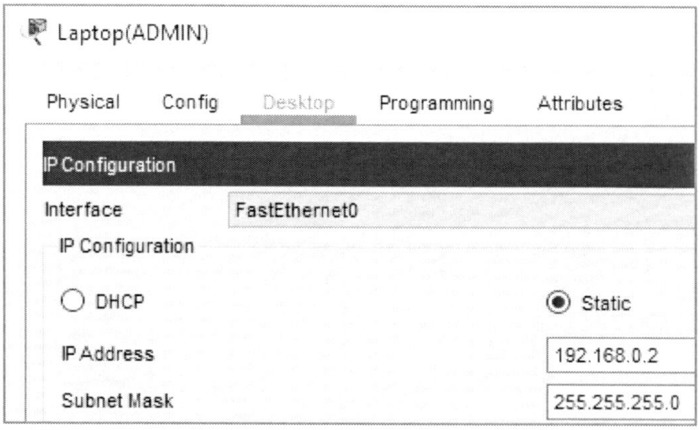

Figure 13.39 Configuring the Static IP Address of the Laptop(ADMIN) Device

Step 3. Launch a Web Browser on Laptop (ADMIN)

On **laptop (ADMIN)** we run a web browser. To do this, select the **Laptop computer (ADMIN),** the Desktop tab, and then the **Web Browser** applet.

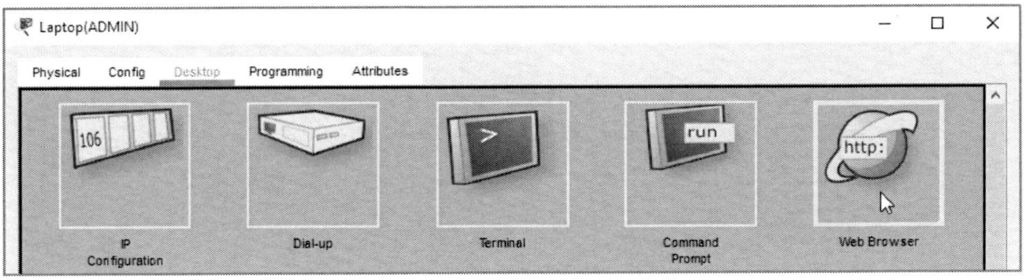

Figure 13.40 Applet Web Browser

Step 4. Enter the default configuration address of the WRT300N router

In the **Web Browser**, in the **URL** field, enter the default configuration address of the router **192.168.0.1** and click the **Go** button.

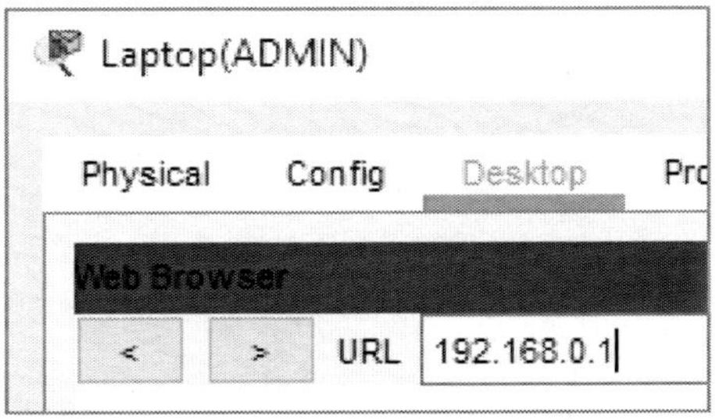

Figure 13.41 Default configuration address for WRT300N

Step 5. Log into the WRT300N router

In the browser, the **Authorization** window will appear, in which we must enter the login and password for the router. By default, these are: **admin, admin**.

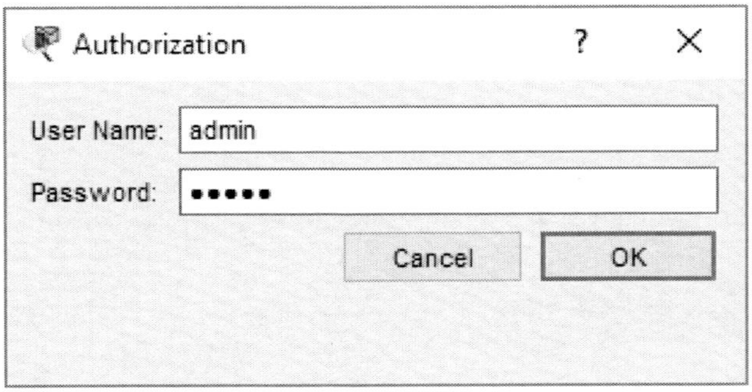

Figure 13.42 Authorizing access to the WRT300N router

Step 6. Enable DHCP Server service

The window of the **WRT30N** router configuration program will appear, in which we must go to the **Setup** menu and the **Network Setup** option.

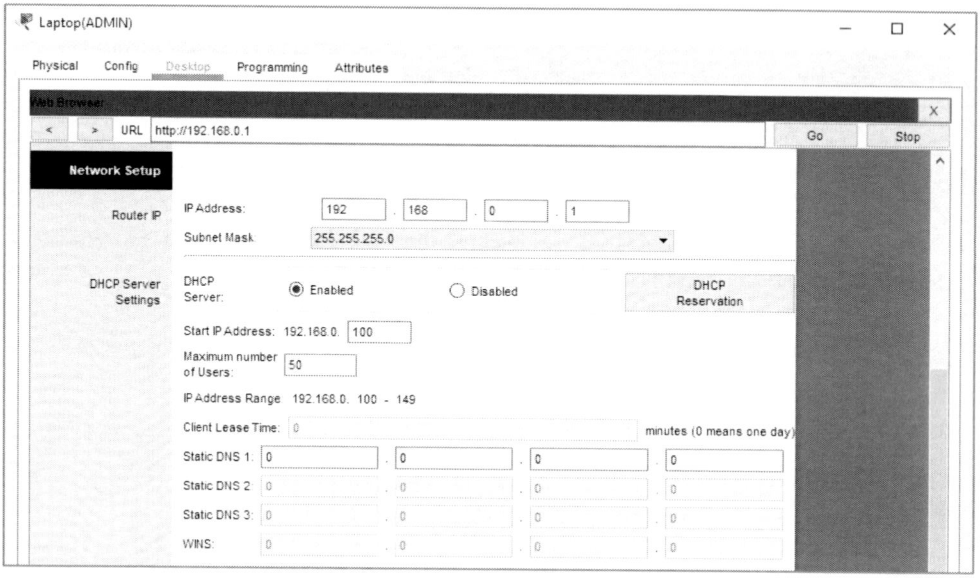

Figure 13.43 Network Setup menu and Network Setup option

We need to set the following fields: **IP Address** to 192.168.0.1 and **Subnet Mask** to 255.255.255.0. You must also select DHCP Server: **Enabled**.

Step 7. Configure the address pool in DHCP

In the Network Setup option there is a section called DHCP Server Settings that we need to configure. In this section, we set the following required DHCP parameters described in the assumptions:

- **Start IP Address** - the first available IP address (in our example 192.168.0.11)
- **Maximum number** - the maximum number of users dynamically getting IP addresses (in our example, four users)
- **Static DNS 1** - DNS server address (in our example 10.0.0.6)

Note: The field named **IP Address Range** contains a range of dynamically assigned IP addresses. It is automatically generated after the configuration is approved based on the values provided in the fields: **Start IP Address, Maximum number**.

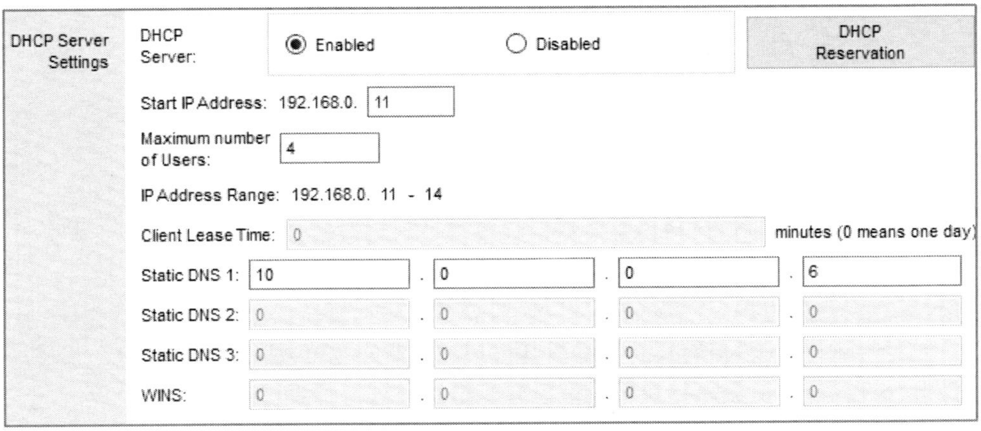

Figure 13.44 DHCP Server Settings section

Step 8. Save the configuration of the WRT300N router

Once the configuration of the DHCP address pool is complete, we must save it so that when the router is restarted, the configuration that we have just done is loaded. To save the configuration, go to the bottom of the screen of the current window and click the **Save Settings** button.

Figure 13.45 Button to save the current configuration of the WRT300N router

We receive a message confirming that the settings have been saved and click on the "Continue" link.

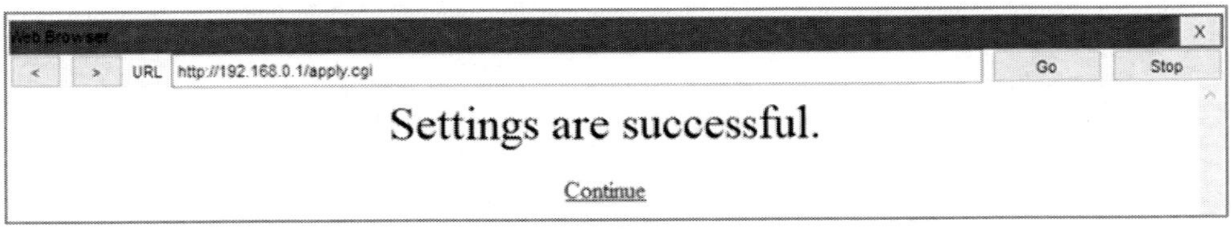

Figure 13.46 A message confirming that the settings of the WRT300N router have been saved.

Step 9. Perform final activities

After saving the router configuration, we check whether the end devices are turned on, connected to the wireless network and whether they have received the appropriate IP addresses from the DHCP service.

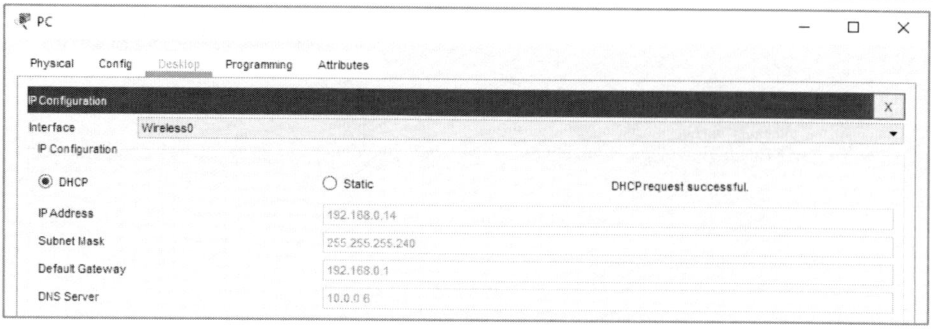

Figure 13.47 Dynamically obtain the right IP address

13.5.2 Configuring DHCP Based on MAC Addresses

This example is a modification of the previous one (addressing and topology are the same). Now we will assign **IP** addresses based on the **MAC** addresses of the end devices. This technique is referred to as **MAC Reservation**. It works by assigning only a specific IP address to a specific physical MAC address.

To configure the DHCP service based on MAC addresses, we must first create a table of **MAC addresses** and corresponding **IP** addresses, which will facilitate our subsequent configuration. The subnet addressing in our example is listed in the following table.

Device name	***MAC address(physical)***	***IP Address (logical)***
PC	**AA:AA:00:00:11:11**	192.168.0.11
Laptop	**AA:AA:00:00:22:22**	192.168.0.12
Smartphone	**AA:AA:00:00:44:44**	192.168.0.14

Table 13.4 Assignment of MAC addresses to IP addresses for end devices.

Step 1. Log into the WRT300N router from a Laptop (ADMIN)

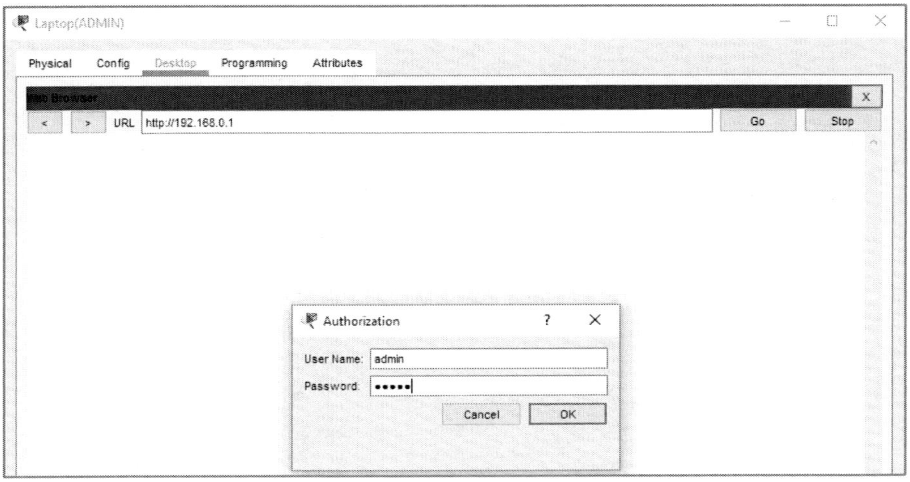

Figure 13.48 Logging in to the WRT300N

Step 2. Configure MAC address assignments

We perform DHCP configuration using IP addresses based on MAC addresses. The window of the **WRT30N** router configuration program will appear, in which we must go to the **Setup** menu and the **Network Setup** option. Click the **DHCP Reservation** button. A dialog box appears that contains the following sections:

- Select Clients from DHCP Tables - selection of clients from the DHCP table,
- **Manually Adding Client** - manual adding of DHCP client,
- **Client Already Reserved** - list of reserved DHCP clients

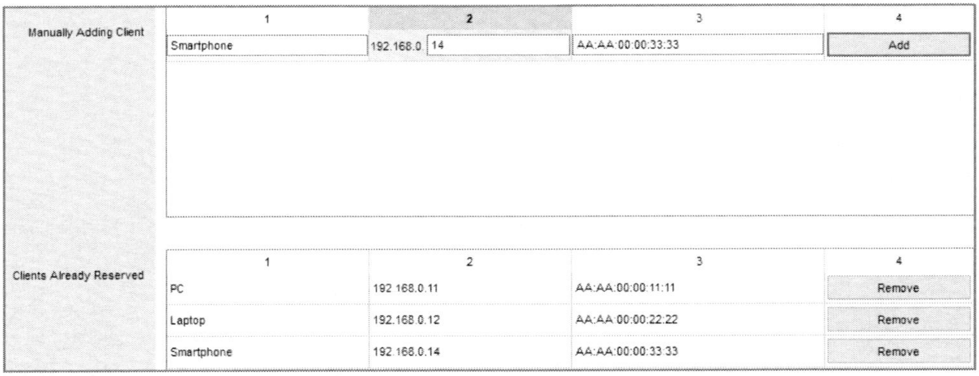

Figure 13.49 Manually Adding Client section

Now we add the names of the end devices, the IP addresses to be assigned and the MAC addresses, thanks to which the server will know to whom to assign which IP address.

Step 3. Save the configuration of reserved MAC addresses

To save the added configurations of MAC address ranges to IP addresses, we need to go to the **Clients Already Reserved** section and click on the **Save Settings** button.

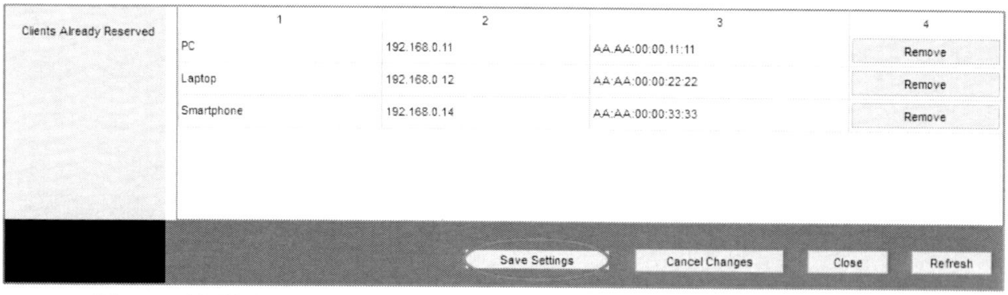

Figure 13.50 Saving settings in the Clients Already Reserved section

Step 4. Perform final activities

After saving the router configuration, check whether the end devices are turned on, disconnect the **Laptop (ADMIN)** device from the **Wireless Router** and proceed to check the DHCP server configuration with address reservation.

Step 5. Verify the operation of DHCP based on MAC addresses

Having saved the configuration of the router, we can see that all wireless connections have been broken for a while and then compiled again, only this time the IP addresses that have been assigned to the end devices match their MAC addresses. We can test it on a **PC** device by checking what address the device has.

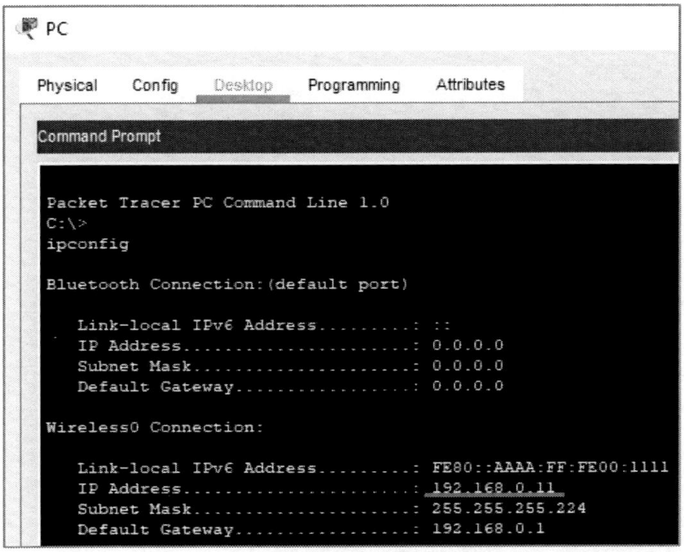

Figure 13.51 Checking the IP address of a PC device

As we can see, the address matches the one that was reserved on the DHCP server for a given MAC address. Now, no other device will receive this IP address.

CHAPTER 14

SKILL EXERCISES – PART III

COMPUTER NETWORKS IN PACKET TRACER

FOR BEGINNERS

14 Skill Exercises – Part III

This chapter contains skill exercises for advanced users to test their skills.

Note – Warning: Remember to periodically save the file state during exercises (keyboard shortcut CTRL+S)

14.1 Grouping Devices and Combine Two Instances of the Program

14.1.1 Grouping Devices

Create the topology shown in the figure below. Then, address the network and end devices appropriately and configure the EIGRP routing protocol (AS 50) so that the two networks can communicate with each other. Then, group devices so that **Network 1** is one device group with the same name, and **Network 2** is the second device group with the same name.

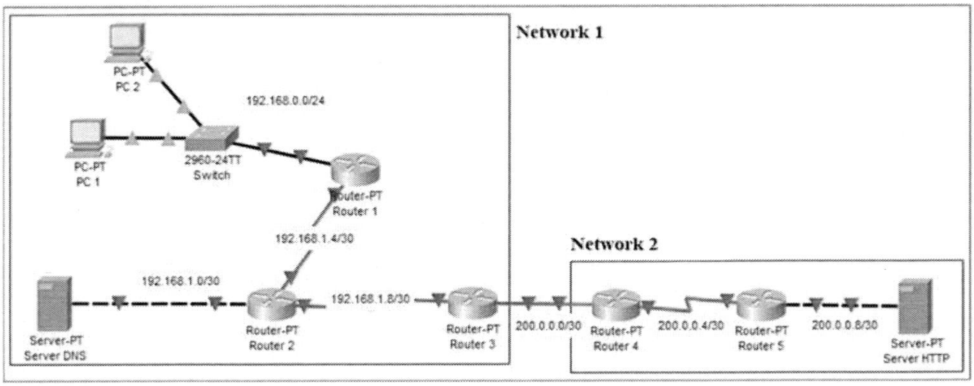

Figure 14.1 Exercise's topology

Solution:

- Create a topology as in the picture, connect the devices to each other using the appropriate cables.
- Address network and end devices according to the scheme and enable interfaces.
- Configure the dynamic routing protocol - EIGRP (AS 50) on all routers taking into account each adjacent network.
- Create a DNS entry on the DNS Server for the address 200.0.0.10 available at **www.http.com**, and create an HTTP page on the HTTP Server on which it will display text "HTTP Page".

- Group devices from **Network 1** into **Area 1** and **Network 2** into **Area 2**.
- Test the connection using the PING command between two groups of devices and try to get the site **www.http.com**, from **PC 2**.

14.1.2 Device Grouping and Multiuser Function

Create a topology as in the figure below. You will need the Cisco Packet Tracer running twice - one time for each area. Once you've created the topology, address device interfaces appropriately and enable them. Configure the OSPF Dynamic Routing Protocol (AS 10) on the routers. Group your devices into two areas: **Area 1** and **Area 2**. Then connect the two instances together using the multiuser function using the **multiuser** password and the corresponding router interfaces.

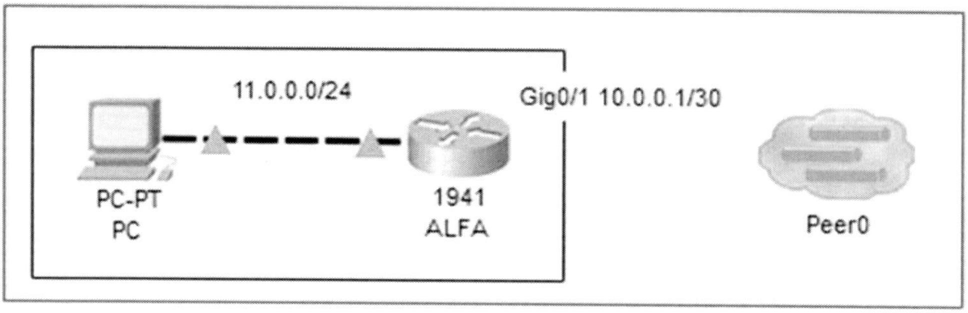

Figure 14.2 Area Topology 1

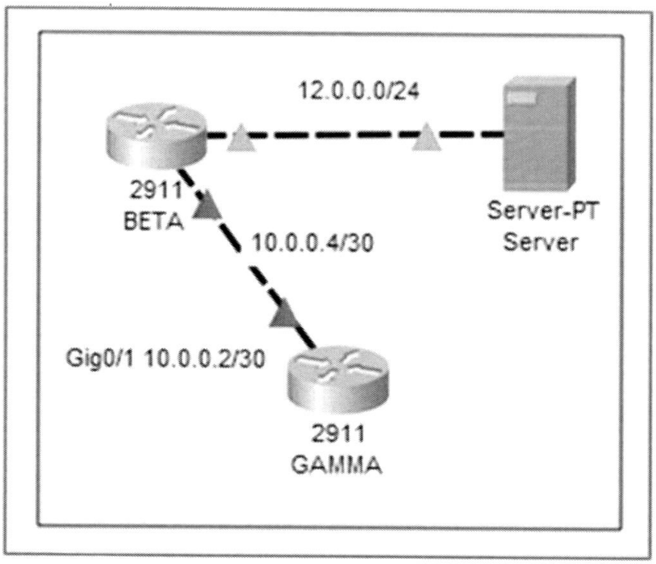

Figure 14.3 Area Topology 2

Solution:

- Following the examples of the two figures above, create a topology in two separate Cisco Packet Tracer windows.
- Address and enable device interfaces appropriately.
- Configure the OSPF routing protocol (AS 10) on the routers. Use router-id to recognize each router.
- Group devices into two areas - **Area 1** and **Area 2**.
- Connect two grouped areas together using the multiuser function. Use the multiuser password and the interfaces shown in the diagram.
- Test the connection between **PC** and **Server** using any available tool.

14.2 DHCP for IPv4

14.2.1 Configuring DHCP on the Server

In the logical topology, this exercise will have four computer workstations, one switch, and one server that will act as a DHCP server. The addresses that the computer stations will receive will be in the range of 192.168.10.10-192.168.10.13 and users who can receive addresses are limited to four. The default gateway address is a fictitious router address: 192.168.10.254, while the DNS server address and TFTP server address are the address of our server.

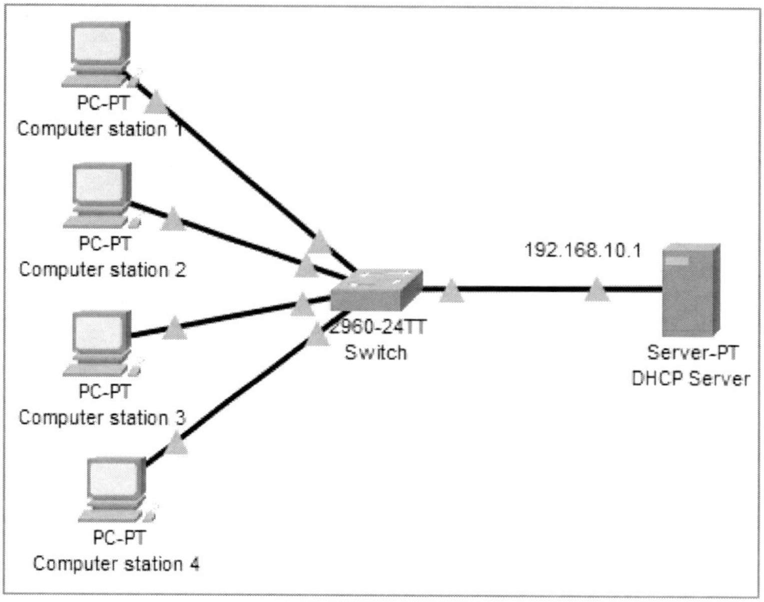

Figure 14.4 Exercise's topology

Solution:

- Create a topology as in the figure above.
- Address the **DHCP Server** device interface.
- Enable the DHCP service on the server.
- Configure DHCP to allocate four addresses in the range 192.168.10.10-192.168.10.13. The default gateway is 192.168.10.254, the server address is the DNS server address, and the TFTP server address.
- On four computer stations, switch IP addressing to dynamic and check that the stations have received the correct addresses.
- If your positions have received the appropriate address, try using the PING command to communicate with the **DHCP server**.

14.2.2 Configuring DHCP on the Router

Create a logical topology that consists of one router, one switch, and five end users. In this exercise, the router will serve us as a DHCP server with a pool called **POOL** and addresses from the 9.0.0.0/24 network. Addresses are reserved from 9.0.0.1 to 9.0.0.10. The default gateway is the address of this router, and the DNS server is 9.0.0.254.

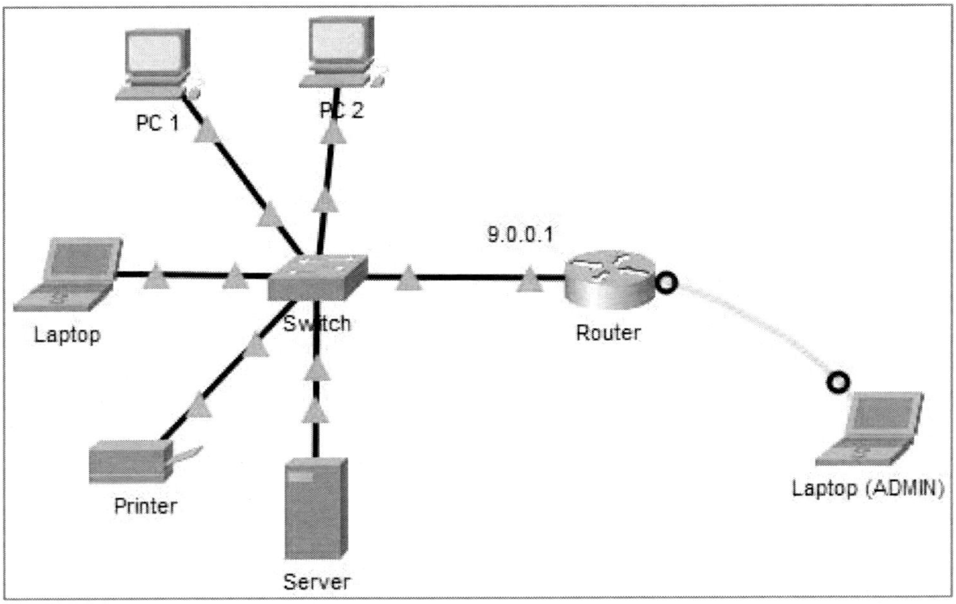

Figure 14.5 Exercise's topology

Solution:

- Transfer the configuration from the figure above to your logical topology.
- Enter the router using the console on **Laptop (ADMIN)** and address the appropriate interface and enable it.
- Create a DHCP address pool called **POOL** with addresses from the 9.0.0.0/24 network, the default gateway that is this router, and the DNS server that is available at 9.0.0.254.
- Reserve addresses in the range 9.0.0.1-9.0.0.10.
- Switch to end devices and assign dynamic addressing to them.
- Test the connection between the hosts and between the end devices and the **Router** device using any tool.

14.2.3 Configuring DHCP on the Wireless Router

In the Cisco Packet Tracer, create a topology such as the one shown in the figure below. The wireless network settings remain the default. Configure the router's Ethernet address to 50.0.0.1/24. The **DNS server** obtains the address dynamically from the DHCP service on the **Wireless Router,** but it has a reservation of the address 50.0.0.254 to its MAC address. In turn, two wireless devices randomly get addresses from the 50.0.0.0/24 pool, which starts giving away addresses from the address 50.0.0.100. The maximum number of users is 10.

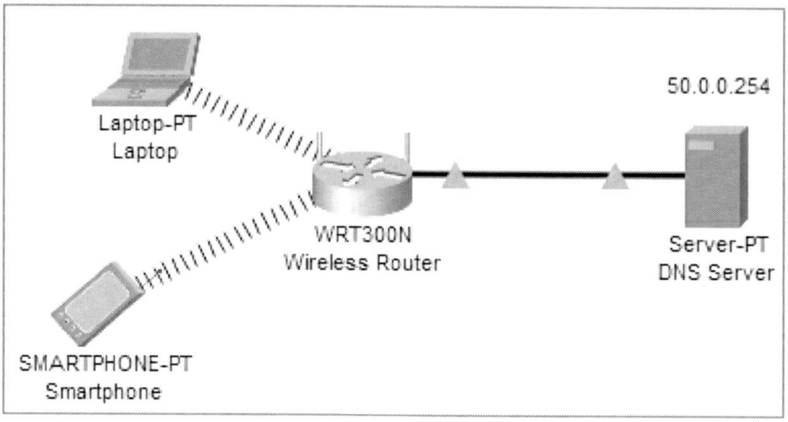

Figure 14.6 Exercise's topology

Solution:

- Create a topology like the one shown in the figure above.
- Configure the Ethernet port on the **Wireless Router** to be assigned the address 50.0.0.1.
- Reserve the address 50.0.0.254 for the MAC address of the **DNS Server** device.
- Configure DHCP on the **Wireless Router** to distribute addresses from the 50.0.0.0/24 network starting at 50.0.0.100 and limited to a maximum of 10 end users.
- From a mobile device - **Smartphone** try to use the `tracert 50.0.0.254`

  command to perform a connection test with the **DNS Server**.

14.2.4 DHCP Configuration on a Server That Is on a Remote Network

The logical topology for this exercise is shown in the figure below. As we can see, we can distinguish four routers (**Up, Left, Right, Down**), a DHCP server at the very bottom and six end users, so-called **Hosts**. Address all devices as shown, and then configure the EIGRP Dynamic Routing Protocol (AS 66) between the routers.

On the DHCP Server device, configure the DHCP service to have three separate pools, named PULA1, PULA2, and PULA3. Each concerns one network - e.g. PULA1 is a pool of addresses at the **Left** router. The default gateways are the corresponding router addresses, and the DNS and TFTP server addresses are the **DHCP Server** device address.

Then indicate to the routers on the appropriate interfaces what IP address the device that acts as the DHCP server has.

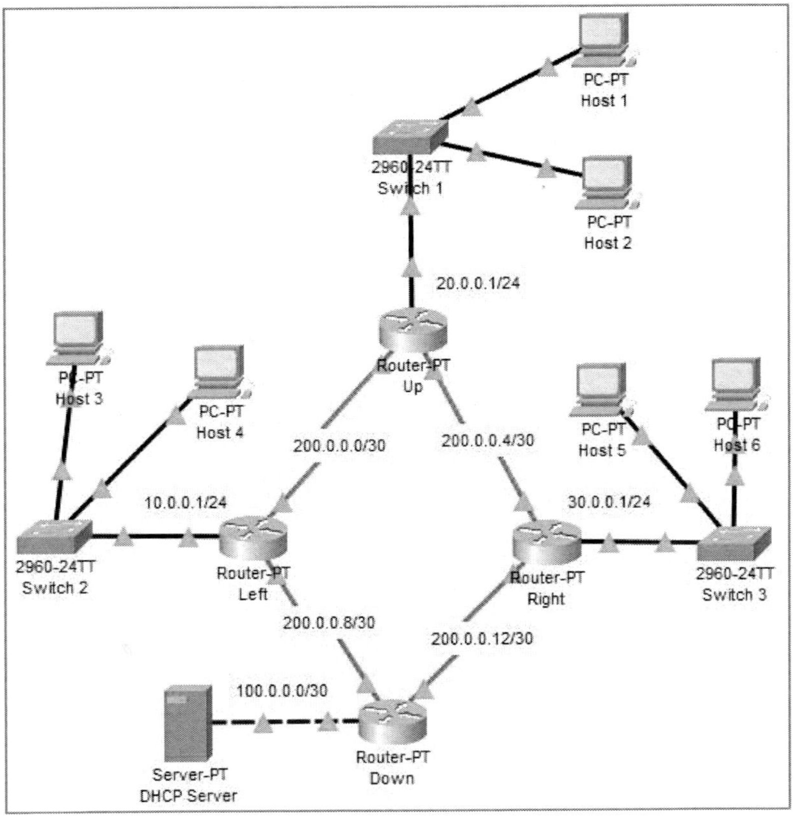

Figure 14.7 Exercise's topology

Solution:

- Create the logical topology shown in the figure above.
- Address and enable the device interfaces accordingly, as shown in the diagram.
- Configure the dynamic routing protocol - EIGRP (AS 66) between routers taking into account each adjacent network.
- On the **DHCP Server** device, configure the three address pools as intended.
- Indicate on the appropriate router interfaces where the DHCP server is located.
- Try to get dynamically IP addresses on each end device - **Hosts**.
- Use the PING command to communicate from each network to the **Down** device.

CHAPTER 15

MISTAKES MADE DURING NETWORK CONFIGURATION

15 Mistakes Made During Network Configuration

The chapter contains descriptions of the symptoms and causes of the most common mistakes when designing and configuring computer networks as well as ways to fix them.

15.1 Wiring or Port Errors

The figure below shows the incorrect use of cables and connecting the correct cable, but to the wrong port, for example, an Ethernet cable was connected to the RS232 console port.

Causes: a simple cable was used between the switches, the computer and router devices were connected to the switch using a patch cable, the computer was connected to the router using a straight cable.

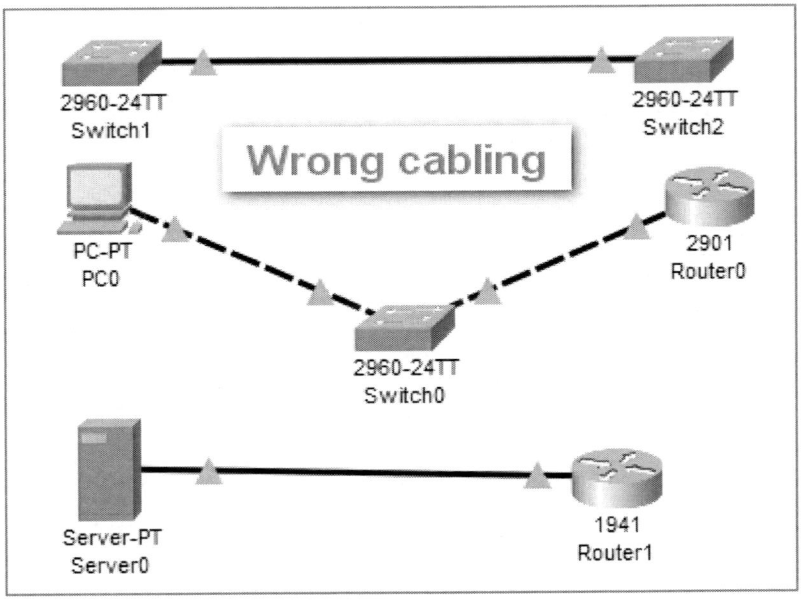

Figure 15.1 Wrong cabling

Repair: switches should be connected using a patch cable, computer and router devices should be connected to the switch using a simple cable, the computer should be connected to the router using a patch cable.

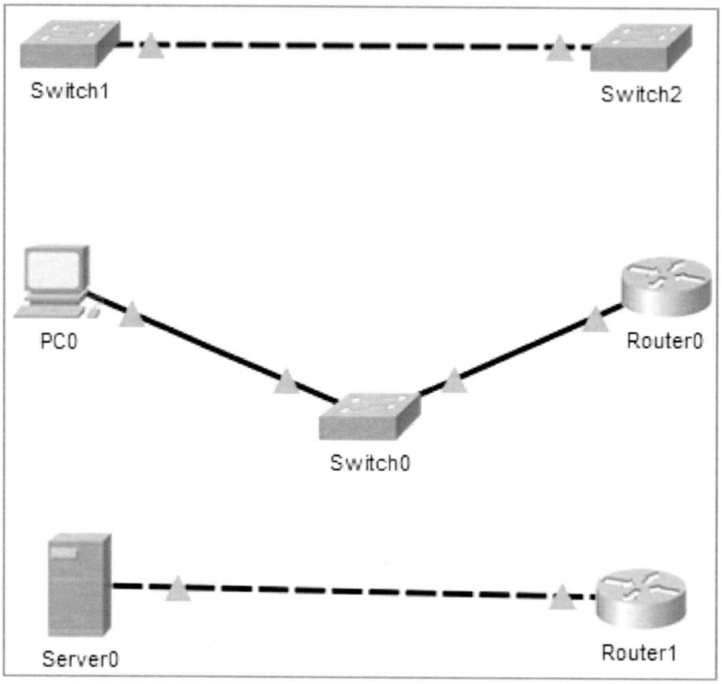

Figure 15.2 Wiring condition after repair

Symptoms: The laptop cannot communicate with the router.

Cause: The correct cable is connected but to the wrong port, i.e. the Ethernet cable is connected to the RS232 console port.

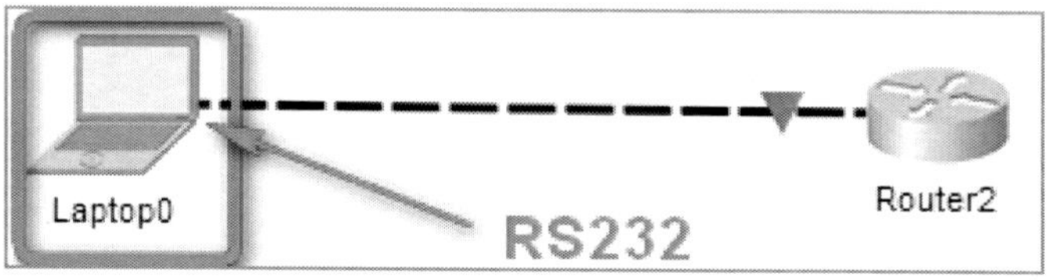

Figure 15.3. Wrong port

Repair: remove the cable from the RS232 port, connect the cable again but to the Fast Ethernet port.

Figure 15.4. Condition after repair

15.2 Device Related Errors

PC0 is connected to the **Switch0** switch. **Switch0** is connected to **Router0**. Why are the interface states on the **Switch0 – Router0** connection disabled (red)?

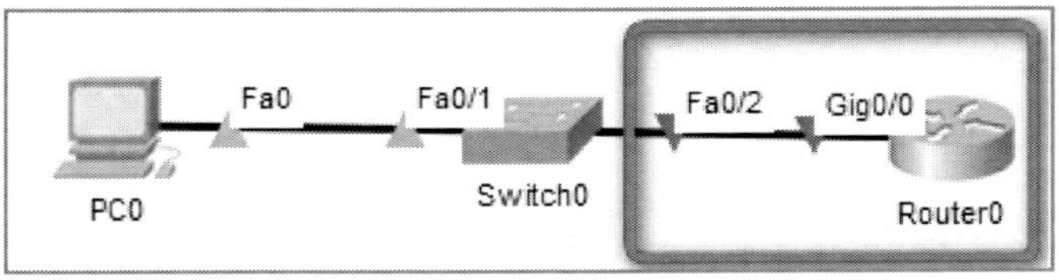

Figure 15.5 Disabled port on router

Symptoms: PC0 cannot communicate with the router.

Cause: The Gig0/0 interface on the router is not enabled. Remember that interfaces are enabled by default on computers and switches, and disabled on routers. Therefore, you must manually enable the correct interfaces on your router.

Repair: Enable the Gig0/0 port on Router0.

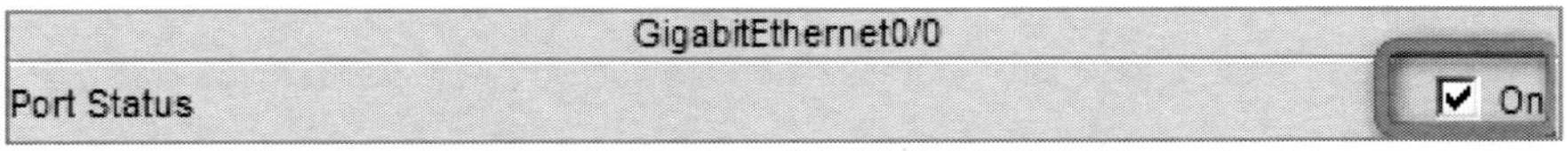

Figure 15.6 Enabled port on the router

15.3 IP Addressing Errors

The figure below and the verbal description show incorrect IP addressing.

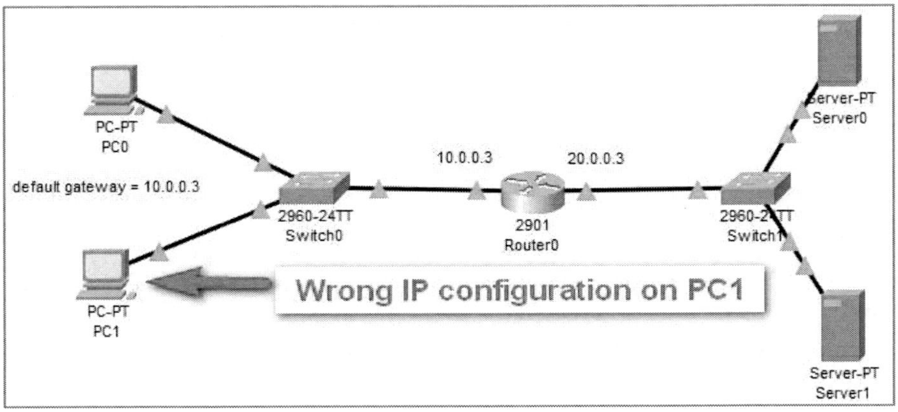

Figure 15.7 Wrong IP configuration on PC1

Symptoms: PC1 cannot communicate with the servers.

PC0 can ping any computer, and PC1 can only ping PC0. Why? The reason should be sought in the addressing of PC1- it can be the wrong IP address, the wrong default gateway or the wrong subnet mask, or for example the computer has been turned off.

Cause: In this example, the error is caused by an incorrect **default gateway** setting. It is set to 10.0.0.2 and this is the address of the PC0.

```
C:\>ipconfig /all

FastEthernet0 Connection:(default port)

   Connection-specific DNS Suffix..:
   Physical Address................: 00E0.8FA8.5968
   Link-local IPv6 Address.........: FE80::2E0:8FFF:FEA8:5968
   IP Address......................: 10.0.0.2
   Subnet Mask.....................: 255.0.0.0
   Default Gateway.................: 10.0.0.1
   DNS Servers.....................: 0.0.0.0
   DHCP Servers....................: 0.0.0.0
```

Figure 15.8 Check your IP configuration

Repair: On PC1, set the gateway address to **10.0.0.3** (the interface address of the router to which the Switch0 is connected.

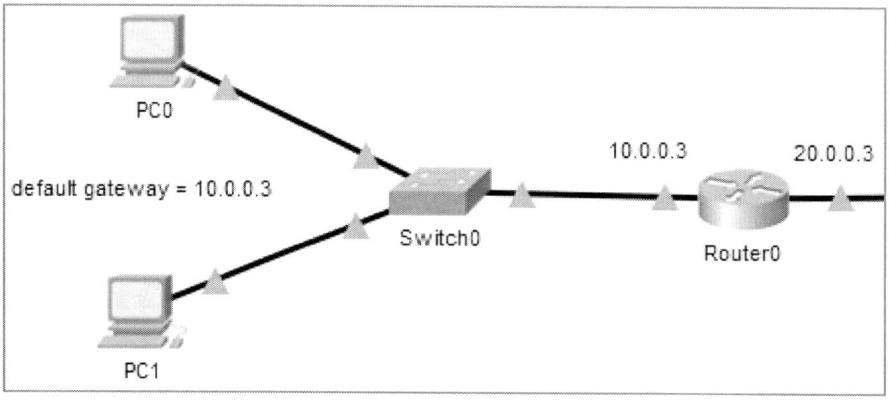

Figure 15.9 Topology fragment with correctly assigned the Default Gateway

The next example shows incorrect IP addressing as well as the lack of a properly configured DNS service.

Symptoms: A request to view a page **www.name.com** from PC1's browser does not end with an error, the page does not appear.

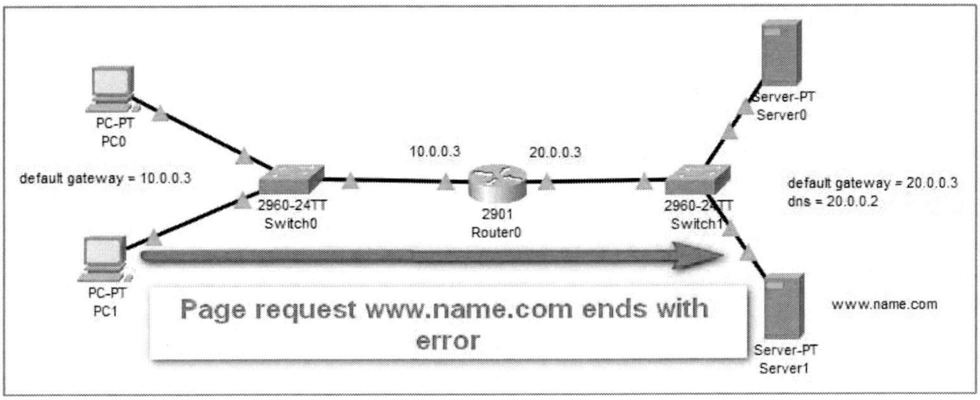

Figure 15.10 Page request www.name.com ends with error

When a PC1 user enters 20.0.0.2 into the browser, a page from **Server1** is displayed.

Figure 15.11 Checking the page by IP address

However, when the PC1 user enters the address of the **www.name.com** the message **"Host Name Unresolved"** will be displayed.

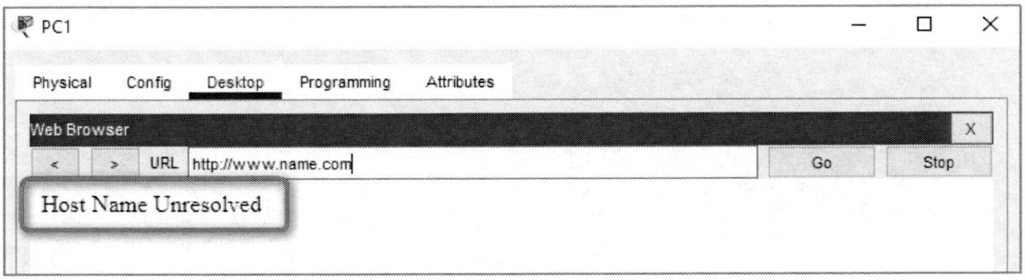

Figure 15.12 Check a page using an HTTP address

The IP configuration is correct because all computers can communicate with each other, which is checked by ping. **Server1** contains a website called **www.name.com**. The server address is 20.0.0.2. This server also acts as a DNS server.

Figure 15.13 Server1 IP Configuration

The IP addressing configuration for Server1 is correct.

Cause: PC1 does not know the DNS server address, or the DNS service is not enabled and configured correctly on Server1.

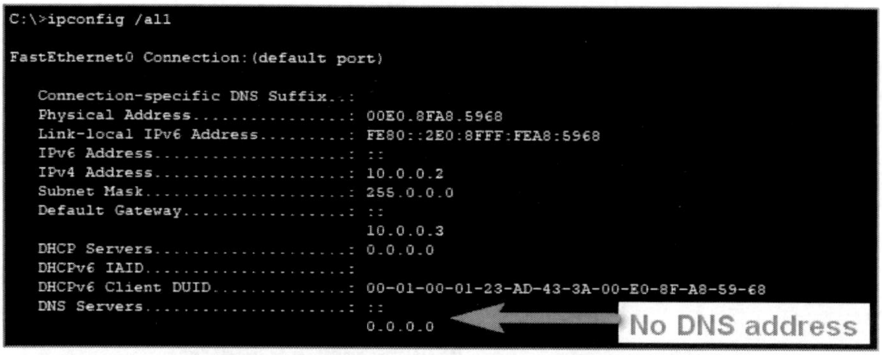

Figure 15.14 No DNS address for PC1

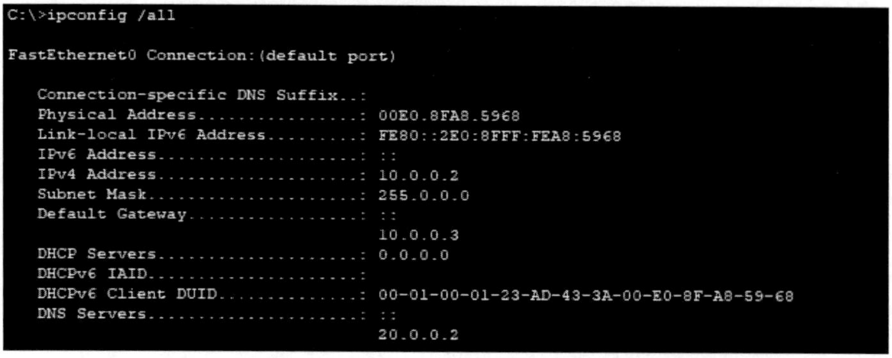

Figure 15.15 DNS address for PC1 set correctly

Fixed: After setting the correct DNS address (the correct address is **20.0.0.2**) on PC1, the error described above still occurs. You must now check the DNS configuration on the server.

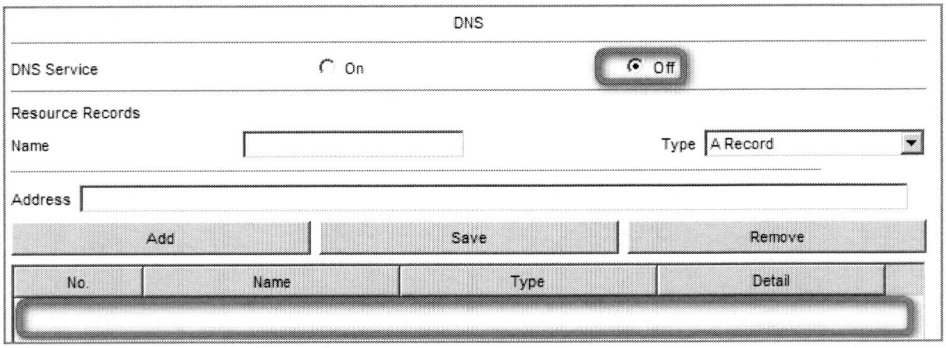

Figure 15.16 DNS status before repair

Fixed: To fix the error, enable DNS in Server1 and add an A-type record that contains the **www.name.com** name and the IP address assigned to that name **20.0.0.2**.

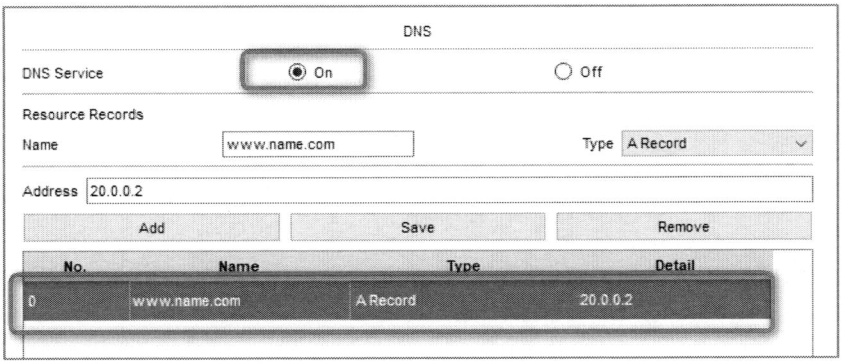

Figure 15.17 DNS status after repair

Then, on PC1, enter the address: **www.name.com** into the browser to check if the error has been fixed.

Figure 15.18 Check a page using an HTTP address

Symptoms: Communication between PC0, PC1 and Servver0, Server1 servers is not possible despite the correct configuration of the routing protocol. The following drawing and verbal description shows the incorrect IP addressing in the router interface.

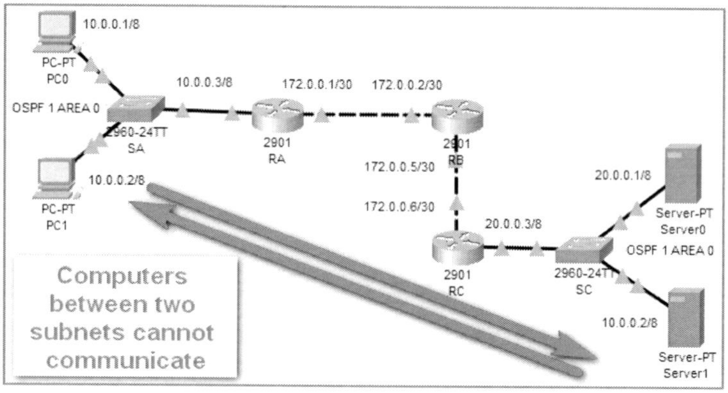

Figure 15.19 Computers between two subnets cannot communicate

The network works in the OSPF protocol in area 0. The configuration of the computers and OSPF has been validated and is correct. PC0, PC1 computers can communicate with each other. Server0, Serverl computers can communicate with each other. Computers from different subnets cannot communicate, e.g. PC1 cannot connect to Server1.

Cause: In the example presented, the cause of the error is the incorrect setting of the interface address (**Gi0/1**) on the **RC** router. It is set to 172.0.0.5 and this address is already used for the interface (**Gi0/0**) in the **RB** router.

Fixed: To fix the error, set the correct address to **172.0.0.6** in the RC router for the **Gi0/1** interface.

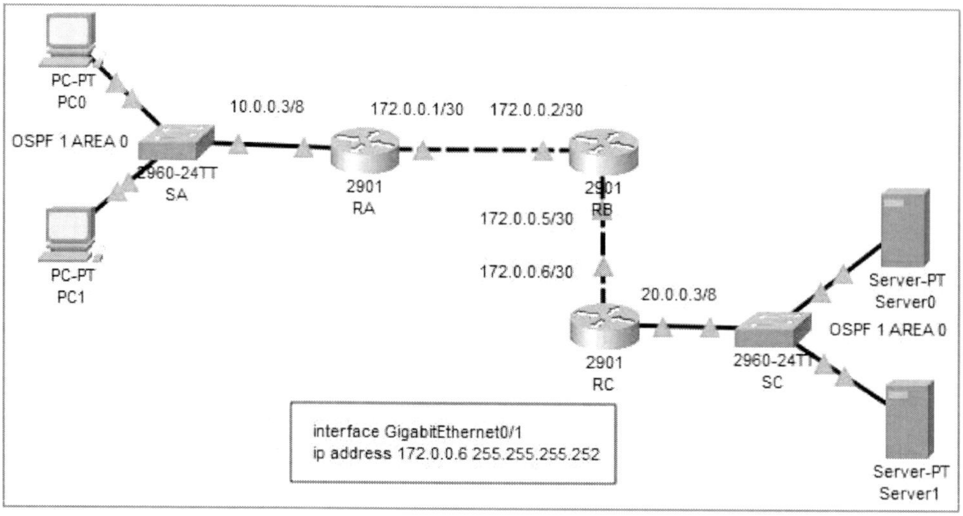

Figure 15.20 Topology after repair

CHAPTER 16

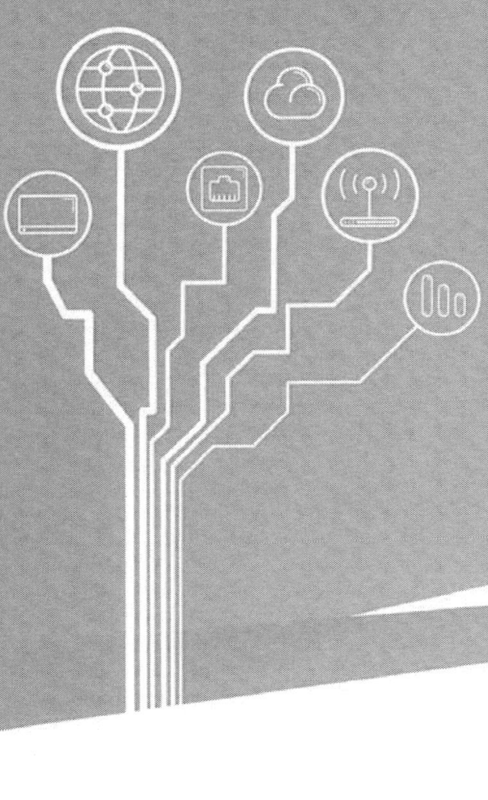

LIST OF THE SAMPLES AND SKILL EXERCISE'S SOLUTIONS

COMPUTER NETWORKS IN PACKET TRACER

FOR BEGINNERS

16 List of the Samples and Skill Exercise's Solutions

This chapter contains a list of sample files and exercise solutions as an addition to the manual.

16.1 The Sample Solution Files

Subsection No.	Title/ Subject	File names
5 . 1	Hubs	Example 5.1.pkt
5 . 2	Repeaters	Example 5.2.pkt
5 . 3	Bridges	Example 5.3.pkt
5 . 4	Switches	Example 5.4.pkt
5 . 5	Access Points	Example 5.5.pkt
5 . 7	Wi-Fi Access Routers	Example 5.7.1.pkt Example 5.7.2.pkt
6 . 1	Transmission Types	Example 6.1.1.pkt Example 6.1.2.pkt
6 . 2	Configurating Network Services: HTTP DHCP FTP SMTP/POP3 DNS Firewall	Example 6.2.1.pkt Example 6.2.2.pkt Example 6.2.3.pkt Example 6.2.4.pkt Example 6.2.5.pkt Example 6.2.6.pkt
8 . 2	Configuring Routers Using the Graphical Interface	Example 8.2.1.pkt Example 8.2.2.1.pkt Example 8.2.2.2.pkt
8 . 3	Configuring Cisco Routers in Cisco IOS: wizard mode, configuration of name, passwords, console port, telnet services and ssh. Configuration of router interfaces, sub-interfaces, dhcp service. Static routing, RIP routing, EIGRP, OSPF. Local definition of router names.	Example 8.3.1a.pkt Example 8.3.1b.pkt Example 8.3.2.1.pkt Example 8.3.4.pkt Example 8.3.5.2a.pkt Example 8.3.5.2b.pkt Example 8.3.5.3.pkt Example 8.3.6.pkt Example 8.3.7.pkt Example 8.3.8.pkt

		Example 8.3.9.pkt Example 8.3.10.pkt Example 8.3.11.pkt Example 8.3.12.pkt Example 8.3.13.pkt
9 . 2 . 2	Configuring Virtual LANs	Example 9.2.2a.pkt Example 9.2.2b.pkt Example 9.2.3.pkt
9 . 3	Configuration Cisco Switches in the IOS: VLAN Configuration Telnet configuration, SSH Basic concepts of REP	Example 9.3.4.pkt Example 9.3.5.pkt Example 9.3.6.2.pkt
10	Physical Topology in PT	Example 10.pkt
12 . 6	Purpose of the Set Tiled Background Button	Example 12.6.pkt Example 12.6-set-tiled-background30x30green.bmp Example 12.6-set-tiled-background30x30yellow.bmp
12 . 8	Multiuser Mode	Example 12.8instance1.pkt Example 12.8instance2.pkt Example 12.8multiuser1.pkt Example 12.8multiuser2.pkt
13 . 2	Configuring DHCP on the Server	Example 13.2.pkt
13 . 3	Configuring DHCP on Your Router	Example 13.3.pkt
13 . 4	DHCP on a Network with Multiple Routers	Example 13.4.pkt
13 . 5	Configuring DHCP on the Wireless Router	Example 13.5.pkt
15 . 1	Wiring or Port Errors	Example 15.1error.pkt Example 15.1repaired.pkt
15 . 2	Device Related Errors	Example 15.2error.pkt Example 15.2repaired.pkt
15 . 3	IP Addressing Errors	Example 15.3.1error.pkt Example 15.3.1repaired.pkt Example 15.3.2error.pkt

		Example 15.3.2repaired.pkt

Table 16.1 List of the Sample Files

16.2 The Skill Exercise's Solutions

Subsection No.	Title	File names
7. 1.	Device-to-Device Connections	Exercise 7.1.1.pkt Exercise 7.1.2.pkt Exercise 7.1.3.pkt Exercise 7.1.4.pkt Exercise 7.1.5.pkt
7 . 2 .	Configure Services on Servers	Exercise 7.2.1.pkt Exercise 7.2.2.pkt Exercise 7.2.3.pkt
11 . 1 .	Configure Devices Using the Graphical Interface	Exercise 11.1.1.pkt Exercise 11.1.2.pkt
11 . 2 .	Routing Protocols, Remote Management	Exercise 11.2.1.pkt Exercise 11.2.2.pkt Exercise 11.2.3.pkt
11 . 3 .	VLANs, Router on a stick, Remote Management	Exercise 11.3.1.pkt Exercise 11.3.2.pkt Exercise 11.3.3.pkt Exercise 11.3.4.pkt
14 . 1 .	Grouping Devices and Combine Two Instances of the Program	Exercise 14.1.1.pkt Exercise 14.1.2area1.pkt Exercise 14.1.2area2.pkt
14 . 2 .	DHCP for IPv4	Exercise 14.2.1.pkt Exercise 14.2.2.pkt Exercise 14.2.3.pkt Exercise 14.2.4.pkt

Table 16.2 List of the Skill Exercise's Solution Files